MW01202076

RAISING VENTURE CAPITAL AND THE ENTREPRENEUR

RAISING
VENTURE CAPITAL
AND THE
ENTREPRENEUR

Leonard A. Batterson

PRENTICE-HALL, Englewood Cliffs, New Jersey 07632

Library of Congress Cataloging-in-Publication Data

Batterson, Leonard A.,
   Raising venture capital and the entrepreneur.

   Includes indexes.
   1. Venture capital—United States.   2. Entrepreneur.
I. Title.
HG4963.B38   1986   658.1′5224   85–30095
ISBN 0-13-752684-9

Editorial/production supervision: *Raeia Maes*
Cover design: *Ben Santora*
Manufacturing buyer: *Gordon Osbourne*

Printed in the United States of America

10   9   8   7   6   5   4   3   2   1

ISBN   0-13-752684-9   025

Prentice-Hall International (UK) Limited, *London*
Prentice-Hall of Australia Pty. Limited, *Sydney*
Prentice-Hall Canada Inc., *Toronto*
Prentice-Hall Hispanoamericana, S.A., *Mexico*
Prentice-Hall of India Private Limited, *New Delhi*
Prentice-Hall of Japan, Inc., *Tokyo*
Prentice-Hall of Southeast Asia Pte. Ltd., *Singapore*
Editora Prentice-Hall do Brasil, Ltda., *Rio de Janeiro*
Whitehall Books Limited, *Wellington, New Zealand*

For Dad,

Leonard A. Batterson, Sr.,

and for those who have

tried and failed, and

tried again;

and for those who having tried,

Succeed

CONTENTS

PREFACE

You are risking a small amount of your capital on this book. As the author is a seasoned venture capitalist, if you read the book for understanding, and put its suggestions into action, you have an excellent chance of achieving an outrageous venture capital-style return on your investment. In fact, the return on your investment may put the average venture capital return to shame. But if you buy the book and it gathers dust, or if you fail to act, you will not be out much capital. Your downside risk is low for the investment—that is, unless you start a business with your capital and then manage to lose it all. In some respects, the venture capital business is not unlike your investment decision in this book. Other aspects of the venture capital business are more involved than the decision process that resulted in your purchase. Together we will explore these crucial distinctions between an everyday purchase and a venture capital investment.

Although the text of the book is neither long nor burdensome, it was written by a venture capitalist who works every day in the venture capital business. The book has been reviewed by several colleagues and friends, who being of good and strong opinions would not agree with everything, but neither would they disagree with most of it. The directories at the back of the book provide the most comprehensive source of venture capital financial assistance to the entrepreneur currently available. Some interesting, helpful people may have without malice been omitted in these directories, and a few may have been included who for some good reason or another would prefer to be left out. Any of these ignored souls who will contact either the author or publisher will be included in a future edition.

The Allstate Insurance Company which has fed, clothed, and helped house the author for the past several years is not responsible for any of the content, but is a great American institution and has provided me with the opportunity to learn and grow in knowledge, and hopefully ability, in one of the most exciting occupations in the world. For this I am more than grateful. My colleagues and superiors at Allstate provide continual comradeship and support in a business that has many highs and lows. Friends to share successes and commiserate with over failures are necessary and appreciated. I am grateful to the deal–doing lawyers of Allstate Financial Law for their construction of flexible yet firm fences which, by providing both investor and entrepreneur with a clear view of their rights and responsibilities, preserve each as a good neighbor to the other.

Charles Rees, currently President of Raffensperger, Hughes Venture Management and former Director of Venture Capital at Allstate, brought me into the venture capital community and I owe him much. Special thanks to Robert W. Cross, one of the finest company turnaround specialists in the business and one who has rescued several distressed companies both for this author and for numerous others during his exciting career on the front lines of the venture capital process. To those entrepreneurs, venture capitalists, investment bankers, consultants, and others who have both endured and supported my efforts to learn and grow in this difficult and exciting business, thanks for the sharing.

Pam Proesel, Sharon Elstner, and Vicki Suhre labored over my indecipherable handwriting and spelling lapses as well as over the typing and proofing of the manuscript. Their efforts are greatly appreciated.

Sandy Morganstein, entrepreneur, founder, and President of the Dytel Corporation has shared, both with the author in the past and with you in this book, his candid and intuitive perceptions on a couple of life's toughest businesses. His company makes an extraordinary product, "The Automated Attendant," which allows a call to bypass an operator or telephone switchboard and get directly through to the desired party. The author hopes that his participation will result in additional product sales as he has made an investment in Sandy's company.

As do almost all entrepreneurial ventures, this one took time away from my wife, Sharon, and daughters, Megan and Caroline, for it was written nights and weekends. They were always supportive and helpful; in this world that's all any compulsive entrepreneur has a right to expect.

Leonard A. Batterson

RAISING
VENTURE CAPITAL
AND THE
ENTREPRENEUR

Part 1

RAISING VENTURE CAPITAL

1

AN AMERICAN DREAM

There is an unspoken promise in America. Many have come, started over, tried hard, made it big, and lived to enjoy it all without doing anything immoral or illegal. This kind of opportunity is remarkable anywhere, at any time, since the first human optimist conceived the idea of progress. America protects and nurtures the thought that we can be better, do better, run faster, jump higher. Progress is why America works. In America getting ahead is not a dream, it is reality for many. For those for whom it is not yet reality, there is the promise that any day now it will be, that it will come sooner here. The embodiment of progress, of America, is the unique American spirit, the entrepreneur. He has roamed, and remade a vast land with his vision and capacity for continually risking and testing his spirit. Kindred spirits in other lands including England, France, Holland, and Japan are catching the vision of the entrepreneurial spirit and are igniting entrepreneurial booms in their lands. Many dreams from this time, these bold creators will be remembered when people gather, wherever they will, and talk of who made their present possible.

You are interested in becoming an entrepreneur by starting a business. After exhausting your personal savings and the funds and patience of numerous relatives and friends you are still short of the capital needed to put the venture into the black, expand your company, and create a successful venture. You go to your neighborhood banker, or even to the "money center" banks downtown, and explain your business idea with considerable skill and enthusiasm. You can't believe it when the banker who gave you the car and house loan and even provided you with a large line of credit on a bank card turns you down flat for a business loan. He tells you with regret that while he would personally like to help out, "the credit policy committee" just won't give him the authority to approve a loan for something as risky as a new business start-up. You head out the door wondering just where you went wrong in your presentation to the banker or whether your new business idea is any good at all. Your particular dream seems only a spectre.

With increasing frequency this scenario is being played out across the world as legions of entrepreneurs seek risk capital financing for their new businesses. Last year in the United States alone it is estimated that over 700,000 new businesses were started. Japan is experiencing an entrepreneurial and venture capital boom as a traditionally homogeneous culture attempts to learn what makes innovation work in the United States. Increasingly, Japanese companies, lead by their strong international trading companies, are exploring investing in early stage companies and observing the process of entrepreneurship. In short order, as methods of venture value creation are learned, it can be expected that venture capital and entrepreneurship will become more firmly established in Japan. U.S. based venture capital companies are setting up foreign operations in anticipation of a worldwide entrepreneurial boom. In the last four years in the United Kingdom more than eighty organizations have been established to support entrepreneurial efforts with their cash and advice—over a 300 percent increase in just four years. Venture capitalists from Holland and other lands have been observed plying U.S. waters as their governments and established interests catch the entrepreneurial fever.

Many of these ventures begun in enthusiasm will have failed utterly within one year of start up, and a large number will not be in business five years from now. A number of these fledgling companies will fail because they could not obtain adequate risk capital (even though it is now more plentiful), particularly during the early, and often, most critical stage of the company's development.

Those few who understand the importance of risk capital, where to find it, and how to get it, significantly enhance their chances of being among the survivors and building a successful company. Major risk capital is presently available from over four hundred venture capital firms being invested by over fourteen hundred professional venture investors. These financial angels make their living backing new ideas and companies that meet their criteria. Hold it, you say. This is beginning to sound like the last visit to the friendly banker. Yes and no. Unlike the banker, the venture capitalist will not usually insist that the money he invests is backed by over 100 percent collateral (or something close). He will roll the dice with you, but will want a piece of your company and will also want a very high return for the high risk he is taking with you in your new venture. Now, you probably perceive the risk as being relatively low in that you will be making it happen. Keep in mind that the numbers are against you and the venture capitalist is very aware of the fragile nature of new businesses. It is very unlikely that he will take a risk with you unless you, your idea, and your potential company have substantial venture capital appeal. You will have venture capital appeal if you:

1. Have a good or unique idea which will make a lot of money.
2. Are willing to give up a good bit of the return on your idea and efforts to compensate the venture capitalist, and his investors, for his risk.
3. Want to build a big, successful company. (At least $25 to $100 million in revenue with real profit)
4. Can accomplish the above financial results in five to ten years.
5. Are willing to work with the venture capitalist as you would a partner.
6. Know a specific business with unusual growth potential very well, and have attracted or are capable of attracting other talented players to your team whose strengths make up for your weaknesses.
7. Recognize your weaknesses but still sleep at night.
8. Are willing to provide your venture investor with an exit for his money within five to ten years.

This is all starting to sound very easy. However, keep in mind that out of the 700,000 previously mentioned new business starts last year, only a couple of thousand were funded by professional venture capitalists. Most venture capitalists who have been in the business for a while receive somewhere between three and six hundred business plans and proposals to invest a year, and after a review of each, will invest in (on an average) one to three new businesses a year. This means to you that unless you are very lucky, or very good, you will not be funded by major venture capital, and, being inadequately capitalized, will most likely join the business casualties for the year.

This book will teach you to be very good and very appealing to the professional venture capital community. It is written to demonstrate how to get your act together, take it on the road, and return home with the capital you need for your business. While there is considerable discussion on how to sell yourself and your company, venture capitalists are very experienced at finding real value in a situation. You will not be able to obtain capital by just being a good promoter or salesman. You must present evidence of real value to the venture capitalist. Remember, he is in the business of selling money (he needs to get his money working to get those high returns for his investors), and he is also in the business of find-

ing and buying great ideas, companies, and people—in short, you. You
have as good a chance as anyone to his capital, if you know yourself,
present your ideas clearly and capably, sell yourself, and know the venture
capitalist and his world. This book will take you into the exclusive world
of high–risk venture capital investing and help you get the money you
need to realize your unique version of an entrepreneurial dream.

2

WHERE THE MONEY IS
(OR KNOWING
YOUR CUSTOMERS)

Before you can raise venture capital you first need to know who has it and who is interested in parting with it, for a risky venture such as yours. You must also know what makes these high–risk financial angels tick and how to get to them. Getting to a venture capitalist is a selling effort, so to be successful in raising venture capital you will need to know and follow the seven keys to effective selling presented in this chapter.

You have tried family, friends, and the local bank in vain to raise the needed start-up or expansion cash so now you turn to the professional venture capital community. As a real profession, venture capital is not very old. Back when the robber barons were on the loose, venture capitalists were usually wealthy success stories like J. P. Morgan who had made it big and had a bit extra to spread around on risky businesses. Later these family fortunes wanted to earn a better return on their money than was available at the trust company (which generally loses real capital) so they hired various business adventurists who the families hoped knew most of the angles shot by wily entrepreneurs. Eventually, adventure capital was christened venture capital (to make it appealing to pension funds and other trust vehicles who put a small portion of their assets into the venture capital funds), and family controlled funds initiated modern venture capital.

During the heyday of the building of corporate America venture capital was not very visible. Not much real money was going into the few venture capital investing partnerships because the capital gains tax was excessive and deadly to the creation of new business opportunities. Eventually both the venture capitalists and the public had enough of non-incentive America, (the capital gains tax was lowered, releasing a flood of capital to the venture industry), President Reagan was elected, and stimulated managers queued up on the corporate rungs determined to try their wings as fledgling entrepreneurs. Soon there were venture capital seminars where money could be raised, *Venture Magazine*, which let people know what other risk-takers were doing and thinking, the major public accounting firms (the Big Eight) set up separate High Tech and venture consulting operations, and corporate America, through its pension funds investing in venture capital partnerships, began to play the game. Entrepreneurship and venturing was trendy. It was an arena where the baby boom generation could go to work, create jobs, and make money to be taxed. The *Venture Capital Journal*, the bible of the venture capital industry, reported in the May 1985 issue that venture capital disbursements to portfolio companies equaled an estimated 3.0 billion in 1984. In 1978 the venture capital industry invested only $550 million. The venture capital industry has become a significant factor in the economy.

Within the industry the flood of investment dollars created a shortage of experienced venture capitalists. In 1977, it is estimated by Venture Economics that each professional managed approximately $3.2 million, whereas, by 1983 the amount was $10 million. While in 1977 there were approximately six hundred venture capitalists, by 1984 the number had risen to fourteen hundred. The situation is: more money available, more entrepreneurs looking for cash, more venture capitalists, but less time for the venture capitalist to look at your deal because he is busy managing more money. You must be very good, or very unique, to even see a venture capitalist. To have any chance to have your deal reviewed, you must know your customer, the venture capitalist.

THE VENTURE CAPITALIST: A PROFILE

Venture capital is a crazy business. Millions of dollars are invested in people, products, and companies who were not even distant acquaintances several months ago. The decisions to invest are made by individualists, working solo or in partnerships, who are generally investing other people's money. Venture capital is also a serious business. In recent years it has fueled much of the job creation of our economy. Jobs are created or lost, individual fortunes rise or fall, new industries are started based on the investment judgement of approximately fourteen hundred high–risk financial angels. Who are these people who make dreams come true?

Venture capitalists are part riverboat gambler, part security analyst, and part entrepreneurial voyeur. They are skeptics and business romantics. Skeptics in that their realism must often temper the optimistic fervor of the entrepreneur. Romantics, in that often they have little real control over operations so must suspend disbelief. This is a business of ambiguity and adversity—ambiguity in that often the venture capitalist must read between the lines, based on his general knowledge and experience, to divine the real state of affairs for an investment—ambiguity in that the investments are often highly illiquid and must be held through good times and bad—ambiguity in that most entrepreneurs have a love/hate relationship with the venture capitalist. They want his money and at times, counsel, but want to be free of limitations and controls. Adversity in that most investments in this risky business go through the valley of the death at least once. Buckminster Fuller once wrote: "Sometimes I only find out where I should be going by going somewhere I don't want to be." Prior to becoming successful, venture capital investments go many places most reasonable men would rather not be. Creative business development often depends on unreasonable men.

Venture capital is the last refuge of the business generalist. He generally provides "know who" rather than "know-how" to his investments. The entrepreneur, as the business specialist, is a provider of know–how. The venture capitalist knows a particular industry, market, or technology. He knows business development. He is a nurturer of growth. He often asks a lot of dumb questions. He knows the pieces of the puzzle that are necessary to create a successful business. Most people involved in business creation build one business in a lifetime; the venture capitalist assists in building many.

Venture capitalists make a few major decisions that really matter, but they matter for a long time. Once an investment decision is made, it is impossible to revoke. The entrepreneur has taken the money and run. Since the venture capitalist often is a minority investor in an enterprise, he must persuade those in control of the soundness of his views rather than insist on his way. Venture capitalists are not in the business of intervention in the day-to-day operations of the business unless absolutely necessary. "If it ain't broke, don't fix it," is a venture imperative. On occasion a venture capitalist will be called upon by circumstances or other investors to assume an operating role, particularly if the individual has operating experience. Generally, this occurs in the most difficult of circumstances, the turnaround situtation. Most venture capitalists would prefer to bring in a strong operating executive or a turnaround specialist. However, on occasion these are either unavailable or the venture capitalist's skills are a unique fit with the operating problems.

This is a business of seeking higher capital appreciation than can be found with any other form of investment. To be successful at this the venture capitalist must figure out what he can sell to whom and what he can buy from whom at a favorable price. What can be sold is either the company, to another company, or the securities of the company to the public. He must consider questions of both fashion and contrariness. Fortunes have been made by buying at a low price when out of fashion and selling when in fashion. Fortunes are also made in the venture capital business by spotting a trend early and funding the creation of fashion. Venture capital is, in part, a business of fashion—one successful company can create a number of imitators seeking to capitalize on the success of the first. Venture capitalists must give close attention and judgment to the role of fashion as well as to the creation of real value. They must also be contrary enough to buck the fashion trend and start a new fashion.

High–risk financial players are calculating gamblers, mentally balancing the risks and rewards. In an individual case the investment may not work out, but the winners will more than compensate for the losers. A venture capitalist is often wrong more than he is right about investment opportunities. This requires a rather unique personal strength—to continue to invest in the face of disappointment and business failure and error in personal judgement, principally about people.

The majority of entrepreneurs are intensely involved with their businesses—to many it is their entire life. It is difficult for them to see the forest for the trees. This close personal identification with their company often makes balanced judgment and perspective impossible. Venture capitalists are experienced providers of perspective—of the long and objective view. Many entrepreneurs are more interested in their enterprises becoming the largest and fastest-growing in the industry rather than the most profitable or best positioned for long-term survival. They are adventurers concentrating on the immediate main chance while venture capitalists attempt to temper exuberance with realism.

Venture capital, at its best, is a network to other people's money. Over several years a venture capitalist will develop a small network—normally five to fifteen key contacts with other venture capital investors. Often the venture capitalist will show his more interesting deals to this personal network and will round up any additional financing required from his personal network. Once an entrepreneur interests a "lead" venture capitalist who has a personal network, the fund–raising effort is less arduous. While these networks are highly individual, generally the network will rely on the lead investor to negotiate the deal, prepare legal documentation, and be the point man in handling the relationship with the company entrepreneur. These venture capital networks are united by past successes and failures and often have a common "style." On occasion one venture capital firm will be a limited partner or investor in another firm, providing a formal financial network tie as well as a personal relationship.

Venture capitalists are prods. They should provide a strong sense of urgency to the company's business development. While the entrepreneur may take the money and run, when the money is gone he often returns to the venture capitalist for more. Experienced venture capitalists will insist that this money is spent carefully and wisely. Part of taking care of venture capital money is accomplishing as much as possible in the shortest possible time. Windows of opportunity are increasingly short and time is money, particularly in a new small company. The effective venture capitalist will help provide a strong sense of urgency.

What of the personalities of these contrary creators of new value— these facilitators of dreams? The backgrounds of the 1400 principal venture capitalists are diverse and yet those in the business have a number of unique and similar propensities.

Most venture capitalists are men of some ego. This is necessary in that they are called on to state unequivocally that they believe in this person or idea, and to back their mouth with their money. Society, bankers, friends, family may believe that the entrepreneur is on occasion confused. The venture capitalist must have both the judgment and ego to sort this out. He must also be a person of empathy. Unless he has a sympathetic appreciation of the struggles of an entrepreneur attempting to create a new company, it is unlikely that any of the real communication necessary for a working relationship will be achieved. An empathic relationship does not mean that the venture capitalist will not be firm in his views or actions, should the occasion demand.

Most successful venture capitalists have intuitive and analytical skills. The analytical abilities are used to figure out what is going on and the intuitive to integrate the information gathered, and act on it. Since the information from an emerging business is often misleading, and the situation ambiguous, often the more experience in the venture industry the better the investment judgement.

Why do venture capitalists endure the rigorous physical demands and mental uncertainties of the business? Perhaps because most believe, with the entrepreneurs they back, that living is risking self from one hour to the next, and because it's both fun and profitable to help create the future.

There are a lot of lists of venture capitalists available. There is one in the back of this book. There is one available from the National Venture Capital Association for postage. The lists tell you where to send your plan, and sometimes to whom. However, most lists don't tell you enough about the customer. You need to know more than where to send a birthday card to your favorite V.C. You need to know his needs and requirements the day he receives your business plan in the mail.

In the first chapter there was the list of the general requirements for venture capital financing. You of course honestly believe that you qualify, and you may (more on this later). You must also meet the specific needs of an individual venture capitalist the day he receives or reviews your particular business plan. At any given moment venture capitalists, like other mortals, are harassed by personal problems, distracted by the possibilities of global disaster, irritated by their bosses and colleagues, and offended by human nature. This is a tough gauntlet for you and your idea to run. You must find the one capitalist in the business who on the Thursday he reviews your plan has put these concerns aside, and who is also interested on this day in tongue cleaners, three-mile–long stores, solutions to the energy problem, or the latest in artificial intelligence, computer generated imaging, or whatever you are selling.

Let's say you send your business plan to five or six venture capitalists from a list. A particular firm has indicated on the list that they are interested in reviewing proposals similar to your idea for a wachamacallit and that they are interested in start-ups. The plan comes into their office and is logged in, and then assigned to the venture capitalist who has indicated to the secretary or deal–logger that he wants to see all the plans looking for money for robotics. Your robotics deal is now on the desk of the robotics specialist for that firm. While he is at peace with the world on your day in question, he rejects your plan because he or the firm is either not interested anymore in robotics deals (because they just did one last week or they just wrote one off last week), or because he is not interested in your niche (machine vision systems) in the robotics area, or because seven investment bankers, brokers, and assorted sources have just sent in other machine vision plans which have their implied endorsement.

Yours is without endorsement (your own excluded), and as they say, what comes in over the transom generally goes out over the transom. Your deal was rejected because your approach and presentation were found wanting. You must first analyze your deal in light of the seven keys to effective selling to have any real opportunity to raise venture capital:

1. Prospecting	(Finding the V.C. who is interested in your deal on the day it is reviewed.)
2. Qualifying	(Learning whether the V.C. is interested in your specific type of deal, and whether there is the time or inclination to pursue it.)
3. Presenting	(Getting the V.C.'s attention over competing plans and creating interest in considering it.)
4. Demonstrating	(Showing and telling why you and your idea or company are truly unique.)
5. Answering Objections	(Professional venture capitalists will raise a host of reasons why not to invest; you must be adept at turning these objectives to your selling advantage.)

6. Closing   (Asking for the money.)
7. Service After the Sale   (Keeping your partner happy and sold.)

You now know that there is a lot more money available than there was previously to finance your business, and that there are more venture capitalists in the business to invest in you. You understand something about their proclivities, prejudices, and habits. You understand that while venture capital is tough to raise, it is not impossible if you follow the seven keys to effective selling of your deal. You are ready to take your first step on the journey toward a successful venture capital close—to begin prospecting for the gold.

3

PROSPECTING FOR GOLD

Prospecting for venture capital can be as time-consuming and arduous as a gold rush. Many other miners and claim jumpers are also searching for the mother lode. You will need the advantage of all the known art plus a little entrepreneurial inventiveness of your own to prevail.

This chapter will provide you with a direct approach to raising venture capital which will minimize the time and floundering required to complete your successful search. You will learn some tried and true approaches including how to define your deal according to the degree of propinquity, maturity, and desire, as well as the avenues of most probable success. Stages of venture financing are reviewed that define which venture capitalists may be shopping for your type of deal.

In gold rush days there were several tried and true methods known to those wise in lode lore. First, there was panning for gold. This approach involved continuously sloshing water around in the pan until the gold settled to the bottom. The venture capital search analogy is to send your business plan to every venture capitalist on every list you can find. The conventional wisdom is that this is a waste of time because venture capitalists run in packs known as syndicates and the syndicates are continuously forming and reforming and talking to each other. Before long they may be talking about your plan if it is interesting, and it will gain a reputation for having been "shopped around."

My guess would be that if your product is truly unique, the credentials of your management team impeccable, and the business plan a gem, the venture capitalists will be squabbling to do your deal. In this rare case, it would make little difference if you advertised your plan on television. Remember the venture capitalist will only fund ½ to 1 percent of the deals he reviews each year. Most entrepreneurs searching for capital would be advised to follow the "dig around in a few sites" approach. This method involves sending your plan to only five or six venture capitalists selected using the following method:

1. Using the list in the appendix find the venture capitalists who are located geographically near your company. Some venture capitalists like to walk or ride their bike to your office. If you are not near any-one, consider moving your operations.
2. It's a waste of time to send your business plan to a venture capitalist who only does leveraged buyouts if you are a seed deal or a start–up company. Make sure you know what stage your deal is in according to venture capital criteria. (See this chapter.) Once you know the correct stage send your plan to five or six who are nearby and handle your stage deal.
3. Check the table in the appendix for individual venture capitalist's deal priorities. This is a list of those deals that each individual venture capitalist is most interested in doing as of right before this book was published. You have now defined your deal according to propinquity, maturity, and desire. You can now put the plan in the mail, and believe you have done your best. Some of the venture capitalists, when they receive your plan, may be wrestling alligators in troubled companies, on vacation, out of money, or just tired. If a few plans come back quick send out a few more.

   The last prospecting method is "gain support from your local sheriff," who in turn can be expected to support your efforts. Here you round up and sell an investment banker, new business lawyer, accountant, or broker (remember a broker is someone who has heard a rumor and is out of a job), or other middleman. The best of this breed has developed working relationships with a handful of venture capitalists. If your plan is forwarded by a middleman who has a venture capitalist's confidence and attention your plan will go to the head of the line. These are valuable individuals both to the time–pressed venture capitalist and to yourself. They can be found most easily through referrals from other entrepreneurs who have walked your way before. In recent years a number of entrepreneurial forums have been organized, such as the MIT forum, where entrepreneurs gather and network their contacts and ideas, local venture capital clubs, the Southern California Technical Executives Network and others.

   Once you have identified the key venture capital contacts, you should interview them to determine their past record in successful venture capital placements. Who do they know, how well do they know the venture capitalist (how fast are phone calls returned), and how many deals have they done together? Also, how much money have they made or lost together in the past? The conventional wisdom is that middlemen are just that—in the way, in the middle. You need a middleman who can open the door for you, and then get out of the way and let you present and sell.

One way of approaching a venture capitalist would be to call and indicate that you would like to forward your plan, but first would like to have some assistance in completing the formal document. Ask if the venture capitalist could suggest individuals who could be of some assistance. This way you may gain the initial interest of the venture capitalist—who would begin to see you as resourceful—as well as the help and backing of a key player in the venture capital support community. Another approach would be to call the venture capitalist if you have a really unique idea, and indicate that you would like to have a meeting to discuss your idea, and learn more about what is required to raise venture capital. Few venture capitalists can refuse a direct appeal to their professional obligations, ego, and desire to help give birth to an idea. Before you call, however, be sure to qualify your prospect according to the three steps in this chapter.

Calling a venture capitalist can be frustrating. While the phone numbers are readily available (in this book), venture capitalists generally travel Tuesday through Thursday and are usually out of the box to a new idea while traveling. When in the office Monday and Friday, they are most often found on the phone or "in conference" with an entrepreneur or management team. Most often these conferences are actually in session rather than an evasion of your call. You must keep calling back, and you must leave word where and when you can be reached. Most venture capitalists feel guilty if they don't return phone calls after the second or third try. Keep trying. Employ the old saleman's techniques of getting to know the secretary on the phone and getting support. If the secretary indicates to her boss that you have really been trying to get through, and looks a little disapproving of the venture capitalist, rather than indicating that some pest has been calling forever, your call is more likely to be returned. Calling other partners, or going over the venture capitalist's head in those institutions that provide venture capital, is likely to end in telephone frustration. No one can play telephone tag like an irritated venture capitalist.

Venture capital fairs are becoming increasingly popular stomping grounds for capital raising. The American Electronics Association–sponsored meetings, particularly those in Monterey and Fort Lauderdale, pack in both venture capitalists and entrepreneurs. At these meetings the capital–seeking company puts on a short presentation to the assembled venture capitalists, and later will meet with those venture capitalists who sign up for individual smaller meetings, where the company can interest the venture capitalists one on one in the business. This approach appears particularly successful for later stage companies with a short window to the public market. Early stage companies generally require more sponsorship than is available in a meat market atmosphere. The AEA is beginning to sponsor a number of regional meetings, which tend to attract venture capitalists from the local area, as well as investment bankers and other intermediaries who may be helpful. In addition local societies are being formed such as the MIT forums, state or city sponsored associations, and various private and public inventor and incubator groups. A referral from an entrepreneur who has been successful in raising capital, and who may be active in your local association, can be most helpful. Business editors at the local paper are generally aware of these organizations and could put you in touch. You may feel a touch like a lamb among wolves at these meetings, but they provide an excellent opportunity to measure your plan and approach to capital formation against your competition. Generally forum sponsors have certain minimal requirements that your organization must meet to participate. Find one that is oriented to your stage company. The MIT format allows the entrepreneur to make a presentation and then take comments and questions from a panel—often composed of a venture capitalist, a business development lawyer, a technical expert, and an investment banker. A venture capitalist will have considerable respect for an entrepreneur who will expose himself and subject his plans to this form of constructive criticism. Those entrepreneurs with the stomach for this form of masochism will reap invaluable capital–raising contacts and will be on the road to successful financing.

Recently venture capital funds have become more specialized. As more money has come into the industry, the larger pools of capital managed by major institutions and a few private partnerships are now in excess of $100 million, with several at cost managing $200 or $300 million. These mega pools will often invest larger amounts than the smaller partnerships, and are the deep pockets that every business can use in case of unexpected adversity. Several of these larger pools have invested as limited partners in the more specialized partnerships. The deep pools must move substantial capital and insure a quality deal flow by financial and personal relationships with the specialized start-up, medical, consumer, and mezzanine venture capital funds. A number of these major funds also have a working relationship with one or several investment banks. The specialized funds provide continuing expertise that the larger pools find difficult to retain, due to the generalist background necessary to invest much money in many different industries and products. On occasion the mega funds will refer your deal to one of their feeder funds.

Traditionally the major institutional funds were the training ground for the venture capital industry. Individuals would join a major bank fund, stay five to ten years, lose and make a little money for the institution, learn the business and move on to the more lucrative private partnerships. When the capital gains rate was lowered and the flood gates opened, with major money moving into the venture capital process, the apprentice system was accelerated. Now an apprentice may stay at his institution three to six years, and then either join with others to raise a fund, or be recruited by an existing partnership.

This information is important to you in raising capital, and in your initial prospecting. Those funds which were recently formed, and there are a number, are generally more anxious and often more responsive in the review of your deal than those which have been around for a long time. The longer the fund has been in existence, the more likely it is to fund deals which are referrals from established intermediaries or from the fund's specific venture capital network. At a number of institutions individuals new to the business are interested in "putting a deal on the books" and are unlikely to have a well-developed personal network. These new funds and new people are hungry. Check out the year the fund was established in the appendix.

David Silver's book *"Who's Who in Venture Capital"* indicates those individuals who have been in the business forever. If you are successful in getting the attention of one of these sages your deal is done, for their network will market your deal. They are particularly busy, and your deal will have to pass a very fine screen. The newer people are more likely to take a shot in the dark with you, and have the time to look at your deal. Should someone new to the industry become your lead investor, it will be more difficult for them to bring others into the deal as your "lead investor" in that they have not yet established a network or a personal following. The older or more experienced venture capitalists are most always a harder sell, but have direct lines to close your deal quickly. The younger members can generally make a decision (with the approval of their senior partner or institution), and they are easier to reach and convince, but will not be able to help round up the rest of the money as easily or quickly. If your deal is in a hot industry, with an experienced management team, doing a unique one-of-a-kind project, the more experienced venture capitalist is probably your best bet. If not, then the newer funds and institutional investors should be a more likely source.

If your concept is hot, this will increase your chance for successful capital raising. Venture capital being in part a business of fashion means that your company's being in fashion or out of fashion will have a major impact on the degree of difficulty you experience. One experienced investor has a treasured photo which was taken on a trip to the sheep country of Italy. The lead sheep is leaping a brook with the rest of the flock in hot pursuit. In this case it wasn't clear whether they all landed in the brook or made it safely to the other side. One investor feels that the group's behavior more closely resembles penguins—kind of running hither and yon in a bunch based on the latest rumor or alarm. Most venture capitalists are that peculiar combination of lone wolf and member of the flock. They must be far enough out ahead to get to the good deals early, but not so far ahead that no one in the network will follow and co-invest. In recent memory the most popular industries have been computer related (most things today seem to be computer related), other electronics, telecommunications and communications, and medical. In the last few years robotics, genetic engineering, health management deals, computer aided design and computer aided engineering have all enjoyed popularity. Hot industry niches appear to be hot for shorter periods. This is consistent with the acceleration evident in the pace of technological change. At the right point in the genetic cycle several years ago venture capitalists would swarm like bees over a quality genetic deal. Today the bloom is off the genetic rose and most venture capitalists will not leave the hive unless you do genetic engineering coupled with stamping out wachamacallits by the gross. In several years this cycle will likely change as genetic firms begin to bring products with compelling economics to market. The moral is—if your deal is hot bring it to the venture capital market now.

Most important to successful prospecting for venture capital is the determination and tenacity to succeed. This requires considerable real self–confidence, a quality which is often apparently available, but evaporates on hard testing. The testing of patience and tenacity which raising venture capital entails helps identify those entrepreneurs with the right stuff. One President of a major institutional fund indicates that in over ten years in the venture capital arena he has seen no deal succeed without passing through the valley of the death at least once. Clearly, building a major new business from the germ of an idea requires individuals of uncommon capacity and strength. It's been said that we accomplish about as much in life as we truly believe in ourselves.

Previously it was indicated that venture capitalists often specialize or categorize their investments by stages and that it is important to locate an investor who is interested in your stage deal. These stages, traditionally, are:

1. Seed Financings   (A wild-eyed inventor with an idea—most major venture capitalists avoid these. For those who specialize, see appendix.)

2. Start–Up   (Generally the rudiments of a management team and a complete business plan—here you need to find a local capitalist who is willing to work with you to complete the elements necessary to build a business.)

3. First Stage	(Generally the product is developed and funds are required to get the production bugs out and go to market.)
4. Second Stage	(Product is going out the door and assets are growing as well as liabilities. Hopefully this will tide you over to positive cash flow.)
5. Third Stage	(Things are really starting to hum and with a bit more push a major business success may be possible. Sometimes also called as mezzanine round.)
6. Fourth Stage	(Also referred to as mezzanine or, hopefully, the stage prior to public market in several months.)
7. Bridge Financing	(A bridge to where? Often to nowhere or too far. Used by venture capitalists often in the form of notes with warrants attached which convert or are rolled into next round permanent financing. Often employed by a company where existing investors want new participants in the next permanent financing—buys time.)
8. Other Plays	(a) Research and Development Financing (seen as a competitive approach by some venture capitalists). Used as a tax–advantaged partnership for product development. If employed must be carefully structured or could mess up later venture capital financing. (b) Leveraged Buyouts. Existing management buys their company from the current owners. Large institutions tend to be major players with help from several specialty funds. (See appendix) (c) Distressed and Turnaround Companies (The author is a former turnaround specialist, as many venture capitalists become). See Part Two, Chapter Four for a description of this activity.

Many venture capitalists will not even consider your idea or company unless it fits with their definition of the correct stage deal. However if the idea is good, the management strong, and the business plan precise, exceptions are made.

If you have been brave, tenacious, and strong and yet have still come up emptyhanded there is still hope. It may be that your idea was just too revolutionary for the venture capital process. Remember, rarely are truly revolutionary products supported by venture capital. This requires quixotic investors more akin to the high rollers of Las Vegas than those involved in the studied process of venture capital.

Normally venture capitalists will not fund a project which they consider to be revolutionary, and they require considerable customer evaluation prior to its acceptance. These deals generally require "deeper pockets" than the venture capital community can provide. Preferred by the industry are those evolutionary products which represent an advance or enhancement over the previous product. These products have an excellent chance of market acceptance based on the prior acceptance by the consumer. There are a few venture capitalists, considered the high–risk concept players, who will consider a revolutionary product or idea. Such products as artificial blood, personal aircraft, or high speed trains would be considered outside the parameters of most venture capitalists.

We started out prospecting for capital, assuming you had first tried friends, family and the local banker. Still available as an alternative to venture capital are local investment syndicates (often structured by business development lawyers or accountants), MESBIC (Minority Enterprise Small Business Investment Company) financing if you are a minority business, and assistance through the SBA (Small Business Administration) and other government agencies.

Now that you know all, or at least most of the short cuts to finding a venture capitalist who will review your deal, as well as how to define your deal according to its particular stage of development, you are ready for the presentation of your idea, plan, or company.

Remember: Never, never, ever give up except to notions of good sense and exhaustion. If you deal in realities, and learn from those venture capitalists who turn your deal down, a successful business can be started and eventually major venture capital raised.

4

PUTTING YOUR BEST
FACE FORWARD

Venture capitalists make mistakes. A number of good ideas and winning people are turned away. Time and the busy venture capitalist wait for no man or plan. You are the seller. You have followed the prospecting suggestions in the previous chapter, and have found and qualified several venture capitalists who have indicated a preliminary interest in your deal. Since their interest is preliminary, you must continue to sell. Very few ideas or companies reach this point in the investment decision process. Your company is now among the select few. If you have reached this plateau, it is because you developed good prospecting skills, and in addition polished your presentation document, the business plan, to a high gloss. Whether you will get the money or not will in large part depend on how effectively your business plan communicates the special nature of your business opportunity, and your ability to make it happen. This chapter indicates what a venture capitalist most wants to find in your business plan and what he most wants to see when he first meets you and your management team.

Business plans are the selling prospectus of venture capital. They indicate what business you will be in, who your friends will be, and your competitors, how much money you intend to make, and how fast. Occasionally, they have been successfully written on the back of the proverbial envelope or the front of a napkin over a business lunch. They outline your promises to your investors, and what return they can expect for their efforts and investment. A business plan, to be effective, should be you. It should be a reflection of your dreams, and your promise. You and your company are going to be unique. Your plan must convey the unusual nature of your investment opportunity.

Venture capital is considered by some to be a glamorous business—variety, travel, dealing with high energy entrepreneurs. There is also plenty of repetition. Try plowing through twenty or thirty business plans and business summaries a month, a few longer than the phone book, and most "me too" ideas. Your plan must set itself apart from the run-of-the-mill. This is not accomplished through fancy binders, reams of computer print-outs, or product and personal endorsements from the high and mighty. Venture capitalists are most interested in the quality, uniqueness, and compelling economics of your business, as well as how well, and in how much detail, you have thought out where you are going, and how you will get there. If you don't first know where you are going, any road will take you there. Venture capital wants a well planned trip.

What is a quality business plan? A quality plan should be a selling document as well as a rational outline of how you intend to build your business. To have a quality plan you must first have a unique business concept or product. If you are seeking financing for the 100th $5\frac{1}{4}$–inch disk drive company or the 1000th data base software company your chances of financing success are remote. Most venture capitalists are looking for evolutionary products or concepts. Of particular interest are those products which carve a small, but not too small, proprietary product niche out of a very large market. If the market niche is too large, predatory competitors will enter, and if too small the company will not grow large enough to support the required rate of return to the investor. The niche must be adequate and protected. Niches can be based on a superior cost advantage, on superior product enhancements, and occasionally on creative distribution and marketing. Most venture firms have traditionally supported those companies which offer productivity improvement to their customers at a real cost improvement over present competition. There are fewer venture firms which will back marketing and distribution schemes. If your deal is based primarily on superior marketing and distribution, be sure your target investors are marketing players. Often the larger venture pools will consider marketing companies while the smaller players are looking for productivity enhancements. Revolutionary products are clearly unique, but these are difficult to finance. Venture capital experience has been that products which may establish a new industry, or at times a new way of life (the light bulb, the automobile, the airplane, in the first half of the century; and today artificial blood, high speed trains, ice ponds for cooling), are essentially visionary projects with an often uncertain and rocky future. Better to bet on a variation of a prior product, like the personal computer, which represented evolutionary growth.

What is unique to one venture capitalist maybe ho-hum to another, and certainly the industry can at times be faulted for funding a nest of clone companies. If you can answer the question in the affirmative that your product will meet an existing or emerging need (three to eight years) in a rapidly growing industry, with superior or compelling economics, then you have met the test of product uniqueness.

Once the venture capitalist knows that you have a unique product or concept, he will turn to the section of the business plan outlining the qualifications of your management team to grow the business. Particularly in a start–up company, no other section of your plan will receive as much attention and diligence. In a start–up, you and your team are the business. You are not sitting around in a huge plant, with a lot of assets and thousands of workers, grinding out product and profit. In a big company mistakes can be made (at times even major errors), a few heads may roll, assets may be redeployed, but generally life goes on as usual. In a small company the same type of error will put the company immediately into major and often fatal distress.

Management is all. Venture capitalists like the type of entrepreneur who "could sell toilet paper off the back of a truck" if need be to keep his business alive. Or, if the current business failed, would start a new business to pay the old investors back. Picking successful business development management is not a science. One experienced venture capitalist believes that "it really can't be done." Experienced investors tend to prefer experienced managers and experienced entrepreneurs. These people have been there before, and the investors are not paying for the mistakes required to learn the business development process. Occasionally, an entrepreneur inexperienced in business management will have the opportunity to direct a venture–backed business start–up, but if he fails to live up to his representations he will be promptly replaced by more experienced managers.

Your plan should be accurate, should be written in concise, clear English, should be realistic, and, above all, should not be undercapitalized. Entrepreneurs are by nature and necessity an optimistic lot and almost always underestimate their financing requirements. A dean of venture capital has said, "you never have too much money." If you need to go back to your backers for more in a second and third round of financing, unless significant milestones have been reached, you will need to give up more of the company to survive than would have been necessary if you had raised sufficient funds in the first round of financing. Most successful business plans contain an executive summary, and a description of the product, market, competition, manufacturing approach, management, selling strategy (including distribution), and five year financial projections. There are a number of excellent books covering business plan preparation in detail.

Generally it is best to send your plan to the venture capitalist by mail, after a brief phone conversation qualifying the venture capitalist's level of interest and availability. A short letter indicating when you spoke, and what about, should be attached. At this point in the process, there is not really much you can do to advance your cause. If you call to determine whether the plan was received, or whether there were any questions, you may be considered a pest. You should receive either a turndown letter or a call expressing further interest within one week to a month. If you receive a turndown letter, a phone call is in order to determine the reasons for the rejection. This information will be helpful to determine the perceived weaknesses in your plan as well as to solicit potential leads from the venture capitalist. During this call you need to be prepared to ferret out the real reasons for the turndown. Venture capitalists don't like to tell entrepreneurs that their plan is ill–conceived, or worse. This tends to be bad for business. Other entrepreneurs hear that a venture capitalist is tough to work with and unreasonable, and perhaps a good deal is missed. You should ask the venture capitalist to be candid because this information could help you correct any weaknesses in your company and business plan. Typical reasons for a turndown which are normally smoke–screens are: "this doesn't fit our portfolio objectives," or "the valuation (price) was too high," or "we just did a competitive company—too bad you didn't write the month before." If what you hear is the typical smoke–screen, it is probable that your plan was not perceived as being sufficiently unique, or your management team is inexperienced in the business. However, remember that it never hurts to ask, and you can always amend your business plan to correct perceived deficiencies. In English class the teacher used to say that poor writing was often due to sloppy thinking; so too in the venture capital business a poor business plan generally reflects either a poor business opportunity, or, more often than not, insufficient prior planning of the business opportunity. Remember, you know that you can build a successful business, but the venture capitalist does not. Your creation of a rational, well conceived, and organized business plan is your best chance to sell him. You must do your homework in advance.

You have successfully completed your business planning and plan, and after several weeks a venture capitalist has called you back, and asked that you and your management team "drop over for a chat." Don't let this nonchalance fool you. Your venture capital financing is on the line in this initial interview. The best advice is to be yourself. We all have several sides to ourselves that we present at different times. Which side or sides would it be in your best interest to reveal, and is there a type that a particular venture capitalist wants to see? As always, honesty is the best policy. While you must emphasize the positive potential of your deal, the venture capitalist is well aware that every deal has its downside and weaknesses. While you should not wear these on your sleeve it does no real harm to discuss your challenges as well as your opportunities. Candor with a partner or potential partner in a business relationship is next to honesty. Since we are talking about investing, and making money, a certain seriousness of purpose is essential. This is really not the time for your best jokes or discussion of your golf game. Some venture capitalists will want to get to know you through a discussion of your deal or business plan. Others may emphasize and review your personal and prior business background. Whatever the emphasis, the key question is whether you are the person who can pull off this business plan, and make major money for the venture capitalist and his investors. After honesty and candor would come intelligence (street smart rather than bookish), vision, energy, and the often rare ability in an entrepreneur to work with and through others—to know when to delegate—and be able to—and when to do it yourself. Most of us, unless we are good actors, will reveal many of these personal traits to an experienced evaluator of people in the course of an hour to two hour initial meeting. The truth is that unless you have many of these traits there isn't much chance that you will build a successful company with or without venture capital financing. Perhaps most important, the venture capitalist will want to discover whether you are a person with great tenacity and staying power, who will continue to lead the company in those most difficult circumstances which come to all new ventures. You must have mettle, courage and when the occasion demands boldness. Most of all, you must never quit until you have made money for the investor. (Part Two, Chapter Three, "High Technology Investing," outlines many of the personal as well as deal characteristics that a venture capitalist desires).

During the initial interview it is important that all members of the management team participate. While the founder or President would be expected to lead the meeting, all key management players should cover their areas of responsibility. If the founder is too dominant, the venture capitalist may draw the conclusion that the business will be run as a one man show. If too passive, the conclusion may be that no one will be in charge. It goes without saying that team squabbling should be avoided. If there are still areas of disagreement among members of the team over key issues, this should be indicated with the positions presented in a businesslike manner. An experienced venture capitalist would not be surprised that business issues remained to be resolved. The venture capitalist would consider it healthy that members of the management team could put this issue on the table for resolution. There will be many other such issues in the course of building the business, and the venture capitalist is more concerned that members of the management team have developed their own method toward crisis resolution, than that they have resolved all pending issues.

This first meeting is to engender confidence—the confidence that you and your team have that certain something required to see it through.

We are talking in large part chemistry, and that intangible feel that you are right for the part. If after many auditions you never get the part, it may be that another role is for you. It is possible, in presenting yourself, to be too good a salesman; to fool both the venture capitalist and yourself. If you sell yourself, you will have to execute your plan. Be certain that you are right for the part.

After the initial interview the venture capitalist, if interested in continuing to pursue your deal, will ask for further meetings, references, and other information on your business opportunity. This is beginning the somewhat tedious and laborious process known in the trade as "due diligence." If you have reached this point you are doing well indeed. The venture capitalist is now about to commit a most precious resource, time, to a thorough examination of your business. The deal is still not sold. No check is yet cut. As you go through this final exam together, you will have the opportunity to further sell your deal through proper presentation, and demonstration, and to finally answer all objections to backing your company.

5

THE FINAL EXAM

An entrepreneur who recently went through a major venture capital due diligence physical noted, at a venture capital seminar sponsored by Deloitte Haskins and Sells: "On the plus side, if you're running the company right, due diligence underscores your credibility to potential investors. The investors reason you're likely to carry on business after you're funded the same way you did before. That's why it helps to have them talk to your customers. But it can also be a pain in the neck. You've got several venture capital firms looking at you and they prefer not to use each other's information. That means you've got to go over the same ground with each of them and, worse, they all want to talk to your customers. The customers aren't interested in being told you've got thirty-three cents in the bank and are desperately looking for funding. Plus, they resent the demands on their time and the occasions when they're interviewed by somebody naive."

Venture capitalists are trustees for other people's money. Most of them, as entrepreneurs, went around and raised funding from a number of institutional sources which are also trustees for other people's money: their job is to be careful while investing in risky businesses. This is a real strain; to let it all hang out, often without control, but still to feel and be responsible. The answer to this conflict is due diligence. Really, this is a legal term for checking things out, or looking before leaping—being prudent before investing, rather than having regrets the night after. The venture capitalist is trying to ask a lot of dumb questions so that occasionally he can form a question worthy of a ten-year-old that illuminates what the company, and the investment, is all about. Starting with a tabula rasa on a subject, and asking illuminating questions which are worthy of a child, is not child's play. This is scary stuff. The ideal image is of a smart, sophisticated, knowledgeable, perhaps even artful, high–powered money man.

The due diligence questions are: What does this do? How does it work? Who will buy it? Why do they want it? How many can we sell? Where can we sell them? Will anyone else make it? What does it really cost to make? Who are these people who want to build a business? Why will they succeed against the odds? Time and again an effective venture capitalist must reveal ignorance. This is not a business for people who need to be smart. The venture capitalist in the due diligence process is revealing vulnerability. However, there is still a sharp edge to this vulnerability. The venture capitalist still holds the gold, and the entrepreneur wants it. Questions begin to grate after a while, and to annoy. The entrepreneur begins to realize that behind the seemingly benign questions is a loaded purpose. Where are the weaknesses in this business plan? Will the management be strong enough to create something out of nothing? The venture capitalist is probing for the tragic flaw and red flag on this investment decision.

The due diligence process itself is rather straightforward. The venture capitalist will call several weeks after the office introductory meeting, and say that it is time to do some additional homework on your deal, and that he expects to be in your area of the world on such and such a date—could you and the key members of your team make a tire-kicking meeting? On the date in question, often enough, you have a critical meeting with a key supplier, or customer, or are just leaving on an all expenses paid junket to China. Cancel these meetings. You need the money and one of the first venture capital tests is a measure of your availability to the venture capitalist. He may invest in you, and in return he wants your time and attention. Not all of it, but enough so that he has a sense of where your head is, at all times. One of the worst feelings in a venture capital investment is to have the entrepreneur forget your name after the money is in the deal. This occurs when the entrepreneur really didn't want professional venture capital—he wanted no–strings money so that he could continue to build his business in his own way without outside contributions or interference.

You want professional venture capital and have cleared your schedule. Be certain that your other key managers are also available on this date. It's very frustrating for a venture capitalist to arrive at your office or plant and find that the marketing staff is on the road selling, or the product development Vice President is attending a management–by–objectives seminar. Common business courtesy requires that the entire business team be available. The venture capitalist is now your number one customer. He will note whether you are smart enough to treat him with the courtesy appropriate to your need. If you treat him appropriately it is likely you will do the same for other critical customers. Once appropriate introductions are under way the venture capitalist will generally either want a tour of your facilities, if any, or will begin to discuss with you key sections of your business plan in some detail. At this point the venture capitalist has completed at least preliminary homework on your industry and has some conception of how you fit in the industry universe.

If you conduct a facility or plant tour it's important to highlight your strengths, pertaining both to people and physical assets. Venture capitalists are of course of various backgrounds. Some have managed plants, some are most comfortable with balance sheets, some focus most on the people. Before you begin the tour, learn enough about your customer to focus the tour toward the venture capitalist's needs and interests. Be sure introductions are made to other key employees, and a feel is provided for the chemistry of your business organization. This is also an ideal time to inspect and demonstrate, if possible, an engineering or production prototype of your product. You can point out the interesting features of your product or manufacturing process which enhance your uniqueness as an investment opportunity. You can show how the device really works in real time. Time is often relatively short in this initial meeting—perhaps one half day—and there will be a lot to cover, so concentrate on the informative and dramatic in this initial tour. Show the venture capitalist what you have that others will want to buy, and why major money will be made.

Of course an inspection tour is not only an opportunity to judge product uniqueness but also a moment to ponder the evolution of your developing business. The venture capitalist is attempting to gauge just how far your company is from positive cash flow and profitability. The price he will be willing to pay, and the terms on which he may be willing to invest, will be strongly influenced by his impressions and conclusions, many of which will be gained during this inspection. This is not a time to withhold and be wary. The venture capitalist is not in the business of stealing other people's business ideas. In such a small industry, he would not be in business for long if he did. Provide full disclosure and treat the venture capitalist as you would a potential partner.

After the plant or business tour the venture capitalist will often want to quiz you and other key managers on your business plans. Some of the questions will be of the ten–year–old variety, but others will be very specific, concerning your forecasts and financial projections. Generally, the earlier the stage of the deal the more questions about management and their capacities, and the later the stage, the more inquiries about margins, profit, and balance sheets. The earlier the stage, the more management depth is critical. In a later–stage company there are hard assets and hard or soft liabilities, and the venture capitalist will want to understand their placement and deployment in support of the company's strategy. In the early–stage deal or start–up, the venture capitalist will want to understand your proposed deployment of the financial assets invested in your company. The venture capitalist will be attempting to judge if and when your company will require more money, and both the upside and downside risk for the investment. Some investments, particularly in soft asset companies such as computer software, have major downside risk in that the product can easily walk out the door with the proprietor. A judgement will be made as to whether you are a business realist, and have sufficient hands–on knowledge of your industry to succeed. The venture capitalist is not in the business of providing the entrepreneur with a business education, and since venture capital is the last refuge of the business generalist, the venture capitalist will want you to demonstrate your specific knowledge and skills.

Some entrepreneurs, particularly those who are seeking later–stage investment just prior to a contemplated public offering, believe that it is most effective, when "whetting the venture capitalist's appetite," to appear relatively aloof and in no real need of funds during this due diligence process. On the one hand this may be effective with newer members of the industry who may start to slobber over your deal and pay up a bit for the deal; in the longer term the relationship generally suffers. Remember that most deals which receive venture capital eventually require more money prior to a successful sale or public offering, and that the real definition of a "mezzanine" deal is often "one that requires a lot of money." If in the long run the venture capitalist believes he has paid too much, too soon, or that he has not really enjoyed full disclosure, you well may pay the price in a later–round cash infusion. A little humility on the entrepreneur's part often goes a long way.

Generally the more experienced the venture capitalist, the more he is interested in the quality of the people rather than in the particular merit of the product or business concept. The old industry adage is that the venture capitalist would rather invest in an A management team with a B idea than a B management team with an A idea. This is because while there are a lot of good ideas around there are few managements that can build a successful business from scratch.

How can you convey the impression that your team is one of the A management teams? As previously mentioned the most important ingredient is to actually be an A management team. If your group is a bit short of perfection—and most are—you should point out what you will be doing to supplement your team and what the projected timing of these management additions will be.

In your discussions it is best to avoid appearing as though you can walk on water. The venture capitalist is looking to back those entrepreneurs who have solid self–confidence devoid of arrogance. The late Pat Lyles, a General Partner of the Charles River Partnership in Boston, used to say he wanted to invest with "I want to do well" egos rather than the "big cheese" mentality. It is not necessary to offer a Las Vegas–style production replete with dogs and ponies, and showgirls. The venture capitalist wants to know that you know your stuff, not that you can create fancy presentations. Save this money for your customers. You should, however, know every aspect of your business plan. It helps to be able to answer off the top of your head rather than pulling reams of computer print–outs from your briefcase. The venture capitalist's questions are an opportunity to demonstrate that you have a carefully crafted business plan, and that you have the ability to alter that plan should circumstances dictate. The venture capitalist knows from experience that circumstances will inevitably change, so investment must be made in those with sufficient flexibility to alter their plans—even those best laid—on a dime, if necessary. A strong showing of rigidity or inflexibility will destroy your fund-raising chances.

The venture capitalist will want to invest with a visionary—a big thinker. After all, this is what creates major market opportunity. But the venture capitalist wants someone who can focus planning on the here and now. It would be a major error in your discussions to raise too many new product or business concepts that you "will cut the venture capitalist in on once this company is funded." A number of entrepreneurs mistakenly believe that the venture capitalist is looking for someone with a million ideas. Not so. The venture capitalist wants someone driven to succeed at the business. Extraneous discussion of other proposals can be a major red flag.

That you sincerely, really want to be rich will be of considerable interest to the venture capitalist. The search is not for empire builders; they are plentiful in large corporate organizations. You need to convey that you are a certified money maker, that you believe religiously that "happiness is positive cash flow," and that you will spend your venture capital as if you just put a second mortgage on your widowed mother's home to raise cash.

If you have already been successful in a previous venture, you will be a hot property for venture capital funding, but you should not wear your wealth on your sleeve—or, if you do, you should convey that you are interested in making even more money. While many venture capitalists are interested in how their investment may contribute to society, this is usually a secondary consideration. If your project is not detrimental to society you are generally well advised to focus your conversation on the financial merits rather than social improvement.

All venture capitalists have certain unique red flags and personal taboos which may kill your deal. These run the gamut from "never invest in software" to the more logical "no company airplanes or boats" unless you are in the airplane or boat business. Should your deal happen to coincide with a venture capitalist's pet peeves no amount of artful persuasion will suffice. Just move on down the road. We all have our particular and peculiar quirks and prejudices.

6

HANDLING AND RESOLVING OBJECTIONS IN YOUR FAVOR

Having successfully passed the due diligence stage of the venture capital funding process, you are now poised to pick up the venture capitalist's check, only to learn that he starts to raise a number of questions or objections to your deal. Or perhaps you have not yet reached the due diligence stage and the venture capitalist is already objecting to your deal or presentation; how can you get past this screen on your way to the money?

There are a number of reasons a venture capitalist will give you if he is not interested in your deal. We have covered those that are a cover for not being at all interested, including "this does not fit our portfolio objectives," "we don't do software deals," "your management team is not complete," and "too early or late stage for us." This type of general objection usually means that the venture capitalist is just not interested in your deal, so if you hear these words your best approach is to find the real objection if you can, and move on to other venture capital sources, perhaps sadder but wiser, with a revised business plan.

If the venture capitalist is interested in your plan, as evidenced by continuing meetings and "due diligence," but continues to raise a number of weighty objections, you are half way home to your money if you are prepared to properly handle these objections. The "I'm interested but leery" objection is generally couched in the following manner: "your projections appear to be high for the market you are addressing;" "your marketing Vice President has never sold in the proposed distribution channels;" "I checked with several of your customers and they feel your product is good but not market tested;" "it appears to me that your research and development budget is short several million dollars over the next two years;" or "you appear to be a one–product company—what's next?" These specific questions reveal that the venture capitalist is now focusing on the specifics of your business plan and beginning to think through your particular business opportunity. If you handle these questions successfully, you will move on to the next step—negotiating the deal. All successful professional salespeople know how to handle customer objections.

Handling customer objections is both an art and a science. An art, in that you are asked to handle a complex human being, and a science in that you can experiment and practice using professional sales techniques prior to facing the actual objections which you must resolve in your favor if you are to finance your company. First, you must have the attitude that you are going to be a need satisfier. You are going to find out what this particular venture capitalist wants on this particular day and you are going to satisfy these needs. Not your own needs. Not someone else's. But those desires of the person before you.

In previous chapters we have discussed and reviewed some aspects of the type of personality who becomes a venture capitalist. However, it would be in your best interest to learn something specific of the needs and interests of the venture capitalist who is getting interested in your deal. This can usually best be accomplished by conveying an attitude of partnership, and by taking an interest in the venture capitalist personally. An attitude of partnership implies that you would not make any major decisions involving the business without first discussing the decision with your lead venture capitalist. By providing the venture capitalist with an opportunity to review your decision, you cement the relationship of trust and confidence with him. Since a venture capitalist is of wide experience in business development, he may also have raised some interesting questions which you had not considered. And you have assured that you will not as readily be "second–guessed" later if your decision does not work out.

Most entrepreneurs fail to develop an attitude of trust and confidence with their venture capitalist because they are by temperament unsuited for a partnership relationship. A number of entrepreneurs are attempting to resolve problems that they have with authority figures by creating their own thing, where they are forever free of oppressive authority. In the initial stages of a company, when the entrepreneur is out on the street trying to peddle an idea, he is generally free to starve and answers to no one. However, once the business is funded, and becomes successful, there is a whole horde of hangers–on, contributors, regulators, con men, tax men, and others who are going to want a piece of the action. If the entrepreneur wants to meet achievement needs and be a big success, the needs of a legion of partners must be addressed. These include, not least of all, the bankers and suppliers who will provide both product and credit, and the venture capitalist who will provide risk capital. Occasionally an entrepreneur does emerge who creates a successful company while minimizing silent partners. He bootstraps his operation on internally generated cash, mortgages house and family's future for seed capital, pays the bank back on high turn inventory, stays a private company, and avoids the "going public" hassle, or goes public but tires of disclosure, buys stock back from the public, and once again becomes a private preserve. These operations are rare today. They are particularly rare in high technology ventures where the "ramp up must be rapid" if the company is to have a prayer of surviving against predatory competition. Those entrepreneurs who successfully temper their authority conflicts, and work with their venture capitalist from the beginning as partners, have the best chance not only to be funded but to both survive and be successful.

Successful sales are consummated when the customer believes that the salesman is on his side—is for his interests. All great salesmen know this truth. This is most readily conveyed when the salesman is actually on the customer's side and is interested in providing service to the customer both before, during, and after the sale. You ask: what possible service does the venture capitalist require? After all, he has the money, and is a person of some recognized power and position, while you are just trying to get started. Like anyone else, the venture capitalist will respond to indications of real personal interest and concern and has his share of the desire to be listened to, and liked. The most successful fund–raising entrepreneurs (some are better at fund–raising than at building a company—more on this later) instinctively begin building a relationship of trust and confidence by discussing with the venture capitalist his most pressing needs, concerns, and interests. For a young MBA just starting in the business the concern may be to not make an early mistake in his first investment decision; for an individual in the business for several years with an institution, it may be an ambition to move from the institution into a private partnership; for the general partner in a private fund, concerns may be raising additional capital or having family squabbles with his other partners.

In addition to business needs we all have our private joys and sorrows where a sincere interest and concern does much to close a sale. If you demonstrate that you "like the venture capitalist" and take a sincere interest in his needs you are far more likely to close your financing than if you make a totally rational presentation of your business plan. Remember that making a sale, even to a venture capitalist, is far from a totally rational process.

In handling specific objections, it must be remembered that objections are reactions on the part of the venture capitalist to a threat. The venture capitalist is trying to slow you down a bit, and regain control of the buying situation. He is uneasy and not in the proper frame of mind for you to close your sale. Often these objections are not real. They are however strongly emotional, and if not overcome, will prevent a sale from being closed.

You may have raised a threat to the venture capitalist's self-image—the one he presents to the world in his business dealings. If you have attempted to get to know the venture capitalist through effective learning and listening, you will at this point have a concept of the venture capitalist's ideal self image, and a key tool in attempting to meet his objections to your deal. Most venture capitalists, like most buyers who control financial resources, have a high need for status. They want to be perceived as being in control of their assets and in control of the buying situation. After all, if you or any other seller is in control, what good are they to their investors who are relying on their investment judgement to insure safety and high returns?

Venture capitalists have all the other needs that human beings have, perhaps more so; these include security, acceptance, achievement, recognition, and relationship. The venture capitalist has patterns of conduct and belief, many of which are unconscious, which you need to attempt to divine and approach correctly. In short, you must know your customer to handle objections. Many entrepreneurs fail to approach the venture capitalist correctly because they project their own value systems on the customer. This is usually fatal. You must also attempt to divine the present mood of your customer. One day the venture capitalist may object to your proposal, whereas the next day you will receive a resounding yes. We are all aware that people have good days and bad, but we rarely act on this insight. We tend to want what we want, rather than really divining moods and putting ourselves in the other guy's shoes.

Most critical to a successful venture capital sale is presenting the benefits to the customer in the most favorable light. Some of these will be economic, since venture capital is in part an economic transaction, and some will be those intangibles of acceptance and partnership mentioned earlier. There are some interesting approaches to making the venture capitalist feel good about himself (and thus feel good about you and your company), which have been proven by entrepreneurs who have successfully raised capital. For instance, the venture capitalist has a need for information about your industry; continue to periodically send interesting articles which will educate about your industry, competition, and product; this approach will not only create comfort about your industry and economic opportunity but will let the venture capitalist know that you are thinking of him and have the enterprise to keep him advised and informed. In addition, periodic updates on milestones achieved or problems resolved are helpful in keeping his attention. If you are visiting his city an invitation to lunch or dinner will provide a chance to further size you up, and for you to show your stuff in another favorable setting. The venture capitalist may not be able to accept on the date you have in mind, but once again you have shown that you are interested, and have a creative, enterprising spirit.

One successful entrepreneur calls this approach "getting in the venture capitalist's face" or "calendar crowding." Whatever the name, you need to get your deal to the top of the pile. There is a fine line, however, between being tenacious and being pushy or attempting to intimidate—never cross this invisible boundary lying somewhere between what is aggressive and what is obnoxious, or you will risk losing the sale.

In your meetings and phone conversations, demonstrate that you recognize that the venture capitalist's time is a most important asset by coming prepared and getting down to business promptly. By these seemingly minor courtesies you convey an attitude of service; that you respect both the venture capitalist and yourself.

You need to find the venture capitalist's hot button—that part of his self-image to which you can direct your appeals most effectively. One successful recent approach was to put several venture capitalists in competition with each other over an attractive deal. In this case one backed out of the deal, but the other's competitive instincts were sufficiently aroused so that he funded the company. This approach requires considerable care, however, for the venture capitalists could decide that the entrepreneur is playing one against the other and the interest of both may be lost. Another approach which has proven successful is to be certain that at least one member of management is known and respected by one or more venture capitalists. In many respects this represents the perfect introduction, for the venture capitalist already trusts and respects one party. By implication the other members of management would be perceived as being capable by association.

Venture capitalists are taking considerable risk and they have a need to attempt to minimize this feeling of risk, or lack of control. To be successful you must satisfy this security need. Some venture capitalists also have a need to dominate a particular situation. This is particularly true of those who have achieved a major position in the business. The alert entrepreneur may have his own needs to dominate, but should remember in a selling situation a little deference can go a long way to successful close. You should not, however, let an attitude of deference indicate that you don't have what it takes to lead your own business.

Selling, even selling your own capabilities, is more a process of listening than it is of direct verbal persuasion. Few sales are closed by the weight of fact or argument. Most are closed because the prospect, in this case the venture capitalist, discovers for himself the merits of a particular course of action. By careful listening, you discover the self image of the venture capitalist and his particular hot button which will allow you to close your funding. You must be very alert during your presentation, and sensitive both to what the venture capitalist says, and to what is said between the lines. Continually recall that the venture capitalist makes few decisions that really matter, but that the one he is facing, in listening to you, is most critical.

Experienced salesmen employ certain proven techniques to overcome a customer's objection and close the sale. These include listening carefully to the objection so that you understand it, and more importantly, hearing the emotion of real objection behind the apparent statement; reducing the level of hostility or opposition by employing an empathic softening statement; converting the objection to a positive question, which you can answer in the affirmative, and finally, asking a closing question which will get you the funding.

It must be realized that many sales, including those of venture capital funding, depend on the balance of evidence or the preponderance of evidence being on one side or another. Few decisions are all or nothing—a complete acceptance or rejection—particularly in a business as intuitive as venture capital. Your task is to move the weight of the positive evidence to your side. This can best be accomplished by moving the customer's emotions to a favorable posture. First communicate to the venture capitalist that you are truly listening carefully to his objection. This is not easy in that he may be indirectly critical of your creation when he says: "I've seen a hundred high resolution graphics deals in the past ten years and not one ever made a dime." One technique is to repeat his objection sincerely so that the venture capitalist is aware that you comprehend. You may be prepared with an answer, but resist the temptation to jump in with your data or argument too fast. You don't want to make the fatal mistake of pitting your ego against the venture capitalist's. Keep the venture capitalist talking because he may come around to the positive aspects of your deal, or may talk himself out of an objection to your deal.

Most customers, including venture capitalists, don't have a large number of real objections to a business proposition. One successful entrepreneur, after being turned down by twenty-seven venture capitalists, had heard every possible objection and was ready with a prepared reply. He closed on number twenty-eight. Generally in a business which depends so much on people, the real objection is either the venture capitalist is not yet comfortable investing in your management team, or the price or terms of the deal are perceived as not compensating for the downside risk. Your task is to continue to make the venture capitalist comfortable with you and your deal. This can be accomplished when, in reply to an objection, after you have conveyed that you understand by repeating the question, you employ an empathic statement which shows that you understand how the venture capitalist feels. Let's say the venture capitalist says: "We really like your deal, but all our funds are committed at present to finance additional rounds in our present deals; perhaps when we raise more money in six months we can take another look at your company." You could reply: "Boy, I can really understand the demands on you—both your time and money—things are really difficult out there right now, but I know that you don't want to let this unique opportunity pass." Your statement, to be effective, must come from the heart and be sincere—if you cannot do this then it is best to leave this unsaid.

Next, by converting the venture capitalist's objection to a question, you add to your positive balance to close the sale. The venture capitalist says, "I really cannot make a commitment until I talk this over with my partners." (Many venture capital partnerships require unanimity on a deal or give other partners a right to veto a given deal.) You say, as a question: "What you are asking yourself is will my partners find this deal to be unique and compelling?" You then take the opportunity to answer this question by once again reviewing, in a non–threatening manner, the unique features of your deal and their fundamental appeal.

Once the principal objection is answered and you have covered in detail the venture capitalist's other concerns, you need to ask for the order. Since the venture capitalist may want to conduct further investigation or to consult with his partners you will not in most cases receive an immediate positive response. Thank the venture capitalist for his time, and attention, and ask when a positive response could be expected.

It should be remembered that the venture capitalist is in most cases a highly sophisticated buyer. It would insult his intelligence and dominance needs for you to attempt to close your deal in a highly aggressive manner. Much better to lay back and let the venture capitalist take the lead as you move to close.

You have learned to meet the venture capitalist's objections to your deal and provide for needs and desires in a selling situation. The next chapter presents the perceptions of an entrepreneur who successfully raised venture capital, as well as the author's comments on his perceptions.

7

"HOW I SUCCESSFULLY RAISED VENTURE CAPITAL"

In this chapter, Sanford Morganstein, President and Chief Executive Officer of Dytel Corporation of Arlington Heights, Illinois, replies to the author's questions concerning the venture capital fund–raising experience from the entrepreneur's perspective.* Mr. Morganstein has successfully raised both seed and early–stage venture capital for Dytel, a designer and manufacturer of telecommunications products providing PBX enhancements. Allstate Insurance Company was the lead investor in Dytel's early–stage financing along with Inco Ltd., C. Itoh (a major Japanese trading company), Robert LaBlanc Associates (a leading telecommunications consulting firm), Northern Capital Corporation of Chicago, and The Enterprise Fund, Houston, Texas.

Question:

What are the main problems facing the early-stage entrepreneur in the venture funding process?

Mr. Morganstein's Reply:

Many venture capital organizations are paying more attention to early-stage financing because of the higher potential returns concomitant with the higher risks that are associated with these investments. The prob-

*Reprinted with permission of Sanford Morganstein.

lem for the early-stage entrepreneur is the great imbalance between the entrepreneur's vital need to raise money, compared to the venture investor's need to participate in any single investment. For the early-stage company, getting funded is an absolute "do or die" situation, whereas for the venture investor there are plenty of companies around to invest in. Perhaps a better way to state this is if an investor passes on a particular investment, his loss is a loss out in the future when and if the company is successful. On the other hand, if a company does not get financed, it is most likely disaster for the company. The investor and the company simply do not have the same level of need to close a deal. One investor told us that many venture investors are looking for excuses for not making a particular investment.

Venture Capitalist's Response:

Mr. Morganstein correctly perceives the imbalance between most entrepreneurs' need for immediate cash, particularly in the early stage company, and the venture capitalist's need to make this particular investment; however, once a venture capitalist focuses a considerable portion of his most important resource (after money), his time, on an investment, he is reluctant to walk away from the investment opportunity unless a major red flag makes an unwelcome appearance. The best time to be raising money, for the entrepreneur, is always when he doesn't really need it—this goes for both debt and equity.

Question:

How does this imbalance cause problems during the entrepreneurial–venture capital relationship?

Mr. Morganstein's Reply:

For one, the venture capital investor is extremely busy—he or she is researching several proposals, is probably on the boards of portfolio companies, and is called on from time to time to assist in some problem situation. When an entrepreneur sends a business plan to a potential investor, he wants an early answer. Given that the venture investor is busy and does not share the company's urgency to make the investment, delays inevitably result. A proposal which is not going to go anywhere will probably get a courteous rejection very quickly, but a proposal that gets attention will take a good deal of time (I expect an average is six months). During this time, of course, the entrepreneur is in limbo.

This same imbalance leads to another problem. The entrepreneur must look under every stone to find his or her funding. Because they are busy, venture investors don't like to compete with each other. If a company is lucky enough to find two potential investors and is working seriously with one of them, one or both of the potential investors may lose interest—they're too busy to waste time on an investment which will not select *them*.

The imbalance could also lead to problems at the negotiation table. Here's where the importance of a good venture investor comes in. The good investor, one who is interested in building companies *and* making a good return, will not try to extract a pound of flesh. The experienced investor will realize that exercising too much power will damage the company if the investment goes forward. Nonetheless, with the present high level of venture money and with a lack of sufficient numbers of experienced investors, many venture capital companies are hiring relatively inexperienced staff people who make it unnecessarily difficult for the company. We have met potential investors who are quite pleased with the imbalance I have described. They perceive that it always works for them. I am not making a comment on the fairness of the process—it doesn't have to be fair—I am only pointing out that the imbalance of the needs of the entrepreneur and the investor is the biggest problem a company has in seeking venture financing.

Venture Capitalist's Response:

While venture capitalists do not like to be rushed into making an investment decision, financings can be arranged in weeks or even days if the particular opportunity is both urgent and rich enough, and the entrepreneur flexible as to the terms of the deal once the price is agreed upon. Most venture capital financings get strung out because the entrepreneur and venture capitalist are really continuing to negotiate the terms of the deal up to the final closing.

Mr. Morganstein is correct in his conclusion that the experienced venture capital investor is interested in a deal which is fair to all concerned. Unfair deals quickly come unraveled, the parties start squabbling, and little or no business gets booked.

Question:

Looking back on the venture funding process, what is your overall opinion of it?

Mr. Morganstein's Reply:

The process of raising venture capital is very difficult. It is fraught with risk and anxiety, as I will describe in some of the following answers. But, there is one particular positive point that I would like to make.

Others have pointed out that American business, in general, is short-term oriented. Despite the fact that many businesses require a long-term view, many corporations get nervous in situations which require more than a year or two to reach profitability. In such situations, a short-term, bottomline–only plan would probably be adopted by the corporation instead of a longer term, albeit more pragmatic plan.

Venture capital is pretty different. Venture investors know that they are in a situation which will require from five to seven years to mature. In this respect, the venture capitalists are more "strategy" oriented, and are more like others—particularly the Japanese—who, on the whole, take a longer term view of business success.

While I think overall that the venture capital process is extremely difficult for the early-stage company, it is certain that if there was no venture capital process, we at Dytel would not have started the Company. The process is difficult and unbalanced, as I have pointed out, but it is certainly one that we entered into with our eyes open. Many times we wished that somehow it could work differently, or that we could put it behind us faster than we in fact did, but overall we learned what it was we had to do.

Anyone who is thinking about immersing himself or herself in this difficult process should be buoyed by the fact that once the investment is made, a long-term partnership will ensue. It provides a real opportunity to create successes which take more time than would otherwise be available. The patience and long view of the venture investors is hard to match anyplace else. It gives the entrepreneurial businessman the time and wherewithal to do his thing.

Venture Capitalist's Response:

There are a number of objections which entrepreneurs may raise to venture capital; it is too expensive; why use it if you don't require it—just bootstrap your operation; takes too long and is too much hassle; too much money in the wrong hands can be worse than too little; and the venture capitalists never really took the time to understand the business and yet intervened in critical decisions. Entrepreneurs still often want the money because as Mr. Morganstein indicates, money which is well and carefully spent buys time, resources, and at times an insurmountable lead over the competition. This lead is critical to success in those industries and for those products which, while innovative, are not one–of–a–kind. Occasionally an entrepreneur comes along who excess cash manages to kill. He can't stand prosperity. Venture capitalists prefer cash conservers. Most professional venture capitalists will take the time to understand your business. The entrepreneur must understand that in ambiguous, risky situations, honest, even honorable men will differ from time to time.

Question:

Why were you successful in raising major venture capital?

Mr. Morganstein's Reply:

We were successful, I believe, because we satisfied most of the classic, textbook criteria that the venture investor looks for. First of all, we have a good management team. Unlike many technological companies, we recognized early the need for strong marketing skills. We spent a good deal of time recruiting the best marketing executive we could find, and frankly, we were lucky to land him. Our Engineering Department had a proven track record of being able to develop and manage the development of similar products. Our production Operations Manager also had done this before. In fact, the biggest weakness in the management team was almost always perceived to lie with me since I had never had complete CEO responsibility despite the fact that I managed staffs and budgets larger than our entire company will be for several years. A good part of the reason we were successful probably had to do with my ability to overcome this objection. I am probably not alone in overcoming this objection. Many extremely successful ventures were started by people who have the necessary skills but simply have not done it before. The literature abounds with examples.

We also had a strong, independent Board consisting of outsiders. They had previously been involved with fledgling companies, and I believe they provided a good deal of confidence for the investors.

Furthermore, we had a new product which had already demonstrated success in the market. Our customer list was impressive, our product's reliability was excellent, and our market was paying good attention to us. In line with having a proven product, we had, to a certain extent, begun to prove the company. We had been in business for two years by the time the investment was closed, and we proved that we could manage in times of adversity and that we were capable of accomplishing a great deal by a combination of skill and extraordinary effort. At the time we went to raise money, we were a very small company being managed professionally like a big company. Our success was most probably tied to our being able to convince investors of this fact.

Venture Capitalist's Response:

The investors backed Mr. Morganstein and his management team despite a lack of CEO experience on Sandy's part because he surrounded himself with a Chairman and Directors with this vital experience, and because he had previous related leadership experience. In addition he has the intuitive ability to make a decision after careful consideration. The team were proven survivors, and had the mark of winners.

Question:

Was it more difficult to raise your seed capital, or your later-stage financing?

Mr. Morganstein's Reply:

I really don't know that my answer to this will be meaningful to others. It was unquestionably easier to raise the seed money, but I think this may have been by chance rather than a result of the nature of raising money.

At the seed-capital stage, the stakes were lower both for the investor and for the company. We were lucky to have raised seed money from those who had strategic interest in participating with us. The early investors were clearly motivated by a desire to create a company in our business area. The profit motive was there as well, but the motivation of the early investors was qualitatively different from the motivation of the venture investors.

Venture Capitalist's Response:

Some of the best seed–capital investors are motivated as much by participation in the creative process of business–building as they are by realizing outrageous rates of return on their capital. By and large the earlier the stage the deal, the more risky, so the returns in both capital and psychic income are generally higher for the initial investor. Early–stage investors endure more uncertainty.

Question:

How do venture capitalists differ? How are they the same?

Mr. Morganstein's Reply:

I have a model of the venture capital community in my mind which because of its generality is probably fraught with error. But, nonetheless, I look at four kinds of venture investors.

First, there is the inexperienced staff person who is learning the business. These people can cause problems, and I don't want to say too much more about them.

Then, there are the experienced investors who are usually principals in a venture investing firm. They're interesting because to a large extent, they themselves are entrepreneurs. These people tend to be very tough on valuation (i.e., the percentage of the company they want) and, in my experience at least, have a bias that they know more about the business than the management team does. On the one hand, this can be good since they will be active participants in the business when it goes forward, but on the other hand, if this attitude is exaggerated, the strong-willed entrepreneur will run into conflict with the strong-willed investor.

Next, is the experienced investor who works for an investment division of a larger institution. In our experience, these tend to be the most fair since they don't have the natural tendency to view profits as only going into their pockets or into those of the entrepreneur. They are more likely to look at the prospect of investing in a company as being wildly successful, or savagely unsuccessful. Because of this, they worry less about who gets which percentage—a big part of zero is zero—a small part of the moon is fine. I originally thought that this type of institutional investor would be encumbered by his or her organization. There is a risk of not receiving the high level management approval needed to make a significant investment. Nonetheless, I suspect that if the lead analyst gives the entrepreneur a reasonable expectation that approvals will be forthcoming, then in all likelihood, the approval will be given even though the process is somewhat slower than that of an entrepreneurial investment firm.

Finally, there is the "seed investor." I include the seed investor in this discussion although some may feel that a seed investor is not a venture capitalist. A seed investor is usually a private person who invests his own funds, although a seed investor can be a strong individual within a large organization which typically does not do venture investing. Usually, of course, the seed investor cannot make the sizable investment really needed to take the company forward, but the seed investor probably does the most to help the company develop.

A seed investor is an early-stage investor who will invest in things that others won't touch. They are as much motivated by the creative urge of sculpting companies as they are by making large returns. The seed investor will give the company an incredible amount of personal time and

will guide the growing company in a non-directive, emphatic, constructive style. The amount of time a seed investor spends is significantly out
of proportion to the funds he has invested because a good deal of his satisfaction comes from growing companies and executives. Seed investors
are one of the best things that can happen to a company.

Venture Capitalist's Response:

While initially an institutional investor may be more objective or de-
tached than an investor from an entrepreneurial venture capital partnership, this detachment is difficult to maintain for any venture capital
investor after the considerable investment of time, energy, and emotion
as well as money that the normal venture capital investment requires.

Question:

*Are venture capitalists really interested in company–building or just
out for a buck?*

Mr. Morganstein's Reply:

There are some venture capitalists who I referred to earlier as seed
investors. They probably share their interests between people–building,
company–building, and moneymaking. But, the tone of the question almost makes it sound like an apology is needed for those who want to make
money but don't care about the growth of companies or people. While
seed investors do indeed exist, an entrepreneur who expects only seed
investors to invest is in for a rude awakening. Not everybody who is associated with the entrepreneur's company has the same expectations of
the company. This is true of both investors and employees. The entrepreneur who doesn't realize that a good part of his job is to take diverse interests and make something of value of it is probably not prepared to make
the compromises needed in the day-to-day management of the company.

We had one venture investor tell us that he doesn't want to make the
entrepreneur a friend—he wants to make him rich. Although no one is
going to have animus towards another who makes him rich, the point that
this investor was making is very well taken. The fuel and lubricant which
makes this whole venture capital machine run is money. Seed investors
are great, and often essential, but there is no reason to curse a daisy because it's not a rose.

Venture Capitalist's Response:

Mr. Morganstein correctly identifies that a company has many constituences and that the CEO must play to their varied needs and mold those needs so that they all contribute to the success of the company. Part of the CEO's job is to create both confidence and value in and through all the company's supporters.

Question:

Are you concerned that venture capitalists will attempt to take over your company later on?

Mr. Morganstein's Reply:

No, I'm not concerned about this, and for a variety of reasons.

Early in our search for a venture investor, we ran across the companies who, if they didn't want to actually take us over, wanted to have a direct day-to-day impact on the company that bordered on being disconcerting. When we were being interviewed by these investors, we felt like we were being interviewed for a job, we felt that we were going to be hired to implement the investor's plan for building a related group of companies. I don't consider the approach as a "takeover," but with such an investor, I would be extremely concerned about the degree of autonomy I would be able to exercise.

On the other hand, the hands-off investor who lets the company do its thing with gentle guidance will undoubtedly play a bigger role if the business later flounders. In fact, I think many venture investments are structured such that the investor can, indeed, gain a majority control of the Board of Directors in the event any of several serious problems occurs. I'm not concerned about this eventuality. One reason is that my natural entrepreneurial optimism doesn't let me spend much time on it; and secondly, if things really do get that bad and the venture investors feel that all or part of management can't do anything about it, then management has failed and the company probably should be taken over.

Venture Capitalist's Response:

Most venture capitalists would rather not run your company—that's why they invested in the entrepreneur. A number of successful venture capitalists have either run companies before and don't want to, or have never run a company and don't want to try. The few that do want to run companies are probably not sure what business they want to be in, operating or investing.

Question:

Why did you choose the venture capital route to financing your company rather than other alternatives?

Mr. Morganstein's Reply:

I don't think we had much choice. We certainly weren't bankable. We may have been able to interest a large company to buy us and merge us into one of their divisions, but no one in our company wanted that. We couldn't have raised more money from our own savings—our seed investors, management, employees, relatives and friends couldn't provide the kind of money we needed.

There may have been many other sources to look at, but notwithstanding the presence of or absence of choice, venture capital was the objective we set for ourselves. We concluded early that venture capital would provide us with the kind of money we needed to position our company through early unprofitable periods. We felt that the venture investor has the necessary long term view to allow us to sacrifice immediate return for long term growth. Finally, we felt that the venture investor would leave management with enough equity to keep us motivated to the highest degree.

Venture Capitalist's Response:

Some ideas are big ideas and they take big money to implement. Time and chance wait for no one.

Question:

What traits do you look for in a lead investor?

Mr. Morganstein's Reply:

The lead investor has several pretty important roles to play, and these roles may be difficult. Once he or she decides to make an investment, he should play an active role in putting the rest of the investment group together (typically, venture investments are made by more than one investor because of the need to share the risk and to make it easier to raise more money should that become necessary).

Just *locating* potential investors is one part of this assistance, and only one reason why this assistance is important. The lead investor has a network of other investors with whom he has probably previously co-invested, and with whom he may be on a Board of Directors. The ease with which an investor can interest other investors says something about how he is perceived by his colleagues. If he can't get anyone to go along with him, he may have previously touted some bad investments, or he may have received poor marks in a Director's role.

Once other investors become interested in the company, the lead investor's role continues to be important, at least until the time the financing is closed. The reason is that consensus on details of the investment has to be arrived at among the company and the venture investors. If there is more than one venture investor, you end up with the situation of trying to find consensus among a diverse and often terribly opinionated and even stubborn group of people. Reaching such consensus is difficult, and the lead investor should be both strong and influential enough to make sure it happens.

It may be just our experience, but it seems that many early-stage financings get done when the company is in a precarious situation. If the lead investor has decided to make the investment, then it is real important for him to ensure that the process of reaching consensus and making all of the finishing touches does not significantly damage the company. The lead investor can do many things during this period. If the negotiation with the other members of the investment group runs into snags, the lead investor should exercise leadership; if the company needs to pay an important vendor/supplier, or pay a debt, then a bridge loan should be forthcoming (remember—the hypothesis is that the investor had already decided to make the investment); if the company needs an individual to complete or augment the management team, then the lead investor should be using his contacts to make resumes available.

I think that our company has a particularly strong Board of Directors who will continue to provide advice and guidance as our company grows. It is important for the lead investor to be someone with solid business experience who will continue to be a major contributor once the venture investment closes. These traits of fairness and integrity, and good sense, will eventually be more important than deal-closing leadership.

Venture Capitalist's Response:

Pick a lead investor who is not only able, considered able by his peers, but who is also willing to work with, and consider the opinion of other investors, particularly in times of trouble. The lone wolf investor as a lead can destroy both an investment syndicate and your company.

Question:

Did you get a fair deal from the venture capitalists?

Mr. Morganstein's Reply:

When the seesaw between investor and company is as unbalanced as I claim it is, it is hard to imagine how it can turn out fairly. Maybe it is a tribute to the venture investors individually that our situation did turn out in a manner which we consider, on the whole, fair. There are aspects of our situation, on the other hand, which we do consider to be unfair. We try to take our situation as a whole. We are quite pleased that we have been financed and that we can now get on with the business of running our business.

We feel we received a fair price for the percentage of the company which we sold, and feel it is particularly fair that the venture investors found a way to accept our valuation of our company provided we meet certain objective criteria.

As I stated at the outset, the process doesn't have to be fair, but if it is terribly unfair to the point of emasculating management and their incentive, then the investor risks managing a non-performing investment. We've had investors tell us that they invest by the golden rule—"He who has the gold makes the rules." So again, the agreements do not have to be fair. But, in answer to your question; yes, on the whole our deal was fair.

Venture Capitalist's Response:

Whether the price paid turns out to be fair depends mostly on the outcome. Selective shopping keeps everyone honest.

Question:

Was the price of the deal important to you?

Mr. Morganstein's Reply:

Yes, but for reasons which may be different from what you would expect. When you look at what the ultimate success of the company will mean to the founders, the price of the deal (meaning, do we give up "X percent," or "Y percent") is pretty immaterial if "X" and "Y" are reasonably close, and even if they are not close, one tends to get lost comparing two very large numbers. We worked very closely with two potential investors, and "X" and "Y" were, in fact, very close. What concerned us, on the other hand, was the fact that both "X" and "Y" were close to 50 percent. The 50 percent number meant that, according to the returns we predicted in our business plan, the venture investor would have had compounded returns of 70 percent per year. This in itself is not a problem; we don't really care about someone else's return as long as ours is fair. But, what the 50 percent figure told us was that the investors viewed us as a very early-stage company and that our achievements—marketing, engineering, and production—were not being given proper consideration. Since the 50 percent figure did not correlate with our notions about desired returns for investors, we could not ascribe the offer to anything but a "venture capital knee jerk." I guess the point of this is that some non-financial considerations get mixed into the entrepreneur's perception of a venture capital offer.

In our case, the dilemma was worked out in a creative way. If we performed according to objective profit targets for the first two years of the plan, we would give up "X percent" of the company, and if we did worse, we would give up "Y percent" where "Y" depended on the degree to which we missed the plan. Also, "Y" couldn't be greater than a certain amount.

We were surprised that some investors later expressed opinions that this sliding scale pricing of the investment based on profit performance over a period of time is a bad approach, and I never fully accepted their arguments. The nature of such a compromise isn't perfect since it could force the entrepreneur into making short-term decisions which could affect long-term profitability. There is no doubt that this risk exists, but the very nature of the entrepreneur/venture investor is long-term anyway, and, in our opinion, the risk is outweighed by the extra motivation we have to perform according to our plan.

Venture Capitalist's Response:

Performance formulas are controversial because they can cause the company's management to place their emphasis on objectives which maximize their pricing but minimize or dilute the company's business performance. They can be used if both investors and management are mature and mostly focused on the success of the business rather than immediate personal gain.

Question:

What was the most difficult part of your experience in raising venture capital?

Mr. Morganstein's Reply:

Since we were pretty far along with two different investment firms, the hardest part was to keep them both interested until we received a firm commitment from one of them. As I mentioned earlier, venture investors are among the busiest people around. Given the large volume of proposals they receive, and our assumption that they have a predilection to turning proposals down, we felt that if either of them decided not to compete with the other, then we would lose a potential investor. My earlier point was that it was of vital importance to us to get funded and of somewhat lesser importance for any given investor to invest in us.

We were, therefore, faced with spending a good deal of time with both investment firms and we helped them with their investigation and due diligence and doing whatever we could to keep them both interested despite their predisposition against competing with each other.

There are other problems, too. We, of course, had to continue to run our business while we spent a good deal of time with the investors. We had also planned to make some important hires, and we didn't know if we could afford to. We did find, however, much to our surprise, that our customers were not overly concerned that investors would call them (as part of the investor's due diligence investigation). Customers did mind when they were called frequently by different investors, but this was more of an annoyance factor, and it didn't seem to raise concerns in the minds of our customers about the company's financial stability.

I think that the rest of the process of raising venture capital, while difficult, is not too different from that which is needed to run the business properly anyway. An investor needs a business plan—so does the company. A company needs a management team—investors need to see it. A company needs satisfied customers, and the investors need to see this as well.

Since investors check out customer references, the company must make sure that its customers are being properly treated. Again, a good company must do this whether or not it is raising venture capital.

Venture Capitalist's Response:

Venture capital is a very time–intensive business and in recent years there have been both more capital and more good deals than in the past. The active venture capitalist is trying to catch the best deals, while helping revive several troubled deals, perhaps raise new capital for his fund (if a private partnership), hire and train new employees, and participate in industry and entrepreneurial meetings and associations. He has a very full plate. The entrepreneur must both respect and obtain his fair share of this time if he is to successfully raise capital. Since the entrepreneur can rarely be sure of financing until the terms are agreed on or the deal closed, it is best for a time to continue to work with several potential investors. Once a lead investor commits, however, it is time to stop courting other's favor.

Question:

How could the venture capital community improve their approach to facilitate the money-raising process?

Mr. Morganstein's Reply:

I am heartened by this question. It goes back to my answer to the first question concerning the obstacles a going company faces in raising venture capital. The fact that the question is asked points out that the venture capitalists realize that all may not be rosy.

First of all, let me point out that the venture capitalists do provide an extremely professional approach. If they're not interested, they let you know very quickly so that you can begin to knock on some other door. Also, despite the fact that they are very busy, they are very good at focusing on the prospective investee company so that when you are working with them, they quickly grasp what your business is about. Further, they have been involved with many companies at similar stages of their development and they can easily point out deficiencies of the company's planned cash flow, inventory, distribution, etc. This experience factor is extremely important and, hopefully, venture capitalists will be careful how they use the "apprentices" who are learning the venture capital business.

The venture capitalists also do a good job of informing prospective companies about what the process is like. Several organizations exist which put on seminars about raising venture capital, and venture capitalists are almost always willing to participate. This book is another example of a service which, hopefully, will help the entrepreneur learn what to expect when trying to raise venture capital. Of course, once an investment is made, the venture capitalist is in an extremely good position to facilitate the company–building process. They usually will be members or observers of the company's Board of Directors. At this stage, they bring their experience and business skills to bear on the strategic decisions facing the young company. Furthermore, they are in a position to help the company with business contacts that the company might not otherwise have. Some refer to this as "know who, not know–how."

Venture Capitalist's Response:

A professional venture capitalist, like the entrepreneur he backs, mostly learns his business through the world of hard knocks. The industry does need to work on methods to help develop new members of the community other than through baptism by fire.

Question:

What criteria did the various venture capitalists use to evaluate your deal?

Mr. Morganstein's Reply:

All of the venture capitalists we talked to considered the strength of the management team to be extremely important. It's probably a cliche to point out that an investor would rather invest in a company with excellent management with an OK product than the other way around. Others, however, feel that if the product is extraordinary but management is only so-so, they can strengthen the management team after the investment is closed. In any case, one of the important characteristics of the management team is its record of success in a situation which is closely related to the situation in the new company. The investors certainly are interested in companies that are doing something new and different. They will be more favorably disposed towards a company whose product or service presents a strong economic incentive for the customer to purchase the product or service.

We would like to believe that one of the criteria used to evaluate the pricing of the deal is the rate of return the investment would provide. As I pointed out earlier, I don't think this was done in our case, and it's very difficult for this to be done in the case of any early-stage company because of the extremely high degree of uncertainty inherent in the young company's own projections.

I think the venture capitalist also looks for a company which is a business area of overall interest to the investor, such as computers, medical equipment, software, etc. Some have mentioned that they look particularly for new market niches and I'm sure that this criterion was used in our case. Also, I think the venture capitalist uses geography as one criterion in making an investment decision. If the prospective company is close to the investor, the company has a better chance—other factors being equal—since the investor would welcome the opportunity to reduce his travel.

Venture Capitalist's Response:

Creative people who can survive ambiguity and adversity are rare but not impossible to find.

Question:

Is venture capital money expensive money?

Mr. Morganstein's Reply:

At first glance, venture capital money is very expensive. An investor is looking for 40 percent to 50 percent compounded return on his investment. If a company borrowed $1.00 from a bank, and paid 15 percent interest per year, at the end of five years the company would pay back $2.01 in an equity situation. At 40 percent, this same dollar would cost $4.38 (you don't usually have to pay back the equity). So, it appears that venture money is expensive, but there's another way to look at it. Most companies which are venture funded are not candidates for bank financing—at least not for the same amount of money which could be made available by a venture investor. Now, let's suppose that an entrepreneur gives up 50 percent of the company to an investor who gets a 40 percent compounded return. This means that the company also gets a 40 percent compounded return on the venture capitalist's dollar, and the company, therefore, turns the $1.00 into $5.38 (the company keeps the equity), which is worth $2.69 to the company's original investors (including the 2:1 dilution). So, the company has a net gain of $2.69. Now, suppose that a bank would lend the company $.10 where the venture investor would invest $1.00. Let's also assume that the company could also increase the value of this $.10 at a 40 percent compounded rate. At the end of five years, $.10 compounded at 40 percent per year is worth $.54. The interest and principal on $.10 at 15 percent over five years is $.20, so the company, in this case, gains $.54 minus $.20, or $.34. Remember, the company in the venture investment case gains $2.69.

Maybe this sounds like an apology for the high rate of return a venture investor gets, but I don't think my example is too farfetched. In many cases, a company could not borrow as much as 10 percent as a venture investor would invest. Overall, you may have to conclude that venture money is expensive, but you get a lot for the price.

I've prepared an interesting chart to help answer the question whether venture capital money is expensive. The chart intends to show what percentage of a venture capital investment a bank would have to lend a company at 15 percent interest for five years for the company to be

Compounding Rate

Dilution Rate	20%	25%	30%	35%	40%	45%	50%
25%	391%	220%	164%	136%	198%	109%	102%
30%	365%	205%	153%	127%	112%	102%	95%
35%	339%	191%	142%	118%	104%	95%	88%
40%	313%	176%	131%	109%	96%	87%	82%
45%	287%	161%	120%	100%	88%	80%	75%
50%	261%	147%	109%	91%	80%	73%	68%
55%	235%	132%	98%	82%	72%	66%	61%

The ratio of loan to equity investment provides equal benefit to the company and gives various dilution effects, assuming a compounded rate of return that the company can achieve with the money. The chart assumes a 15 percent interest rate on borrowed funds for a period of five years.

"whole" compared to an equity investment. The vertical axis shows how much dilution the company would suffer, and the horizontal axis gives hypothetical returns the company could achieve with the money from an equity investment, or bank loan. The contents of the table shows what percentage of an equity investment a bank would have to loan for the loan to be as valuable as the equity investment.

Venture Capitalist's Reply:

On a scale of one to ten an experienced venture capitalist can locate your deal. Take some of the risk out of the deal for him, and he may give you a better price.

Question:

What techniques did you use to sell your deal?

Mr. Morganstein's Reply:

I believe that a good venture capitalist is motivated by the desire to build companies as well as the desire to make big returns. In our company, all of key management was very enthusiastic about our business, our potential, and what we had already accomplished. We made sure we communicated our enthusiasm to each potential investor and hoped it was infectious.

But, overall, I think that techniques used to sell the company to an investor are similar to those used to run the company. We tried very hard to get trade press coverage of our new product. The coverage was impressive and very positive, and we used reprints with potential investors and continue to use them for potential customers. We started early to present ourselves as a company with a strong commitment to customer service. Our customers and investors both liked this. The investors were favorably impressed with us because they spoke to customers who had had the benefit of our customer service. We were in business for two years before we raised venture capital, and were able to point out to potential investors that we could manage our business, and plan and perform according to plan.

There were a couple of things we did which fall outside this premise which were specifically related to attracting venture capital. One of these tactics was chosen particularly to raise our proposal to a higher degree of attention than it would have otherwise received from the busy venture capitalists. I became personally involved in a nonprofit organization which supported other entrepreneurial companies. I got to meet several venture capitalists through this organization, and I believe that when the time came to present our business plan, it was somewhat easier for me.

Venture Capitalist's Response:

Once the money is raised the real work of company–building begins. An entrepreneur who can sell a venture capitalist should have sufficient skills to sell his product. However, neither venture capitalist nor entrepreneur should ever forget that the product marketplace is often less forgiving than the deal marketplace of venture capital. Some entrepreneurs are better at selling their vision than at closing product sales.

Question:

Several venture capitalists turned you down. What did you learn from these rejections?

Mr. Morganstein's Reply:

Grace.

Some of the reasons for the rejections we had anticipated as problems and risks associated with our new business. When it came to rejections because of problems we knew about, we felt disappointment, but didn't learn very much from it. These rejections did, however, remind us that we should perhaps focus on these problems and try to meet them.

Some of the rejections made little sense to us. My favorite is the "fear of competition" rejection. We have a unique product and if it is any good, there would certainly be competition. The opposite pole of this kind of rejection is the one which is based on the uniqueness of the product. This produces fear of there being no market for the product. We felt that the people who turned us down because of "fear of competition" fall into the category of those who are looking for reasons not to invest. They could have just as easily turned us down out of concern that our market wouldn't develop.

Maybe my view of this comes out of hubris, but overall, I don't think we learned valuable lessons from rejections. A venture capitalist who turns a particular investment down feels that the problem he or she sees can't be fixed. Otherwise, he would invest and then participate in fixing the problem. Maybe we would have felt differently if someone had told us that they would invest "if. . . . " Actually, we did get one such rejection from someone who didn't like our initial valuation of the company. He said that he would "consider" the proposal if the price were different. By the time we received the rejection, we had, in fact, already modified our initial valuation and were too far along with our ultimate investor to go back and start a price negotiation with the new one.

Question:

Would you do it again?

Mr. Morganstein's Reply:

Not soon.

8

PRICING YOUR DEAL

It is apparent by now that while venture capital is exacting for both the entrepreneur and the venture capitalist, it is not exact. There is constant interplay of a variety of human emotions, including greed and avarice, as well as creativity and common purpose. This is as true in pricing a venture capital deal as in any other aspect of the business. This chapter provides an introduction to venture capital pricing which will provide a leg up when taking the venture capitalist on over price. You will learn how a venture capitalist prices a deal, whether price really matters, and how to position your deal for a fair but favorable price. Many are misguided when it comes to venture capital pricing. They mistakenly believe that the only deals which venture capitalist's will do require that the company become a one hundred million dollar company within five years, and that the return on investment to the venture investor must exceed fifty percent per annum. Not so; a number of venture capital firms are interested in singles, doubles, and triples, as well as home runs—at least the majority are. Some, however, will only look seriously at home run deals.

Before you go to see the venture capitalist, you should have a good idea about how much of your company you want to sell, for what price. In considering pricing and his risk, the venture capitalist will be looking at several factors including how much he can expect to make if the deal goes as projected; how much he will lose if it goes bust; what is likely to happen if it just does o.k.; how you and he will eventually part company, and he will get his money out; and how much time he is likely to spend working with you to make the company a success. Most venture capitalists are more interested in those deals where the entrepreneur and his team have a personal investment in the company. For these "entrepreneur at financial risk" deals, more attractive pricing is available. Some experienced investors believe that the level of risk in the later–stage deals is actually equal to the early–stage and therefore will require a substantial return at any stage. The particular stage at which a deal will be categorized is somewhat in the eye of the beholder, so the entrepreneur will be best served by casting his deal in the most favorable, but also realistic light.

Keep in mind also that when venture capitalists attempt to raise money from their investors, a number will state in their prospectus that their prior investments have achieved 40 percent to 60 percent compounded rates of return. For some of these firms this is pure fiction at worst, and at best stretching the point. Most of these computations involve the inclusion of unrealized capital gains which represent mark-ups over prior round financings based on the value paid by adding a new outside investor. The most realistic return measure for a venture capital fund is cash on cash, or the actual cash generated from income received from the investments, return of principal, and capital gains minus capital losses and provisions for loss. A smaller venture capital pool should, over the life of the partnership, realistically expect to achieve a 20 percent to 25 percent return per annum on investment. The larger pools of capital (anything over $100 million) would be doing well to be in the 15 percent to 20 percent annual return range. Larger pools tend to generate more losses in that they are involved in a large number of investments, and they are more inclined to take the occasional crapshoot that the smaller fund will avoid.

Venture capitalists generally want their money back within five to eight years, with the emphasis on the early return of capital. Like any business, the more rapid the turnover of inventory—other things being equal—the more profit. A real aggravating deal for the venture capitalist is when a deal enters the "land of the living dead." This is the deal that over six or seven years develops into a $10 or $12 million dollar revenue company which is making a little bit of money. Usually the entrepreneur and his team are drawing down adequate salaries and have long ago given up the dream of becoming a major company. They have little incentive to give up the good life and go public, if possible, and/or merge into another company. In brief, the venture capitalist is stuck. He is now tying up both time and money in a no results deal—perhaps it would be better from his perspective if the company went under.

Somewhere between 5 and 15 percent of the deals fail utterly and completely. The venture capitalist is wiped out, as is the management. Most of the money has been contributed as common stock or some equivalent of common, such as the so–called "California preferred." There is generally a long line of hungry creditors, because prior to failure, most venture–backed companies have the credibility required to talk other businesses into providing credit.

The venture capitalist's so–called downside risk of the deal going south is a difficult call. Certain types of deals—the more creative software deals, those that require a lot of money to make any progress, such as the development of new materials processes to be marketed into entrenched industries, and medical deals that may chew up years in the FDA (not to mention exorbitant amounts of investors cash)—are clearly long on the downside. Many investors will avoid these deals completely. Those that will play will exact more than the usual pound of flesh, and they should. The venture capitalist can get totally killed in these plays.

Occasionally a venture capitalist will take part of his investment in debt or convertible debt with a cap or call, and part of the investment in common stock or a convertible preferred. This split approach provides the venture capitalist with some protection of capital plus good return if the deal does as projected. The company gets a lower rate on the debt portion, and the right to clear up the debt if more equity can be raised later, internally or from the outside, at more favorable terms than the initial deal.

Entrepreneurs rarely believe that they are going to require additional money beyond the initial round of financing. Venture capitalists know from long experience that it always takes more time and money than anyone imagined to create a new business. The unexpected always arises to test the staying power of both entrepreneur and venture capital investor. New business approaches eat money.

If an entrepreneur raises the exact amount of money, give or take 10 percent, to reach a major milestone in his business plan such as the completion of product development, or the obtaining of major contracts, or the actual sale of the product, and the financial and venture capital markets are not involved in a major correction just when he is seeking additional funding, it is probable that he will raise money at a higher or the same valuation as long as he retains the confidence of his prior investors and they agree to put up minimum "show money" or "confidence money" so that new investors will see that the old are putting their money with their mouth. In many cases, experience demonstrates that the company would have been better off taking what money it could, when it was available. The old saw about bankers lending you money when you don't need it, and refusing when you do, applies in some degree to all financial markets. Within reason, get it when you can.

One venture capital school holds that "price doesn't matter." In a perfect world with perfect hindsight this is true. If a deal is a total write-off, price doesn't matter; if the deal goes to the moon and returns barrels of cash, no one cares what they paid, other than they would have preffered to have invested earlier. Its base hits where the price matters, and these will comprise much of the normal portfolio. When a venture capitalist invests, he cannot be sure of the outcome; which will shoot the moon and which will be putouts. Price does and should matter to both the venture capitalist and entrepreneur, but it should not matter too much. In those deals where the entrepreneur can be fairly confident that he may not require too many additional rounds of financing (such as when product development has been completed), he can afford to be more flexible as to price. If it is probable that a number of additional rounds will be required, his equity is his gold and should be guarded carefully.

Ultimately price is set by the vagaries of the market more so than by the calculation and permutations of the venture capitalist or entrepreneur. In the venture capital marketplace, price is often in a period of readjustment depending on the influence of a variety of factors, including how much venture capital is available, how much has been invested in various stage deals, the current capital gains rate, the stage of the public market (how possible and how rich are initial public offerings), and the bullish or bearish temperature of the venture capital community. Price, as has been mentioned, is also a function of geography, and how much squabbling you can create, among venture capitalists, for your opportunity.

Price is the measure of value. In a deal it is the place where minds meet and agree on a mutual satisfactory exchange—the venture capitalist's money in exchange for participation in an opportunity which will produce a future earnings stream which will compensate for the risk assumed. What is risk to one man may be adventure to another. What is rejected by one, may be accepted by another. A bargain, to one, may be a holdup to another.

Venture capitalists worry a lot about a concept called valuation. This means that if you offer 50 percent of your company to a venture capitalist for $1 million your company is now valued or has a valuation of $2 million. Your 50 percent is now valued at $1 million. This is mostly play money. It does not become real money until you pass go by going public or selling your company to another company. Venture capitalists are very leery about paying too high a valuation. For several reasons. No one likes to be thought of as overpaying for a deal. This reflects on the investor's sanity if not judgment. If you overpay for several deals, the word may get around and every hungry investment banker with an overpriced deal will be knocking at the front gate. In addition all your friends in the business will send you those deals where they are trying to round up money at a higher price. You want to be in their better deals early, not their shopped deals late. One successful venture capital group has well deserved reputation, which they occasionally flaunt, for being slow, cheap, and thorough in the business. While they may miss a number of the high flyers, they are following the classic investment strategy of buying low and selling high.

Entrepreneurs who err on the side of giving up too little of their company, or giving up too much, can wind up short of capital and unable to raise it later at any price. This is particularly dangerous in any industry where intense competition is expected. Often in hotly contested high tech ramp–ups such as the personal computer market or the mass of disk drive companies, the ability to raise capital at the opportune moment in the right amount is what seperates the winners from the losers. Only those companies with the resources to survive the slings and arrows of outrageous fortune have the staying power to continue to test their mettle in the marketplace.

Recently one personal computer manufacturer raised way too little venture capital in his first round financing, when the opportunity was open to raise considerably more. The company then attempted an abortive private placement which was derailed when personal computer stock prices plunged in reaction to several well publicized debacles including shareholders lawsuits, before going back to its original backers who responded with tight fiscal conditions and terms. This was the classic financing error of not taking all the money that was offered, when it was offered, but rather believing that you could out–think and out–guess the capital markets for a particular industry. Experienced stock pickers have found that it is very difficult to forecast major market moves, much less the window of opportunity for money raising for small, risky high growth ventures. Cash is king. You can't ever have too much.

Entrepreneurs naturally want to hold on to as much of their company as possible through the various stages of financing. They quite correctly reason that the less of the company which is given up at any one stage, the more or less that can be given up later if more money is required, as well as the more there is for themselves, management, and employees. The money–raising entrepreneur is attempting a difficult balancing act—trying to determine in an ambiguous business situation how much capital is enough. Generally the earlier the stage of the company, the more difficult the money–raising equation. The truth is that it is normally close to impossible to accurately forecast cash requirements for an early–stage company. All the spreadsheets in the world, combined with all the venture capitalists and all the financial Vice Presidents, will most of the time fail to do so. Here, as in many areas, the best guide is entrepreneurial intuition, combined with a few sharp pencils to define the most probable cash requirements. Perhaps more important than an accurate cash forecast is keeping in mind, and warm at all times, a variety of financial sources, either in case your current investor group gets tired and closes their wallets, or because additional investors are required in later–stage financings to support the company on to operating success. Foreign investors seeking to enter the venture capital game, or large established corporations interested in a window on a particular technology or industry, may enter the investor syndicate to provide support for the company and the early–stage investors.

While many entrepreneurs are concerned about losing control of their companies by selling more than 51 percent to the investor group, the more savvy recognize clearly that any time major money is taken from either a bank or an investor, and a significant business is being attempted, a large measure of control has already passed to the company's supporters even if voting control is still retained. These fragile business endeavors are built more on the continuing confidence of all support groups than on careful distinctions concerning control. The trick, in the question of what percent of your company to sell for how much money, is like most business endeavors: to reach a good trade where you get a little more than you give—after all, this is what is known as making a profit. Don't be overly hung up over percents—strike a good deal.

Individual venture capitalists will vary in their approach to pricing. Some will be very flexible and highly intuitive. Others will go over the numbers in considerable detail, perhaps even warming up their calculators while you watch, or showing you their calculations run on their portable personal computer at various profit and return scenarios. Whatever the method, before you commit yourself to a valuation for your deal, go out in the marketplace and find out what is currently being paid for a company such as yours.

Many venture capitalists have certain rules of thumb under which they operate such as; "I would never pay more than $10 million for a start–up" or "the highest valuation we have ever paid was $30 million" or "we will only pay up on a deal if we can see that it will really be big, a potential billion dollar company." You may want to tailor your price to their conceptions. Remember; if money cannot be raised, price will not matter.

9

NEGOTIATING A FAIR DEAL

Knowing how to price your deal and how the venture capitalist thinks about pricing provides information useful to your upcoming negotiations with the venture capitalist. However, realize venture capitalists are experienced negotiators. Most come to the table with a good idea of what they want as to terms, price, protection, and company disclosure. They have been there before. If you are a first or even second or third time entrepreneur your previous experience may have produced exceptional negotiating skills, but you are negotiating on the venture capitalist's home court and, in effect, playing his game with odds stacked against you, for he has the gold. You will need to know the objectives, attitudes, and strategies that he will bring to your negotiations. While this chapter may not make you an effective negotiator you will at the least be forearmed. Even though the venture capitalist may be making the rules, most will negotiate on a fair and reciprocal basis for several reasons: they are interested in learning more of your trading and negotiating skills. Many very successful business men are excellent traders; they always seem to wind up with the better part of the bargain while retaining the good will of their adversary. A start–up business has limited resources, and the effective trader can acquire these necessary start–up resources on the most favorable terms. The venture capitalist, being an experienced trader of money for opportunity, will want to reach a fair deal with the entrepreneur. He does not want his partner–to–be to enter the relationship believing that he has been taken unfair advantage of in the discussions and exchange. Taking unfair advantage in a close working relationship leads to continued rounds of one–upmanship and eventually the relationship ends. No one makes money when distrust and animosity rear their heads. Expect the venture capitalist to be protecting his interests, but not acting like the often imagined "venture vulture."

A number of venture capitalists love to negotiate. Others, being essentially more analytical rather than interpersonal, actually shun the activity. If your deal is perceived as being fair from the beginning, and providing the expected rate of return, these members of the community will with few exceptions take your deal as presented. A few of the legally trained members love to strut their stuff and will debate many of the more mundane details. Others will leave this to their counsel. Be aware that there are a number of typical standard clauses in a normal venture deal and venture capitalists will generally be rather inflexible on these points. (See Chapter Ten, Part One, Deal–Doing Lawyers.)

Usually at the initial meeting, the venture capitalist will open the discussion by inquiring as to your perception as to a fair price or valuation for the company. You should not toss the ball back to him by asking, "What do you want to pay?" The venture capitalist is now a buyer, and he wants to be in control of the negotiating process; let him. You should respond with your valuation and price, and explain why this valuation makes sense. If it is in tune with market realities, it may be accepted with little or no bargaining; if not, the negotiations could be protracted. After the venture capitalist has completed his due diligence, he will ask you to his office and outline price, terms, and conditions, and generally explaining any real divergence from your point of view. Although normally if there was a real difference in price, this would have been raised and resolved at an earlier date, before he had invested both time and money in completing his due diligence. If the terms are reasonable, and in line with your realistic expectations, it would be better to accept them on the spot rather than engage in an agonizing reappraisal of your position. The venture capitalist wants to know that you are decisive, where you stand, and what you are willing to accept. In addition, if you delay it is possible that a "red flag" will emerge, and the venture capitalist will not continue to extend his offer indefinitely.

Closing the normal venture deal is an art form of its own. Once you and the venture capitalist have reached agreement on terms, this oral agreement will often be set to writing in a term sheet or letter of commitment. A number of venture firms will not provide a letter of commitment. Most letters of commitment that are drafted provide so many "outs" that they are of little real legal value, although perhaps some psychic support. At this point some entrepreneurs begin to relax, believing that the deal is completed and they can go home. Not so. A venture deal isn't over until its over—until the signed documents of closing, and the money, have changed hands. The terms sheet or letter of commitment should be viewed only as the general framework and outline of agreement on major points, with additional negotiating to come over minor points, and the occasional drop dead showdown point prior to final closing. The completion of the legal documentation process itself becomes the final stage for negotiation.

Most entrepreneurs locate a strong lead investor who will make the first and largest commitment to his financing. The lead investor will also play a role in negotiations with other investors. This role may vary. The more experienced venture capitalists who have a successful track record as lead investors may do all the negotiating with the company and communicate the results to other members of the eventual syndicate. The lead investor will attempt to bring both entrepreneur and other investors together in a workable partnership. Occasionally a lead investor may be of less experience, or other strong, normally lead investors are going to invest, and they will want to negotiate directly with the company and the lead investor as well. This form of negotiating can set the entrepreneur up for the good and bad guy approach as the lead plays the good guy, and the other investors ask for the tough terms which the lead may or may not feel are important. Some entrepreneurs attempt to put the responsibility on the lead investor to "bring the other investors in line" with the entrepreneur's expectations. This is self–defeating in most cases because the lead investor can easily begin to feel that he is being used by the company and become hostile. If you find yourself in a dual negotiation with several venture firms, the best approach is to deal with each as individually as possible and not attempt divide and conquer.

Books on negotiating technique, such as "How to Get Everything You Always Wanted Out of Everybody," outline a variety of dazzling gambits so that you get what you want while the other guy never realizes that his pants are missing. While these gambits can be effectively deployed in the hands of an experienced negotiator, most first–time entrepreneurs will find the vast majority counterproductive. What you really need to know is how strong is your negotiating position from the outset. This is normally a function of several factors imcluding how far along you are toward a producible product, the strength of your management team, how hot your industry is (both on the stock market and off), and whether you have managed to create a venture capital auction for your deal. If you discover along the way that you have a highly marketable deal, your position will be strong in negotiation, and correspondingly you will yield few points on reasonable valuation and terms. As you move toward the weaker end of the spectrum, more will be given up to complete the funding. The entrepreneur must ultimately make a trader's judgment as to the real interest of his suitors, and his corresponding negotiating strength.

Once this judgment is correctly made, and conveyed to the venture capitalist, most other matters will be quickly settled.

It's always nice to be able to come to the table from a position of maximum negotiating strength, or to further this position as you dicker. If you have a deal in a hot industry, you may be able to create "gold rush fever" for your company, and set up the "venture capital auction." In this case a number of strong lead investors are slobbering over your deal, and you will be able to pick and choose from among the best. This is known as the cat/bird's seat. It is as easy to fall off this seat, as to get on it in the first place, so it is critical when taking this approach that the potential lead investors do not believe that they are being pitted against each other. This can be accomplished by allowing each equal access and equal time in the due diligence process, advising the potential investors that there are others interested in the company, disclosing the identity of the other potential investors where appropriate, and encouraging the investors to all get together in one syndicate and support the company as co-leads. If the deal has sufficient potential, the investors will swallow their pride, give up the lead role, and all participate.

An effective intermediary can be helpful in reaching accommodation with the venture capitalist. The investment banker or lawyer can buffer the entrepreneur's rough edges, if any, and present, in a softening manner, issues which might if presented directly cause the deal to disintegrate. The venture capitalist will, however, become uncomfortable with the deal if the use of an intermediary restricts his access to the entrepreneur. Intermediaries must both be judicious and be used judiciously. They are often employed in the later–stage deals where they can explain and filter excess baggage which might interfere with a closing.

While these firms are helpful in putting the deal together, they should normally withdraw from the field as the final deal is negotiated, unless the entrepreneur desires that a particular individual lead his negotiation with the venture capitalists. The venture capitalist will, however, much prefer to negotiate directly—principal to pricipal—so the entrepreneur should be very sure of his level of interest before involving an intermediary, in the final negotiations, in the role of negotiating for the principal. Investment bankers, when employed in structuring a deal, must be familiar with the venture capital process or a lot of work may go under the bridge, and fail to meet the venture capitalist's needs. Many investment bankers, over the years, have been in and out of the venture capital marketplace, following the investing cycles. It is best to deal with an investment banker who has steady and continuing contact with the venture capital community.

Bankers and venture capitalists tend to have different personalities and objectives. Thus, bankers are rarely helpful to the entrepreneur in the venture capital raising process. The exception would be those few bankers who have developed a real specialty in high–risk lending and the contacts which make informed judgments possible. Several accounting firms have, over the years, specialized in assisting entrepreneurs. A list of several law firms who are interested in this type of business is included in the Appendix. These firms will generally assist in everything from business plan preparation, to financial projections, to providing venture capital introductions. They are an invaluable aid to the first–time entrepreneur and can provide many short cuts based on prior learning.

Once the deal is cut the entrepreneur is often hungry for his operating money but in dealing with a closing, patience is the best counsel. If cash is tight while documents are being prepared, some firms will provide a cash advance in the form of a demand note, perhaps with warrants required, until the deal is closed. The demand note generally bears interest at prime or a point or two above, and is rolled into the final security at closing. Stay flexible in this process, you are almost home.

Most of the time there is a final gunfight just before the closing. Everyone's getting married and remains a bit jittery just before the ceremony. Entrepreneurs are not sure they really want a partner who some day might kick them out and take over the company, and the venture capitalist doesn't want to put up with last minute revelations, which should have been previously disclosed, or at–the–wire unreasonable demands. There seems to be something in human nature which creates seller's and buyer's remorse—perhaps a bit of personal insecurity. Practically every deal goes through these last minute showdowns and is closed. An effective deal–making lawyer is essential. His is the art of the carefully crafted compromise which keeps the parties talking and moving to the final signing. Here it is very helpful if a closing date has been set, at least several weeks in advance, of which all parties are aware. Such a deadline keeps last minute points to a minimum, and provides a final drop dead date. A number of these points will vanish of their own lack of seriousness when a minor compromise is suggested. Remember most of the major terms were agreed upon long ago.

The major points to remember in a venture capital negotiation are:

1. It's only money.
2. Once the terms are agreed upon, keep your sense of humor; the deal will close.
3. Hire a deal–making lawyer.
4. Let him do his job.
5. Show up at the closing to collect your check (unless it is wire transferred).
6. Cash the check.

There are several things to avoid which could kill the deal:

1. Turning the negotiation into a personal competition with the venture
   capitalist (the ego fault).
2. Forgetting that price is not everything.
3. Pitting the venture capitalists against each other.
4. Having your brother-in-law, the divorce lawyer, close the deal.
5. Shooting yourself in the foot at a final showdown.

10

DEAL–DOING LAWYERS

Your supporting player in the negotiating process should be a lawyer who knows how to say yes as well as no—the rare deal–doing lawyer. There are a lot of different types of lawyers plying their craft. There are ambulance chasers who specialize in personal injury litigation; there are real estate lawyers who are effective in anything from a house closing to setting up a real estate limited partnership syndication; there are labor lawyers who can handle anything from an age discrimination case to an appearance before the National Labor Relations Board. There are lawyers who specialize in going to court, and those who can best keep you out. There are those attorneys whose advice will keep you out of jail or help you get out if you are in jail. There are numerous branches of business lawyers: some who are best with large corporations; others are specialists before the Securities and Exchange Commission; a few are tax experts and will assist you in paying less and retaining more of your income. There are lawyers who know how best to say no; and then there are the few really proficient lawyers who know how to say yes or yes but. These are the deal–doing lawyers, and they are a rare breed.

Legal training teaches its future practitioners to think of the worst possible case or result which may befall a client, and then to advise the client of the innumerable disastrous ramifications which may occur. In law school this is known as the cloud of "fat caution." Many lawyers are living, breathing, walking, talking examples of fat caution; even worse, often overly aggressive examples of fat caution. This trait makes it constitutionally impossible for the vast majority of lawyers to see or believe in the positive side of anything. Given human nature and their exposure, in their practices mostly to the downside of the human equation, the pessimistic view expressed by most lawyers works out that way often enough. They are often right, which makes them even more pessimistic as they age in the harness of the practice of law. However, for your deal you do not need the pessimistic lawyer. Your temperament and his are likely to be as the sunny side and the dark side. You want the rare deal–doing attorney who will protect your interests while not inserting his particular bias in the way of closing the deal. He should be familiar with the venture capital process, and not just a friend of a friend who used the attorney on a house closing several years ago. Familiarity with the venture capital process will mean that a number of issues which would concern the pessimistic attorney will be understood and dismissed before they become an argument by the deal–doer. If he is really good, he will have the skill, experience, and talent to come up with a creative legal solution to help bridge the gap over those business points on which the parties may disagree prior to closing.

An experienced venture capital lawyer is relatively rare, though generally available if a diligent search is conducted. Venture capital areas such as the San Francisco and Boston areas have the more prominent venture practitioners, and an appropriate reference from your venture backers or others may get their interest and attention. How difficult they will be to retain will depend in part on the activity level of the current venture capital cycle. An effective deal–doing venture capital lawyer will not only understand the law as applied to venture capital in its general business, securities, tax and other legal aspects but will himself understand the particular problems of the start–up and small business as a business entity. The best of these lawyers is more than capable of acting as a valued advisor to the emerging company, and will often serve as Secretary to the corporation, though not normally as a member of the Board of Directors of the venture–backed company.

Some ventures do not have the luxury of being located in a town or state with highly experienced venture capital counsel. In this case, the choice is between using good local counsel—someone who is interested in growing into an effective venture capital counsel—or finding sufficient local counsel and supporting their efforts with a review by one of the experienced out–of–state law firms. It's familiar practice on many matters for the law firm which gets the business to farm out work in which they lack real experience to a more specialized firm. You should be certain that the principal lawyer you retain on your venture deal will either actually do the work on your deal or will retain close supervision over his younger colleague if he delegates the work to a junior member of the firm. Another consideration is to be certain that your selected attorney will be readily available to close your deal rapidly once essential business points have been agreed upon. The climate for a venture capital deal can alter rapidly while waiting around for your attorney to draft documents, so it's critical to have an attorney who can move the paper once essential business points have been agreed upon. In this connection, if an overly protective attorney is engaged, he will "lawyer" the deal to death and take forever to complete the work while the venture capitalist burns. The effective venture capital lawyer knows what points are critical, what points can be dispensed with, and what points are really worth hard negotiation. He also knows that once the documentation is completed and the deal closed, the legal papers will be filed, in most cases never to be opened again, and the ongoing relationship of the venture capitalist and the company will be far more critical than his handiwork. He will work at all times to keep this relationship amicable and positive.

By and large the venture capital community prefers at all cost to stay out of court. Besides being bad for future business, once a venture deal winds up in court the venture capitalist will generally lose his investment. Fragile start–ups simply will not normally survive serious acrimony and lawsuits. Professional venture capitalists get sufficient experience with bankruptcy court to want to avoid any other legal entanglements. They want to be your partners, not litigants against you.

Normally the lawyer for the venture capitalist will draw up the required legal documents. The money is his, so it is best to let his attorney start the process even though you realize that this will provide him with some negotiating advantage. Once you receive the documents, read them and make sure that they represent the deal you have agreed to, and then forward them to your venture attorney for his review.

There are a number of fairly standard venture capital documents with which it will help to be familiar; these documents will vary in both form and substance depending on the nature of the business deal. Generally if the venture capitalist believes that he has been fair or generous on price he may insist on a tougher document or instrument to protect him on the downside. Also, if he views the risk in the deal as being unusually high he will insist on additional protection, in the majority of cases. This is not unusual and should be both expected and respected. Nothing to get upset about and spoil the relationship. Stan Golder of Golder, Thoma, and Cressy, one of the more successful and most experienced venture capitalists, has said: "You name the price, and I will name the terms; you name the terms, and I will name the price." Continue to keep firmly in mind that the venture capitalist is continuously balancing mentally his risk and reward, and attempting to make adjustments according to these perceptions.

The lawyer for the venture capitalist will take the term sheet which was agreed upon and negotiated between the company and the venture firms, and will review its provisions to determine whether the terms are clear, understood by both parties, and complete. On some occasions it is considered necessary by counsel, particularly in the more complex deal, to redraft the term sheet so that there is a real meeting of the minds which can be expressed, and replicated, in legal terms. This exercise, while time–consuming, can be useful in those deals which may break new ground as to structure and terms. If the deal is relatively straightforward a redraft of the terms may simply be a way for the attorney to run up his bill. Most law firms still bill by the hour, and while the entrepreneur should feel free to request that the venture capitalist ask his law firm for an estimate of the billable hours, he should also be alert, as the documentation proceeds, for excessive lawyering.

Once the term sheet review is complete, the attorney will proceed, normally working from a letter or check sheet provided by the venture capitalist which relates additional non–negotiated terms that he wants in the final documentation. Occasionally an entrepreneur will be surprised at some of the additional terms which the venture capitalist will raise, believing that these should have been raised and negotiated earlier in the process, prior to the completion of the term sheet. These entrepreneurs feel a bit sandbagged by the venture capitalist who appears to come in with additional points after the negotiations are complete. While this criticism is on occasion justified, normally the points raised by the venture capitalist, such as anti-dilution provisions, majority vote to approve a merger, financial reporting, etc., are not deal–breaking points. Those entrepreneurs who are sensitive to such matters should be certain to have a working knowledge of normal venture capital documents prior to the agreement on the term sheet, and specifically negotiate those provisions which they believe to be onerous. Once the term sheet is negotiated the venture capitalist will tend to treat other provisions as somewhat standard and be rather inflexible on these later points.

The principal venture capital document is the stock purchase agreement, which comes in several colors and shades. Normally venture capitalists will want to purchase either common stock or, more often than not, a form of convertible preferred security with some of the attributes of common stock and some aspects of the more secure preferred stock issue. Essentially the venture capitalist is trying for some of the best of both worlds, the liquidity of common stock coupled with the security position and liquidation preferences of preferred stock.

The principal provisions of the document are: the housekeeping terms of the deal, such as how much stock is being purchased at what price; when and how it will be paid for; the venture capitalist's ownership in the company; and a list of those positive items which the company agrees to perform such as providing financial statements and letting the venture capitalist attend the board meetings, if not actually join the Board of Directors, etc. There are also a number of negative covenants—that is, a list of those things you agree not to do such as sell control of the company out from under the venture capitalist, pay you and your relatives fat salaries or dividends, sell additional stock without the venture capitalist's approval, decide that making hedge hoes is not profitable, or go into the model airship business. There are also a number of items of default which may mean that the venture capitalist will be able to exercise what is known as a majority voting right event. The exercise of this event by the venture capitalist would not be a cause for rejoicing by the entrepreneur; it generally means that the venture capitalist has just exercised his right to take control of the Board by electing a majority of its members. While this right is rarely exercised, its existence gives the venture capitalist a powerful hammer to persuade the entrepreneur to carry out the venture capitalist's wishes and views, should circumstances warrant or the venture capitalist desire. The actual exercise of the majority voting right event is very cumbersome in most circumstances and could lead to time and money–consuming litigation. If, on going into a deal, the venture capitalist is overconcerned about matters of company control, he will generally insist that the control stock is placed either in present escrow or in a voting trust over which the venture capitalist has substantial influence or outright control. Most entrepreneurs resist either of these control options and, unless rather desperate for cash, generally are successful in opposing their inclusion in the legal documents. Normal majority voting right provisions would be: failure to meet any outstanding debt obligations which are not cured within thirty days; exceeding certain debt/equity ratios; working capital falling below certain prescribed limits; and insolvency or bankruptcy. In some cases failure to provide financial statements would be a majority voting right event, but not normally.

From the venture capitalist's perspective, failure to include "lack of timely financial statements" as a condition can be a serious oversight in that many of the majority voting right tests are based on financial results. If the statements are not available, it would be difficult if not impossible for the venture capitalist to call a majority voting right event in that the critical proof of noncompliance would be noticeably absent. Should the company be in default, it will want certain provisions included which will allow a timely cure of the default, and these should be carefully negotiated. The venture capitalist will also include certain provisions which provide specific protections and additional benefits to the equity he has invested in the company. These equity provisions normally include several demand registration rights for the venture capitalist, where he can request the company to register his shares in a public offering at the company's expense. While this right is once again rarely exercised, its existence means that the entrepreneur will also remember that one of his objectives must be to take the venture capitalist out of his deal after a reasonable period.

Particularly important today, when a number of later stage financings are being put together at lower prices than the prior rounds, is the anti–dilution provision. This provision means that the venture capitalist's position will be protected in whole or in part through the issuance to him, at no charge, of additional stock if necessary to protect his value in the company when additional financings are undertaken. In practice often the venture capitalist will waive this right, if necessary, to accomplish a financing which will keep the company moving along its business plan, or solvent.

A final critical section of the legal documentation is the representations and warranties—promises that certain things are as represented, including: that taxes are paid to date; that the company is not in default; that financial statements are correct; that the company has complied with all state, federal, and county laws; and most important, that there have been no material adverse changes in position since the last financial statements. This issue becomes critical in many venture capital deals in that often the entrepreneur neglects to mention, and the venture capitalist and his attorneys may fail to discover, a critical piece of information that if disclosed prior to the financing being completed, would have either caused the financing to fall through or would have resulted in a lower price having been paid for the company's stock. There is a fine line at times between what might be called entrepreneurial extravagation, and outright misrepresentation, but most experienced venture capitalists are more than aware when they have been a victim of the latter. Such misrepresentation can sour the relationship at best and may call for the venture capitalist to either demand a lower price for his present stock, through an adjustment, or provide the spark which will trigger a demand for a much lower price on the next round if conditions are adverse. Most entrepreneurs with a skeleton in the closet would be better served by getting all the information out on the table initially rather than waiting for it to bite them later and risk poisoning the relationship.

Finally, the lawyers will, as they are inclined, try to define any tricky terms in the document which may be subject to misinterpretation. In this connection if it is a performance deal, definitions of net income or income before tax can be quite critical, and the entrepreneur should be exceptionally careful to be certain that what is included and excluded in these tests be carefully defined. The last section will include the conditions for a successful closing, and while these are not generally fatal, if not complete they will delay a closing to a later date. Here the company will need a certificate of incorporation, bylaws, attorneys' opinions that all is o.k., corporate authorizations, etc. One memorable closing was held up while the lawyers argued over what state's law would apply should a lawsuit ever result over the terms of the deal. This type of issue should never arise at the closing but should be worked out by both sides well in advance of closing. There are sufficient substantive issues which can get in the way of the closing without work and worry over minor matters. In addition to the closing documentation the venture capitalist may want employment agreements, agreements as to purchase and sale of founders' stock should a founder leave the company, and non-competition agreements.

Some venture capital firms have more of a legal orientation to their deals and require more of the entrepreneur in the way of documentation. Others, often the more experienced, want adequate documentation but do not engage in legal overkill, and will in fact resist efforts by other members of the investment syndicate to make the transaction too complex. Deals can get so complicated that the parties can never remember what they agreed to do or refrain from. Like most things in business it is normally best to keep legal documentation as simple and straightforward as the lawyers will permit. Finding that lawyer who can get it right the first time without extensive and expensive redrafting is key to legal peace of mind.

Should the entrepreneur be involved with a venture capital syndicate, he and his attorney will in most cases come up against a gaggle of attorneys. Each member of the syndicate may have his own attorney review the documents, and this will mean that each lawyer will have a few points of his own to improve the deal, and the protection of his client. Here it is best to let the attorney for the lead investor discuss these points with other investor's counsel, and sort out which should be included and presented to entrepreneur's counsel and which should be discarded.

Attorney fees are a troublesome point. Lawyers get paid more for working more hours or for providing real added value to a deal by assisting in negotiating deal-breaking points. Many attorneys really want to work; particularly those in firms with a number of young associates whose fees can contribute handsomely to the senior partners' income. Legal fees can be kept to a minimum by minimizing arguments and redrafting of the agreement, and by having necessary materials in order and complete when presented to the attorney for inclusion with the closing documents. As previously mentioned, careful negotiation of the terms of the deal will greatly assist in capping legal fees. For the normal convertible preferred security deal, without any extras, fees for the investor's counsel, which the company will generally be required to pay prior to closing, will range from approximately $15,000 to $25,000. Too much redrafting and argument can, in a major city, raise these fees to well over forty thousand. One entrepreneur, on receiving a high legal bill from investor's counsel in a first round financing, requested and got a cap on fees in the second round, but then proceeded to argue over a number of points such that the investors, when presented with the bill of their counsel—over the minimum the entrepreneur agreed to pay—were as unhappy as the entrepreneur was on the first round. A world without lawyers would be an inexpensive place indeed.

Occasionally a second closing will be held because other investors have been rounded up after the first closing, or the company wanted to close quickly due to a cash shortage. Lawyers charge to close as well as to draft and open, so fees for this additional service should be contemplated if a second closing is being considered. Just as there are deal breaking and deal making lawyers, there are also fast and slow lawyers, and those who will attempt to really run up the fee, and those who will be more judicious with the company's limited assets. The entrepreneur must consider in each case what his requirements are for counsel, and once again always request an estimate from investor counsel. If there are various firms in the investment syndicate, do not pay the bills for all their attorneys, just those of the lead investor.

On occasion if you deal with a venture capital institution, you will face both inside and outside counsel. The inside counsel will normally act as the legal coordinator and run interference for the outside counsel, and on occasion, for the venture capitalist who will refer some points on which he wishes to prevail to the inside counsel as "legal questions."

If in your mind these are not legal issues, but rather essential business issues, they should be settled directly with the venture capitalist rather than allowing him to refer the issue to counsel—this will only work against the entrepreneur's self-interest.

Now and again an entrepreneur will get his ego involved with the legal process itself and attempt to win at the legal points and add up his negotiating score against the venture capitalist. Remember this is a business deal, and like most good deals everyone must come out a winner if anyone is to win. Legal documentation time is not the time to be scoring points, but to get the deal down right, complete, carefully, but once accomplished to have established a continuing relationship which will work once the documents are put away and most often forgotten.

11

SERVICE AFTER THE SALE

The documents are put away, the lawyers paid, and after considerable effort, you have successfully prospected, presented, negotiated and closed your venture capital financing. The check has cleared the bank, and you have cleared up a number of pressing outstanding bills from impatient creditors. You are recovering from the late night staff party celebrating solvency, and considering your next business moves now that, for the moment, cash flow problems are behind. Your real work is really just beginning; building a company, as well as keeping your newly–won, most important customer, the venture capitalist, happy after the sale. Before they invested, as a condition to closing, the venture capitalists insisted that within one-hundred-twenty days you hire a first class Chief Financial Officer. You explained that "Mabel, who has kept the books for the last three years could do the job," but this fell on deaf ears. You can't understand why the venture capitalists want a Chief Financial Officer, other than to keep one eye on you, and one eye on their money. This requirement certainly couldn't have anything to do with accurate financial controls and procedures in that the proverbial two shoebox system has worked for a long while. Telling Mabel about her new status is not going to be fun, particularly when she is personally completely loyal to you, the founder. In addition to the trouble with Mabel, the venture capitalists mentioned that they would like a new Board of Directors named, including three of their number, but excluding several of your old cronies who have helped the company achieve its present status. Being a good old boy who votes with the founder, plays graybeard, and smokes cigars will no longer qualify for a Board seat. The venture capitalists also insist on an audit committee prior to the company "going public," and a compensation committee whose principal mission appears to be to limit the founder's outrageous salary and perks, not to mention imposing some restraint on the seven relatives and other hangers–on on the payroll. Venture capital is apparently going to require some attitude readjustment on the entrepreneur's part if he is to continue to build a successful business.

The most difficult but awfully critical readjustment occurs with old cronies who were with the entrepreneur in the early, tough days. Any worthwhile leader feels a real sense of obligation to those who provided encouragement, support, and gave part of their lives to build a dream. United States Presidents have on occasion had a difficult time letting old supporters go when they were no longer effective. A company that is undergoing rapid development goes through many corporate stages very quickly. Normally these stages which will occur over a ten, twenty, or thirty year business life are compressed in a three to five year development cycle. In the more normal business development cycle, attrition and normal life cycle changes "solve" many of the old crony problems, some gracefully move aside and others have the time and the resources to grow with the company.

The normal venture capital supported rapid "ramp up" does not have the luxury to support a nurturing employee development program in most cases. If the company is to compete effectively and meet its business plan, the old cronies must become just that, old cronies. Entrepreneurs who are not equipped to face the real pain of human readjustment, and avoid staffing with individuals who maybe highly competitive with them, usually fail. Often a place can be found in the new scheme of things for the early employee, but it may not be in as visible a leadership position. The entrepreneur generally does the employee no favor by keeping him in a position which is beyond his capabilities in a company expanding geometrically.

Recruiting new management for a growth mode is at best difficult, even if the entrepreneur has accepted its necessity. Several alternative methods are most frequently employed: the use of the executive search recruiter; assistance by the venture capitalists (who are in a sense professional qualifiers); referrals by the Board of Directors; and the less fashionable run an ad and interview method. Most of these can be effective if the entrepreneur has, with the advice and consent of the venture capitalist and key members of the Board of Directors, carefully reviewed the necessary prerequisites for the job, and determined what type of personality would fit with both the entrepreneur's style and the emerging company culture.

The executive search method is an interesting approach for those who have not been through it. A number of major executive search firms

are actively interested today in working with the venture capital–supported company. They reason that there is a good chance that the company will be successful if supported by venture capital, and that eventually
they will get their fee for the work. Generally their fee is a substantial
percentage of the first year's salary, usually a third. This approach is not
cheap. Some firms will, however, take up to one half of the fee in the form
of warrants or other equity–oriented compensation. Once the fee is agreed
upon the search firm will, with the company's assistance, draw up a job
specification which outlines the required personal and work characteristics, what the person is to do, the pay, etc., and the firm will attempt to
size up the company culture—who can get along with the entrepreneur.
Like anything where a buck is involved, some of the firms are very professional and really interested in whether there is a proper and hopefully
continuing fit between the eventually successful candidate and the company. Others really don't care, and are interested in making a sale and
moving on to the next flower. Or they are interested in staying with the
same flower, and pollinating it a number of times as various "successful
candidates" prove unsuccessful in holding on to the job. Most firms, once
the specs are agreed upon, will then begin to use their various sources to
locate prospective candidates. These sources are gained by approaches
varying from sending letters to names gleaned from various industry list-
ings, or from the business press, to calling old industry contacts, dusting
off the latest computer probe of the firm's data banks (where lie résumés,
gathering computer dust), and direct calls to the prospective candidates
by either the search principal or research associate. The firm is interested
in coming up with seven to ten candidates who on paper are close to the
specs agreed upon with the company. Once these immortals are located
and convinced that it is in their best interest to hazard a new future and
fortune by consenting to an interview, the search firm will then review
this chosen list with the company to determine their interest. Often in a
difficult search the chosen list will include a few ringers who are making
too much money to consider a move (but like to shop around so they can
feel good), whose spouses have said that the last move was the last move,
who don't want to leave their spouses, or who really like it where they
are with their friends and expect to be promoted shortly to CEO, but just
in case their best laid plans don't work out want a back door handy. There
are always a couple on the list who just never should have made the list.
By the time all the sorting and interviewing has taken place there are a
couple of candidates remaining who the company finds of interest and
who want the job. The search firm then helps the parties get together on
salary, perks, etc., just as any self–respecting broker would, who wants to
earn a fee. (Normally fees are payable even if no successful applicant
shows up to the party and/or is selected.)

The freebee method of executive search is to ask the venture capitalists in your deal, and your new Board of Directors, if they know anyone who may be qualified for the position, after you have worked up your own specifications for the job and discussed it with them. Venture capitalists receive a number of résumés from job seekers every week and occasionally one of these is of real interest to a portfolio company. The venture capitalist may also be working with another portfolio company where an effective player is exiting because he doesn't get along with the founder or is tired of that business, or for some personal reason. A number of venture capitalists have a little black book or a little black disk with a memory of possible management candidates filed by what they do best. Don't be shy in asking for a peek in this book. The venture capitalist is your partner and likes to contribute more than money. Assuming that you have assembled an outside Board of Directors who can be helpful and have broad industry contacts, they can contact some of their friends and find you another candidate at no cost to you. Another effective method is to contact various alumni placement offices of leading universities and business schools that compile lists of out–of–work and soon to be out–of–work alumni. If you are not an alumni, and this maybe a requirement to access these lists, then you probably know someone who is, and can get the list for you. Newspaper ads such as those in *The Wall Street Journal* can be useful, and despite impressions to the contrary, people are occasionally hired through the papers. The problem with the papers is that you have to sort through a whole gaggle of miscellaneous garbage before hitting pay dirt. Often the jobs that are advertised are those no one in their right mind would want; that is why they are being advertised.

Recruiting an effective Board of Directors is as critical as selecting the key members of your management team, if not more so. An effective venture capital–backed company Board is called upon to help provide strategic direction for the company, assist with suppliers, bankers, investors, and other critical contacts, help provide effective incentives through stock options, and advise and consent on major capital spending and operating matters. The most effective Boards are not composed of lawyers, bankers, and insurance salesmen, but rather of seasoned business executives, entrepreneurs, and venture capitalists who understand something of the industry in which the company is engaged. Occasionally consultants with broad industry contacts are useful, particularly if they are entrepreneurially oriented. The best Boards are entrepreneurial but also serve a trustee function. They are, in effect, a review and a check on the actions of management, which, in pursuit of its immediate goals, may either throw the baby out with the bath, or fail to put the proper operating structure in place prior to implementation of its aggressive plans. The Board is also entrusted with proper reporting and auditing of results, which is critical in those companies which are first public. To have an effective Board, the entrepreneur should, with Board consent, develop a reporting format which provides the Board with information required to properly direct the business, and then see that the board receives that information a week or so prior to each meeting, and that a critical review of key operating areas is undertaken at each Board meeting.

Achieving the real confidence of the Board is critical to the entrepreneur. Without this confidence, the entrepreneur is not likely to remain CEO for an extended period. It is important to the entrepreneur that his relationship with each Board member is one of full and complete disclosure, and that Board members are consulted on a regular basis regarding key decisions.

Occasionally the board may be called upon to consider replacing the CEO because the company is not meeting its business plans. This will be a tragedy for both the company and the entrepreneur, without a close working relationship having been established previously. Board review of operations requires the management to focus its time and attention on the most vital issues rather than on those operations with which it is most comfortable.

Find a banker who is more than just a money lender. High growth requires strong and deep bank lines to see the company through ever accelerating inventory and receivables expansion. The best bankers understand the company, its management, and the industry environment. Rather than panicking and calling the loan as business turns down and difficult, they attempt to bring others into the banking syndicate to provide additional credit capacity. They are willing to work with your venture capital backers rather than remain at odds (which is often the case). Major suppliers are also a source of expansion capital, and a resource should cash become tight. Relationships with the largest and most important of these should not be left to the purchasing manager or operations manager, but should receive the time and attention of the entrepreneur. In difficult times, three of these suppliers with over $5000 overdue can put the company into bankruptcy, so their continuing support is imperative. Suppliers are good sources as to what is really happening in your industry in that they are selling to your competition. They generally know who is strong and who is weak in the industry. In the electronics industry there are several senior credit managers whose opinion on the probable survival of a company will either cause a company to survive or fail, and around which smaller suppliers will rally in time of trouble. Suppliers should be informed on a regular basis as to the company's progress.

The venture capitalist doesn't just go away after he has invested in the enterprise; however, there are varying degrees of activity depending on the approach and policies of the particular venture capital firm. As a rule, the earlier the stage of the investment (i.e. seed, start–up, 1st round investment), the more active the venture capitalist in either following or participating in company decisionmaking. Most venture firms, particularly the private partnerships, will want a seat on the Board of Directors, and will attend and participate in the vast majority of Board meetings. All venture capitalists will want to be informed of any major adverse changes in the company's business or prospects promptly after this information is available. All are interested in positive developments, and would appreciate this information as well—in a business where a lot is negative it's good to hear good news. Generally the lead investor will be the most active in a particular investment, but this is really a function of the approach of the particular venture capitalist. Some have many investments so the amount of time they can spend on any one deal is limited. Others have fewer and prefer to spend a good deal of time with each deal. From time to time the work load of a particular venture capitalist can change very abruptly (due largely to problem situations arising), and likewise the attention and focus on your company may diminish. Finally some investments just don't require much time—they hit their business plan almost from day one and the venture capitalist can more productively spend his limited time elsewhere.

Prior to accepting an investment from a venture capitalist, it would be helpful to talk with other companies in his portfolio to determine whether his particular style will be compatible with yours. Recently a few venture capital firms have become more like operating holding companies—in some cases actually founding or co-founding a business and/or acting as a key member of the management team on a fully participating basis. These operating–oriented firms will normally make fewer investments but they watch each egg much more closely. With this approach the intention of the venture capitalist may be to actually be the operating entrepreneur. Of course, in part, the degree of active involvement will be a function of the amount that a venture capital firm has invested in your deal, and what percent of the portfolio this represents. For the larger institutional funds and partnerships an investment of $1 million to $2 million would not be considered particularly significant. An investment above $3 million would have their full attention. For the smaller funds a $1 million to $2 million investment would be quite visible and would have their full attention. Generally if your level of risk is perceived as being higher, the higher the level of attention to your deal. If you need help in certain areas where the venture capitalist is knowledgeable, such as finance, or in some cases operations or technical aspects, the venture capitalist will lend a hand if you ask. The venture capitalist will also provide support if your management team is not complete or found seriously lacking to any degree.

In the case of distressed situations the venture capitalist can be expected to take a very active role, particularly if he is the lead or co-lead investor. Here he will become involved in operating decisions, and may actively press for management changes. Chapter Four, Part Two explores the subject of company turnaround in depth.

As previously indicated a number of venture capitalists are closet entrepreneurs. Those in the private partnerships are active entrepreneurs in their own small business of business finance and development. They enjoy the entrepreneurial process and like entrepreneurs. They want to participate and want to help. Treat them as you would want to be treated, as a real partner in your plans and dreams. It's only in your best interest.

Eventually the venture capitalist will want to take his money out of your deal—to exit. He prefers to do this through a well-timed public offering or through a profitable sale of the company to a larger company. He hopes this will occur in years five through seven of the investment, although he would not be disappointed if it happened earlier. He may also exit in a less preferred form, either through a sinking fund, where you pay him off over a period of time, or where he sells his interest back to you or to others in one lump sum. Occasionally if you are reluctant to let him cash in his chips, he may intimate that he will call a demand registration which can force you to undertake a public offering. In practice the exercise of a demand right rarely occurs since its presence in the agreement is generally sufficient to prevent its exercise. Venture capitalists will insist that this right is present; this is a deal-breaking point. There is a time for all things and there is a time to part. Venture capitalists and entrepreneurs usually know when they are mutually ready to dissolve the relationship. This most often occurs when both parties have accomplished their objectives. The venture capitalist will realize the return he expected if the company goes public or is sold, and the entrepreneur will realize personal and business liquidity. In venture capital most things are for sale at a fair price.

The determination of whether the company will either remain public or private is more than just an economic issue, as we will explore in the next chapter.

12

PUBLIC OR PRIVATE

The vast majority of venture capital is invested in private companies which the venture capitalists hope one day will become public entities. They long for this public exposure for several reasons: first, so that their chips invested in the company can eventually be cashed; and because in a sense a public company, for a venture capitalist, is a visible indication of his success which will be noticed and recognized by his peers. Until the public offering, the venture capitalist has been laboring on behalf of the company mostly in anonymity, while the entrepreneur and others are recognized and highly visible. Everyone likes a little glory. Also this success will be noticed by entrepreneurs looking for capital, and most would prefer to have a successful venture capitalist as an investor, so the venture capitalist may secure a stronger deal flow from his visible successes. Of less publicity but still important, particularly financially, are those companies which are merged or sold to other companies or investors. This "public or private" decision often determines not only what the ultimate return on invested capital is for the company and its venture investors, but also whether the company is just a shooting star in the public market but never a real ongoing successful company. This chapter explores the pitfalls and pratfalls of the public or private choice.

After a time many venture capitalists will put subtle pressure on a company to "go public" if it is financially sound, and well positioned for such an undertaking. This can be accomplished in a not so subtle manner by calling a registration right, where the company must in effect offer shares for sale to the public. These demand registration rights are incorporated in almost all venture capital financings. Public offerings, particularly if the company is premature, can be undertaken in haste with both venture capitalist and entrepreneur regretting their impetuousness.

A private company can be a thing of beauty. There is little or no SEC to report to; lawyers and accountants play less of a role, and rake off fewer chips for their services; directors, if not old chums, tend to be helpful and loyal to the founder; contact with stockholders is generally direct, rather than through the press, which magnifies most information; everyone involved with the company is calmer and more at ease outside the glare of public purview. The entrepreneur with a bit of the buccaneer may operate a bit on the edge, and on occasion, over it, in his private company world. Private companies were invented by and for the entrepreneur's satisfaction.

A public company is opposed to the reasons most entrepreneurs start their own company—to get away from authority. To be private is to be one's own. It is to be secret; not under public control or scrutiny. To be public is to be open to the view of all. Those entrepreneurs who are attempting to avoid authority should examine their needs and motivations prior to a decision to go public. A public offering may be a good decision for the company, but a bad or uncomfortable decision for the control-sensitive entrepreneur. Most entrepreneurs who are extremely sensitive to authority or to working with others, when the others have strings attached, never build their business beyond several employees. They are content to work as consultants, mom and pop shops, or small family businesses. They enjoy the perks available to the small businessman such as an automobile write-off, tickets to the hockey games, the mother in law on the payroll. Big, visible, and public is not what they really want of life. Small, quiet, and invisible is beautiful. A number of entrepreneurs are in conflict: they want to be invisible and manage their companies like the small family controlled company while enjoying the benefits of a public company. These conflicted entrepreneurs are generally uncomfortable with venture capital financing. They really want to do and have it all for themselves. Until the entrepreneur resolves this conflict to some degree of reconciliation or exhaustion a public offering should not be undertaken. It will almost always be bad for the health of the company and the entrepreneur. To "know thyself" is fundamental to successful living after a public offering.

The public entrepreneur is ensnared in authority. The government, his lawyers and accountants, numerous stockholders, public relations and stockholder relations firms, the union if any, and his competitors, all seem to know his own business and how to run it better or at least more conservatively than the entrepreneur. Then there is the public market and its analysts. The stock market analyst wants to make his reputation by learning what he can about the company before his colleagues and competitors have a scoop on the company's business situation or earnings. Those analysts that follow the stock and whose firms make a market in the stock are basically adverse to bad news and to the ups and downs of business development. When news about their company is distressing, they get lots of phone calls from nervous brokers and stockholders who their brokerage firm has put into the stock as being a possible real winner. At times the brokerage firm may have a Director on the Board, who, while knowing the financial markets, may not really know much about operating a business. All of this means pressure, and lots of it, to report favorable earnings, no matter what the long term effect on the company's competitive position. A developing company often succumbs to this pressure, books or tries to book questionable sales as revenue, and later must reverse its earnings announcement under fire from either its accountants and lawyers (who are correctly worried about their liability—being sued by other lawyers representing irate stockholders) or from the SEC which is attempting to protect the public from the fraudulent scheme and, it appears at times, from itself. The reality of unbookable earnings may be that the revenue which cannot be recognized is actually more bankable than other revenue, which, having definite payment terms (but from shakier customers), is considered bookable because technically the customers have committed to pay for it at a certain date.

This anomaly has occurred often in various high technology businesses such as personal computers, where major OEM customers will order product which can not be booked because of uncertain payment dates, but is in fact more real and certain than the bookable orders from miscellaneous marginal distributors. When these earnings could not be recognized several companies were forced to either not report the earnings or recall earnings already reported. Since the P.C. industry was under a spotlight due to its high public profile (it appeared that one half of all journalists were writing about personal computers, as they once wrote of Genetic Engineering), the impact of not showing a continuing stream of earnings, no matter how shaky, was to undermine supplier, investor, and banking confidence and spook an investment community just waiting for news of the latest computer casualties. In a public company earnings must be qualified by the rules, and if either the rules are trifled with, or expectations are disappointed, a company may fail not on its fundamentals, but on its failure to live up to its expected promise. Business is tough enough without having to live up to promises that you didn't make, but that were made by others to others in your company name. A public offering subjects the entrepreneur to the greedy and at times vicious side of stockholders who believe that the only purpose for their investment is to see it increase consistently, and have no patience with management which fails its expectations however unreasonable.

For the venture capitalist, the public offering and the shares of stock in the companies they have financed are the product of the venture capital industry. If the venture capitalist tends to encourage his companies to go public prematurely, he does a major disservice both to the public, to his companies, and to the venture capital industry. During booming new–issue markets this pressure can be difficult to resist because as companies go public the venture capitalist can report some realized gains and receive or seek additional financing for his venture funds, as well as perhaps distributing several dividends to investors. Like most excess, this catches up with everyone at a later date. Stocks boom and bust, the public gets weary, and the new business process undergoes another cycle.

Even a successful public offering can leave the early–stage company open to the sin of raising too little money too soon. The public market is like riding a tiger; when he is hungry you keep throwing him raw meat, and when he is full he doesn't want any more, so you just keep riding until he is hungry again, and wants more meat. However, it is exceptionally difficult to time when he will be really hungry. Sometimes he is just a little bit hungry, and will only take so much meat. A company hits the offering window and goes public, but the underwriters are only able to sell one half to two thirds of the stock that the company needs to sell to maintain a competitive financial structure. Competitors who are better positioned, are luckier, or earlier, raise all the money they require for the near term and ride out the competitive storm. Your company raised too little money too soon. The consequences of this will be unsettling at best, and at worst, fatal. Now that the stock is public, a number of investors who are only interested in private companies (which can be taken public), such as most venture capitalists, will decline to invest in your company unless your stock is priced as a total steal. These venture investors are interested largely in getting in early and getting out at high price, not in buying the stocks of public companies which are undercapitalized for their industries at bargain prices. The few firms who specialize in emerging public companies will normally exact their penalty price for the perceived high risk in the undercapitalized public company. Should the premature public company fail to achieve the continuing strong support of its principal underwriters (either because they are out of business or gun shy), they may be unable to raise any money, at any price, even in the public market through a secondary offering. This will be particularly true if, following the law that markets go up and down, the market is down or on the way down when you need the money. Once again "get all the money you can when you can" operates with ruthless efficiency.

A public offering is not always a realistic possibility; the market may be depressed so maximum value cannot be realized; stocks in your industry group may be temporarily out of favor; the company cannot afford the expense of an offering or, in certain fields such as medical, long term prosperity may be enhanced by an alliance with a major company, bringing the required deep pockets and broad distribution capability. The sale of the company or merger with a complementary business can be a successful alternative both for the entrepreneur and the venture capitalist. Before the sale of the company is undertaken the entrepreneur should decide whether he is emotionally prepared to part with his creation; and if so, whether he is prepared to accept a realistic price. Most entrepreneurs believe that they would sell their company; after all everything has its price and everything is for sale to the profit–maximizing economic man. However, once the day of reckoning approaches, many entrepreneurs will experience seller's remorse and refuse to conclude the sale. They simply cannot bring themselves to part with their dream and lifetime work. They are often rightly concerned whether they will play an important role under new ownership, and whether their employees and cronies will receive a fair shake under professional management and often absent ownership. These fears can in part be alleviated if the owner negotiates a long term contract for himself and key employees, and ensures that careful job descriptions are contained in these contracts. Very often the new ownership will be pleased, and consider it a real plus if present management who brought the company to its current success will stay on with the company after the sale. In many cases continuing management is required for a sale of the company at anywhere near full value. As for price, generally the entrepreneur will need to accept something less than the figure that he believes represents the true value for the company. Here discussions with investment bankers and venture capitalists can be useful, particularly since the venture capitalist, if he is an investor, will not be anxious to sell his position at any less than realistic full value.

Entrepreneurs should of course be aware that the sale of a major asset such as your own business can trigger unfavorable tax consequences, and plan accordingly. Without adequate tax planning the sale of the company can result in substantial liability, which may not be able to be met by cash on hand if a non–cash sale is concluded. Most venture capital–supported companies are relatively free of relatives and other hangers–on, and are often managed less as a close corporation, and more as a small company trying to become a large one and go public. By being managed for results, a sale to a larger company generally has fewer glitches.

Occasionally fast–growing companies find themselves in the public or private offering alternative trap. Well meaning but hungry underwriters make their appearance at the top of the new–issue market, and a firm advises that it can raise $15 million for your private company through a "private placement" (sale to a few sophisticated investors, several of which are major U.S. institutions and others overseas); a second firm offers to take the company public with a firm commitment to raise $25 million in the public market which is currently ravenous for stock in your industry. It appears that the underwriters and the public are willing to throw money at your company. Your apparent strong position, however, is grounded on shifting sands—the fickleness of all financial markets. The sheep will run together, and very fast, when pursued by rumors and reality. Several analysts lead a few investment seminars with the argument that demand for your product may not be what they had originally projected so investors should lighten up on stock in your industry. (This is a good game for the brokers—the analysts project that the economy will buy umpteen million of whatever is popular and sell a lot of stock, then the demand "fails to materialize" and the analysts downgrade the stock, resulting in much selling off, which results in additional profits for the brokerage firms.) Several companies in your industry start laying off employees due to less demand than projected (unfortunately some managements are often misled by the same analysts who hype their stock); suppliers of these companies get as nervous as the banks, customers get even more nervous, and competitors spread rumors of the company's impending demise; soon the downward progression of unrealized expectations sinks the company, or at best mortally wounds the company's public financing opportunity. The private placement is called off some time before the public offering fiasco in that normally sophisticated investors tend to smell the wind, and panic before the public market. You are shut out at the window.

Investment bankers are financial shepherds to the fledging company. They are experts in advising a company how and when to raise venture capital in the public market. Some have extensive networks of contacts who they have made money for on other deals, and therefore, can arrange a private placement for a company with reasonable fundamentals without much fuss. A quality investment banker is interested in earning a fee, the lifeblood of his business, but will not advise a company to seek a public offering unless he truly believes, based on substantial evidence, that the company is ready to undergo the rigors of a public offering, and survive in the aftermarket. Various investment banking houses are good at different activities and have various standards to judge a company's readiness for a public offering. Most reputable houses require a company to have sales in excess of $10 million, net income of at least $1 million for the current year, and reasonable rates of growth which exceed industry averages by some margin. The best houses conduct a thorough management review as well as operating and financial audits prior to offering stock to the public. If the offering fails, either before or after the stock is offered for sale, the reputation of the investment banking firm, and the individual underwriter, is tarnished.

Investment banking is an aggressive, highly competitive business. If you have a successful company, the competition for your underwriting will normally be intense. As in venture capital, the selection of your lead underwriter will be the most crucial decision. On his shoulders will rest the eventual success or failure to form an effective syndicate, and sell out the offering. It's difficult for the investment banker to perform this service alone so it's important that he be supported by an effective in-house team. Underwriting new companies is a highly cyclical business, as is the stock market for new issues, and there are times when a new–issue underwriter is a bit hungry for business, and may tend to oversell both himself and the entrepreneur on the advisability of a public offering. The entrepreneur, particularly during these hungry times, must keep and retain his own independent perspective on the appropriateness of an underwriting for the company.

In raising any kind of money, either debt or equity, the best time is when you really don't need it. This is also the best time to establish a working relationship with a potential underwriter. Many underwriters will serve as unofficial financial advisors to a new and promising firm for no real fee, in the hope that when an offering or other major transaction comes along, they will be in the first seat to obtain the business. Remember that you are seeking a professional financial advisor who is an expert in the corporate finance market; in addition it helps immensely for a fledgling company if the underwriter understands in a hands-on manner how to manage and operate a business. A number of underwriters lack this essential skill of business development expertise. They are most effective in underwriting mature, established businesses, but fail to appreciate the peculiarities of the new venture. Your venture capitalist, attorney, accountant, or member of the Board of Directors would all be excellent sources to recommend an underwriter. Be sure to interview a number of potential underwriting candidates, as the venture capitalist or others may have their own special relationships which they would tend to favor.

Various underwriters will manage deals with various levels of perceived market risk. The "penny stock exchange," or the Denver exchange, is known for the low priced, high flying, high risk deals that the respectable houses will not touch. Normally, if the stock is to be priced on the initial offering at below ten dollars a share, the more established investment banks are leery in that this is the current price which separates the quality issues for new issues from the more speculative issues. This number will change from time to time depending on the flow of the market. Some houses specialize in making markets in particular specialized issues such as computer, medical, or telecommunications. This house may have strong institutional contacts who desire these specialized issues, and will make the important institutional market in your stock. Other firms have strong retail distribution or will support the stock for some time in the aftermarket due to their greater financial resources. Other firms only want to be perceived as managing the cream of the new–issue offerings, so you may need a pedigree to interest these underwriters.

"I never met an underwriter who could predict the state of the stock market at the exact moment a new issue will come to market." Most underwriters will attempt to accomplish this impossible feat of market timing. The reason they try is that it is perhaps the most important question, but sadly one where they most always come up short. Since the stock market is a bit like a big lottery, the failure to predict the market by those in the supposed "know" is not surprising. It is perhaps a credit to their resilience that they will continue to try. This means that you should not be surprised, though perhaps disappointed, if you must either withdraw your offering from the market or cut back the number of shares offered, the price, or both. This lottery aspect of a new stock offering means that it should not be exclusively relied on for continuing funding of the new company. A new company is in real trouble if a public stock offering is the only way to either compete or bail it out of prior difficulties. A few companies have managed to make the market window and survive through a new–issue offering, but you must be feeling lucky to leave your company's future solely to this fickle device. If you succeed, the rewards can be substantial; a higher price perhaps than could be achieved in a private sale (because it is now a more liquid stock—though sometimes not much), the opportunity to offer meaningful options to your employees, the prestige and visibility of a public entity, the chance to use paper to acquire other companies, rather than cash, and the feeling that you have arrived in the big time. Offsetting these benefits are the aforementioned glare of public and press scrutiny, the pressure for continuing good news, the tendency to shoot the messenger bearing bad news, the hassle of reports, forms, more bureaucrats, calls from the insane and disgruntled, etc. In addition, a bigger fish may start buying up your stock if you get real successful, take you over, and kick you out of a job and your office. You may long for the good old days of being poor but less visible and more secure.

Investment bankers and venture capitalists sometimes seem like the same type of fish to the entrepreneur—they are both earning fees, or income, or capital gains, off his hard work. There are several distinctions between the two breeds. An effective investment banker is generally more of a salesman than the average venture capitalist who often takes the orientation of a buyer. The investment banker must first sell the successful company on retaining his firm as the company's underwriter in competition with many others, then he must keep the company sold on his services until he can undertake a major transaction, must then sell the company's stock to savvy investors or to the public market, and then must keep selling the company to help maintain the price in the aftermarket. Not surprisingly, the investment banker is attuned to the market, and to what kind of company the market will now buy at what price, and in what amounts. He is a market animal. The venture capitalist is generally more concerned with creating value, the investment banker with helping set and realize value in the marketplace. Recently several investment banking houses have been successful in combining in some form or another the dual functions of venture capital or business development and underwriting, or making a market in a company's stock. While a few have for a short time been successful, it remains to be proven whether these somewhat contradictory roles can be housed under one roof successfully for an extended period. Unless a strong Chinese wall is established and maintained, there is the tendency for the venture capitalist to do deals that the underwriters believe they can sell, thus neglecting their necessary role in the process of business development. It takes a firm hand at the helm at the investment house to keep these combustible functions apart.

Now and then an exceptionally strong investment banker will bring a deal to a venture capitalist, induce the venture capitalist to make an investment, and then attempt to act as the lead financier on the deal in place of the venture capitalist. Unless the investment banker is highly experienced in business development, or in the business of a specific industry, this approach will often lead to conflict between the investment banker and the venture capitalist with various other investors splitting their allegiance between venture capitalist and investment banker. Following the thought that success has many fathers and failure is an orphan, both venture capitalist and investment banker will want to achieve the maximum recognition and visibility from the successful deal; this can lead to considerable infighting unless relationships are managed adroitly by the savvy entrepreneur. Here the entrepreneur will want to maintain the good will and advice of both parties without alienating either party. Generally this can be accomplished by looking to the venture capitalist for those subjects either affecting the investment syndicate or matters of business development, and to the investment banker for the state of the public markets. These are large egos, however, and the entrepreneur will sometimes wonder who is really trying to help his company be successful. Each relationship must be looked at objectively, and favorites avoided.

Professional venture capitalists believe that a little bit of a big company is just as good, if not better, than a big piece of a small company or of an unsuccessful company. Since venture capitalists are not generally interested in small companies because these do not normally provide exceptional rates of return, the entrepreneur must look into his own soul for the answer to the private or public dilemma and to his own peace of mind. On occasion a mistake may be made, a public offering undertaken, and then at a later date the company is taken private once again. This is however a relatively rare occasion, generally possible only when the company is cash rich and its stock selling well off of normal market or real value. Public or private is a question whose answer, once determined, is difficult to reverse.

AFTERWORD

Venture capital in some form has been with business enterprise as long as one man had something extra, and was willing to risk it based on the ambition, talent and efforts of others. Adventuresome capital, when supportive of those souls in our society who hear a different drummer and venture on the frontiers of the known, nurtures a free and prosperous society. It may not be the last, best, hope of mankind, but it is essential to make the rather unique entrepreneurial dream of freedom and opportunity come true.

Part 2

OTHER MUSINGS ON RISKY BUSINESS

INTRODUCTION

The successful entrepreneur is a person of many parts. He is also called upon to play many parts in the development of a growing company. As a person of creative vision he must first see the world according to a distinctly different reality than is immediately apparent to mere mortals. As the inspiration and driving force behind the establishment of a fragile creation he must be a person of uncommon focus and intensity. He must dream clear dreams that never were and that others never see. Perseverance is his most critical stock in trade. He must be resilient enough to stand in the most pressing times of trouble. His ear must be fine tuned to the yessayers of the world rather than the naysayers. Often the only real credit will be that the attempt was made when no one else would venture forth. Flexibility coupled to an imaginative disposition permits openings to be found where none appear to exist. This is his age, his time and element; for the world appears to be coming around once again to the need for new forms to provide substance to varied perceptions of what we are about and where we are tending. Once again, as in olden times, when fabrics shift the entrepreneur is called forth to engage danger and the uncertain, proving that only in risking ourselves from day to day do we truly live. Admission of error is difficult when the vision is so clear, but a necessary companion in crossing over from ambiguity to a full and necessary comprehension of reality. Winning and losing is not really what his day is all about. It is about being unfettered and unbounded and finding self. These "Musings on Risky Business" are dedicated to the secret place in all of us that knows how much we can be if we continue to dream our dreams and apply the best we have to the work of the world.

13

EYE OF THE TIGER

Entrepreneurs are never entirely alike nor entirely different. They are driven by their own particular demons to attempt to create their own unique destiny. They are generally very uncomfortable with authority imposed from without, whether in the form of the corporation or the imposition of another's will. Many as children were unable to be true to themselves while attempting to conform and placate an overwhelming parent. Their characteristic hostility to authority, and the limitations they sense it imposes, is a response to these childhood chains. Many attempt the often futile effort to live both without limits but also without limitations. The best of the breed may avoid authority and situations they cannot control, but know their own limitations.

The United States provides an opportunity unique historically among nations for flexing entrepreneurial muscles. Here with considerable luck and pluck the classic entrepreneur's drives can be turned to fun and profit. Where there is an opportunity to succeed there is also the opportunity to fail. You can go bankrupt here, you can fail, but you can also start over if you have the will and courage. Entrepreneurs often fail because there seems to be no other way to learn their trade with its combination of vision and the practical.

Entrepreneurs are often misfits who simply don't mesh with the corporate culture. They don't fit in. Their independent ideas and vision and willingness to act decisively are not normal behavior at most corporations. Corporations move carefully, rationally when at their best, and mostly by consensus. Any new idea must be carefully sewn and gradually nurtured to survive the corporate political environment. Entrepreneurs are totally impatient with this process of censensus and accommodation. They don't like to fail, but it is not necessary for their survival not to fail, which is true at many American corporations. They are often the best, the brightest, and the most driven of the corporation's employees. Even with the limitations often imposed by the corporate structure, they will produce great achievements. The average corporation, however, has trouble with great achievement. It is too exceptional and makes corporate leadership feel guilty and uneasy. Uneasy because the leadership sees something of greater potential value than its own leadership, and guilty because its rewards can in no manner truly compensate for the exceptional contribution which the corporate entrepreneur may make to the bottom line. The entrepreneur in the corporate environment is the one who seems to say that the corporate emperors have no clothes, and that they are underworked, overcompensated, and perked into lethargy. The entrepreneur doesn't have much patience for the chain of command. It slows him down and delays his accomplishment. It is to be subverted or ignored. This is not comforting to those whose authority is not always based on personal contribution, but rather on institutional authority and support. The entrepreneur is not interested in getting along by going along. He wants to get going.

What seems to have happened in our society is that in several generations we went from a nation of essentially independent farmers and shopkeepers to a nation of centralized capital and centralized authority. This centralized capital required workers to make it productive, and through various inducements ("you can't keep them down on the farm once they're making real money") enticed the independent farmer, laborer, and shopkeeper to give up their independent way of life for the security provided by working together with others in a common, more centralized endeavor. This has not been all bad. There was a lot of poverty and hardship on the farm. Hours were long, and work often backbreaking. Pensions and social security nonexistent. Little time for culture, education, or the finer things of life for most of farm society. The cities, the factories, the corporation promised and often delivered a better life for many. Like most good things, there was a price for this comfort and security. It was not just that the corporation eventually meant giving up independent views for the good of the whole; it was that if we rely too much on others we forget how to do for ourselves, to roll up our sleeves and really work. Many have been seduced by this offer of a free lunch, and forgotten how to really work. It's not unusual for an entrepreneurial company to hire someone from a major corporation and find that this individual really doesn't want to work hard and well. He is more interested in consumption and reward than productivity and contribution. Corporations give a lot of lip service to the idea of hard work, but the dependence they encourage negates the message.

Planning, as practiced in large corporations, tends to dwell on assembly of the plausible or politically acceptable alternatives, and eliminating these one by one until the most likely course presents itself—hopefully the course of greatest probable success. Most corporate planning departments are inhabited by the overly analytical members of the corporate staff, rather then the more intuitive who are found on the line. They attempt to find out what is unacceptable and then focus on the acceptable. The entrepreneur, however, subconsciously focuses on what is acceptable and rarely consciously considers other alternatives or the probability of failure. He is engaged in creating the future, and tends not to look back either in anger or regret. Because much of this focusing on the acceptable is unconscious, it is necessary for the entrepreneur to have considerable experience, both positive and negative, in his field, to successfully choose a course with a high probability of success.

Until recently, when entrepreneurs were spoken of it at all, it was not quite as criminals, but certainly as a fringe element of dubious reputation and intention. This was a product of the fifties mentality when national and international mass markets were being created as a direct result of mass production techniques, which where honed to a fair thee well during the wartime emergency. With advent of the computer and computer controlled manufacturing (robotics), it became possible to create specialized products for smaller or niche markets, and to manufacture these specialized products in almost custom quantities. Suddenly the need for the entrepreneur was back and the technology was available to produce items which were highly specialized and customized, but still in mass quantities. This revelation, coupled with the hot breath of the Japanese and other low cost labor competitors to the United States led to a resurgence of the American entrepreneur. It had been a long time coming. J. P. Morgan and the gang made money concentrating most things in mass, and now the new entrepreneur was making fame, fortune, and the cover of *Time* by breaking things apart. Economics continued to prove that as in most human events necessity is the mother of both invention and fashion, just as new invention may call forth a new necessity and fashion.

There are a number of inducements in this country not to be an entrepreneur. Corner offices, expense accounts, club memberships, administrating rather then creating; the stuff of the modern corporation is available to many with a decent education and moderate ambition. Most of the time corporate organizations deliver on their essential promise, which is, in return for time and attention, a decent standard of living, not too much work, and comradeship. Corporate highs will not be too high, but then again the lows are not too low. Great nerve not normally required. The good life.

Entrepreneurs reject all of this. They are not really interested in the good life; rather their own life. They come in several shapes and sizes. They have something to demonstrate to themselves, to the world, to their parents, to the future. They make most normal people a little uncomfortable. Small talk is not their strong suit. Oh, they will talk at length, but mostly about their particular creation. Some would say their singlemindedness is boring if not offensive, but then their dedication and persistence are admirable. The brightest of the lot will stay away from wild escapades and mad chances unless pressed to the wall by negative cash flow and howling creditors. Their risks are more calculated. They know intuitively which cards have been played, which remain to be played, and what cards their competitors are holding. They may even have an ace or two up their sleeves.

Successful entrepreneurship requires a man of passion. You really have to care about what you are doing. No half measures here. Some have been known to make pacts with the devil (often in human apparel) to start or save their company. When their backs are to the wall, their best efforts are called forth. They can live off the land while constructing their palace. These are not easy people to live with or to love. Their time is not really their own so it will never belong much to their friends or family. They are bringing forth a new order, and this leaves little time for little else. They can really be infuriating at times, but show great charm in the pursuit of their objectives. If you get involved with one as a friend, employee, or spouse, chances are your life will be one of considerable intensity. Never a dull moment. It's possible they might lose it all, so never go into it for the money, only for the living.

Building something from nothing teaches a good deal about what life is often really all about. The process requires mostly faith and considerable courage. An entrepreneur often does not win the first time. He is learning this trade and developing his intuition. Many lesser mortals will wish him to fail, including those he calls friends. He may lose his home and have to start over. His wife and children may not have all the things others of his apparent ability and resourcefulness are able to provide for their families. To those of more placid disposition he may even appear a little unstable. He experiences a certain amount of pain—in our world this appears to go with the territory of original creation.

Our society has often made the prophets, persons of vision, artists, entrepreneurs, and others pursuing their own distant drum pay for their gift of creation. It's as if their unique talent is a threat to the self esteem of those who are more conformist and less creative. Of course they are a real threat to whatever is established, whether in art, business, science, or government. Their discoveries, inventions, and creations may well drive out the old if they prove over time to have greater utility or interest.

These unique individuals are necessary to a society like ours, which depends on the market that requires the new and useful to sustain its momentum, and on the media which craves the new and interesting to both sell and entertain. This is why we honor them when they succeed, and praise their creations and success. Success truly does have many fathers. Failure remains the proverbial orphan.

The entrepreneur is not principally interested in power over others, although this may result from his efforts. Most are driven by a need for achievement and for the right to create their own unique vision. In fact entrepreneurs often get themselves in trouble when they get or become corrupted by their success, and become more interested in power over others, or the trappings of success, forgetting or becoming unfaithful to their animating vision. If their underlying motivation is the acquisition of material things, fame, or success in the eyes of the world, they are often unable to keep the clear head and vision required of the true innovator and creator. Like Galahad of Arthur's Court, in losing their virtue, they lose their gift and exceptional power, becoming mere mortals. Of course it is only human that success corrupts, and the creative power lost. Perhaps that is why there are not very many repeaters as true entrepreneurs. Not too many who fail have the courage to come back, and those who succeed make the pages of *Venture* and begin to enjoy the good life.

Most entrepreneurs are eventually faced with the fact that most people around them don't really want their efforts to succeed. The human race does not honor its prophets until they are successful or dead. Finally the entrepreneur realizes that he is really out there all alone, and that the only way to vindicate himself is to make a success of his venture. To accomplish this he must peel away some of the veneer of civilization and the trappings of ordinary existence, and casting his fate into his own hands, take real responsibility for his own life, without the apparent comfort of a paycheck or the support of family and friends. This is the reason entrepreneurial networks can be critical to entrepreneurial success. They provide the support and occasional succor which society and family and friends may deny the fledging entrepreneur. They are a role model for the successful long journey. They say: "we did it, and you too can." Taking responsibility for yourself is not something that most of our society encourages, from the government to the large corporation; the trade is, you contribute and support us, and we will take care of you. Many have come to realize that often this is a false promise uttered by a false prophet, and that maturity as well as real financial security comes from self–reliance and from occasional reliance on other independent spirits for guidance and support.

Entrepreneurial activity is by necessity and nature intense and all–consuming. Working closely with the average entrepreneur is akin to proximity to a blast furnace. A high degree of personal commitment and dedication is required. The employee is signing on for a voyage which may lead to the ends of the earth. Working in an entrepreneurial company can be hazardous, particularly if the entrepreneur does not allow the same degree of freedom and creativeness to his employees as he himself demands. It can also end abruptly if the entrepreneur is the type who has difficulty with those who may disagree with his interpretation of the vision. Some entrepreneurs reserve all interpretation unto themselves. If being an entrepreneur is chancy, working with and/or for one can be even more hazardous. Most successful entrepreneurs have a rather unusual ability to know what they want, if perhaps being a little uncertain always where they are going. The most creative are more interested in the creative journey, rather than on what distant shore they land; however, they are quite clear that they want to take the voyage in a certain size ship, headed in a Northwest direction, with a cargo of selected inventory, and crewed by hand–picked sailors. They are possessed of an intuition of what will be most immediately useful. They know what to have available to seize the unexpected opportunity or to fend off danger. The successful entrepreneur develops an instinct about what will be good for him and draws to him the helpful. He is also a ready improviser. If he does not happen to have at hand the stuff to fashion and give form to his dreams, he will find it wherever it lays. In any situation he is able to divine the most useful and creative combination, and bring the opportunity around to his liking. Living off the land is his specialty, planning generally a rather obscure ritual practiced by his larger more established competitors.

Many of the successful entrepreneurs that venture capitalists support are in their late thirties to early forties because these are the years when combined experience and energy are at their peak potential. Any younger, experience will be insufficient, any older, and energy and daring are likely to be lacking. Now and then successful entrepreneurs will emerge in their early to late twenties, but these are often market–driven success stories, which may be closer to winning the state lottery than representing a real entrepreneurial effort. The beginnings of the personal computer industry with Apple Computer is an example of this market–driven kind of success. Apple's later history of struggles, renewal, and revival with the successful introduction of its Macintosh line and the IIc appears more akin to true entrepreneurship.

When the going gets tough, the successful entrepreneur gets tough. Entrepreneurs can be tender on people and tough on results in good times, but in lean times the successful are often tough on both. They are wily survivors and have been known to push the lame and crippled, as well as their investors, from the lifeboat if necessary to continue their activities. For the hardiest of the breed, bankruptcy, either company or personal, is insufficient to dampen their spirit. They will simply open a new shop down the street, and continue business as usual. Previous investors are likely to be little noted or remembered after down-the-street success. The most intractable problems are likely to be viewed as opportunities, and a worthy test of the entrepreneurial mettle. These people thrive on adversity, and on occasion, will only rise to the heroic effort when called upon to do so by exceptional circumstances of the severest adversity. The normal everyday challenge is boring, but in a major crisis that is why they live and work. This is a business for survivors, not necessarily for nice people.

Entrepreneurs know how to get out and get going—morning, evening, and afternoon. They will call you on Saturday, Sunday, holidays, and at any time with their visions and concerns. They are really always working and planning their next move, examining the risks in their decisions, and acting, always and ever acting. This is a restless bunch, rarely happy if not shinning in use and motion. The successful are busy and focused. No purposeless activity here; each step along the byway is intended to lead to a highway to somewhere. Time is more than money. They are not self starters—they never stop.

A calculated boldness is characteristic of most successful entrepreneurial ventures. This is the world of the darling and audacious, of the strikingly unconventional. New trails in the forest are being blazed. High technology entrepreneurs are often particularly bold in their conceptions and constructions. Their companies are working on the frontier, pushing the window of the known world back a bit. This is larger than life activity—a deviation from the normal and average human behavior. This is not just gambling or crap shooting. Bold strokes are carefully calculated and often meticulously implemented. Betting the whole company is occasionally required by events but most successful entrepreneurs labor mightily to avoid being pushed into this corner of possible no return. Too much work, sacrifice, and effort was required to build the company to lose it all on one chance throw of the dice.

Recently, with the establishment of a large number of venture–supported companies in almost every interesting market niche in the high technology area, it has become increasingly difficult to avoid the "betting the company" syndrome in order to establish the necessary leverage to rise above the pack and become one of the survivors. Needless to say more companies in high tech are failing and will fail in the future as betting the company becomes a structural requirement for eventual success. This phenomena is particularly apparent in the world of the personal computer industry, and its related peripherals where hundreds of companies are attempting to gain a toe hold over a limited market opportunity. Betting the company is more often required today because product life cycles are shorter, which means that the company's whole financial position may be required to develop the next generation product before adequate profits to provide financial stability can be wrung out of the prior product introduction. Over time many experienced entrepreneurs will shy away from these excesses and more stability will return as this activity proves increasingly unsuccessful.

Much of the higher risk entrepreneurial activity has occured in Silicon Valley and its environs in California because a culture is established where it is possible to rebound fairly quickly from business failure. Boldness is encouraged in this environment where networks are readily available to help place unsuccessful entrepreneurs in new entrepreneurial ventures, and where a number of the managers in venture–backed companies are normally participating in their second, third, or even fourth business start–up. Boldness is noticeably lacking in the industrial Midwest, where conformity is rewarded, and where it is much more difficult to become reestablished after business failure. In much of the Midwest "things that don't work out" are regarded as personal failing rather than the often unavoidable slings and arrows of outrageous fortune. Once the matter becomes personal or is viewed by the business community in this context, both personal and business recovery becomes difficult. Those communities which want to encourage entrepreneurial activity not only need to begin to establish networks of money, information, and assistance, they need to look to their own values and attitudes before an entrepreneurial environment will emerge. History teaches from the Renaissance to Elizabethan England that the brave and bold are in large measure a product of their place and time. Infertile soil will discourage even the hardiest of adventurers.

Is entrepreneurship really just the pursuit of happiness and satisfaction cloaked in the disguise of the adventurous businessman? Do entrepreneurs ever find happiness and satisfaction, or is there some compulsive torment and neverending quest to eternally create the new, to reinvent time, to continually rediscover fire? Many entrepreneurs clearly find immense satifaction in their work and undertakings. It is very rewarding to get up in the mornings and begin a creative activity where the structure of what you do is your creation, largely under your control, and direction, and which may turn up a number of challenging surprises during the day. This is great fun and for those who for whatever reason are uncomfortable or feel restricted in more structured or circumscribed environments, it is as necessary to happiness as breathing. While entrepreneurship can be frustrating, painful, and difficult, for some, it is the only world they can inhabit in any real personal peace. For others of more accommodating but equally adventurous disposition, entrepreneurship is not so much an escape from the authorities of the past but rather the opportunity to fully explore the present. It is an arena where the full and complete use of powers and talents is called forth. While corporate America produces job descriptions and normally asks employees to do their job and not some other, the entrepreneur is not circumscribed by the walls of a job description or limited in what he may accomplish, by the insecurities of his superiors, or the necessity to wait his turn until others ahead of him in the corporate pecking order retire. His field is wide open, and he can attempt whatever broken field running he is able to perform. He is free to both succeed and fail, and perhaps most of all to be himself. In a world where many are not themselves and want others to be like them, this may be as close to happiness as he is likely to come.

14

WHY OUR CORPORATIONS CANNOT INNOVATE

Last year the IBM Corporation spent over $3 billion dollars to maintain its technical supremacy. This was more money than the entire venture capital industry invested altogether. Over the last ten years it is estimated that all major U.S. corporations added virtually no new jobs to the American economy, whereas venture-backed companies created thousands of new jobs. Our major corporations, with their combining, merging and taking over, are making headlines but not opportunity. They are by and large trustees of assets which they carefully manage with the fidelity of a trustee rather than the vision of the entrepreneur. Occasionally a few lone voices in their midst issue a call for innovation and change and for the encouragement of the maverick spirit in the corporate world. These calls often fall on deaf ears. Why?

Our giant corporations are not only prisoners of the inertia created by their size and complexity. They are captives of their essential constituency, their institutional stockholders and lenders, the major money center banks and the stock market. This captivity to a sponsorship which encourages stability over risk–taking creates overly hierarchic and bureaucratic organizations where not making a mistake is valued over taking a chance. How does all this work?

The stock market is no longer the province of the small investor. A recent article in *The New York Times** noted that "The little guy has been

*From "How the Institutions Rule the Market," November 25, 1984. Copyright © 1985 by the New York Times Company. Reprinted by Permission.

frightened by the growing influence of the big institutional players . . .
their ability to buy and sell millions of dollars of stocks at a crack has led
to wild price gyrations that can enrich or wipe out small investors in a
week or two. And that has driven many away from the whole game, perhaps for good." Periodically, there are rumors of the small investors'
hoped–for return like the prodigal son, but he never seems to make it to
dinner. It's unclear who is out searching for him, but let's assume that it
is the hungry retail broker who doesn't have any institutional business.
Mostly this broker is going hungry. The *Times* reports: "Institutions are
now responsible for 60 to 65 percent of volume of the Big Board, while
Wall Street houses trading with their own money . . . account for 25 to 30
percent of all trading—down from 33 percent in the late 1970's." The little
guy is no longer a real factor. The top institutional investors and their
agents are moving most of the money. Most of these investors are paid to
play it fairly safe. After all, they are investing pensions—widow and orphan money—for real. These investors don't like surprises—good or bad,
they only provide upset. If the news is good, the management must be
taking some way out risks with the equity investment, which will turn to
garbage tomorrow. If the news is bad, well, who likes bad news; it only
sends the stock down. The major investors in our major corporations like
things on an even keel. How do they get this? Managements who don't
keep things on an even keel find their stocks not recommended, which
means that business starts bouncing around, until they bounce out of their
jobs. Investing for the long term by company management is not appreciated because it doesn't move up short term earnings, and thus the price
of the stock, and once again, it will provide some kind of a positive or
negative surprise which no one saw coming. If the analysts who are paid
to see momentous events coming don't know about them, what good are
they? In brief, we have this zero sum game going where everyone gets his
except we don't take many chances, create any new jobs, or build for the
future. Those in power, whether Democrats or Republicans, don't want
to change the pension rules on investing too much, because under the
current rules of the game they obtained power, and governments prefer
stability to those things that may go to the moon or crash in flames. Wars,
revolutions, South Sea Bubbles, and other means of economic collapse are
never good for the reigning politician's health or longevity. All this business then about the rebirth of the corporate entrepreneur just won't work.
The deck is fully stacked. It's not in the self interest of any self–respecting
Chief Executive Office to promote entrepreneurship in the major American corporation. Until the country really wants to see more real economic risk–taking, nothing will happen. Usually in the history of nations,
as outlined by Toynbee, major change will not occur until an exceptional
challenge produces a like–minded exceptional response. At the moment
the Japanese challenge, while annoying, does not seem sufficient, and the

Russian Empire appears on its way to eventual economic collapse. Its bureaucrats and planners have apparently failed to establish any real risk–taking within the system. While there are a number of people who will value security for a while, particularly when their history has not provided much, eventually they start to feel secure and adventuresome and start to undermine the system that prevents the fulfillment of their now deepest desires.

Since at the moment no extraordinary challenge is on the horizon—although these do tend to show up unannounced and out of breath—we can't expect much innovation and entrepreneurship from major corporations. We will need to look to our last, best hope, the American entrepreneur—which corporate America almost killed in the fifties but is making a strong resurgence. He is coming back for several interesting reasons. Americans believe in progress and opportunity in their very being — equal opportunity is the American promise. We want things better for our children and our children's children. With the baby boom and the Mexicans coming over the leaky border there are a lot of people going to be looking for economic opportunity. If the politicians fail to provide it, they will be out of office. The politicians know that the pension fund–stock market–corporate American system which elected them is not going to provide the required homes, jobs, and satisfactions, so they are looking around for someone who can. They have rediscovered the classic American entrepreneur as the new American hero.

The only way entrepreneurship will have a chance is to continue to lower the capital gains rate, set free some additional pension fund investment for risky business, and get the media lionizing entrepreneurial heroes so people in middle America know what is going on, and get interested in taking a few calculated chances rather than sitting around watching television. It appears that all of this is starting to work. Last year over 700,000 companies were started in the U.S. vs. a handful in 1958. Last year more money went into venture capital than ever before in the history of man (although less than the IBM research and development budget). Those in the venture capital business see people coming out of the corporate closet in increasing numbers, and ready to make a try for it on their own. People are beginning to wake up all over America and leave their security and passivity behind.

How would it be possible for our corporations, the custodians of successful entrepreneurs of the past, to shake off financial and operating inertia and emerge in the vanguard of the new entrepreneurial age? First, the tyranny of the stock market, the stock analyst, and the pension funds must be broken. This could be accomplished in several ways. The small investor could return to the market in record numbers, diluting the influence of the larger blocks of money, but this appears unlikely. Even should the small investor return, it is probable that his orientation would be less long–term than the money managers, and more likely to panic and sell on the first downturn in earnings and rumors of same. Visionary corporate leaders who have lived with the problem of short–term results could come together and begin to attempt to educate both the public and the money managers on the requirement for a longer–term view if American commerce is to retain its position in the world economy, or the government could intervene and through tax and other incentives reward longer–term oriented investors for the additional risk which they believe they are assuming. It appears probable that only a change in government–controlled incentives will be sufficient to shock and alter the present psychology of the investment community. A complementary approach would be to alter our banking system so that banks would be encouraged to provide, and corporations to obtain, a higher proportion of their total capitalization through debt rather than equity financing. This approach has in part permitted Japanese companies to focus more on long–term research and development and less on creating immediate earnings. In addition, changes in dividend policy and its taxable consequences as well as continuing incentives for longer–term research and development spending could promote a longer–term outlook in the corporate suite.

All of these financial incentives and changes in the investment environment, however, will prove insufficient unless the leadership model of the corporation moves from the administrative and ministerial to the entrepreneurial and innovative. Many American corporations have established over the years a particular franchise. These continuing franchises may be in the retail business, insurance, oil, banking, credit cards, cars, or dog food. They were organized to provide goods and services to mass American and worldwide markets, and have performed this not inconsequential function effectively and efficiently. Many of these markets are mature, and simply don't require much in the way of innovation. The goods that are provided do a more than adequate job of meeting the requirements of the market, and change in the product would be unnecessary, confusing or both. Not much innovation is expected or required from these industries, and it is probably best if these corporations simply expire or continue doing what they do best without bestirring themselves from gentle slumber. Other corporations of a more aggressive, innovative, and entrepreneurial inclination are beginning to search for solutions to their entrepreneurial-trustee dilemma. They are aware that various technical, demographic, and culture changes are occurring which are calling forth new approaches to changing market realities. Often the initial thrust, because it is the least resistant to change, is to position the corporation in new markets or industries which exploit the corporation's current strengths. This is attempted both by acquisition and through internal development of new business opportunities. Thus Sears has acquired a number of companies in the financial services sector where their loyal customers of middle America can be provided an array of real estate, brokerage, and other services, building on their established consumer trust and wide customer base. IBM has established internally generated business units which operate on a more autonomous basis, free from incursions from the corporate staff. These IBU (independent business units) are used by IBM in businesses where innovation and fast market response are critical to success—their first major success occurred with the successful production and introduction of their personal computer using the IBU as the organizational form.

Operating like a separate new company, the IBU has considerable freedom from the demands of the parent, and the ability to act with alacrity. Initially there were six units at IBM: personal computers, software, robotics, medical test equipment, computer-aided design and manufacturing, and network computing services. Now there are others. The leader of the IBU at times appears to act and speak as if the Chief Executive of a smaller, more specialized company. Later, as in the case of the personal computer IBU, the unit may be reabsorbed by the parent as the business matures. It's a form of internal venture capital followed by internal corporate acquisition. It permits initial creativity and later mass implementation of the creation.

The IBM, IBU technique is emerging as a possible model to solve the entrepreneurial–trustee dilemma. In addition to changing the form of the organization, incentives must be structured which will encourage and promote entrepreneurial activity. Major corporations have more problems with inadequate entrepreneurial incentives than any other aspect of the entrepreneurial process. In most corporations the higher you move up the corporate ladder, the more you are paid, both in salary and bonus. It is considered unseemly for a lower level employee performing an innovative task which may contribute much to the corporate coffers to be paid more than the boss. The rejoinder from the entrepreneurial ranks is that "I had a better year than the boss so I should be paid more." While on the surface this may appear to be true, it raises several difficult issues in a corporate setting: officers in most major corporations are similar to a military cadre; they have responsibility for the care and feeding of the organization; may be relieved of command if events do not turn out well; worked their way up through the organization through effective and loyal behavior; and are the final repository of the corporation's values, dreams, and culture. This cadre is well paid both for past and future service, and because it is in power. To pay an innovative entrepreneur more than the boss is often viewed as indicating that the lowest should be highest, and as a threat to the corporate power structure. This is particularly true if the established power structure is not really innovating but playing a trustee's role. There is always the fear that someone will argue "how tough is it to be a trustee and collect a big salary?" "What have you done for the corporation lately?"

This fear is not groundless, as the recent controversy over large bonuses paid to various automotive executives makes clear. Most forget that the bonuses were paid because the corporation met its goals, and would not have been paid had the goals not been accomplished. Of course in America there is always the part of the American psyche that contains an element of disdain for those who are not working with their hands or in the shop—perhaps this is a carryover from our agricultural past and industrial inheritance. In the information age, with most of the work force engaged in handling communication and information, this attitude will fade further into the collective unconscious. Players and superstars in professional sports have long since exceeded the salaries of the team manager. It has not gone without notice that this has created some big egos on the part of the players, and on occasion considerable independence and not a little insubordination. There is an unspoken managerial fear that this superstar ego problem could be communicated throughout the organization with resulting loss of control and discipline. Those corporations which choose the route of innovation, and thus will be the survivors in a more heterogeneous age, will need to begin to resolve the issue of entrepreneurial compensation. For this to be effective it must apply throughout the organization—to all who are in a position to make a major entrepreneurial contribution. Salary differential would still exist between those in the executive suite and the typing pool, but the imaginative, innovative contribution would be fully rewarded either through substantial bonuses or stock incentives. Innovative compensation will be a requirement of the entrepreneurial corporation of the future.

Maverick thinking and action are essential for any real progress to occur within a corporation. How can they be nurtured and encouraged? Other than through a restructuring of financial rewards, they must come from the top. Top management must change its thinking and cherish the mavericks within the organization. A clear message must be sent that these individuals, like the sacred beasts of Eastern religions, are to be free to wander the halls and regale passersby with their visions, encouraged in their mind–stretching schemes whenever possible, and provided necessary financial support, especially when there is a little extra to spend on the future. Top management support for the offbeat will work wonders. Company bureaucrats will at first be amazed and privately wonder about the sanity of senior management but this will pass as they continue to support policy in whatever form or substance. Eventually the more adventuresome from the bureaucracy will form alliances with the more communicative of the visionaries, and the corporation will become known as a place that encourages independent and creative projects, thus attracting more of the same. Occasionally maverick approaches will be disruptive and upsetting to normal procedures, but this is a small price for innovation.

Another approach to encourage mavericks is to re-examine the real checks and balances which exist among the various corporate departments, and determine if some of them are blocks to the independent creative approach. Most large corporations have a formal or often informal series of relationships and review procedures, which can stifle the more creative members of the company. Good ideas never surface because they are reviewed to death. Often these reviews reflect the balance of power which has been worked out among the various operating and staff departments. An innovative idea or approach comes from an operating department, but first it must be reviewed by the financial staff, then by the legal staff, then the marketing and public relations staffs. By the time it reaches the light of day, it is either amended, diluted, or avoided. The original proponent is fully exhausted and disgusted. Large corporations tend to accumulate checks and balances which once served some larger and vital corporate purpose, but have since outgrown their usefulness and are retained because they always were and always will be, or because without them the incumbent in that job would be out of work. A review of those procedures and the elimination of those which do not directly contribute to corporate objectives will encourage innovations to come to the light of day. Without top management support this will never occur in most corporations, but nothing is more critical to provide the environment where the offbeat will flourish.

Trustee managers should be encouraged to use their political and administrative skills to shield and get the corporate staff off the back of the innovative, entrepreneurially inclined corporate producers. Such a role, for corporate management, is an effective use of the considerable talents for conciliation of an effective trustee manager. He in effect is the shield and catalyst which encourages and protects entrepreneurial behavior within the corporate structure. Such managers, when working in tandem with effective entrepreneurial producers, more than earn their substantial compensation. They permit the force, size, and resources of the large organization to be brought to bear in a focused and productive manner by the entrepreneurial innovator. They smooth the rough edges which often exist between the maverick entrepreneurial spirit and the corporate monolith. Those corporations which both honor and reward the contributions of the innovator and the conciliator and mesh their talents will be formidable. American ability to manage complexity will have at last been effectively united with American vision and imagination.

Corporations will also need to surrender some of the "let's not do anything too different or unusual because this may wind up in the papers and tarnish our image with the public" problem. Many American managers are trained to avoid any hint of controversy. Communications which are not carefully tailored and packaged by the public relations department are to be avoided, and expressions of views which are not company line are prohibited.

Why this requirement for the corporation to seem to speak with one voice, and a bland one at that? The mavericks often prefer controversy over silence, the interplay of ideas over corporate quiet. Corporate communication is a real problem. If everyone in the corporation felt free to speak his mind on corporate policy, the world would have no idea what the corporation stood for, was trying to accomplish, or was all about. A guy on the loading dock would be saying one thing one day, and the Chairman of the Board would come out with something else the next. The world would be confused, not to mention employees, customers, and suppliers. In a world where a lot of hungry reporters make a good living jumping on the sensational and misrepresenting or hyping the actual, communications discretion and control apppears necessary for corporate survival. However, the maverick likes to speak his mind, often without limitation as to subject, content, or listener. Some corporations have solved this dilemma by essentially allowing free speech within the corporation, but prohibiting or limiting it outside the company.

The maverick who violates this prohibition is brought to heel. Besides dislodging several effective corporate mavericks, such a solution fails to provide the maverick personality with the interplay, on a one on one basis, with the world which is often required to stimulate and enhance his creative capacity. The maverick becomes uncomfortable with these limitations and leaves for more open spaces. Initially corporate public relations departments should be encouraged, and should encourage corporate mavericks to enjoy free outside contact on those issues which do not violate corporate policy, and should loosen the reins on those issues which are perceived as being matters of company image. Often a company in fact has many different images depending on the relationship which a particular customer had with the company for good or ill, so one more will not really hurt much. In addition the P.R. department should be encouraged to permit free outside speech within certain limited and carefully defined arenas. Thus a maverick should be without limitation in speaking before certain industry groups or within industry publications, but would be prohibited from outrageous remarks in the public press and local newspapers. Perhaps there is no completely satisfactory solution between the maverick's need for self expression and the corporation's desire to protect itself, but the attempt needs to be made if mavericks are to be retained within the corporate family. The most creative among us need the freedom to express and circulate their ideas and contributions.

15

LOOK FOR THE LIONS

"Look for the Lions" was written by the author to provide understanding to the entrepreneur, and the financial community, of the common elements and problems inherent in investing in technical companies. In recent years high technology investing has become the dominant vehicle for venture capitalists, and can be expected to gain a large percent of available funds in the future. The article, reprinted below,* was first published in the December, 1984 edition of *Investment Decisions* and will be particularly useful to the technical entrepreneur in gaining insight into a venture capitalist's concerns prior to making a technical investment decision.

Early in the world magicians applied both faith and the rudiments of science to astound. When magic lost its sway and faith was unbundled from science, man discovered fire and the electric current. High technology replaced high magic as the shaper of destiny.

Today technology is knowledge and information structured and harnessed to do the work of the world. High technology represents advanced knowledge and information more tightly and more economically bundled. It may also represent an unusual insight into the unity and association of things. Its life is only a moment, for today's high technology is tomorrow's toaster. It is an ever receding star.

High technology is a unique investment category. Its mere mention conjures up wondrous feats, unleashed demons, and excessive financial

*Reprinted by permission of W. R. Nelson & Co.

returns. There are several dominating characteristics of high technology investments: a product or service with a high knowledge or information content; which can be repeated consistently and economically; which cannot be duplicated by others too quickly or too accurately; which provides the critical window of opportunity; which is likely to be superseded in short order by more advanced applications. These unique investments represent the cutting edge of our commerce and science based civilization.

Many venture investors and entrepreneurs attempt the hazard of seeking new fortune through the creation of high technology companies only to be waylaid by perils viewed in retrospect to be all too familiar; squabbling and unfocused management, unbounded ego, products with one more engineering change before shipment (when the documentation weighs more than the product—ship it), products finished for ghost markets, products that don't work, salesmen who can't sell and accountants who won't or can't count. These distresses are, of course, present occasionally in low tech as well as high tech ventures. High technology investments are subject to their own peculiar forms of distress.

High technology must provide reproducible results for commercial success. When technical prototypes are flawed, products produced based on these prototypes often don't work and take so much time and money to fix that everyone is worn out before the payoff. High tech failure could, on occasion, be avoided if it could be determined in advance whether a particular technology will work consistently. One litmus test favored by investors, is to attempt to judge whether the particular application represents merely a new application of a known technology or whether the inventor is attempting to extend the state-of-the-art, or even worse, creating a new art. The technical investment decision often gets down to how many old concepts have to work in an old way, how many old concepts have to work in a new way, how many new concepts have to work in an old way, and how many new concepts have to work in a new way. A related issue is the technology which creates a new market or an entirely new industry—the new concept working in an entirely new way. Recent examples include micro computers and user–friendly software, biotechnology, and advanced robotics. Investor over-reliance on technical experts to evaluate leading edge technology can produce highly misleading conclusions. The expert is generally familiar with the current state-of-the-art, but may often lack the imagination to correctly perceive creative extensions of the art. If the expert earns his living evaluating the creations of others, it is unlikely that he will still be highly creative himself. He is, in essence, a critic rather than a creator. A new technical achievement may represent a threat to his expertise in that if the technology achieves market acceptance, a new level of expertise and new experts may be created. While investor reliance on experts is not always to be avoided when the technology is radical and pushing known limits, the only real expert may be the innovative technologist.

High technical advance represents the search for unity in hidden likenesses and the application of a new unity to the world's work. As J. Bronowski has written, "The progress of science is the discovery at each step of a new order which gives unity to what had long seemed unlike." Radical technical innovation comes from the mind and hand of those who are open to further explorations of the essential unity of all experience. Its very nature is more akin to the world of wonder than the experience of the expert. Investors in a new technology must, at times, make their own leap of faith and for a moment suspend disbelief in favor of wonder. These investment opportunities call on all of the venture capitalist's intuitive skills.

While in some cases disbelief must be suspended for a time as to whether a technology will work, careful analysis must be undertaken as to whether the interesting technology will meet a market need. For a company to grow from a technology, the technical result must always be acceptable to a sufficient number of customers. If there are competitive technologies, the result must either be better in a general sense, and capture segments of various product applications, or better in a very specific sense and capture all or most of one segment. Technologies fail the market test which are not quite up to satisfying a general or specific market requirement. The product may not be fast enough, the definition precise enough, the cost low enough, the features broad enough, the size small enough. A successful technology must deliver enough to the customer. It is not sufficient to be merely interesting. The technology must be ready for the market and the market ready for the technology. There is nothing like a customer for a new technology to gain investor acceptance.

A successful technology must, in addition, have market staying power. Technical markets are subject to rapid alternation. Established technologies are often brushed aside by a more responsive technology. For the new technology to gain a foothold and stay long enough to earn a fair return for the risk, the product may need to be 100 percent cheaper, 50 percent faster, and provide advanced enhancements. Technology, by its nature, is destructive of the older order. It must be strong enough to drive out the old and to withstand for a time the challenge of future innovation.

While for a period an investor in a new technology must suspend disbelief for the technology to incubate, investors must also continuously monitor whether the technology is approaching consistency. This is particularly necessary in most small technical ventures where funds and time are limited. Realism tempers optimism, and for those innovations where discrete technical gates can be identified, progress at these junctures should be identified and expected. Slow cooking is essential to most high technology success, but the world's expectations need to be considered.

Pricing of the high technology deal is often considered more of a science than an art. Its parameters are expressed in the mathematics of the 30 percent to 50 percent expected rate of return. However, of course, each deal does not return the expected 30 percent to 50 percent. A few fail utterly, on several a little is lost or what is invested is returned, a couple make the expected return and if luck holds maybe one is a major home run. This distribution bares a closer resemblance to a certain randomness than to science. The artistry of the venture capitalist is often in limiting losses. A good poker player knows that if losses are kept to a minimum on those hands which are discarded, it is often only necessary to win a few substantial hands to win the game. One thoughtful investor believes that "price is of no real importance" in the investment process. For the wildly successful deals or the abject failures this is often true. If an investor pays $.50 for a stock and later sells out for $20.00 the winnings are not that different had he paid a penny a share. If an investor loses all his money, does it matter whether he paid a dollar or a dime? Pricing is perhaps only important for investment's singles and doubles, not for its triples, home runs, or putouts.

Most early–stage venture capital pricing today is really set by the market, which is a function of the location of the deal, what investors are involved (particularly as lead or co-lead investor), the trendiness of the technology, the economic potential of the deal (big pot or average), and the perception of risk (crapshoot or no brainer). In areas such as Silicon Valley and Route 128, where there are substantial resources and easy access to resources, prices tend to drift higher. Popular technologies now appear to succeed each other as often as the latest hit videos command premiums. Technology deals have commanded premiums because they can be sold publicly or privately for premiums. When and if the time arrives that the venture capital product, its securities, cannot be sold for a premium if issued by technology–based companies, then technology pricing will decline. As windows of opportunity narrow, due to the compression of technical development created by an increase in the number of experienced venture capitalists with more money to spend, and therefore more similar deals, the value of an advanced technology per se, as compared to low tech or no tech investments, will decline.

Technology investments are very enticing and, therefore, difficult to exit. There is an ever present promise that just a little bit more time and money will complete the product development or persuade a reluctant market of the product's compelling economics. Most venture capitalists will continue to be "patient money" if the cost performance benefits are still available and if confidence in management remains. Confidence generally remains if management is continuing to focus on the task at hand and has been frugal with investment capital. Increasingly emerging technologies, particularly in telecommunications (due to the Bell System breakup), have found post–venture capital backing with established companies bringing the deep pockets required for final product completion and market roll–out.

Technical ventures often flounder because the technologist tries to do it all or thinks he can. Few inventive and scientific minds have the skills required to lead a fast–growing company, but a number have the inclination to try. In part, this is a manifestation of the healthy ego drive which is required in technical and scientific development to endure the repeated failure which may preceed a major breakthrough. Once the creation is produced, the drive to create a technology or product may become the drive to build a company—to take the technology to market. This drive may be productive if the technologist realizes that complementary skills in finance, production, marketing, and administration must be added to his technical abilities if a successful company is to be created. Where an inability to work with or communicate with other members of a management team exists, the venture investment can flounder.

Occasionally, an innovative entrepreneur assembles, or has assembled around him by others, the appearance of an effective management team. On paper, all the required bases are covered—aggressive marketer, meticulous yet innovative financial officer, a hands-on manufacturer who knows how to deliver a quality product—all of whom relate to and share the vision of the founder. Such quality teams can represent the illusion of opportunity if the technologist is not a business realist who is willing to listen and learn from other members of management. Many venture capitalists believe deals are more successful where a lion is leading a herd of buffalos rather than a buffalo leading a pride of lions. Lions are brave, tenacious, loyal, aggressive, and fast on their feet. They are also very rare. Many deals fail today because money is available and buffalos plentiful. Look for the lions but look for lions who will accept input and advice from all the best sources.

Occasionally, investors back a technologist who made a major creative step early in his career and has since been searching for the Holy Grail. With a few notable exceptions, major technical and scientific breakthroughs have been the province of the young and are once-in-a-lifetime intuitions—generally occurring in the second or third decade of life when wonder is fresh and the mind open to a new ordering of experience. The young create the illuminating metaphors which call forth a more satisfying conception of reality. Like exceptional athletes, unusual technical innovators tend to burn out early. Investors often fare better putting their money on the young when new industries are being created.

An ego driven technologist may be highly secretive regarding his invention. He is concerned that it may be stolen, but in addition sees the invention as a reflection of himself and is truly concerned that it and he may be rejected by the investment community and the marketplace. These market–reluctant technologists require that considerable trust be generated prior to full disclosure of their invention, and a continuing effort is required to maintain that trust. Once the technologist feels in his gut that investors believe in his vision and share it, communication can be achieved and real progress made.

High technology investment is not for those who are looking for something easy. It requires a real sensitivity both to the unique potential of a particular technology and the technical process, as well as to the unique character of many technical entrepreneurs. Finally, it must be recognized that often the best laid plans go wrong. That the development and nurturing of a new technical business is a fragile endeavor. That luck often plays a more important role than pluck. That most, if not all, companies are at some time in the valley of death. That many of these will emerge if supported by patient risk capital. That this is a risky business not for the fainthearted either as venture capitalist or entrepreneur. That it's important to come back from setbacks, even those which most say are fatal. One man made it big on his thirteenth try.

16

HOW TO TURNAROUND
A FAILING BUSINESS

For over twelve years the author has been involved in the turnaround of troubled companies. Like many things in life he happened on his first challenging situation when he returned to St. Louis after Harvard Business School. One thing led to another and he eventually learned a good deal about this always challenging, arcane art. As a practicing venture capitalist, he prefers not to be involved in troubled situations, but the venture capital business, by its nature, eventually involves calling on the skills of business revitalization. Most venture capitalists have in their little black book several business revitalization wizards upon whom they may call on in a pinch. These efforts, while not always successful and rarely satisfactory to everyone involved, are an important part of the venture capital process. A reading of the following article, will provide information on a situation that both the entrepreneur and venture capitalist labor to avoid.*

Businesses often fail which have the capacity to survive. Experience indicates that a carefully crafted turnaround approach can save a failing company. Studies on the rise and decline of business organizations show that many successful companies at some time in their history experience periods of decline. Those companies that survive and prosper find a way to overcome adversity and turn challenge to advantage. If the measured response to the challenge is carefully constructed and directed, the company will emerge stronger and more profitable for the experience.

Some Turnaround Success Stories

Consider this story, for instance, A major company on the New York Stock Exchange closed its two largest divisions, reducing its net worth to several million dollars. The interests of twenty insurance company and bank lenders, representing major money center institutions as well as participating regional and local banks, were at risk. Without the continuing support of all lenders, the timely completion of work in process, and the collection of substantial receivables from New York City, the company would fail.

This company was once listed among the Fortune Second 500. It was highly profitable. Capacity, employment, assets, and owner's equity were expanding. Loss of financial and operating momentum was at first hardly noticed. There were several cost overruns, late deliveries put profit margins under increasing pressure, and lenders questioned projections more closely. Cost overruns on major contracts continued, one of the company's customers required major retrofit work caused by inadequate engineering, and other customers' concern increased. Almost without notice, the company began to fail.

Had this company employed the strategies and techniques of "business as usual" in this unusual but increasingly common situation, the company would no longer exist. By employing specialized turnaround strategies and techniques, company management turned a distressed situation to competitive advantage.

Here is another such story. A worldwide producer of equipment for the brewery, soft drink, and glass industries experienced an unprecedented backlog of orders for its proprietary electronic bottle inspection equipment. The electronic manufacturing facility could not meet the surging demand. Delivery on major machines as well as parts was adversely affecting the company and product reputation. Ownership recognized the problem, and a complete manufacturing turnaround was planned, initiated, and completed. Within a year, the backlog was substantially reduced, an experienced manufacturing management team in place, financial and cost controls established, and the facility and manufacturing processes improved.

After the turnaround, this subsidiary company contributed significant operating income to its parent and helped finance a needed expansion of the parent company's product line. The company's management had faced the unpleasant facts of insufficient capacity and inadequate manufacturing organization. Because management faced reality, the company's reputation as an efficient producer was enhanced.

First Step in a Turnaround

Facing and recognizing reality is the critical first step leading to a business turnaround or revitalization. An objective view of the true situation provides lenders, employees, and stockholders with the necessary confidence that critical issues are being addressed. Should these key support groups feel that the facts are incorrectly perceived or not perceived at all, the revitalization will never begin. Objectivity in the best of times is difficult, but in a time of stress it is impossible without outside advice. This advice can be provided by lenders, lawyers, accountants, and turnaround business consultants.

Deciding if a Turnaround is Worthwhile

With the aid of outside counsel, owners and management should ask whether the company is experiencing a major decline in economic performance or simply a temporary slowdown. Comparison of key financial and performance ratios with past downturns should reveal the true situation. If a major decline is indicated by the analysis, management should next consider whether in this specific case the revitalization effort is worthwhile and whether it will succeed. A business turnaround requires the exceptional effort and personal commitment of owners and management similar to that required in a start-up venture. A true turnaround is, in effect, a starting over. If the return on investment in time, money, and emotion will never be recovered, then the turnaround may be simply an exercise to save a wounded ego rather than to achieve a worthwhile economic result.

Distinguishing Between Need for Ego Gratification and Sound Economics

The distinction between initiating a turnaround for ego gratification and initiating one for economic gain is often subtle, but it needs to be addressed. It is particularly important to address this issue in those companies which are controlled by a sole stockholder who is also the company founder. Establishing a carefully crafted turnaround plan with appropriate expected return on investment will assist in separating questions of ego reinforcement from those of sound economics. If the turnaround motivation is strongly related to ego, it is often impossible to make sound operating decisions while the turnaround is in progress. The company founder will continue to intervene in operating decisions to obtain the required ego message. Making a specific agreement with an owner in advance as to the turnaround management's scope of authority can be helpful in these situations.

Companies will on occasion require a turnaround because the talent, experience, and personality of the founder or key managers are no longer adequate to meet the new requirements of changing competitive and economic circumstances. The talent required to start up a business may not be the same talent required to manage for profits and growth over the long term. The entrepreneur may be bored with details of day to day operations. The founder may excel in the particular discipline required to establish the business, but the name of the game may change. A number of computer companies were begun successfully by engineers, only to falter when marketing expertise was the way to win. Unless the founder of a company recognizes his or her limitations, the company may fail.

Preparing the Turnaround Plan

Once it is determined that the turnaround effort is worthwhile, that there are sound economic reasons for proceeding, and the role of the founder is resolved, a turnaround plan should be prepared. Unlike normal operating plans, the turnaround strategy selected will have one chance to succeed. The choice of an approach must be correct the first time; however, many minor modifications are made as circumstances change during implementation.

Short-Term Survival Plan

An initial short-term plan should be developed which is aimed at business survival. Long-term strategic success will follow only if the company is a short-term survivor. Management should consider the probability of bankruptcy, when this might occur, and what resources may be available in the near term to avoid this unfavorable result.

If projected cash flows indicate that only an immediate infusion of additional equity will save the situation, consider whether the opportunities available to the business, if viewed as opportunities rather than as problems, are likely to attract the required capital.

After a search of several years, a small business computer manufacturer was recently able to attract capital when the management of the company, assisted by a turnaround consultant, developed a business plan which focused investor attention on the company's prospects rather than on past results.

Turnaround capital can often be found through the sale of underutilized assets, collection of overdue receivables, extending credit terms, refinancing, and reductions in the work force or employee compensation as well as through turnaround equity. It is mandatory that sufficient staying power is available to complete the revitalization. If company debt–to–equity ratios are out of line with industry norms, liquidation or asset reduction may be the only viable approach unless the product is sound and positioned in a growth industry. If the latter is the case, capital can often be obtained if a sound operating plan is established which will permit the restructured company to participate in industry growth.

Long-Term Competitive Strategy

Once the short survival plan is in place, management should develop a long-term competitive strategy consistent with the short-term plan. Difficult trade-offs will be required. Should employees be released whose experience is the key to long-term success? If assets are liquidated to survive and ease cash flow pressures, will these assets need to be replaced later at higher cost? Supplier relationships may be strained that will be critical when the company returns to normalcy. As a rule, give up as little of the future as necessary to stay in business, and keep those resources which are critical to preserve the future. By devising a probable competitive approach for the return to health, critical difficult resource choices can be more easily made.

Consider whether the company is in an industry which substantially outperforms most other industries. If it isn't, the company must outperform most other firms in the industry to achieve a return on investment which will ensure its long-term survival. For the best chance to outperform other industry firms, the company will need to concentrate its limited resources on the successful development and careful implementation of one strategy.

Companies that through planning become the overall industry cost leaders are often the most successful competitors. In effect, through their low cost base, they have the staying power to weather the severest competitive challenge.

Another highly successful competitive approach is to offer a unique product or service or one which is perceived as being unique by the consumer. Generally, a company requires a turnaround in part because the product or service being offered is a "me-too" item which is not significantly different from what the competition is offering. Differentiation can be achieved by improvements in product quality, by reductions in price, by offering a unique feature with wide appeal, or through an unusual marketing approach coupled with effective promotion. The real successes have often been achieved by doing the same thing just a bit differently than the competition. Uniqueness provides competitive protection and allows superior profit margins. Uniqueness in a turnaround requires imagination of a high order, but if achieved, it offers the most dramatic results.

"Find a need and fill it," the often quoted marketing prescription, is a turnaround nostrum as well. Turnaround companies often have failed to define their markets or have defined them too broadly for their limited resources to have competitive effect. A company with limited resources cannot be all things to all customers. Specialization can be the most effective competitive weapon against a full line competitor. Selecting a market niche defined by customer type, product line, territory, or promotion reach may provide a leadership position and will result in concentration of scarce resources.

Revitalization presents unique opportunities to redefine a competitive strategy. A company may cut costs and achieve a low cost position, or it may begin to offer a unique product or service. It could also redefine its markets so that scarce resources are most effectively employed.

Detailed Operating Plan

After the development of a competitive strategy, a detailed turnaround operating plan should be prepared. Generally the focus of the operating plan will be to increase revenue, reduce cost, restructure liabilities, or sell off assets.

Establishing a turnaround operating plan requires a detailed review of functional operations. A manufacturing company offers significant turnaround opportunities on the plant floor. Ask whether improved procedures or training will significantly reduce labor content or material usage. Are there significant bottlenecks in the production flow which are reducing output and increasing cost? Is supervision of the work force appropriate to the manufacturing task? Does manufacturing management ask for and encourage innovation, or is management resistant to change? Do employees believe they can make a difference in their work, and are they heard by management? The answers to these questions, once action has been taken on them, has saved several companies.

Management should rethink the effectiveness of every asset employed in the business. One highly effective technique, the management audit, involves retaining an outside consultant to evaluate the effectiveness of all resources employed in the business. Priorities are established for the more effective use of assets.

A business may require a revitalization because management sold the wrong product to the wrong customer for the wrong price. It is no longer sufficient to simply sell a product. Those companies which have prospered have developed effective marketing strategies. They have addressed and answered the question of what the consumer needs or wants, and what consumer needs or desires the company can best fill employing its limited resources. Unless a company has an internal method of continuing to evaluate the changing requirements of the market, eventually it will offer a product or service with no demand. Companies which have traditionally emphasized engineering or manufacturing are particularly subject to this form of blindness.

For instance, consider the situation in which an electronics company was controlled by a parent with a track record of success in the design and manufacture of major mechanical equipment. Customers would purchase mechanical products as a matter of course. The parent believed that the same automatic purchasing behavior would evolve for the electronics company's products. It therefore made a major investment in the development of a new electronic machine with a much higher selling price than that of the current successful and adequate machine. The new product offered engineering advantages over the old but little in the way of improved performance. The result was that customers were not as willing to accept as face value innovations in electronic products as they were to accept changes in mechanical products. The machine was designed without a market. This illustrates a common situation: companies which are very good at a functional process often require a turnaround because their very competence blinds them to the lack of a market. Revitalization efforts must first focus on what markets exist and how they can be sold with limited resources.

Revitalization often requires management changes. Existing management may be neither incompetent nor dishonest but simply so involved with the problem that it cannot see the forest for the trees. Management may have created the problem and may be reluctant to give the problem up. The situation may be unsuccessful as it is but more comfortable than the uncertainty of change.

Selection of Management Team

Once the short-term and long-term turnaround plans are developed, a turnaround management team should be selected. Because of the similarity of a turnaround to a start-up, it is often useful to have a predominance of key managers with entrepreneurial skills combined with the determination to implement the plan. Individuals with a strong sense of priorities, who will finish one task before moving to another, are crucial. While organizational norms may be respected, they cannot be allowed to interfere with plan implementation.

The turnaround team will be most successful if milestone guidelines are established and regular meetings are held to track progress, overcome resistance to change, and identify new operational opportunities as they are made apparent. Often it is most effective if company leadership during the initial stages can be placed in the hands of a turnaround specialist. After the revitalization is completed, the specialist will move to other efforts. The feelings created by dislocation and change will go with him rather than staying with the remaining management.

Conclusion

A carefully crafted and effectively implemented turnaround will save a failing business in many cases. A turnaround is a difficult effort. Decisions are made under the press of events and under stress. Success will be maximized if the prospects for success are carefully reviewed prior to the starting over. Stress can be minimized if decisions are made in accord with a revitalization plan. Hard work, true, but if it succeeds, the effort is well worth it to all concerned.

17

THE VENTURE VULTURE

WANTED: DEAD OR ALIVE

Nurturer of the Young Company or Predatory Financial Mercenary

Description:	Flushed with green; occasionally beady–eyed visionary seeking and feasting on outrageous returns of capital.
Mates:	After diligent investigation and extensive documentation.
Habitat:	Wherever entrepreneurs roam: principally North American Continent.
Range:	From Silicon Valley in the west to Route 128 in the east; north to Minnesota; south to the Everglades.
Comments:	This creative, irascible member of the order Falconiformes present throughout history. Emerging from recent obscurity to preeminence. Nests near other members of the order close to major universities, deal–doers, wild-eyed inventors, and plumed entrepreneurs. Lack of bountiful feeding ground results in scarcity in some areas.

Educate Disc flies toward the tall building at the speed of a $500,000 per month cash burn. The entrepreneur, an experienced product developer, has a shaky grip on the controls as the company spirals toward financial disaster. Suppliers and bankers start to circle, anticipating the probable impact. Just before the company crashes and burns, the venture vulture swoops in, removes the entrepreneur and founder, feeds cash to the starved company, names its own man President and CEO. The venture vulture wins again, and the naive entrepreneur is out with only his options "fully diluted." An occasional outcome of a venture capital investment.

Advanced Jogging Devices develops personal fitness monitoring and fitness enhancement software for use with the home computer for the weekend athlete. After raising and spending $2 million from several savvy venture vultures, the company discovers that weekend joggers are too busy running to bother to purchase its product. The company files for Chapter eleven and the venture capitalist writes off his entire investment. The entrepreneur moves several doors down the street, and sets up a new shop, Advanced Cardiac Monitoring and Diet Centers, using the same core software developed for the jogging deal. While the venture vulture is trying to figure out whether the entrepreneur expropriated his software, the Cardiac Centers flourish coast to coast; the company goes public; the entrepreneur cashes out a large portion. The venture vulture creeps to his silicon nest with one more lesson on how he can lose his principal. A possible outcome of a venture capital investment.

Outer Dimensions Restaurant Extravaganzas approaches an experienced venture capital investor with a carefully crafted business plan proposing the development of a prototype restaurant of the future which would provide good food and drink, as well as a different life experience at each sitting. While eating Veal Oscar, the patron, depending on the program for the evening, could be rocketed through the universe to a strange new world, return to those thrilling days of yesteryear with Billy the Kid, or enter the hidden world of the supernatural and bizarre. A full tummy and sufficient action created by advanced projection and sufficient stereo surround sound with computer and laser imaging enhancements are enough to provide any diner with fast digestion.

A few venture vultures, who made big money in another restaurant deal, take a crapshoot based on the concept and the experienced management team, who have just come off a rescue mission, successfully reviving a major hamburger chain headed for hamburger heaven. After considerable difficulty with the prototype, the dinners, the help, and assorted other hassles endemic to a start–up including several additional rounds of major investment by the venture capitalists, the company after three years turns a profit and by year eight is ready for a public offering. The entrepreneurs and venture capitalists make a modest return on their labor, risk and investment. The base hit venture outcome—a more often than not conclusion.

A brilliant medical technologist, after years of mixing various formulas in the back of his brother's drug store, finds a recipe for artificial blood. The product carries oxygen, requires no blood typing, can be stored at room temperature, is not toxic, is composed of all natural ingredients, and carries no viral or other infection on transfusion. The product has been tested on several small animals and appears to work, but is years and many millions from FDA approval. Several concept venture investors write the business plan, recruit an experienced business management team to complement the technologist's skills, and a new company is launched with the potential, if successful, to save thousand of lives; the payoff years away, but potentially enormous. A possible home run for the venture vulture, and another potential outcome.

Over the past several years venture capitalists and the venture capital industry have received considerable notice and publicity. Some articles lionize the venture capitalists as financial ministers to an unproductive economy; others raise the spectre of the venture vulture feasting on outrageous returns of capital created by the sweat and courage of the entrepreneur. Based on my own experience as senior investment manager in the Venture Capital Division of the Allstate Insurance Company, one of the oldest and largest participants in the venture capital industry, I believe both of these extreme characterizations to be incorrect. The venture capitalist's role is neither as vulture or financial angel. Rather, at his best, he is a consummate business generalist employing skills unique in the management of high risk business development—skills forged in the discipline of trial and error, win and lose. His is an interesting world of the survival of the adroit, lucky, and prepared.

The venture capitalist is also a catalyst facilitating an ever accelerating process of change in the products, form, and birth and death of business organizations. His work as the manager of business development is speeding up the rate at which products, markets, and technology are created and destroyed. This is at its heart a revolutionary activity in that old technologies, companies, and products are destroyed or brushed aside by the force of the new. Paraphrasing Niels Bohr, the venture capitalist is at once an actor and a spectator in the drama of company creation. This is a dynamic activity along the lines described by Joseph A. Schumpeter when he described capitalism as a process of creative destruction. The venture capitalist is a principal actor in Schumpeter's evolutionary process of competition. As Schumpeter argues, "Competition is by nature a form or method of economic change and never can be stationary. . . . The fundamental impulse that sets and keeps the capitalistic engine in motion comes from the new consumer's goods, the new methods of production or transportation, the new markets, the new forms of industrial organization. . . . It strikes at the very foundation of all existing firms and organizations and tends to destroy while it creates the new; a never ending stream of creative destruction." Accepting this view leads to the conclusion that the substantial influx of venture capital into the economy over the past several years, coupled with a resulting near tripling of the number of active venture capitalists, has the potential to work a profound transformation in the pace of competition, and ultimately in the structure of both our business organizations and economy as the successful companies of our industrial past are displaced by those with the ability to bob and weave, enhance the creativity of the increasingly dominant information and knowledge workers, and respond on a dime to the ever more rapidly changing needs and desires of the customer.

Money can be made in the venture capital business two ways: either the venture capitalist must be an amazingly astute judge of people and business opportunities, or he must earn it the hard way by working daily to develop successful businesses. Often in the venture business the companies which are the easy winners are apparent from the first board meeting after the close of the financing: everything is just right; the management team is reasonably united, knows how to run a business, and the marketplace is waiting for the company's products with great expectation.

These rare easy winners, if more numerous, would make venture capital a relaxed way to earn a living. Nothing worthwhile is ever easy; if it was, everyone would be doing it. This old saw applies to the way venture capitalists really make their money, by working with, or replacing company managements who have run up on the rocks of business distress. As the prime manager of high–risk business development, the venture capitalist's role is principally that of a manager of adversity, while the entrepreneurial management team generally functions as the management for business opportunity.

Adversity arises for a number of reasons including ineffective management; product introduced without a market; product development not completed on time and budget; sales and revenue outrunning financial controls; and either selection of an inappropriate channel of distribution, or failure to effectively sell into the channel selected. More often than not the entrepreneurial team in hot pursuit of their opportunity will run up against one or more of these dashers of dreams of independence and glory. The venture capitalist, who until now has functioned more as the resident skeptic and general provider of "know who," now becomes the manager of adversity.

A company while on its maiden entrepreneurial voyage wound up on the rocks of overexpansion and product glut. The venture capital investors attended a hastily called board meeting. The deal and the company were coming unglued. Earnings appeared to be a disaster in the face of rapidly shrinking revenues, due to a slowdown in sales created by too much product coming to market during the normal summer slowdown. The banks (which were loaned to the limit), and the numerous suppliers were expected to gather momentarily to attempt to recover what collateral they could. The management team, who until a few weeks before appeared to be multimillionaires due to their paper stock holdings, were astounded at the swift turn of events. All holes were fast flooding. The venture capitalists realized that unless they acted this investment would be a significant write-off. The investment syndicate immediately contacted their most effective and crisis–tested rescue specialist. Fortunately he was available, having recently wound down another mission. Driving down at rapid speed from his home just outside San Francisco, he arrived at Rickey's Hyatt House to await a potential summons from the board meeting. The call from the venture capitalist was terse and brief: "We have a company in dire straits, not sure that we can effectively insert you into the operation; the entrepreneur has a control position, but he will be under extreme pressure from banks and suppliers. Please be ready and on call nearby tomorrow."

The venture capitalist who had flown in from Boston the night before attended a pre-Board meeting dinner. He found the President of the company before dinner. The President explained that even though the company was in a difficult position somehow the company would survive. As the President talked, the venture capitalist began to form a picture of a hard-pressed management team. This team would not be able to rally the support necessary to restrain nervous banks and creditors, and convince them of the company's continuing viability. The venture capitalist mentioned that he had asked a consultant who specialized in troubled business situations to come down to the company for discussions as to how he might be able to assist the company in their time of trouble. Company management embraced this suggestion with honest relish.

Most venture capitalists don't want to be directly involved in the day to day management of business adversity. They have extremely demanding schedules created by the responsibilities inherent in monitoring from five to ten separate investments. They must be close enough to their investment to know when a company is moving toward the rocks, and then must intervene when their psychological and financial leverage is the greatest. When necessary this intervention will take the form of parachuting in their own rescue or turnaround specialist. Generally this rather extreme step is taken only when either management appears unequal to the task ahead, and cannot see the forest for the trees they have planted, or when management has lost the critical confidence of the other key players, the banks and suppliers. When possible the venture capitalist will stop short of the rescue technique and work with existing management to rebuild both their confidence and confidence of key outsiders. A venture capitalist's willingness to work with management rather than against them, depends largely on his continuing belief in their honesty both with him and with themselves, and on his continuing confidence in their business judgement and willingness to give their all to bring the company back from adversity to opportunity. Ultimately the venture investor's loyalty is to the success of the investment, not to a particular management team, but the best of the breed will provide for those who have been straightforward and were defeated by an unfortunate turn of events.

The venture capitalist is an agent for positive change in adverse business circumstances. He brings with him to the troubled company a library of reality, gained in numerous other business battles, and is prepared to act decisively should circumstances warrant. Venture capitalists are well compensated because their library of business reality is only gained through going through the valley of death innumerable times. Reality and objectivity are the venture capitalist's stock in trade, and the principal value which he brings to a developing business. His work is as a facilitator of value—intervening only when required. The venture capitalist who ignores reality, whether of the marketplace, or the particular circumstances of the investee company, is doomed to extinction.

Most successful venture capital deals today are team efforts. Rarely is the lone wolf entrepreneur the predominant role model or leadership vehicle. The venture capitalist would prefer to invest in a lion leading a herd of buffalos rather than in a pride of lions led by a buffalo, but he truly favors a strong lion leading other lions. Lions who can effectively lead other lions are rare creations in the business jungle. Lions have real trouble working together; they tend to devour each other unless order is maintained by the strongest. But the strong often prefer to travel surrounded by admirers and errand runners rather than by potential rivals for pride leadership. Once in a while a lion comes along who reasons that if he leads other strong lions, his team will rule the jungle. The venture capitalist wins by backing lions led by a big, strong lion.

A business development management team must consist of players with a variety of skills and abilities. The big lion will play quarterback, and he is the business generalist, whether entrepreneurial visionary or aggressive business manager. Other team members include the Vice President of Sales and Marketing, the Financial Vice President, the Vice President of Manufacturing, and the Vice President of Engineering. Weakness in any one of these critical positions can kill a company very quickly in the venture capital world where windows of opportunity are very narrow. The management chain is only as strong as the weakest manager. Many venture management teams are only partially formed when the venture capitalist invests. If the venture capitalist is a seed capital investor he may be backing the wild–eyed inventor wandering around accompanied only by his ideas; if the investment is made at an early stage, a technical en-

trepreneur may be joined by a sales or marketing executive who has decided to take a shot at the entrepreneurial challenge after years with a
large company. A partially formed team can mean more or less risk for
the venture capitalist. Since he is investing in people who can make business ideas work at a profit, normally the more complete the team, the less
risk. However, the contrary may be true if one team member or several
fail to perform in an entrepreneurial environment. In these cases the venture capitalist often wishes that he had worked more with company management to form the team. Seed capital investors often prefer this early–
on investment precisely because they participate in team formation. Venture capitalists become very intuitive about which people will work out.

Cannonball Communications, Inc. was founded in early 1979 by a
big, strong lion. He started out in his early years, working around Washington D.C. in a variety of regulatory staff legal jobs, and eventually came
to lead several regulatory agencies. When it became apparent that the Federal Communications Commission was moving to deregulate much of the
world of telecommunications he smelled that another gold rush in communications would soon be on, and was determined to have his share.

Contacts with a number of high level lawyers and other corporate
executives provided initial seed capital as well as the rudiments of a Board
of Directors. Applications were filed for a wide band of available spectrum. Licenses were eventually received which permitted the company to
set up and operate a modest operation which soon produced positive cash
flow, though of minimal amount. To operate the initial venture, a corporate controller was selected, as well as a highly knowledgeable and experienced expert on the operation and use of broadcast and microwave
spectrum. Eventually the controller could be and was supplemented with
a polished Vice President of Finance. As the company continued to develop, with the award by the FCC of additional parking rights on the spectrum, the company was subdivided into separate subsidiaries each headed
by a very capable operating President, backed by his hand–picked team.
The Board of Directors was enhanced with the addition of several venture
capital investors highly knowledgeable in telecommunications strategy,
and eventually with several outside industry operating executives of national repute.

For a considerable period, the entrepreneur resisted the inclusion of
outside experts on the Board, perhaps fearing being second–guessed by
these potential Monday morning quarterbacks, or simply out of loyalty to
his former directors who would need to retire from the Board. The team
worked because there was considerable opportunity, in the many businesses the company was involved in, for the able and exceptional to strut
their stuff, and because all major players received equity participation in
the venture. The entrepreneur had the personal strength and vision to
recruit lions to his team whose skills complemented his own. Over a pe-

riod of time this effort was not without considerable stress and strain as various aggressive members of the team attempted to obtain more autonomy and authority, but the big lion was able to contain and rebuff these assaults on his authority with minimal damage to the egos of lesser lions or to his company as a whole. His people skills were equal to the task not only of assembly of a first rate team, but of orchestrating their individual contributions for full fidelity.

The relationships between this entrepreneurial team were based more on mutual respect and need for each other, than on close personal ties or having worked together in a prior venture. The sharing of mutual crises is effective in the establishment and effective performance of venture management teams, and some venture capitalists prefer to invest only in teams who have worked together in the past.

There is a unique and at times peculiar chemistry which unites business development management teams. Struggle over insurmountable odds brings out the best or the worst whether in combat or in business start-ups. Those teams which fail to develop the requisite chemistry usually fail to do so because the entrepreneur is a visionary, but not a leader. He is either indifferent to moulding people together into a common effort or he pits his subordinates against each other in order to maintain iron control over the venture. His continual stirring of the pot and rattling of cages keeps the troops continually off balance and the company from meeting its business plan. Suspicion and doubt replace trust and confidence, and the "can do" attitude required for success in the face of adversity. These weak teams simply fold and slink away unless rebuilt by the venture capitalist operating in the rescue mode. The managers spend all their time and energy trying to watch and manage each other, rather than manage business growth.

Educate Disc, mentioned as going into a $500,000 per month cash burn before crashing, practiced this highly combustible form of ineffective personal chemistry before dying. The entrepreneur, assisted by a start-up venture capitalist assembled a management team which in (on paper) all respects qualified as an experienced, effective team. However, the entrepreneur never joined the team. He continued to do his own thing, and often failed to include other team members in his schemes and dreams. This failure also led to a lack of feedback on his plans from other team members, whose views and opinions came to be as well-informed about industry direction as that of the entrepreneur. The niche selected by this entrepreneur was moving faster than even the most united team could effectively manage, so the company never had a chance. The venture capitalist tried a rescue mission, but without a major infusion of cash, which he was unwilling to make based on progress in team formation and unity, the company failed. As much as anything the lack of everyone getting together, and pulling together doomed this venture. In a start-up business people are the whole company; assets are insufficient to provide a fall—back position except for the briefest of periods if the people fail to work out and work together.

Once the entrepreneurial management team is in place and pulling together, the relationship between the team and the venture capital backers becomes crucial for business success. For a considerable period, these relationships tend to be one of considerable testing. The entrepreneur probes to determine what control the venture capitalist is inclined to exercise over his business strategy and day to day operations: does he attempt to tell the entrepreneur how to run the business or is he content to make policy and people suggestions, playing the role of skeptic; is he going to be highly assertive and aggressive, or more laid back in his positions and postures? If the entrepreneur takes a step with which the venture capitalist disagrees will this be used later to unseat the entrepreneur if he is unsuccessful up to that point? What kind of relationship does the venture capitalist want: friend, mentor, director, critic? For his part the venture capitalist wants to determine if this entrepreneur is honest with himself and with the venture capitalist. Does he believe his own promotion? Is the agenda he presents his real agenda? How up front is he and straightforward? Will he bounce back from failure, and from the probable necessity to reduce his expectations? Can he both lead and manage or will the company need a manager? Will he lie about future events to induce the venture capitalist to put more money into the deal at a later date or can he be counted on only for the usual entrepreneurial extravagation? If the venture capitalist is fair and gives rather than takes the odd shilling will the entrepreneur reach for all the chips or pass a fair share to the venture capitalist? The answers to these questions determine the tenor of the relationship.

The most effective entrepreneurs tend to treat the venture capitalist like their most important customer, which he is, in the early stage of a deal. The entrepreneur attempts to know his important customer: his tastes, habits, needs, requirements, prejudices, and goals. If possible he attempts to know him in a variety of settings and circumstances. If assistance can be provided to the venture capitalist which does not compromise the venture capitalist's integrity, the entrepreneur provides the favor. Most of all he listens and respects the advice of the venture capitalist, if not always implementing it. He looks to the venture capitalist as a valuable partner and resource which money cannot buy, but a patient ear can acquire. Like any customer the entrepreneur treats the venture capitalist with personal and business consideration and respect.

Many entrepreneurs mistakenly view the venture capitalist as their adversary rather than as a valued customer and supporter. Relationships which begin on an adversarial footing seem to always end that way, to the detriment of the entrepreneur. The entrepreneur who forgets that "he who has the gold makes the rules" more often than not loses both the support of the venture capitalist and, on occasion, control of the company. There is an art to conducting spirited negotiations with a valued customer and still maintaining the confidence and support of the customer. The venture capitalist does not expect or desire the entrepreneur to roll over and play dead in the name of harmony. He will be trying to cut a tough but reasonable deal in any future financings and expects no less of the entrepreneur. Like any close relationship the venture capitalist expects that this one will have its highs and lows, and will not sever the relationship over a minor point while in a low period.

Proper chemistry between the entrepreneurial team and the venture capitalist is the critical ingredient. They have to both like and respect each other. If either group believes that this relationship will not be a pleasant experience then it should never be entered into. Life is too short and venture capital deals too long not to enjoy the relationship. Some venture capitalists are too interested in the business concept, or the potential huge return, or the fancy technology. "Never invest in a man you cannot and do not like" should be the first rule for investment success in a business development project.

Since venture capitalists have different approaches and temperaments the management team must also do their homework, and not just take their money from any available source. The source of the money will be as important as its availability. Venture capitalist and entrepreneurs should spend more time getting to know each other, and less worrying over the size of the market and the competition. Analysis should give way to close chemistry. This is a marriage and all the best reasons for proceeding will never replace enjoying the experience.

Living happily ever after is best accomplished when venture capitalists and entrepreneurs keep each other fully informed as to their changing expectations and views. A venture capitalist who has a full checkbook, having recently closed a major fund, will have a different perspective on the same deal when his cupboard is bare at the end of an investment cycle. His views will also change if the entrepreneur fails consistently to meet his business plan goals. The entrepreneur, for his part, may begin the business with one product strategy, run into rough sledding and need to change his direction on the proverbial dime. At least once a week the entrepreneur and the lead venture capitalist will normally discuss major business issues to avoid a communications gap. They then continually modify their perceptions of reality jointly. This joint alteration of perceptions is critical in that most venture companies are operating in an ever changing marketplace where market and product reality changes often. Only those who are talking together will stay together.

The venture capitalist's and entrepreneur's expectations of each other need to be highly realistic. Venture capitalists are exceptionally busy, attempting to invest increasingly large accumulations of capital; monitor an expanding number of portfolio companies; develop the experienced venture management talent required for growth; and assist in the rescue of troubled portfolio companies. Some investors are busier than others: they invested more money during the last up cycle than they can now effectively manage. These venture capitalists find they are now trying to put their finger into an increasingly large hole in the dike. They do not really have the time to be providing effective advice and good counsel to their companies. Those entrepreneurs who have a venture investor in these adverse circumstances will be generally disappointed in the management assistance and advice received from these investors. A number of venture capitalists, however, kept their powder dry during the last boom, and are now in the cat bird's seat, having both the time to contribute to their companies, and also the money available for new reasonably priced opportunities—avoiding past excess, they expect to profit.

Entrepreneurs should ask their potential venture backers whether they will be able to provide both their money and their time. If they are on their first venture with minimal management experience, the lack of the venture capitalist's time could prove in the future to be the critical difference between success and failure. Realism on the part of both venture capitalist and entrepreneur as to the level of the venture capitalist's involvement will enhance significantly the probability of success both in the relationship and in the business.

A well structured board of directors contributes significantly to the nurturing of a new enterprise, and both complements and supplements the contributions of the venture capitalist to business development. Most entrepreneurs where the venture capitalist is a minority investor, as is usually the case, want to have a majority of the board "friendly" to management and its interests. They reason that in case of a fight with the venture capitalist at a later date, a friendly board will improve their chances of survival. This is rarely true. He who has the gold eventually gets to make the rules. A "friendly" board structure simply means that it may take the venture capitalist longer to enforce his rules. The entrepreneur also feels more comfortable continuing to receive advice from those who assisted him in getting his venture this far along, and reasons "if it ain't broke, don't fix it." The venture capitalist on his part wants at least several board seats if not an outright majority to insure that his views, concerns, and interests are represented and heard. He will work hard to insure that all board members are effective contributors rather than graybeards and cronies. Other than being a Board member himself, the venture capitalist will often insist that another experienced operating executive fill a seat—best of all is an executive from the industry with wide and deep knowledge. Some entrepreneurs "get the shakes" when the venture capitalist proposes experienced operating talent for the board.

They are frankly afraid of being second–guessed and on occasion contradicted. One company's second round financing came perilously close to collapse when the entrepreneur at the last minute refused board seats to investors who he perceived as being "unfriendly." The investors wondered, not surprisingly, whether they really wanted to be part of a club that didn't want them. Eventually a compromise was struck with the lead investor joining the board and representing all other investors. This was, however, at best a patch up, and investors are still uncomfortable with the arrangement. This early rancour continues to spill over into other aspects of the relationship and is a major business problem for this company. The strains created by an "uncomfortable board" will haunt the entrepreneur.

The board of directors is particularly critical to a new enterprise because the accelerated rate of change in a new company demands seasoned hands at all stations; because the board's "conservatism" tends to balance entrepreneurial enthusiasm; because the board is a source of business talent which is relatively inexpensive compared to the unaffordable cost of a corporate staff to carefully research and brief management on issues; and because the board is a great source of "know who." Venture capitalists estimate that several years ago a new enterprise could take five to seven years to develop. Today, with many players in each market niche, if the company is not established within the first three years, it may never be. Rapid technical change and the resulting business pace leave all but the most fleet of foot behind. The new company must in addition cope with a monumental array of issues created by government regulations, increased public awareness, and the lust of the marketplace for the ever new, exceptionally compelling, and least costly solutions to personal desires and society's ills. Large corporations "staff" many of these issues and problems; the emerging company in pursuit of its opportunities requires the immediate judgment and intuition of the experienced venture director to continue forward momentum. Time is insufficient to run down the details, and construct compelling cases. The emerging company must be down to cases swiftly or be bypassed by the more intuitive, swifter competitor. The experienced venture director brings balanced judgment and intuition to the company's swift deliberations.

Entrepreneurs have been known to run off half-cocked, and the board can provide a firm, restraining hand. While entrepreneurial vision is focused on the far horizon, the rest of the company forgets to catch up, and without a restraining Board maybe forced to play catch–up. If events are out of hand, catch–up may not be possible. An effective mix is for the entrepreneur to focus his attention (but not all his time) on company opportunities, and the board of directors making certain that someone is minding the store. Eventually a number of venture–backed boards insist that a chief operating officer be selected whose attention to detail will complement the entrepreneur's occasionally unfocused energy. A board will in addition provide critical outside supporters, such as lenders and suppliers, with the confidence that management's actions and initiatives are subject to review and discipline.

The best boards know a lot of helpful people. From arranging key future customer contacts to providing sources of information on critical competitive thrusts and opportunities, the effective venture capital board member is a working member of the business development team. Effective board members tell the entrepreneur what he never hopes to hear, and have the ability to really burn the CEO and management team when required. Their willingness to be more than direct, and without mercy, if need be, gives the company a major competitive advantage. A positive board provides criticism of unsurpassed clarity, assisting the business development management team in shaping and nudging its business into competitive condition. The fine venture capital board member is a unique contributor from the venture capitalist's bag of the tricks of growth.

Another escapee from the bag of tricks is the venture capitalist's rescue or turnaround artist who is brought into a troubled situation when the lenders are on the window ledge threatening to jump, the management team wandering around the halls in aimless shock, and the bankruptcy lawyers on call. These one–eyed foxes, expert in the containment of crises, have perfected the art of staying cool and keeping everyone else cool and believing while the ship is righted. Their principal skill is the immediate infusion of leadership of a high order. Stepping into the middle of a fire fight is neither for the timid or faint of heart. Their business is decision, and the restoration of confidence. Today's rescue specialist is not just a chopper of heads or a trimmer of bloated assets. The high technology venture deal, particularly, can be short on hard assets to shrink. The business of these companies is information ordered to a higher degree of complexity. Looking around in the back of the storeroom for excess inventory which cannot be sold because it is obsolete will not save the company. Today's rescue specialist is dealing with intangibles more than bringing cash flow and outgo into line. When opportunities, even in the best of times, are perishing in nanoseconds, the rescuer must sort for the ones with the longest and surest staying power. The baby must not be thrown out with the bath. This is the arena of the sure–footed billy goat.

Just waking up dazed management requires extreme measures. One rescue operative, on failing to notice any signs of life, told management they were "the most aimless collection of morons ever assembled to promote disorder." This management got mad, and got even. First they fired the crisis manager. But he was reinstated with the help of the suppliers, lenders, and the venture capitalists. The entrepreneur fought the turnaround at every turn. He was losing control; all that he had worked for, planned for, and dreamed about—the business was going. Deep in the forest he could no longer see the tree tops. Directors were called into emergency sessions. Discussions moved to rump board sessions with several directors gathering, dissolving, and recombining in their search for solutions. The storm eventually spent itself; the parties reconciled, and began digging out of the mud.

The days that the entrepreneur and the venture capitalist spend together in the trenches either permit and facilitate the formation of a bond of respect, admiration, and mutuality, or they can lead to the relationship being terminated short of financial success by what is known in the busines as falling out of love: the entrepreneur and the venture capitalist communicate only when essential, often on formal matters; the venture capitalist may withdraw from the board of directors, if possible recovering part or all of his capital at either a loss or breakeven.

Venture capitalists will not give up on either an investment or an entrepreneur without a struggle, so normally the venture capitalist will withdraw only if the entrepreneur proves to be unethical in his business practices, refuses to consult, or as is more often the case decides to run the business for himself, family, and friends rather than for the investors. The early warning signs of entrepreneurial excess begin to show, including: excessive perks, fancy cars, new offices, long vacations, funny financial statements, revolving controllers, and relatives in all the wrong places. Strong members of the management team begin to depart and only those that agree with the boss are left around. These can never be reached after 5:00 p.m.

The signs of a company's being managed only for the entrepreneur's interest do not normally appear only after the first blush of real success, but in retrospect are there all along: the entrepreneur who is more interested in what he can take out of the company, rather than in what he is building with others; who is not particularly interested in earnings which could create a public offering opportunity, but rather in raking off pretax goodies; whose vision becomes clouded by the quick and dirty fix rather than putting the necessary pieces in place to construct a business for the long future; whose interest in the fast ramp up exceeds the plausible or prudent; in the end, whose decisions are motivated by what is good for him rather than what serves the interest of the enterprise. This kind of entrepreneur is not a good candidate for venture capital funding, but is now and then funded because he is available and can appear attractive, to either the inexperienced venture capitalist learning the ropes of the business, or to the fund that has too much money chasing too few good deals which is willing to shoot craps with those who want it all now, and will attempt to use their friends and supporters. "Me first" entrepreneurs create some of the longest days for venture capitalists, as a successful relationship is impossible.

Successful venture capital-entrepreneurial relationships are formed when both parties have a good concept of who they are and what they want from the relationship. Some deals from the beginning just go right. One knowledgeable venture capitalist believes that you have a good idea from the first board meeting whether or not the deal will ultimately prove successful. The management team and the entrepreneur know what they are attempting to accomplish, move in an aggressive direction toward their goals, are willing to remain flexible in the pursuit of their goals, realize and act as if time and money are in short supply, and possesses a highly focused sense of urgency. They feel hot breath on their backs.

Getting off to a good start, or love at first sight, helps the relationship flourish. One entrepreneur with an early–stage company designing and manufacturing telecommunications equipment calls the venture capitalist occasionally even if there is nothing momentous to report. He is just stay- ing in touch and continuing to form a relationship. The venture capitalist is his most significant customer, and while he does not believe that the customer in this case is always right, he should always be informed and sense that the entrepreneur is considering his reactions in managing the business. As in many close relationships, what happens between the lines is often more important than its seeming rational content.

The developing business goes through a process of moving from an initial state of instability through equilibrium to stability. A developing enterprise is initially unstable because it lacks a sufficient financial base to weather adverse conditions; its internal personal relationships lack the cooperation required to move assets forward; there is little or no accept- ance from the outside, necessary to gain community or industry confi- dence in the business attempt; and the lack of profit and positive cash flow—the normal measure of how well the business is doing—is minimal or nonexistent. The elements of the required business mix are in flux and have not yet jelled into a company with staying power. Eventually, given sufficient time, money, talent, and effort these various elements combine to form a stable enterprise. However, if they are left on their own, unat- tended, rather than moving toward greater organization, entropy, or the winding down of the system, enters the mix and leads the organization toward increasing disorganization. Occasionally, however, a random event, unexpected and out of the blue, enters the life of the company and leads to enhanced organization and greater stability. Experienced entre- preneurs and venture capitalists often would prefer blind luck to calcu- lation and their best laid plans. "The moving finger writes, and having written, not all our efforts, or all our tears will cancel half a line." Time and chance enhance all.

Business innovation often arises under conditions which promote non–average behavior. When conditions are the most adverse and the wolf at the plant gate, the organization reaches down inside and meets an ex- traordinary challenge with exceptional effort. Necessity is the mother of invention. Random events and fluctuations can also lead an organization down an unforeseen path toward greater instability. In this case the venture capitalist, acting as a necessary agent, intervenes and, attempting to forestall fate, smooths out company lows and makes the random if not predictable then at least manageable. He assists in the transformation of instability into value, usefulness, and order. In this view the venture capitalist is an agent of necessity, intervening when appropriate in the affairs of a company to nudge, cajole, and shove the company back on a track toward stability when the random and unexpected derail the enterprise. The venture capitalist is neither vulture nor financial angel, but rather a major participant with entrepreneurial management in the formation of a unique business development management team with approaches, techniques, and a style of its own.

If all bets were sure, and the business development process easy, everyone would be doing it. Over the lifetime of a venture capital partnership average rates of return, while higher than most forms of investment, are not vulturous, perhaps twenty percent over the life of a well-managed fund. This represents fair compensation for the often difficult business of dream making.

18

THE FORESEEABLE FUTURE*

Human beings as a species are undergoing the growing pains of early adolescence. Our sun is relatively young among the stars and we will grow with it to maturity. Like adolescents, we are still developing the tools, concepts, environmental understanding, and judgment which will serve us when we come to full realization and exercise of our powers. The tools that are emerging will be much more useful than the rudimentary implements that we now use to scratch from the earth a meager existence for many. Enhancements to present known and working technologies and their future combination and integration into more complex entities provide a window on those things of our childhood which we will carry to our adulthood. Advanced materials, robotics, computers, biotechnology, electronics, medicine, and telecommunications within the next one hundred years will mate in unimagined wonders. Many of these hybrids will arise in our lifetime. Consider the visible difference in the world as current development trends merely continue on established paths without major shift in perspective as to how the world works.

Our computers are processing more complex information for less money at faster speeds. Soon they will be fully programmed to talk with us, to listen to us, and to assist in making knowledgeable if not wise decisions and judgments. They will become extensions of ourselves. It will

*Various articles published in *High Technology Magazine* over the past several years on specific technologies stimulated the author to write this chapter on the convergence of various technologies to shape our future. These thought are presently being expanded by the author into a book on the future of technology.

be a while until they actually think in the way and of the things we do. It does not appear that this will happen until first we know a good deal more about how the human brain works than we do now, and until this information can be encoded in silicon or a successor medium. Recent theories and models of the human brain postulate that the brain performs many operations at the same time rather than one at a time like today's digital computers, and that it processes information in an ambiguous manner rather then in the yes/no, black/white style of the computer. It was thought that the brain might work somewhat like a digital computer with the individual processors or neurons exchanging information through electrical impulses. This mechanistic computer model, however, failed to explain how the brain could process exceptionally complicated information and patterns often arriving from several different sensors such as the eyes and ears at the same time, and sort out reality from fantasy. It stretches the imagination to comprehend how the more than ten billion processors in the brain could be so wired together to effectively transmit and exchange information. It appears that the neurons may work together in "families" and that these "families" may work together and communicate by means of the electromagnetic fields that we know are present in the brain. What we call mind is related to these brain field effects and the relationship between these effects and the individual processors. It may be that certain neuron "families," through association or formation of the electromagnetic field, form "tribes" or associations which create various thoughts, ideas, or impressions, and assimilate complex information and order it into what we know as reality, or fantasy, or dreams. It seems likely that the brain also relies on certain repetitive patterns or codes (programming) which it uses as a form of shorthand to process information and then store it in its memory cells. Using past encoded experience which is recalled from memory (both long and short term, similar to the computer's temporary and permanent storage), the brain, in an associative manner, compares what it knows of the world with what its sensor mechanisms are telling it of current reality.

The future then may hold a computer working in an associative manner, utilizing various field effects, so that all the processors of the computer would be linked through a continuous electromagnetic field, and the processing of information, its storage or recall, sensing, perceptions, ordering of information and output to the body would take place, simultaneously, instantaneously, continuously, and parallel. Such a computer would mimic closely the functions of the human brain and could be considered to possess a "consciousness" unique to its state.

It is interesting that what we know and theorize concerning the operation of the human brain has a number of common elements with the operation of present computers. Both have memory capacity, both process input and receive it, both transmit information from memory to processor and from processor to memory. It appears that our subconscious mind is beginning to construct rudimentary clones perhaps one day capable of duplicating or surpassing in some respects its power and function. The strands of DNA which create and order life as we know it and construct the human brain have created an entity with the potential power of self replication utilizing currently inanimate matter. While this is the stuff of science fiction, based on what is now known, theorized, and extrapolated, it appears likely. Our computers will resemble ourselves.

In his illuminating book, *The Micro Millennium*, Christopher Evans* defines intelligence as "the ability of a system to adjust appropriately to a changing world, and the more capable of adjusting—the more versatile its adjusting power—the more intelligent it is." He then goes on to argue that there are six factors that permit a creature to be versatile or flexible in the manner in which it adjusts to its environment. These factors are: sensation, or the ability to capture data; data storage, or how much information can be stored; processing speed, or how fast the information can be handled; software modification speed, or the speed and ease with which the entity can alter its software or programming and/or produce new programming when conditions require (as well as the ability to make its own modifications); software efficiency, which means that little of the processing power is used in running the program and that it is error-free or nearly so; and finally, the range of tasks which the sofware permits the entity to perform. Using this definition of intelligence, Evans then sets up a scale to rate various creatures against the scale. This scale is useful in demonstrating the large difference which currently exists between computer and human intelligence today. If humans were at one million on the current scale, today's computers would be at about 1000—essentially beating humans in only one category—processing speed. This should give humans cause for comfort, except that Evans notes that it took man several hundred million years to reach his present position, whereas the computer has made some considerable progress after only twenty-five years of comparable evolution. Evans also argues that human evolution required that man have huge software packages to reproduce, eat, maintain bodily systems, etc. A computer will not have these requirements and can concentrate only on the software required for intelligence. This should lop a number of millions of years from the computer's evolutionary time scale. It has already been possible for a computer to pass man in one highly specialized area—playing chess, where computational power is critical. Evans then looks to the fact that in areas of scientific advance, progress tends to accelerate. As computer hardware and software develop, the machine itself will be able to help improve its own hardware and software. This is already happening in the use of the computer to design and prototype new electronic circuits and computer architecture. Such projects

*Washington Square Press, New York, 1979.

as the Japanese Fifth Generation Project are the precursors to the ultra-intelligent machine of the future envisioned by Evans. Given the acceleration of the rate of change, it appears probable that by the late twenty-first century, these ultra-intelligent machines will co-exist with man.

It is also apparent that as our understanding of the ordering of the genetic code, or DNA, and its expression in brain function continues, so too will our ability to create increasingly complex codes to direct, control, and increase the functions and power of our computer system. It is being made manifest that we can apply the rules, codes, and patterns that govern human nature and human life to inanimate matter such as the silicon of a computer chip. Most interesting efforts are underway to create biological computers that use the molecules present in nature to transmit electrical energy and information as well as store it. These biocomputers based on carbon rather than silicon would be composed of the most predominant element essential to human life. Depending on the complexity of their architecture and the sophistication of their programming, these biocomputers could begin to resemble the human brain in their abilities. Molecular computers would permit much smaller computers operating at unimagined speeds. Configured in either digital or analog form depending on the architecture, these biocomputers would be capable of either on/off functions, as are current computers, or, in the analog form using enzymes as the "processor," would be capable of continuous computation more associated with that used by the brain. A fully functioning molecular computer is thus possible with the ability to appreciate ambiguity. Experts anticipate that if this line of inquiry continues unabated a basic prototype of a biochip could be constructed within the next decade, and a true biological computer by the twenty-first century. Understanding the processes of the human brain will thus allow further development of silicon-based computer architecture as well as contributing to the development of the architecture of the biocomputer. The inanimate is becoming animate, and the animate, but disassociated, more complex. Something along these development lines occurred in human evolution. Within the next several years, it is expected that the first biosensors, a combination of electronics and biology, will make their first useful appearance. These sensors will permit physicians to regulate insulin flow to the body where required, track various concentrations of chemicals in the blood, and even turn on or off an implantable drug dispenser. These electronic organic connections are the first real union of the manmade and the artificial, representing the fusion of life and non-life. This process involves molecules of a body chemical adhering to enzyme-coated membranes which form a second chemical which reacts with a third producing an electrical potential which can be detected.

Biological science and computing science are converging. Merely continuing along paths of present awareness and inquiry will one day create life very much as we know and experience it. Since we do not understand what consciousness is, it is uncertain whether the entity created will be conscious, but it appears that we will not be able to note the distinction. Clearly momentous questions will be raised as mankind takes on God-like powers. Questions of when life begins will once again rage, similar to the present unresolved questions over abortion, and the beginning of human life. Will life begin the moment the final chip is plugged in, or when the power is turned on, or only if and when consciousness is achieved?

Adding additional fuel to this raging debate will be the further development of genetic engineering technology. The early 1980's witnessed the introduction of a new machine with the capability to automatically synthesize DNA. These gene machines string together DNA building blocks to build custom DNA sequences. Relying on purely chemical methods and electronic controls the machines buildup a single strand of DNA one nucleotide at a time. With this method, it is currently possible to build fragments of DNA up to sixty nucleotides long. While currently only fragments can be produced which are used as probes to isolate genes for commercially valuable proteins such as interferon, in fact, in several cases, entire genes have been synthesized. As the gene machine technology develops, it will be possible to construct genes thousands of base pairs long. Gene machines are within our vision which will replicate the genetic code for a human being and/or his replacement parts. It might then be possible to home-grow a human being or to use our full understanding of these codes to provide biological or biologically determined programming to silicon-based machines.

Until the era when true new life forms can be homegrown and programmed on demand from carbon materials, parallel developments can be expected in the enhancement of silicon-based entities, and other artificial constructs formed from more hardy and durable materials. Stronger then steel, able to withstand incredible heat, and lasting nearly forever, impervious to corrosion, are the next generation ceramics.These materials, (often defined as solids), that deliver superior mechanical, thermal, or electrical performance (over metals or plastic) in high stress environments, contain conglomerations of microcrystals. Their heat resistant, anti-corrosive properties, and resistance to wear make them ideal candidates for environments where carbon entities dare not tread. They are also candidates for use with high power electronics where heat dissipation is a major concern. The combining of advanced materials with artificial vision systems and advanced computer control in the field of robotics promises a world or worlds populated by artificial humans or robots. Machine vision companies are now applying information about how humans "see" to the construction of artificial vision for robots and other mechanical and electronic equipment. These systems, while currently crude, have the potential as more is understood about human vision to provide inanimate hardware with a faculty which will prove to be a critical element of consciousness—the accurate perception of the physical environment. Human vision as we know it requires immense processing power and memory capacity as well as an ability to take an accurate guess about what is perceived when the image is ambiguous. At the time when field processing is better understood in the human brain, it may be that these field effects will be utilized to provide human vision systems for machines. As the memory capacity and processing power of our computers increase, the power will be available to develop fully functioning machine vision systems. Carbon-based entities, such as human beings, did not come to their full capacity without evolutionary struggle. Machine vision evolution is at a primitive stage, but offers a window on consciousness to the inanimate. It appears that these mechanical robots will emerge at an earlier date than the fully functioning biocomputer, and it can be expected that as materials research produces more durable ceramic or other unknown materials of increasing durability, flexibility, and longevity, these robots will come to resemble higher life forms. As computer technology becomes more dextrous, it would then be plausible to imagine that these beasts will take on more intelligence, perhaps one day emerging as the dominant species or a co-equal species with carbon-based life forms. The day could come when walking on the earth or wherever would be fully carbon-based life, silicon-based life, or a combination of carbon, silicon, ceramic and other worldly materials and alloys. These life forms would be inhabited by minds created naturally and artificially. What we now call artificial would become natural. Human evolution would continue but with direct human intervention. It goes without reflection that several or perhaps all of these life forms could be immortal as we now comprehend the term. The ethical questions will be complex. Would bringing out a new model obsolete the old, or could the old be upgraded? For those that could not be upgraded at all or too easily, would this be legal death or would there be no death at all as we experience it? This is the boundary where religion, mystery, and science will meet and may result in some better or final understanding of why we are here and where we are going.

At the very least, medical science through its understanding of the aging process and the mind and the body will be able to extend the life of the entire system and repair or replace the parts as they become worn through repeated use or misuse. Combining the best of new materials, surgical advances, and biochemistry with the function of living cells has recently resulted in a variety of manmade devices replacing human organs and body constituents. Prominent among these symbiotic artificial devices are the artificial heart, bone regeneration, artificial skin, tendons, joints, and artificial blood vessels. Within the near future artificial blood, artificial muscle tissue, liver, pancreas, and kidneys are possibilities. Most interesting, and a model for future devices, is an artificial skin which simulates skin function in keeping infection out and retaining fluids. Cells from the body migrate into a pattern as outlined by the artificial skin. The artificial skin is not rejected by the body because the stimulated interface between the skin and the body is not recognized by the immune system as being foreign and, therefore, subject to rejection. Artificial blood investigations are under way and have been patented, utilizing all natural ingredients, and when mixed in the correct recipe under controlled conditions will recreate the chemistry and function of human blood, including efficient oxygen transport and dissemination throughout the body. This product, a combination of inventive and scientific insight gathered from many fields, including chemical engineering, anesthesiology, and pharmacology promises to eliminate the necessity of blood typing prior to transfusion, and provide a sterile product free from possible contamination from AIDS or other blood transmitted diseases.

Genetic engineering offers the promise that genes may instruct a mixture of the requisite soup to self-organize and create life. Medicine will be stronger and stranger than fiction.

These momentous developments are based on an appreciation of what man has put in place in his first years of life. They do not depend on a breakthrough in our perspective, or a massive shift in fundamental understanding, such as might occur either due to contact established with life forms of other worlds (which most scientists believe the statistical evidence for is overwhelming), or due to a new scientific tour de force such as the long awaited unified field theory or another bedrock understanding of the properties of matter, space, time, and destiny. Nor does it take into account the possible impact of an emerging world cosmic consciousness where minds begin to merge and act in concert as one. These are interesting speculations, some of which will probably come true, but they take us beyond what we know. It may be that something unexpected will raise the race to majesty if we just get through the next few decades, but it is becoming clear that merely the expected will be enough.

The rush to cosmic consciousness will be hastened by telecommunications revolution's momentum toward a fully and instantaneously connected world. In the very near future it will be possible to know, through satellites, nationwide paging, cellular phones, and body locators and communicators, what is happening in the world almost at the moment it occurs; for anyone in the world to communicate with another at any moment. While this is not telepathy, it is very close. The world will be one and open. What this says for the survival of those governments based on concentration of authority is clear.

It will be possible to have what you want when you want it because at some point in their development, our intelligent machines will begin to reproduce themselves out of readily at hand renewable materials. Eventually, factories will not only automatically reproduce robots, but the factories will clone themselves. New automated manufacturing systems are making their first appearance in U.S. factories. Known as "flexible systems" these manufacturing processes can alter their procedures on computer command to produce an assortment of parts, and can simultaneously be programmed for new parts or to accommodate design changes. These flexible systems permit the production of a wide variety of product types and styles on command at reasonable cost. They are a force for diversity and toward more custom and unique products and away from mass production. Once robotic systems are developed which can repair the equipment as well as load the machines, utilizing expert vision systems, manufacturing will be moving toward the self-replicating factory of the future.

Evolution is moving toward heightened consciousness and self-awareness. Technology and human intervention is playing a more prominent role in this development. Evolutionary events which once took millenniums are taking decades, years, months, and days. The factories of the future will result in a world of super-abundance, eliminating a principal impetus to war—poverty and economic competition—the survival of the fittest. As economic competition wanes, most ideological competition will be replaced by shared values of freedom, usefulness, creativity, and peace.

We humans are at an early age. Sometimes we try to walk before we can run, but even this is growth. Run we will. From the mud of the earth, risen to the rim of the stars, mankind will face in certain maturity his own beginning and perhaps never end. And then at one time, man's reconciled consciousness, focusing with fondness and acceptance on a troubled childhood, will recall those who went before as children and made their present eminence possible.

19

AFTERWORD: TECHNOLOGY, MYSTERY, AND SCIENCE

The last years of the twentieth century are creating a technology base which will propel human beings on dramatic unanticipated highways and byways in the second millennium. Much of the drive for this technical surge, unseen since the early years of this century is due to the technical entrepreneur. He is taking concepts from the great labs of our universities and from our corporations where entrepreneurs may incubate, but not flourish, and turning them into products and markets. Rarely a day passes that we do not learn of some breakthrough development in biotechnology, electronics, robotics, materials, computer science, artificial intelligence, and medicine which will soon change the way we live. Exploration no longer takes place on the high seas, but rather all around us.

Mystery is ever present in our world. From ancient times humans have wanted to know who they are, why they are here, and where they are going. Science and its counterpart technology attempt to get into the essence of things and provide tentative answers to these resounding questions. Mystery then calls forth great quests. It challenges humankind to send probes and sensors into unknown waters in the mind and in both time and space. It produces people of genius who perceive relationships and draw together distant strands into more encompassing unity. Mystery beckons and humans continuously answer the call to knowledge, understanding and wisdom. With each successive unveiling of mystery our awareness of the most basic questions of purpose and existence become both more simple and more profound.

The lives of scientist and entrepreneur are a kaleidoscope of change, chance, feedback, modeling, prediction, evidence and theory. Each, through work, is transforming the lives we live. The entrepreneur lives in a world of change and chance. Few companies make it big without a major assist from lady luck or without preparation for her arrival. Risky business is in constant motion and unless the entrepreneur sets up correct feedback on actions, in the form of controls and by listening to the pulse of the organization, he tempts failure. The entrepreneur is in the business of predicting what the right thing will be in that he must always sell his product. He looks to evidence of consumer behavior and constructs models in his head of how he will pull together the elements of a successful company. Like science there are always new possibilities, new worlds to explore. Each is engaged in a creative process, in the attempt to leave something in place which might be important or at least helpful.

Like entrepreneurs, scientists often have large egos—they need them to survive failure and uncertainty and blind alleys. Scientists of course have a rage to know and to uncover part of the world, whereas the entrepreneur seems to be trying to put it back together in his own way. Each, however, leaves something unique which wasn't there before. Scientists are often thought of as loners plugging away in the lab or in contemplation until by happenstance or brilliance a discovery is made. Entrepreneurs also live their lives to a different drummer. The technologist or creative engineer doesn't appear too dissimilar from the scientist. He wants to take what is known and apply it to the work of the world. The entrepreneur may measure his success more in the size of the company, or jobs created, or profit earned; the scientist and technologist may find their satisfaction in other moments. Each is seeking something for themselves as well. The coin of the realm is just different. There is a community of tenacity which all pioneers share. They not only must rearrange the old order, but they are out there alone on the other end of the limb. This loneliness involves courage of a high order.

Whether a specific entrepreneur will prevail depends in part on exquisite timing. A number of personal computer companies were founded prior to the successful launching of Apple computer. Being in the appropriate milieu and being exposed to the right combination of linked circumstances provides in many cases the stimulation and resources required to found a company. Areas such as Silicon Valley and Boston's route 128 have provided such an entrepreneurial milieu. Others are feverishly attempting to imitate these original primeval entrepreneurial soups. In the case of Apple the right people, with the right product, with the right advisors did one creative selling job on a public which was sufficiently conditioned by the media and other opinion trendsetters to want personal computing power. A short time later in the same personal computer industry another window of opportunity opened when IBM joined the fray, and it appeared to some that a compatible machine could be offered piggybacking on the probable development of an IBM personal computer standard. As recent events demonstrate, neither the Apple approach nor the "clone" approach have been without risk. Future opportunities in this industry, including artificial intelligence, telecomputers which combine phone communications capabilities with computer memory and processing power, and other networking and multiuser tasking will also require exquisite timing.

Writing in *Science and Human Values*, J. Bronowski argues, "There never was a great scientist who did not make bold guesses, and there never was a bold man whose guesses were not sometimes wild. Newton was wrong, in the setting of his time, to think that light is made up of particles. Faraday was foolish when he looked, in his setting, for a link between electromagnetism and gravitation. And such is the nature of science, their bad guesses may yet be brilliant by the work of our own day. . . . For in science, as literature, the style of a great man is the stamp of his mind, and makes even his mistakes a challenge which is part of the march of its subject." Even as the scientist, the bold entrepreneur will often be mistaken, plugging down unmarked roads on a journey leading more toward apparent failure than success. In attempting to call forth a new conception of reality, the entrepreneur can be forgiven for occasional confusion between reality, and reality as he sees it. For it is only in this visionary, search called forth by a personal vision, that new patterns of understanding emerge. Particularly in the world of deeds, but also in the world of ideas, the connection between dreams and reality is but a small step.

The scientific pursuit, like the entrepreneurial is always incomplete. New, more revealing information is always coming to the fore which obsoletes old theories and conceptions of reality. The marketplace of the mind, like the marketplace of goods and services, is continually in flux—the established, entrenched dogma a parallel to a dominant product position, both soon to be eroded by a more useful or complete explanation or satisfaction of needs. These fluxes bring home the matter of our ignorance and a certain humility which is essential both to successful entrepreneurship as well as to great science. It's only by not being sure of all the answers that we continue to ask the unanswered and perhaps unanswerable questions. New questions beget new opportunities, and new opportunities a new platform from which to view the world and conceive of new questions.

As always, some are fearful of the unknown. They believe that if we find out something, we may not always use it wisely or to good purpose. There is plenty of recent and past history to support this view. Our science and technology have produced horrifying weapons and dreadful possibilities. But evil has always been with us, perhaps programmed in our genes or perhaps just part—the downside—of mystery. Certainly what we discover opens larger vistas both for good and evil. We have to hope that the more we know and understand the more likely we are to direct our actions to beneficial ends. Perhaps we are nowhere safe, free, or aware, when afraid. It appears that it is in our way to continue to unravel our possibilities.

Lately science, as practiced by individuals of genius, and technology, in their support, are working in tandem with each other. Historically, technology or applied science has been disdained by those who are interested in "pure" science. However, over the centuries an exceptional breakthrough in our ability to perceive the world has been followed shortly by quantum improvements in our ability to conceive it. Increasingly powerful technologies such as computers, lasers, and genetic engineering are providing the tools to power new explanations of our whereabouts. We can expect clearer answers in short order. We can also expect improvements in the way we live. There will be more goods to go around, manufactured by fully automated computer controlled factories of the future, which eventually will self–reproduce and maintain themselves. This will not be business as usual. Everyone will have more than enough, obliterating economic competition and survival as one of the prime ingredients of war. Our energies will turn more to exploration; to the stars and beyond. This will all take a little time, so in the meantime, there is a lot of opportunity for the entrepreneur and his supporter, the venture capitalist.

Our task will be to continue to penetrate to the center of existence, and to find once and always what was always and forever known. Soon we as a species will learn to listen to our deepest and most searching intuitions and to discover both within and without ourselves a remarkable destiny. Technology and science are leading us up out of the mud toward wisdom, compassion, and occasional grace. With such tools, and hope, truly we will not be the last of our race nor the last race.

APPENDIX A

CHECKLISTS TO ASSIST IN SUCCESSFULLY RAISING VENTURE CAPITAL

CHECKLIST ONE: RATING THE UNIQUENESS OF YOUR BUSINESS PLAN

Business plans which are viewed by the venture capitalist as being highly unique have a significantly better chance of being funded than those which contain nothing unusual. Most venture capitalists will review at a minimum several hundred business plans each year so yours, to be carefully considered, must grab the venture capitalist from the start. You want to produce a plan which will be funded, not write a great first novel. Remember that the business plan is a selling document, and perhaps your first and last chance to get the venture capitalist's attention and interest.

My business plan is a selling document because:

_____ I present compelling economics (if successful in building a company a lot of money will be made by all).

_____ I have a unique product, service, or concept (something that a large number of customers need and will pay for and that will be difficult for competitors to duplicate quickly).

_____ My product is an evolutionary rather than a revolutionary product (doing something a little bit better or different rather than creating something you are not sure anyone will buy).

_____ The product addresses a large market opportunity (in the billions of dollars is better than millions of dollars).

_____ We will sell to a small but highly profitable segment of a large market (a protected niche).

_____ Our product is faster, better, or much cheaper than anything on and about to be on the market.

_____ Productivity improvement is key to our product.

_____ The management team is complete.

_____ The management team is experienced in the business we are attempting to build.

_____ The management team wants to build a business rather than create a bunch of fancy products that no one wants.

_____ The management team is hungry to make money.

_____ The management team was successful before at building a business, or failed but learned what they need to know to be successful at this opportunity.

_____ We have assembled or will assemble an experienced board of directors.

_____ The board of directors will be consulted and not serve as window dressing.

_____ The plan is accurate and written in concise, clear English.

_____ The plan calls for adequate capital.

_____ The plan gives up enough of the company to the venture capitalist to compensate for the risk. (Generally enough to result in a 40 percent to 60 percent rate of return annually.)

_____ The plan contains an executive summary, a description of the product, market, competition, manufacturing methods, management, selling, marketing, and distribution strategy, and five year financial projections.

_____ I've been working on building this business for a while and so far have survived and not given up.

_____ My plan conveys the impression that I am looking for a business partner as well as money.

The more selling points a business plan contains the more likely the business plan will be funded by major venture capital. For those wild-eyed inventors, wandering around in the financial wilderness in search of funds, there are individuals who specialize in helping assemble the business plan, and often the management team, around a product, service, or idea. These start-up helpers range from brokers who want a fee for selling the idea, to lawyers, business plan writers, and seed fund venture capitalists who will help organize the plan and company as well as support the effort with their seed capital.

CHECKLIST TWO: STEPS IN SUCCESSFULLY RAISING VENTURE CAPITAL

Successfully raising venture capital is an established process and your chances of success are enhanced if all bases are covered in a logical progression:

_____ Develop a unique product, concept, or service.

_____ Develop an outline of what is required in people, money, organization, strategy and tactics, and other assets to build this particular business.

_____ Assemble a management team with the ability to successfully build and operate this business.

_____ Prepare, with the assistance of the members of the management team, a clear, concise business plan representing the "game plan" of how the business will be operated and financed.

_____ Identify those venture capitalists who are most likely to review a business plan in your industry and stage of development. (Use the venture capital directory in Appendix B.)

_____ Mail the plan, with a cover letter indicating why the plan is unique, to four or five selected venture capitalists.

_____ Call the venture capitalist in several weeks to determine the status of your plan if a reply has not yet been received.

_____ Meet with the venture capitalist to initially present your deal.

_____ Prepare for "due diligence" meetings with the venture capitalist to continue to sell your deal.

_____ Negotiate with venture capitalists over deal structure and price.

_____ Complete investment syndicate formation by entrepreneur and lead venture capitalist.

_____ Obtain commitment by all venture capitalists in the deal.

_____ Prepare legal documents of closing (time to involve your deal-doing attorney).

_____ Officially close the deal.

_____ Work with the venture capitalist after the sale.

_____ Cash out for the venture capitalist through a sale, merger, or public offering.

CHECKLIST THREE: OBTAINING A STATE OF MIND CONDUCIVE TO RAISING VENTURE CAPITAL

Several authors, combining the best of the ways of Eastern mysticism and relaxation techniques with Western competitiveness, present approaches to obtain your goals which permit the participant to "go with the flow" rather than against the grain. This "oneness with what you are doing" approach permits the objective, in this case raising venture capital, to be obtained with a minimum of hassle, anxiety, and difficulty. The author has observed that those who are successful in raising venture capital obtain a state of mind as well as an understanding of the process which promotes and permits success. Administer this self-awareness review to determine whether your stuff is right:

_____ I would rather be rich than be the big cheese.

_____ While I want to be rich, I would rather build a successful company.

_____ While I want to build a successful company, I would rather be creative and effective in what I do everyday.

_____ I work effectively with peers, but not well for another.

_____ I want the best around me in my products, employees, investors, and other supporters, but if they are not available I will on occasion compromise, but not too much.

_____ I am afraid to fail and admit it, but succeeding is okay.

_____ I will work both very hard and very smart to obtain my goals.

_____ I accept that in this life it is difficult to have everything, at least at one time, and that it will be necessary at times to surrender personal life for business success.

_____ I know in what way I am truly unique, and what it is that I want to bring to the world.

_____ I will let my family and friends know that it's not that I am not interested in them, but that this is just something that I have to create for a time.

_____ I will never give up.

_____ If forced to give up by adverse circumstances, I will start over.

CHECKLIST FOUR: VENTURE CAPITAL MYTHS AND LEGENDS

Just as it is important, in raising venture capital, to examine your state of mind prior to undertaking the trip, it is also useful to disabuse yourself if necessary of myths, legends, and folklore which perfuse the industry. Reliance on myth can lead to wrong action and much wasted time, money and effort. Consider whether:

_____ Venture capitalists are interested only in a high return on their money, not in working together to build a successful business.

_____ Raising venture capital is easy. Money can be obtained in a couple of weeks.

_____ Being a great promoter is all it takes to build a successful business.

_____ If the venture guys make a few bucks on their investment this is sufficient to satisfy.

_____ Since venture capitalists don't operate a business, they don't really understand my problems.

_____ Most venture capitalists have never met a payroll.

_____ Venture capitalists like to make a lot of money on their deals, but they don't mind losing it.

_____ Fancy technology deals get all the venture capital money today.

_____ Venture capitalists will leave me completely alone to run my business unless I really mess up.

_____ If the business begins to fail the venture capitalist will never step in and find someone else to run the company.

_____ A good business operator can run a business in any industry.

_____ Given sufficient time and money, poor management can be fixed.

_____ You have to know someone on the inside to raise venture capital.

_____ Most venture capitalists are nice guys, perhaps a little world weary. If they were really bright, they would be running their own companies.

CHECKLIST FIVE: FINANCING VEHICLES AVAILABLE AT VARIOUS GROWTH STAGES OF A TYPICAL HIGH-TECH, "FAST-GROWTH" COMPANY*

Stage of Corporate Growth	Financing Vehicles Available	Venture Capital Considerations
Conceptual Stage ("Seed" or idea stage to start-up stage, which is evidenced by ideas, a preliminary business plan, and a prototype)	Seed Capital and/or First Round: • Private Funds • Grants/Endowments • R&D Partnerships • Joint Ventures	Venture capital funds are generally not widely available, due to the "extravagant risks." However, it may be available if IPO market looks strong.
Start-up/Initial Operations Stage (Comprehensive organizational structure, a good business plan, a regular production schedule)	Midround or Developmental Round Financing: • Private Funds • Government Programs • Bank Loans • Industrial Revenue Bonds • Private Placements • Joint Ventures • Venture Capital	Companies are likely to seek and find venture capital funds if the management, market, and product considerations are sound.
Rapid Growth Stage (Company breaking even or showing a profit; accelerated product demand; inadequate cash flow to meet expanding operations)	Expansion or Third-Round Financing and Mezzanine or Growth Stage Financing: • Bank Loans • Industrial Revenue Bonds • Private Placements • Joint Ventures • Public Offerings • Venture Capital (all types)	Companies are most likely to seek and receive venture capital as this stage is reached.
Maturity Stage (Steady product demand; established market niche; slower growth)	Financing Available: • Bank Loans • Debt Instruments • Public Offerings —Common Stock —Preferred Stock —Bonds • Leverage Buyouts • Mergers and/or Acquisitions • Some Venture Capital	Some venture capital firms specialize in leverage buyouts and acquisition; otherwise, venture funds are generally not available, due to low return on investment.

*With the permission of Deloitte Haskins & Sells.

CHECKLIST SIX: METHOD TO PRICE YOUR VENTURE CAPITAL DEAL

Remember what a leading venture capitalist said: "You tell me the price, and I will tell you the terms; you tell me the terms and I will tell you the price." Through effective structuring of the venture capital terms, the venture capitalist can offer you a price which you will find fair and acceptable. You must remember, though, that this price has a price. For example, perhaps your deal's price is tied to a performance formula where you give up more of the company if certain goals which you commit to achieving are not reached by a certain time. Or perhaps the venture capitalist buys common stock rather than preferred and can easily obtain voting as well as actual control of the company if projections are not realized.

Venture capital pricing is in part a money market, and like any market its pricing will vary with the laws of supply and demand. If you have a deal which is perceived as being "hot" practically anytime is a good time to raise venture capital. However, if your deal is a good deal but not overwhelming, then your timing in raising capital can be critical. Generally the venture capitalist will pay a higher price for your deal at those times when it is possible for him to move his product, your company securities most readily—during a hot new issues public stock market. During other less heady times, venture capital valuations tend to be more realistic and lower, reflecting real value. Below are several examples of approaches to venture capital pricing.

The Market Method

Venture capital investors have a good idea of which industries are in fashion and which out of fashion, and of the risk-reward profile for the particular industry and stage of your deal. They will have a fairly accurate conception of what price your deal might bring from another venture capital firm. However, since this is not an exact market you might be able to obtain a "better" price at another firm, but remember that the terms may be more difficult to make up for the lower price, the firm less helpful later on, or the chemistry between entrepreneur and venture capitalist absent. Price is not all that matters in a partnership, although it is important to the later relationship that both parties to the deal consider it a fair deal. The following approach is the market method of pricing:

——— Bring your deal along to the highest stage possible on your own prior to seeking venture capital. This will maximize your price.

——— Discuss possible valuations of your deal with your attorney, accountants, investment bankers, and any friendly venture capitalists prior to establishing your price.

———— Select a valuation which is reasonable in light of market realities, a bit on the high side, perhaps, so there is room to negotiate. Not so high that the venture capitalist feels that you are so far out of the ballpark that working with you will be a waste of time.

———— Try your valuation on several venture capitalists, one of whom you will be attempting to secure as your lead investor.

———— If your valuation fails to pass the "snicker test" with several venture capitalists, revise the valuation downward.

———— Remember that most venture capital financings require more than one round of equity infusion prior to positive cash flow. Don't sell so much of the company that there is none left for you.

———— If you sell one-third of your company for $1 million the valuation or value of your company is set at $3 million.

There are several theoretical methods to value companies for venture capital financing which are discussed from time to time, such as paying two times current or next year's projected revenues, or some multiple of earnings over the next five years. All of these may be considered in pricing a deal, but the author believes that these are mostly a distraction from marketplace pricing mechanisms.

CHECKLIST SEVEN: SOURCES OF VENTURE
CAPITAL FINANCING

_____ What I can beg and borrow from myself, family, and friends.

_____ The local bank or finance company (collateral most always necessary).

_____ Grants and endowments (particularly useful for high tech products).

_____ Research and development partnerships. (Find the local packager in your neighborhood.)

_____ Joint ventures with companies and corporations. (Generally the company must be fairly far along before a major corporation can be interested. Your attorney or accountant may be able to introduce you to a small company looking for new products.)

_____ The public market. (Some concepts have sufficient sex appeal to be taken public by a new–issue underwriter without sales or earnings. Several firms specialize in this form of concept underwriting.)

_____ Industrial revenue bonds and other governmental assistance. (A number of state governments are setting up programs and funds to back new business start–ups and provide jobs to their communities—contact the local business development agency for a list.)

_____ Private placement of your securities through a local investment banker. (Some local or regional investment bankers will attempt to raise money for your deal, and perhaps even invest most of their fee in the deal to prove their good faith to new investors. Once in a while a venture capitalist will take a piece of this action.)

_____ New venture incubators. (While these hatcheries for new ventures may or may not have funds available they can be invaluable in contacts to financial sources.)

_____ If all else fails, try hanging out around the local clubs or watering holes where successful businessmen and investors gather. One entrepreneur raised rescue money by spending his last dollars on a first class coast to coast air ticket and successfully solicited the first class section for the $10,000 needed to save the business.

CHECKLIST EIGHT: MOST PROBABLE VENTURE CAPITAL OBJECTIONS TO YOUR DEAL AND YOUR READY, EFFECTIVE REPLIES

_____ The deal doesn't meet our portfolio objectives. (The soft turn-down—you need to ask what the objectives are, which generally boils down to making money, and explain how your deal will accomplish this objective.)

_____ "An old deal is a bad deal." (If your deal is musty with mileage, it needs to be presented in a new light to secure venture capital. Explain that the reason you haven't sold any product for the past fifteen years was because you were concentrating on the development of a one of a kind product which is now perfect.)

_____ Your product is so revolutionary that no one will understand it or want it. (You need to develop strong market research and preferably at least several major customers who will swear that people will want the stuff. Interestingly enough, most venture capital–backed companies fail not because the product could not be developed or produced but because an insufficient number of people really wanted to buy the product.)

_____ This product will never work. (Pert charts which show the step by step requirements to get the product to work can be useful in converting the doubting venture capitalist. He can then take this document to his consultant on the technology and ask him whether the device will ever work, and soon enough to beat the competition.)

_____ Your management team never made a nickel. (This is a tough objection. It can be overcome by demonstrating that your prior experience has prepared you to be on the "cutting edge" of making money—that you and your team are an undiscovered talent waiting for the call, and that the venture capitalist will both be remembered as a wise man and make a lot of money by taking a chance on you.) (It is also helpful to surround yourself with Directors or perhaps a Chairman who has made money before. The venture capitalist will figure it might be catching.)

_____ We don't do seed capital deals, or, no leverage buyout for us. We are an early–stage investor. (Some venture capitalists do specialize. If you ascertain you are in the wrong hands ask for a reference to a friend.)

_____ Your management team is incomplete. (Ask the help of the venture capitalist in recruiting and building the management team. Stress that he can play a major role in building the team that will run the business.)

_____ Your business plan lacks focus. (There is perhaps nothing so threatening to a venture capitalist as a company without focus. Time and money are in short supply in the early stage company and must be spent effectively and efficiently. Redefine what it is you are trying to do.)

CHECKLIST NINE: REVIEW OF READINESS FOR "DUE DILIGENCE" PHYSICAL

_____ Complete management team is available on date of venture capitalist's visit.

_____ Key customers, suppliers, bankers, accountants, attorney, and other involved parties are alerted to expect calls from the venture capitalist inquiring about the company's status.

_____ If money was obtained from earlier investors, all securities laws are either fully complied with or omissions are corrected.

_____ References for all key management personnel are contacted and advised of probable venture capital inquiries.

_____ A listing of key personnel, business, customer, and vendor references is prepared for venture capital review.

_____ The management team has reviewed the strengths and weaknesses of the business plan including any holes in the financials, and is prepared to answer questions and objections as well as sell the opportunity.

_____ Your team knows who will buy your product in what amounts and at what price. Backup material for these sales assertions is available.

_____ The team presentation to the venture capitalist has been "disaster tested." The tone will be self–confident but not overly promotional.

_____ The office and plant look like a business is being conducted.

_____ You normally hide your brother-in-law in the broom closet—take him out of the closet with any other relatives and let the venture capitalist know that you are being up front.

_____ Treat the venture capitalist like your most important customer, which for the moment he is. Pick him up at the airport or wherever, but not in the back of the office delivery truck.

_____ Answer all questions on the facilities tour. If you lack the latest automated equipment, say so, but indicate your plans to obtain it if finances permit, and if it is in the business plan.

_____ The plant tour can be a time to shine. Don't hide your assets, whether of people or plant.

_____ Convey your "big vision" of the company and industry.

_____ Don't ask to use the new venture capital money to take out your prior investment in the company. The venture capitalist will be much more inclined to invest if he knows you are financially at real risk.

_____ Indicate your flexibility as to other investors which the venture capitalist might want to bring into the investment syndicate, unless you just cannot work with a particular investor. If this is the case say so.

_____ If possible, have your financial information up to date, and if you can afford it, a recent review or an audit of your statements.

_____ Your attorney should be certain that all corporate housecleaning including satisfactory bylaws, qualifications to do business, incorporations, etc., are in order. If yours is an early–stage or seed company, the venture capitalist will be less demanding in this regard.

_____ Treat the venture capitalist as you would a partner.

CHECKLIST TEN: SPOTTING A DEAL-DOING LAWYER

_____ Check Appendix E in this book for attorneys recommended by the leading venture capital firms as proficient in entrepreneurial law.

_____ Contact several listed attorneys, describe your plans to them, and set up an appointment.

_____ Determine whether the attorney is familiar with the venture capital process. Inquire as to past venture capital deals worked on.

_____ Probe for approach to the role of the attorney in the fund-raising process. Does the attorney view the process as essentially adversarial or as a cooperative venture where the objective is to reach a deal which is perceived as fair to all parties?

_____ Attempt to define the level of negotiating skill. Discuss your particular deal as it is now taking shape, and ask for any suggestions which could improve the deal. Determine whether these suggestions are positive or negative.

_____ If a law firm, rather than a solo, what attorney in the firm will handle your particular deal? Will you be passed off to a junior associate or work with the senior partner?

_____ If a law firm, does the firm as a whole have the specific skills in corporate, tax, securities, creditors' rights, business development law which you may require in the life cycle of your business?

_____ Will the attorney push you for a seat on the board of directors, or is he content and competent to serve as a valued advisor?

_____ Does the particular lawyer who will work on your deal have the time available to close your deal within your allotted time?

_____ Does the lawyer have a working knowledge of the principal venture capital documents?

_____ Ask the lawyer for his estimate of the bill for his services in writing.

_____ Determine the attorney's reputation for veracity and the overall quality of his work by contacting references on prior deals. Ask references about specific examples of creative legal business solutions which the attorney devised, which broke a deadlock, and allowed a prior deal to move to a smooth close.

_____ Is this a "deal-doing" attorney who will keep you out of court rather than encourage you to sue?

CHECKLIST ELEVEN: REFLECTIONS PRIOR TO
UNDERTAKING A PUBLIC OFFERING

_____ Would I rather be highly visible or invisible?

_____ Can the company afford the additional cost both to go public and to remain public?

_____ Will I or my Financial Vice President have the patience required of those running a public company with stock analysts, stockholders, and various forms of government regulation?

_____ Do I want to run the company with an eye on the latest quarterly earnings report card, or is it important to preserve the flexibility to manage the business for the long term?

_____ Is my company far enough along in its development and in its financial progress to achieve success as a public company?

_____ If I go to the public market now will I be able to go to the same market later if additional funds are required to finance the business? Will a public offering, even if successful, negatively affect raising private money at a later date?

_____ Is a public offering necessary to provide a real advantage over other competitors?

_____ Is the price that can be obtained for your company's stock in the present market a fair valuation for the company?

_____ Could a better financial valuation be obtained in a private sale of stock?

_____ Will my company and industry support the growth expectations of the stock market?

_____ Am I trying to go public at the "worst time," when I really need the money, rather than at the best time when I really could get along without it?

_____ Will my stock be priced with those companies that are considered quality stock picks or with the dogs?

_____ Have I been able to enlist a quality investment banking house to undertake my offering?

_____ Overall, will I live to regret going public?

GUIDES THROUGH THE ENTREPRENEURIAL WILDERNESS

New Venture Strategies, Karl H. Vesper, Prentice-Hall, Inc., 1980.

Entrepreneuring, Steven C. Brandt, Addison-Wesley Publishing Co., 1982.

Who's Who in Venture Capital, A. David Silver and Roland Press, John Wiley & Sons, 1984.

Venture Capital Handbook, David J. Gladstone, Reston Publishing Co., Inc., 1983.

How to Sell Anything to Anybody, Joe Girard, Warner Books, 1979.

The New Alchemists, Dirk Hanson, Little, Brown and Co., 1982.

Raising Venture Capital—An Entrepreneur's Guidebook, Deloitte Haskins & Sells, 1982.

Strategies for Going Public—An Entrepreneur's Guidebook, Deloitte Haskins & Sells, 1983.

Forming R & D Partnerships—An Entrepreneur's Guidebook, Deloitte Haskins & Sells, 1983.

The Entrepreneur's Manual, Richard M. White, Jr., Chilton Book Co., 1977.

Venture's Guide to Investing in Private Companies, Arthur Lipper III, with George Ryan, Dow Jones-Irwin, 1984.

Venture Capital—Where to Find It
National Association of Small Business Investment Companies, Membership Directory. The guide is available at $1.00 per copy from:

The National Association of Small Business
Investment Companies
1156 15th St. NW
Suite 1101
Washington, DC 20005
202 833-8230

National Venture Capital Association Directory, available from:

The NVCA
1655 North Fort Myer Drive
Suite 700
Arlington, VA 22209
703 528-4370

The directory is free, but enclose a stamped self-addressed envelope with $.80 postage.

High Tech—How to Find and Profit from Today's New Super Stocks, Albert Toney and Thomas Tilling, Simon & Schuster, 1983.

Pratt's Guide to Venture Capital Sources, 8th ed., Edited by Stanley E. Pratt and Jane K. Morris, Capital Publishing, 1984.

Databook of Venture Capital Sources for High Technology Companies, Richard Loftin, Financial Data Corp., 1981.

The Corporate Finance Sourcebook, The Zehring Company, 1985.

Appendix C

VENTURE CAPITAL
DIRECTORY

ALABAMA

FIRM NAME: Private Capital Corporation

ADDRESS: 1625 First Alabama Bank Building
              Birmingham, AL 35203

PHONE: (205) 251–0152

SBIC ____   VENTURE CAPITAL FUND ____   MESBIC ____   OTHER _X_

TYPES OF FINANCING PREFERRED (Stages): Under unusual circumstances will do start-ups; generally prefer lower mature financings—is often growth capital

MINIMUM DATA REQUIRED TO CONSIDER FINANCING: A thorough business plan with good financial information

GEOGRAPHIC PREFERENCE: Southeast—easily reached from Birmingham, Alabama

INDUSTRY PREFERENCE BY FIRM: Communications/Media/Health Care ventures of all types/Computers/Manufacturing Companies involving proprietary products or technologies

INDUSTRY PREFERENCES BY INDIVIDUAL FIRM MEMBERS: N/A*

YEAR COMPANY ESTABLISHED: 1973

FUNDS UNDER MANAGEMENT AT COST: N/A

MINIMUM SIZE INVESTMENT: $500,000

PREFERRED SIZE INVESTMENT: $500,000–$1,000,000

WILL FIRM SERVE AS LEAD INVESTOR: Yes

NUMBER OF DEALS COMPLETED IN THE LAST 12 MONTHS: 2

AMOUNT INVESTED IN LAST 12 MONTHS: $700,000

AVERAGE TIME REQUIRED TO COMPLETE A DEAL:
    (From Initial Contact to Closing)   Shortest time for $2.5 million deal was 10 days; longest time for $500,000 deal was 13 months

ARIZONA

FIRM NAME: Greyhound Capital Management Corporation

ADDRESS: 1110 Greyhound Tower
              Phoenix, AZ 85077

PHONE: (602) 222–8816

SBIC ____   VENTURE CAPITAL FUND _X_   MESBIC ____   OTHER ____

TYPES OF FINANCING PREFERRED (Stages): Seed/start-ups/first stage/second stage

*N/A stands for not available

MINIMUM DATA REQUIRED TO CONSIDER FINANCING: Executive summary

GEOGRAPHIC PREFERENCE: USA

INDUSTRY PREFERENCE BY FIRM:
Computer Hardware/Software
Telecommunications
Electronic Data Processing
Semiconductors
Electronics and Electrical Component
Optics and Lasers
Media and Technology
CAD/CAM

INDUSTRY PREFERENCES BY INDIVIDUAL FIRM MEMBERS: N/A

YEAR COMPANY ESTABLISHED: 1979

FUNDS UNDER MANAGEMENT AT COST: $25 million

MINIMUM SIZE INVESTMENT: Seed to $250,000

PREFERRED SIZE INVESTMENT: $500,000–$750,000

WILL FIRM SERVE AS LEAD INVESTOR: Yes

NUMBER OF DEALS COMPLETED IN THE LAST 12 MONTHS: 13

AMOUNT INVESTED IN LAST 12 MONTHS: $8.1 million

AVERAGE TIME REQUIRED TO COMPLETE A DEAL: 9 months
(From Initial Contact to Closing)

FIRM NAME: **SunVen Partners**

ADDRESS: P.O. Box 5190
               Phoenix, AZ 85010

PHONE: (602) 254–3944

SBIC ___ VENTURE CAPITAL FUND _X_ MESBIC ___ OTHER ___

TYPES OF FINANCING PREFERRED (Stages): Seed/research & development/start-up/first stage/leverage/buyouts

MINIMUM DATA REQUIRED TO CONSIDER FINANCING: Annual sales—nominal

GEOGRAPHIC PREFERENCE: Southwest USA

INDUSTRY PREFERENCE BY FIRM: High Technology/Media and Communications

INDUSTRY PREFERENCES BY INDIVIDUAL FIRM MEMBERS:
Scott S. Eller, General Partner
Karl Eller, General Partner
F. Wesley Clelland III, General Partner
Hembrecht & Quist, General Partner

YEAR COMPANY ESTABLISHED: 1984

FUNDS UNDER MANAGEMENT AT COST: $20.6 million

MINIMUM SIZE INVESTMENT: Seed to $100,000

PREFERRED SIZE INVESTMENT: $300,000 plus

WILL FIRM SERVE AS LEAD INVESTOR: Yes

NUMBER OF DEALS COMPLETED IN THE LAST 12 MONTHS: 14

AMOUNT INVESTED IN LAST 12 MONTHS: $4.2 million

AVERAGE TIME REQUIRED TO COMPLETE A DEAL: N/A
(From Initial Contact to Closing)

CALIFORNIA

FIRM NAME: **Arscott, Norton & Associates**

ADDRESS: 375 Forest Ave.
                          Palo Alto, CA 94301

PHONE: (415) 853–0766

SBIC ___   VENTURE CAPITAL FUND _X_ MESBIC ___   OTHER ___

TYPES OF FINANCING PREFERRED (Stages): Start-up and early stages

MINIMUM DATA REQUIRED TO CONSIDER FINANCING: Business plan

GEOGRAPHIC PREFERENCE: Open

INDUSTRY PREFERENCE BY FIRM:Computers/Telecommunications/Medical

INDUSTRY PREFERENCES BY INDIVIDUAL FIRM MEMBERS: N/A

YEAR COMPANY ESTABLISHED: 1978

FUNDS UNDER MANAGEMENT AT COST: $75 million

MINIMUM SIZE INVESTMENT: $250,000

PREFERRED SIZE INVESTMENT: $1 million plus

WILL FIRM SERVE AS LEAD INVESTOR: Yes

NUMBER OF DEALS COMPLETED IN THE LAST 12 MONTHS: 11

AMOUNT INVESTED IN LAST 12 MONTHS: $8 million plus

AVERAGE TIME REQUIRED TO COMPLETE A DEAL: Varies
(From Initial Contact to Closing)

FIRM NAME: **Arthur Rock & Co.**

ADDRESS: 1635 Russ Bldg.
                          San Francisco, CA 94104

PHONE: N/A

SBIC ___   VENTURE CAPITAL FUND _X_ MESBIC ___   OTHER ___

TYPES OF FINANCING PREFERRED (Stages): Early stage

MINIMUM DATA REQUIRED TO CONSIDER FINANCING: N/A

GEOGRAPHIC PREFERENCE: Northern California

INDUSTRY PREFERENCE BY FIRM: Technology

INDUSTRY PREFERENCES BY INDIVIDUAL FIRM MEMBERS: N/A

YEAR COMPANY ESTABLISHED: 1961

FUNDS UNDER MANAGEMENT AT COST:N/A

MINIMUM SIZE INVESTMENT: $100,000

PREFERRED SIZE INVESTMENT: $500,000

WILL FIRM SERVE AS LEAD INVESTOR: Yes

NUMBER OF DEALS COMPLETED IN THE LAST 12 MONTHS: N/A

AMOUNT INVESTED IN LAST 12 MONTHS: N/A

AVERAGE TIME REQUIRED TO COMPLETE A DEAL: N/A
   (From Initial Contact to Closing)

FIRM NAME: **Associates Venture Capital Corporation**

ADDRESS: 425 California St.,
                Suite 2203
                San Francisco, CA 94104

PHONE: (415) 956–1444

SBIC ___   VENTURE CAPITAL FUND _X_ MESBIC _X_ OTHER ___

TYPES OF FINANCING PREFERRED (Stages): First and second stages

MINIMUM DATA REQUIRED TO CONSIDER FINANCING: Business plan and
   pro formas

GEOGRAPHIC PREFERENCE: None

INDUSTRY PREFERENCE BY FIRM: Electronics/Medical Products and Ser-
   vices/Energy Projects/Water

INDUSTRY PREFERENCES BY INDIVIDUAL FIRM MEMBERS: Walter P.
   Strycker

YEAR COMPANY ESTABLISHED: 1978

FUNDS UNDER MANAGEMENT AT COST: MESBIC—$1.2 million; VEN-
   TURE—$1.5 million

MINIMUM SIZE INVESTMENT: $50,000

PREFERRED SIZE INVESTMENT: $150,000

WILL FIRM SERVE AS LEAD INVESTOR: Yes

NUMBER OF DEALS COMPLETED IN THE LAST 12 MONTHS: 3

AMOUNT INVESTED IN LAST 12 MONTHS: $650,000

AVERAGE TIME REQUIRED TO COMPLETE A DEAL: 90 to 120 days
   (From Initial Contact to Closing)

FIRM NAME: **AVI Management, Inc.**
                (Associated Venture Investors)

ADDRESS: 3000 Sand Hill Rd.
                Bldg. 1, Suite 105
                Menlo Park, CA 94025

PHONE: (415) 854–4470

SBIC ____   VENTURE CAPITAL FUND _X_   MESBIC ____   OTHER ____

TYPES OF FINANCING PREFERRED (Stages): Seed or start-up/first round

MINIMUM DATA REQUIRED TO CONSIDER FINANCING: Business plan

GEOGRAPHIC PREFERENCE: Santa Clara County, California

INDUSTRY PREFERENCE BY FIRM:Electronics/Computers/Lasers/
    Communications/Software/Semiconductor Production Equipment/Industrial
    Automation/Computer Peripherals

INDUSTRY PREFERENCES BY INDIVIDUAL FIRM MEMBERS:
    Peter L. Wolken—Electronics/Computers/Semiconductor Production Equip-
        ment
    David Sturdevant—Computer Software and Systems
    Chuck K. Chan—Lasers/Industrial Automation/Computer Peripherals

YEAR COMPANY ESTABLISHED: 1982

FUNDS UNDER MANAGEMENT AT COST: $20 million

MINIMUM SIZE INVESTMENT: Seed to $100,000

PREFERRED SIZE INVESTMENT: $300,000

WILL FIRM SERVE AS LEAD INVESTOR: Yes

NUMBER OF DEALS COMPLETED IN THE LAST 12 MONTHS: 2

AMOUNT INVESTED IN LAST 12 MONTHS: $2 million

AVERAGE TIME REQUIRED TO COMPLETE A DEAL: 60 days
    (From Initial Contact to Closing)

FIRM NAME: **Bay Venture Group**

ADDRESS: One Embarcadero Center
                  Suite 3303
                  San Francisco, CA 94111

PHONE: N/A

SBIC _X_ VENTURE CAPITAL FUND ____   MESBIC ____   OTHER ____

TYPES OF FINANCING PREFERRED (Stages): Seed financings/Start-up financ-
    ings

MINIMUM DATA REQUIRED TO CONSIDER FINANCING: N/A

GEOGRAPHIC PREFERENCE: San Francisco Bay area

INDUSTRY PREFERENCE BY FIRM: Optics and Lasers/Pharmaceuticals/
    Proprietary Technology/Communications/Computer Hardware and Software/
    Electronic Data Processing/Electronics and Electrical Components/Environ-
    mentalControl/High-TechnologyManufacturing/MedicalEquipmentandInstru-
    mentation/Medium Technology

INDUSTRY PREFERENCES BY INDIVIDUAL FIRM MEMBERS: All inquiries to
    William R. Chandler

YEAR COMPANY ESTABLISHED: 1981

FUNDS UNDER MANAGEMENT AT COST: N/A

MINIMUM SIZE INVESTMENT: None

PREFERRED SIZE INVESTMENT: $200,000–$500,000

WILL FIRM SERVE AS LEAD INVESTOR: Yes

NUMBER OF DEALS COMPLETED IN THE LAST 12 MONTHS: 6

AMOUNT INVESTED IN LAST 12 MONTHS: N/A

AVERAGE TIME REQUIRED TO COMPLETE A DEAL:N/A
   (From Initial Contact to Closing)

FIRM NAME: **N. C. Berkowitz & Co.**

ADDRESS: One Sutter St.
                   San Francisco, CA 94104

PHONE: (415) 788–4120

SBIC ___   VENTURE CAPITAL FUND ___   MESBIC ___   OTHER _X_

TYPES OF FINANCING PREFERRED (Stages): First stage/second stage/seed cap-
   ital/bootstrap funding/turnaround funding

MINIMUM DATA REQUIRED TO CONSIDER FINANCING: Business plan with
   heavy emphasis on product or service information. Two years, financials if
   turnaround

GEOGRAPHIC PREFERENCE: West Coast, although will look all over world for
   larger turnaround or special situations including divestitures

INDUSTRY PREFERENCE BY FIRM:No retail; otherwise will examine all legit-
   imate situations

INDUSTRY PREFERENCES BY INDIVIDUAL FIRM MEMBERS: N/A

YEAR COMPANY ESTABLISHED: 1958

FUNDS UNDER MANAGEMENT AT COST: N/A

MINIMUM SIZE INVESTMENT: None

PREFERRED SIZE INVESTMENT: $250,000

WILL FIRM SERVE AS LEAD INVESTOR: Yes

NUMBER OF DEALS COMPLETED IN THE LAST 12 MONTHS: 1

AMOUNT INVESTED IN LAST 12 MONTHS: N/A

AVERAGE TIME REQUIRED TO COMPLETE A DEAL: 60 days
   (From Initial Contact to Closing)

FIRM NAME: **Blalack–Loop, Inc.**

ADDRESS: 696 E. Colorado Blvd
                   #220
                   Pasadena, CA 91101

PHONE: (818) 449–3411

SBIC ____ VENTURE CAPITAL FUND ____ MESBIC ____ OTHER _X_

TYPES OF FINANCING PREFERRED (Stages): Early stage/start-up stage

MINIMUM DATA REQUIRED TO CONSIDER FINANCING: Business plan

GEOGRAPHIC PREFERENCE: California

INDUSTRY PREFERENCE BY FIRM: High Technology/Innovative Products/Unique Management Capabilities

INDUSTRY PREFERENCES BY INDIVIDUAL FIRM MEMBERS: N/A

YEAR COMPANY ESTABLISHED: 1969

FUNDS UNDER MANAGEMENT AT COST: In excess of $50 million

MINIMUM SIZE INVESTMENT: No minimum

PREFERRED SIZE INVESTMENT: $500,000–$5,000,000

WILL FIRM SERVE AS LEAD INVESTOR: Yes

NUMBER OF DEALS COMPLETED IN THE LAST 12 MONTHS: 3

AMOUNT INVESTED IN LAST 12 MONTHS: $9 million

AVERAGE TIME REQUIRED TO COMPLETE A DEAL: 60 days plus
(From Initial Contact to Closing)

FIRM NAME: **Capital Formation Consultants, Inc.**

ADDRESS: 185 Front St.
                  Suite 201
                  Danville, CA 94526

PHONE: (415) 820–8030

ADDRESS: 1720 Ala Moana Blvd.
                  Suite 1506B
                  Honolulu, HW 96815

PHONE: (808) 949–0544

SBIC ____ VENTURE CAPITAL FUND _X_ MESBIC ____ OTHER ____

TYPES OF FINANCING PREFERRED (Stages): Start-up or second stage

MINIMUM DATA REQUIRED TO CONSIDER FINANCING: Business plan and
background

GEOGRAPHIC PREFERENCE: Any

INDUSTRY PREFERENCE BY FIRM: Any

INDUSTRY PREFERENCES BY INDIVIDUAL FIRM MEMBERS: Any

YEAR COMPANY ESTABLISHED: 1979

FUNDS UNDER MANAGEMENT AT COST: $18 million

MINIMUM SIZE INVESTMENT: $500,000

PREFERRED SIZE INVESTMENT: $500,000–$1,000,000

WILL FIRM SERVE AS LEAD INVESTOR: Yes

NUMBER OF DEALS COMPLETED IN THE LAST 12 MONTHS: 2

AMOUNT INVESTED IN LAST 12 MONTHS: $2 million–$5 million

AVERAGE TIME REQUIRED TO COMPLETE A DEAL: 90 to 120 days
(From Initial Contact to Closing)

FIRM NAME: **Carlyle Capital Corp.**

ADDRESS: 444 S. Flower St.
Suite 4650
Los Angeles, CA 90017

PHONE: (213) 689–9235

SBIC ＿＿   VENTURE CAPITAL FUND ＿X＿   MESBIC ＿＿   OTHER ＿＿

TYPES OF FINANCING PREFERRED (Stages): Second stage or more advanced/leveraged buyouts

MINIMUM DATA REQUIRED TO CONSIDER FINANCING: Business plan plus financials

GEOGRAPHIC PREFERENCE: USA Based

INDUSTRY PREFERENCE BY FIRM: Entertainment/Communications/Leisure

INDUSTRY PREFERENCES BY INDIVIDUAL FIRM MEMBERS: Raymond A. Doig/Dennis Stanfill

YEAR COMPANY ESTABLISHED: 1983

FUNDS UNDER MANAGEMENT AT COST: $25 million

MINIMUM SIZE INVESTMENT: $500,000

PREFERRED SIZE INVESTMENT: $1 million—$3 million

WILL FIRM SERVE AS LEAD INVESTOR: Yes

NUMBER OF DEALS COMPLETED IN THE LAST 12 MONTHS: 4

AMOUNT INVESTED IN LAST 12 MONTHS: $14.95 million

AVERAGE TIME REQUIRED TO COMPLETE A DEAL: 4–12 weeks
(From Initial Contact to Closing)

FIRM NAME: **Catalyst Technologies**

ADDRESS: 1287 Lawrence Station Rd.
Sunnyvale, CA 94089

PHONE: (408) 745–1110

SBIC ＿＿   VENTURE CAPITAL FUND ＿X＿   MESBIC ＿＿   OTHER ＿＿

TYPES OF FINANCING PREFERRED (Stages): Seed/first stage

MINIMUM DATA REQUIRED TO CONSIDER FINANCING: Summary business plan

GEOGRAPHIC PREFERENCE: Northern California

INDUSTRY PREFERENCE BY FIRM: Computer Hardware/Communications/Consumer Products/Electronics

INDUSTRY PREFERENCES BY INDIVIDUAL FIRM MEMBERS: N/A

YEAR COMPANY ESTABLISHED: 1983

FUNDS UNDER MANAGEMENT AT COST: 8.25 million

MINIMUM SIZE INVESTMENT: $50,000

PREFERRED SIZE INVESTMENT: $100,000–$250,000

WILL FIRM SERVE AS LEAD INVESTOR: Yes

NUMBER OF DEALS COMPLETED IN THE LAST 12 MONTHS: 4

AMOUNT INVESTED IN LAST 12 MONTHS: $1.25 million

AVERAGE TIME REQUIRED TO COMPLETE A DEAL: 60 days
(From Initial Contact to Closing)

FIRM NAME: **Central Valley Venture Capital Corp.**

ADDRESS: 3621 Tina Pl.
                Stockton, CA 95206

PHONE: (209) 931–2505

SBIC ____   VENTURE CAPITAL FUND _X_   MESBIC ____   OTHER ____

TYPES OF FINANCING PREFERRED (Stages): All stages

MINIMUM DATA REQUIRED TO CONSIDER FINANCING: N/A

GEOGRAPHIC PREFERENCE: Central Valley (California)

INDUSTRY PREFERENCE BY FIRM:Agricultural Technology/Others

INDUSTRY PREFERENCES BY INDIVIDUAL FIRM MEMBERS:
Thomas M. Gibbs III, President
Newell Jackson, Vice president

YEAR COMPANY ESTABLISHED: 1985

FUNDS UNDER MANAGEMENT AT COST: N/A

MINIMUM SIZE INVESTMENT: $100,000 or less

PREFERRED SIZE INVESTMENT: $100,000–$200,000

WILL FIRM SERVE AS LEAD INVESTOR: Yes

NUMBER OF DEALS COMPLETED IN THE LAST 12 MONTHS: N/A

AMOUNT INVESTED IN LAST 12 MONTHS: N/A

AVERAGE TIME REQUIRED TO COMPLETE A DEAL: N/A
(From Initial Contact to Closing)

FIRM NAME: **CFB Venture Capital Corporation**

ADDRESS: P.O. Box 109
                San Diego, CA 92112

PHONE: (619) 230–3304

SBIC _X_ VENTURE CAPITAL FUND ___ MESBIC ___ OTHER ___

TYPES OF FINANCING PREFERRED (Stages): Later stage

MINIMUM DATA REQUIRED TO CONSIDER FINANCING: To be determined

GEOGRAPHIC PREFERENCE: West Coast

INDUSTRY PREFERENCE BY FIRM:Communications/Biotechnology/Research
and Technology/Computers and Peripherals/Fine Chemicals

INDUSTRY PREFERENCES BY INDIVIDUAL FIRM MEMBERS: N/A

YEAR COMPANY ESTABLISHED: 1983

FUNDS UNDER MANAGEMENT AT COST: $1.2 million

MINIMUM SIZE INVESTMENT: $100,000

PREFERRED SIZE INVESTMENT: $200,000

WILL FIRM SERVE AS LEAD INVESTOR: Yes

NUMBER OF DEALS COMPLETED IN THE LAST 12 MONTHS: 5

AMOUNT INVESTED IN LAST 12 MONTHS: $1 million

AVERAGE TIME REQUIRED TO COMPLETE A DEAL: 90 days
(From Initial Contact to Closing)

FIRM NAME: **Charter Venture Capital**

ADDRESS: 525 University Ave.
Suite 1500
Palo Alto, CA 94301

PHONE: (415) 325–6953

SBIC ___ VENTURE CAPITAL FUND _X_ MESBIC ___ OTHER ___

TYPES OF FINANCING PREFERRED (Stages): Seed/start-up/first stage/second
stage

MINIMUM DATA REQUIRED TO CONSIDER FINANCING: None

GEOGRAPHIC PREFERENCE: None

INDUSTRY PREFERENCE BY FIRM: High Technology/Electronics/Biotech-
nology

INDUSTRY PREFERENCES BY INDIVIDUAL FIRM MEMBERS: N/A

YEAR COMPANY ESTABLISHED: 1982

FUNDS UNDER MANAGEMENT AT COST: N/A

MINIMUM SIZE INVESTMENT: $100,000

PREFERRED SIZE INVESTMENT: $250,000–$500,000

WILL FIRM SERVE AS LEAD INVESTOR: Yes

NUMBER OF DEALS COMPLETED IN THE LAST 12 MONTHS: 10

AMOUNT INVESTED IN LAST 12 MONTHS: N/A

AVERAGE TIME REQUIRED TO COMPLETE A DEAL: 3 months
(From Initial Contact to Closing)

FIRM NAME: **Churchill International**

ADDRESS: 444 Market St.   9 Riverside Rd.
                25th Floor   Weston, MA 02193
                San Francisco, CA 94111

PHONE: (415) 398–7677   (617) 893–6555

ADDRESS: 545 Middlefield Rd.
                Menlo Park, CA 94025

PHONE: (415) 328–4401

SBIC ____ VENTURE CAPITAL FUND _X_ MESBIC ____ OTHER ____

TYPES OF FINANCING PREFERRED (Stages): First, second, and third stages

MINIMUM DATA REQUIRED TO CONSIDER FINANCING: Detailed business
    plan

GEOGRAPHIC PREFERENCE: None

INDUSTRY PREFERENCE BY FIRM: Advanced Materials/Artificial Intelli-
    gence/Communications/Computer Integrated Manufacturing/Computer and
    Computer Peripherals/Semiconductors and Support Technology/Software/
    Test and Measurement Equipment

INDUSTRY PREFERENCES BY INDIVIDUAL FIRM MEMBERS: N/A

YEAR COMPANY ESTABLISHED: 1978

FUNDS UNDER MANAGEMENT AT COST: $97.2 million

MINIMUM SIZE INVESTMENT: $250,000

PREFERRED SIZE INVESTMENT: $250,000–$1,200,000

WILL FIRM SERVE AS LEAD INVESTOR: If approved by investment committee

NUMBER OF DEALS COMPLETED IN THE LAST 12 MONTHS: 22

AMOUNT INVESTED IN LAST 12 MONTHS: $12.675 million

AVERAGE TIME REQUIRED TO COMPLETE A DEAL: 2 months
    (From Initial Contact to Closing)

FIRM NAME: **City Ventures, Inc.**

ADDRESS: 1880 Century Park East
                Suite 413
                Los Angeles, CA 90067

PHONE: (213) 550–0416

SBIC _X_ VENTURE CAPITAL FUND ____ MESBIC ____ OTHER ____

TYPES OF FINANCING PREFERRED (Stages): Second or third stage/expansion
    financing/management buyouts

MINIMUM DATA REQUIRED TO CONSIDER FINANCING: Business plan con-
    taining current financials, projections, and management backgrounds

GEOGRAPHIC PREFERENCE: No preference

INDUSTRY PREFERENCE BY FIRM: Communications/Medical and Industrial Instrumentation/Analytical Instruments/Computer-Related Products/Chemical Products/Commercial Industrial Products/Consumer Products and Services

INDUSTRY PREFERENCES BY INDIVIDUAL FIRM MEMBERS: All partners handle inquiries in all areas of interest to firm

YEAR COMPANY ESTABLISHED: 1982

FUNDS UNDER MANAGEMENT AT COST: $2 million

MINIMUM SIZE INVESTMENT: $100,000

PREFERRED SIZE INVESTMENT: $200,000–$350,000

WILL FIRM SERVE AS LEAD INVESTOR: N/A

NUMBER OF DEALS COMPLETED IN THE LAST 12 MONTHS: 5

AMOUNT INVESTED IN LAST 12 MONTHS: 1.15 million

AVERAGE TIME REQUIRED TO COMPLETE A DEAL: 4–12 weeks (From Initial Contact to Closing)

FIRM NAME: **CommTech International**

ADDRESS: 545 Middlefield Rd.
              Suite 180
              Menlo Park, CA 94025

PHONE: (415) 328-0191

SBIC ____ VENTURE CAPITAL FUND ____ MESBIC ____ OTHER _X_ (Technology development and commercialization fund)

TYPES OF FINANCING PREFERRED (Stages): Seed and early stage/technologies that can form basis for start-ups

MINIMUM DATA REQUIRED TO CONSIDER FINANCING: Full description of technology/patent protection or other proprietary aspects/comparison with competition and markets

GEOGRAPHIC PREFERENCE: Western U.S.A.

INDUSTRY PREFERENCE BY FIRM: N/A

INDUSTRY PREFERENCES BY INDIVIDUAL FIRM MEMBERS: N/A

YEAR COMPANY ESTABLISHED: 1983

FUNDS UNDER MANAGEMENT AT COST: $12 million

MINIMUM SIZE INVESTMENT: $100,000 seed capital

PREFERRED SIZE INVESTMENT: $500,000 plus

WILL FIRM SERVE AS LEAD INVESTOR: Yes

NUMBER OF DEALS COMPLETED IN THE LAST 12 MONTHS: 1

AMOUNT INVESTED IN LAST 12 MONTHS: $3.5 million

AVERAGE TIME REQUIRED TO COMPLETE A DEAL: Variable; 6 months–1 year
(From Initial Contact to Closing)

FIRM NAME: **Continental Capital Ventures**

ADDRESS: 3000 Sand Hill Rd.   555 California St.
               Building 1, Suite 135   Suite 5070
               Menlo Park, CA 94025   San Francisco, CA 94104

PHONE: N/A   N/A

SBIC ____ VENTURE CAPITAL FUND _X_ MESBIC ____ OTHER ____

TYPES OF FINANCING PREFERRED (Stages): Start-up financings (first major round)/second and third round financings

MINIMUM DATA REQUIRED TO CONSIDER FINANCING: Business plan or executive summary

GEOGRAPHIC PREFERENCE: Pacific and mountain time zones

INDUSTRY PREFERENCE BY FIRM: Communications/Computer Hardware and Software/Electronics and Electrical Components/High Technology/Energy/ Manufacturing/Medical Equipment and Instrumentation/Medical Sciences/ Optics and Lasers/Proprietary Technology

INDUSTRY PREFERENCES BY INDIVIDUAL FIRM MEMBERS:
Frank G. Chambers   Lawrance A. Brown
William A. Boeger   Donald R. Scheuch

YEAR COMPANY ESTABLISHED: 1959

FUNDS UNDER MANAGEMENT AT COST: $35 million

MINIMUM SIZE INVESTMENT: $100,000– $250,000 (minimum initial commit-
                         ment)
                         $1,250,000 (maximum initial commitment)

PREFERRED SIZE INVESTMENT: $250,000–$1,000,000

WILL FIRM SERVE AS LEAD INVESTOR: Yes

NUMBER OF DEALS COMPLETED IN THE LAST 12 MONTHS: 11

AMOUNT INVESTED IN LAST 12 MONTHS: $4.8 million

AVERAGE TIME REQUIRED TO COMPLETE A DEAL: 30–45 days
(From Initial Contact to Closing)

FIRM NAME: **Cornell Capital Corp.**

ADDRESS: 2049 Century Park E.
               #1200
               Los Angeles, CA 90067

PHONE: (213) 277–7993

SBIC _X_ VENTURE CAPITAL FUND ____ MESBIC ____ OTHER ____

TYPES OF FINANCING PREFERRED (Stages): Initial or seed money

MINIMUM DATA REQUIRED TO CONSIDER FINANCING: N/A

GEOGRAPHIC PREFERENCE: Los Angeles, California, or New York City

INDUSTRY PREFERENCE BY FIRM: Non-high Technology

INDUSTRY PREFERENCES BY INDIVIDUAL FIRM MEMBERS: N/A

YEAR COMPANY ESTABLISHED: 1980

FUNDS UNDER MANAGEMENT AT COST: N/A

MINIMUM SIZE INVESTMENT: $100,000

PREFERRED SIZE INVESTMENT: $100,000 plus

WILL FIRM SERVE AS LEAD INVESTOR: Yes

NUMBER OF DEALS COMPLETED IN THE LAST 12 MONTHS: 8

AMOUNT INVESTED IN LAST 12 MONTHS: N/A

AVERAGE TIME REQUIRED TO COMPLETE A DEAL: 3 months
(From Initial Contact to Closing)

FIRM NAME: **Crosspoint Venture Partners**

ADDRESS: 1951 Landings Dr.
Mountain View, CA 94043

PHONE: (415)964-3545

ADDRESS: 4600 Campus Dr.
Suite 103
Newport Beach, CA 92660

PHONE: (714) 852-1611

SBIC ____   VENTURE CAPITAL FUND _X_   MESBIC ____   OTHER ____

TYPES OF FINANCING PREFERRED (Stages): Start-up stage technology companies

MINIMUM DATA REQUIRED TO CONSIDER FINANCING: Executive summary of product, market, and people

GEOGRAPHIC PREFERENCE: West Coast, Northwest, Rocky Mountain, Southwest, and Midwest

INDUSTRY PREFERENCE BY FIRM: Communications/Computer Software and Systems/Computer Peripherals/Medical Products and Instruments/Semiconductor Devices and Equipment/Industrial Automation and Controls/Instrumentation/Related Service and Distribution Businesses

INDUSTRY PREFERENCES BY INDIVIDUAL FIRM MEMBERS:
Frederick J. Dotzler—Medical
James F. Willenbory—Computer Software
William P. Cargile—Communications and Computer Peripherals
John B. Mumford—Industrial Automation and Controls/Semiconductor
Robert A. Hoff—Medical and Computer Related

YEAR COMPANY ESTABLISHED: 1972

FUNDS UNDER MANAGEMENT AT COST: $65 million

MINIMUM SIZE INVESTMENT: $50,000

PREFERRED SIZE INVESTMENT: $500,000–$1,000,000

WILL FIRM SERVE AS LEAD INVESTOR: Typically, lead or sole investor

NUMBER OF DEALS COMPLETED IN THE LAST 12 MONTHS: 16

AMOUNT INVESTED IN LAST 12 MONTHS: $10.5 million

AVERAGE TIME REQUIRED TO COMPLETE A DEAL: 30 days
(From Initial Contact to Closing)

FIRM NAME:　　**Developers Equity Capital Corp.**

ADDRESS:　　　9201 Wilshire Blvd.
　　　　　　　Suite 204
　　　　　　　Beverly Hills, CA 90210

PHONE:　　　　(213) 278–3611

SBIC _X_ VENTURE CAPITAL FUND ___ MESBIC ___ OTHER ___

TYPES OF FINANCING PREFERRED (Stages): Growth financing for ongoing
concerns

MINIMUM DATA REQUIRED TO CONSIDER FINANCING: Comprehensive
business plan

GEOGRAPHIC PREFERENCE: West Coast

INDUSTRY PREFERENCE BY FIRM: Diversified portfolio; firm has expertise in
the real estate development field

INDUSTRY PREFERENCES BY INDIVIDUAL FIRM MEMBERS:
Larry Sade　　　　　　　　　　Mark Brandstein
Dennis J. Shea

YEAR COMPANY ESTABLISHED: 1964

FUNDS UNDER MANAGEMENT AT COST: $1 million

MINIMUM SIZE INVESTMENT: $75,000

PREFERRED SIZE INVESTMENT: $75,000–$100,000

WILL FIRM SERVE AS LEAD INVESTOR: Yes, particularly in real estate

NUMBER OF DEALS COMPLETED IN THE LAST 12 MONTHS: 8

AMOUNT INVESTED IN LAST 12 MONTHS: $480,000

AVERAGE TIME REQUIRED TO COMPLETE A DEAL: 2 months
(From Initial Contact to Closing)

FIRM NAME:　　**Diehl, Brown & Co.**

ADDRESS:　　　1201 Dove St.
　　　　　　　Newport Beach, CA 92660

PHONE:　　　　(714) 955–2000

SBIC ___ VENTURE CAPITAL FUND ___ MESBIC ___
OTHER _X_ (investment firm)

TYPES OF FINANCING PREFERRED (Stages): Initial

MINIMUM DATA REQUIRED TO CONSIDER FINANCING: Business plan

GEOGRAPHIC PREFERENCE: Southern California

INDUSTRY PREFERENCE BY FIRM: Technology

INDUSTRY PREFERENCES BY INDIVIDUAL FIRM MEMBERS:
Michael Henton—Medical, Electronics
Jack Norberg—Software
R. R. Diehl—Financial Institutions

YEAR COMPANY ESTABLISHED: 1978

FUNDS UNDER MANAGEMENT AT COST: N/A

MINIMUM SIZE INVESTMENT: $200,000

PREFERRED SIZE INVESTMENT: $250,000

WILL FIRM SERVE AS LEAD INVESTOR: Yes

NUMBER OF DEALS COMPLETED IN THE LAST 12 MONTHS: N/A

AMOUNT INVESTED IN LAST 12 MONTHS: N/A

AVERAGE TIME REQUIRED TO COMPLETE A DEAL: 90 days
(From Initial Contact to Closing)

FIRM NAME: **Douger, Jones & Wilder**

ADDRESS: 3 Embarcadero Center
                   Suite 1980
                   San Francisco, CA 94111

PHONE: (415) 434–1722

SBIC ____   VENTURE CAPITAL FUND _X_   MESBIC ____   OTHER ____

TYPES OF FINANCING PREFERRED (Stages): All stages

MINIMUM DATA REQUIRED TO CONSIDER FINANCING: Business plan

GEOGRAPHIC PREFERENCE: Northwestern, western, and southwestern USA

INDUSTRY PREFERENCE BY FIRM: N/A

INDUSTRY PREFERENCES BY INDIVIDUAL FIRM MEMBERS: N/A

YEAR COMPANY ESTABLISHED: 1981

FUNDS UNDER MANAGEMENT AT COST: $86 million

MINIMUM SIZE INVESTMENT: $250,000

PREFERRED SIZE INVESTMENT: $750,000

WILL FIRM SERVE AS LEAD INVESTOR: Yes

NUMBER OF DEALS COMPLETED IN THE LAST 12 MONTHS: 12

AMOUNT INVESTED IN LAST 12 MONTHS: $10 million

AVERAGE TIME REQUIRED TO COMPLETE A DEAL: 90 days
(From Initial Contact to Closing)

FIRM NAME: **EMC II Venture Partners**

ADDRESS: 701 East B St.
Suite 1500
San Diego, CA 92101

PHONE: (619) 239–6866

SBIC ____ VENTURE CAPITAL FUND _X_ MESBIC ____ OTHER ____

TYPES OF FINANCING PREFERRED (Stages): Early stage financings pre-
ferred/pre-seed/start-up/first and second stages/will also finance leveraged
acquisitions

MINIMUM DATA REQUIRED TO CONSIDER FINANCING: Business plan describing key aspects of management, the market opportunity, product, or service intended to exploit the market opportunity, projected financial results
over 5-year planning horizon, and capital requirements

GEOGRAPHIC PREFERENCE: Principally Southwest for start-up; no preference
for later stage

INDUSTRY PREFERENCE BY FIRM: None; investment policy not restricted

INDUSTRY PREFERENCES BY INDIVIDUAL FIRM MEMBERS:
Ray W. McKewon—Various
Allan J. Grant—Various
Hans W. Schoepflin—Various
Bradley B. Gordon—Various

YEAR COMPANY ESTABLISHED: 1980

FUNDS UNDER MANAGEMENT AT COST: $11 million

MINIMUM SIZE INVESTMENT: $250,000

PREFERRED SIZE INVESTMENT: $250,000–$1,500,000

WILL FIRM SERVE AS LEAD INVESTOR: Yes, will originate

NUMBER OF DEALS COMPLETED IN THE LAST 12 MONTHS: 2

AMOUNT INVESTED IN LAST 12 MONTHS: Approximately $1 million

AVERAGE TIME REQUIRED TO COMPLETE A DEAL: 6–8 weeks (varies with
(From Initial Contact to Closing)   nature of project)

FIRM NAME: **Enterprise Venture Capital Corp.**

ADDRESS: 1922 The Alameda
Suite 306
San Jose, CA 95126

PHONE: (408) 249–3507

SBIC _X_ VENTURE CAPITAL FUND ____ MESBIC ____ OTHER ____

TYPES OF FINANCING PREFERRED (Stages): First and second stages

MINIMUM DATA REQUIRED TO CONSIDER FINANCING: Annual sales/profits
projected after 1 year

GEOGRAPHIC PREFERENCE: West Coast region

INDUSTRY PREFERENCE BY FIRM: Diversified

INDUSTRY PREFERENCES BY INDIVIDUAL FIRM MEMBERS: N/A

YEAR COMPANY ESTABLISHED: 1983

FUNDS UNDER MANAGEMENT AT COST: $1 million

MINIMUM SIZE INVESTMENT: $50,000

PREFERRED SIZE INVESTMENT: $100,000

WILL FIRM SERVE AS LEAD INVESTOR: Yes

NUMBER OF DEALS COMPLETED IN THE LAST 12 MONTHS: 8

AMOUNT INVESTED IN LAST 12 MONTHS: $725,000

AVERAGE TIME REQUIRED TO COMPLETE A DEAL: 2 months
(From Initial Contact to Closing)

FIRM NAME: **Euro/America Technology Investments, Inc.**

ADDRESS: 2121 S. El Camino Real
                 Suite 1000
                 San Mateo, CA 94403

PHONE: (415) 345–8523

SBIC ____   VENTURE CAPITAL FUND __X__   MESBIC ____   OTHER ____

TYPES OF FINANCING PREFERRED (Stages): All stages

MINIMUM DATA REQUIRED TO CONSIDER FINANCING: N/A

GEOGRAPHIC PREFERENCE: USA/Europe

INDUSTRY PREFERENCE BY FIRM: Any

INDUSTRY PREFERENCES BY INDIVIDUAL FIRM MEMBERS:
Flemming Fischer, President
Allan Robb, Vice-president

YEAR COMPANY ESTABLISHED: 1983

FUNDS UNDER MANAGEMENT AT COST: N/A

MINIMUM SIZE INVESTMENT: $100,000 or less

PREFERRED SIZE INVESTMENT: $100,000–$200,000

WILL FIRM SERVE AS LEAD INVESTOR: Yes

NUMBER OF DEALS COMPLETED IN THE LAST 12 MONTHS: N/A

AMOUNT INVESTED IN LAST 12 MONTHS: N/A

AVERAGE TIME REQUIRED TO COMPLETE A DEAL: N/A
(From Initial Contact to Closing)

FIRM NAME: First California Business and Industrial Development Corporation

ADDRESS: 3931 MacArthur Blvd.   130 Montgomery St.
                 Suite 212   6th Floor
                 Newport Beach, CA 92660   San Francisco, CA 94104

PHONE: (714) 851–0855   (415) 392–5410

SBIC ____ VENTURE CAPITAL FUND ____ MESBIC ____ OTHER _X_

TYPES OF FINANCING PREFERRED (Stages): Start-ups/second stage/buyouts/ acquisitions/owner-occupied facility/equipment

MINIMUM DATA REQUIRED TO CONSIDER FINANCING: 3 years financial statements and tax returns, business history, management resumes, financial statements of principal, cash flow pro forma

GEOGRAPHIC PREFERENCE: No preference

INDUSTRY PREFERENCE BY FIRM: No preference

INDUSTRY PREFERENCES BY INDIVIDUAL FIRM MEMBERS: N/A

YEAR COMPANY ESTABLISHED: 1978

FUNDS UNDER MANAGEMENT AT COST: $5 million

MINIMUM SIZE INVESTMENT: $75,000

PREFERRED SIZE INVESTMENT: $500,000

WILL FIRM SERVE AS LEAD INVESTOR: N/A

NUMBER OF DEALS COMPLETED IN THE LAST 12 MONTHS: 12

AMOUNT INVESTED IN LAST 12 MONTHS: $4 million

AVERAGE TIME REQUIRED TO COMPLETE A DEAL: 60 days
     (From Initial Contact to Closing)

FIRM NAME: Genesis Capital Limited Partnership

ADDRESS: 20813 Stevens Creek Blvd.
                 #101
                 Cupertino, CA 95014

PHONE: N/A

SBIC ____ VENTURE CAPITAL FUND _X_ MESBIC ____ OTHER ____

TYPES OF FINANCING PREFERRED (Stages): Start-up/first and second stages

MINIMUM DATA REQUIRED TO CONSIDER FINANCING: Business plan

GEOGRAPHIC PREFERENCE: West Coast

INDUSTRY PREFERENCE BY FIRM: Communications/Computer Related/Electronic Components and Instrumentation/Industrial Products and Equipment/Medical

INDUSTRY PREFERENCES BY INDIVIDUAL FIRM MEMBERS: N/A

YEAR COMPANY ESTABLISHED: 1982

FUNDS UNDER MANAGEMENT AT COST: $20 million

MINIMUM SIZE INVESTMENT: $100,000

PREFERRED SIZE INVESTMENT: $300,000–$600,000

WILL FIRM SERVE AS LEAD INVESTOR: Yes

NUMBER OF DEALS COMPLETED IN THE LAST 12 MONTHS: 6

AMOUNT INVESTED IN LAST 12 MONTHS: $2 million

AVERAGE TIME REQUIRED TO COMPLETE A DEAL: 3 months
    (From Initial Contact to Closing)

FIRM NAME: **Girard Capital, Inc.**

ADDRESS: 9191 Towne Centre Dr.
                  Suite 370
                  San Diego, CA 92122

PHONE: (619) 457–5114

SBIC ____   VENTURE CAPITAL FUND _X_   MESBIC ____   OTHER ____

TYPES OF FINANCING PREFERRED (Stages): Early stage/start-up/buyouts

MINIMUM DATA REQUIRED TO CONSIDER FINANCING: Business plan

GEOGRAPHIC PREFERENCE: Southwest USA

INDUSTRY PREFERENCE BY FIRM: Communications/Computer Related/
    Distribution/Electronic Components and Instrumentation/Energy/Natural
    Resources/Genetic Engineering/Industrial Products and Equipment/Medical/
    Real Estate/Financial Services

INDUSTRY PREFERENCES BY INDIVIDUAL FIRM MEMBERS: N/A

YEAR COMPANY ESTABLISHED: 1976

FUNDS UNDER MANAGEMENT AT COST: $25 million

MINIMUM SIZE INVESTMENT: $250,000

PREFERRED SIZE INVESTMENT: $500,000

WILL FIRM SERVE AS LEAD INVESTOR: Yes

NUMBER OF DEALS COMPLETED IN THE LAST 12 MONTHS: 1

AMOUNT INVESTED IN LAST 12 MONTHS: $500,000

AVERAGE TIME REQUIRED TO COMPLETE A DEAL: 120 days
    (From Initial Contact to Closing)

FIRM NAME: **Glenwood Management**

ADDRESS: 3000 Sand Hill Rd.
                  Building 3, Suite 250
                  Menlo Park, CA 94025

PHONE: (415) 854–8070

SBIC ____   VENTURE CAPITAL FUND _X_   MESBIC ____   OTHER ____

TYPES OF FINANCING PREFERRED (Stages): Initial and early stage financing

MINIMUM DATA REQUIRED TO CONSIDER FINANCING: Detailed business plan

GEOGRAPHIC PREFERENCE: Western USA

INDUSTRY PREFERENCE BY FIRM: Computers/Telecommunications/Instrumentation/Robotics-Automatics/Engineering/Semiconductor-related Equipment

INDUSTRY PREFERENCES BY INDIVIDUAL FIRM MEMBERS: N/A

YEAR COMPANY ESTABLISHED: 1982

FUNDS UNDER MANAGEMENT AT COST: $17 million

MINIMUM SIZE INVESTMENT: $50,000

PREFERRED SIZE INVESTMENT: $500,000

WILL FIRM SERVE AS LEAD INVESTOR: Yes

NUMBER OF DEALS COMPLETED IN THE LAST 12 MONTHS: 8

AMOUNT INVESTED IN LAST 12 MONTHS: $3.5 million

AVERAGE TIME REQUIRED TO COMPLETE A DEAL: 3–6 weeks
(From Initial Contact to Closing)

FIRM NAME: **Glover Capital Corp.**

ADDRESS: 199 S. Los Robles Ave.
                #625
                Pasadena, CA 91101

PHONE: (818) 795–6910

SBIC ___   VENTURE CAPITAL FUND ___   MESBIC ___   OTHER _X_

TYPES OF FINANCING PREFERRED (Stages): Second expansionary

MINIMUM DATA REQUIRED TO CONSIDER FINANCING: 3 years of financials; meeting with senior controller and chairman

GEOGRAPHIC PREFERENCE: Pacific Basin

INDUSTRY PREFERENCE BY FIRM: Direct Mail Catalog/Light Manufacturing/Service Organization

INDUSTRY PREFERENCES BY INDIVIDUAL FIRM MEMBERS: N/A

YEAR COMPANY ESTABLISHED: 1983

FUNDS UNDER MANAGEMENT AT COST: $1 million

MINIMUM SIZE INVESTMENT: $50,000

PREFERRED SIZE INVESTMENT: $100,000

WILL FIRM SERVE AS LEAD INVESTOR: Not usually

NUMBER OF DEALS COMPLETED IN THE LAST 12 MONTHS: 3

AMOUNT INVESTED IN LAST 12 MONTHS: $650,000

AVERAGE TIME REQUIRED TO COMPLETE A DEAL: 1 month
(From Initial Contact to Closing)

FIRM NAME: **Golden Gate Investments, Inc.**

ADDRESS: 2121 S. El Camino Real
San Mateo, CA 94403

PHONE: (415) 345–9900

SBIC ____   VENTURE CAPITAL FUND _X_   MESBIC ____   OTHER ____

TYPES OF FINANCING PREFERRED (Stages): Seed/start-up/troubled company/complex situations

MINIMUM DATA REQUIRED TO CONSIDER FINANCING: N/A

GEOGRAPHIC PREFERENCE: USA, Asia, Europe

INDUSTRY PREFERENCE BY FIRM: Any

INDUSTRY PREFERENCES BY INDIVIDUAL FIRM MEMBERS:
A. Larry Lundsey, President

YEAR COMPANY ESTABLISHED: 1972

FUNDS UNDER MANAGEMENT AT COST: N/A

MINIMUM SIZE INVESTMENT: $100,000 or less

PREFERRED SIZE INVESTMENT: $300,000–$600,000

WILL FIRM SERVE AS LEAD INVESTOR: Yes

NUMBER OF DEALS COMPLETED IN THE LAST 12 MONTHS: N/A

AMOUNT INVESTED IN LAST 12 MONTHS: N/A

AVERAGE TIME REQUIRED TO COMPLETE A DEAL: N/A
(From Initial Contact to Closing)

FIRM NAME: **Grace Ventures Corporation**

ADDRESS: 630 Hansen Way
Suite 260
Palo Alto, CA 94304

PHONE: (415) 424–1171

SBIC ____   VENTURE CAPITAL FUND _X_   MESBIC ____   OTHER ____

TYPES OF FINANCING PREFERRED (Stages): All stages

MINIMUM DATA REQUIRED TO CONSIDER FINANCING: Business plan (except seed financings will review product and marketing concept paper)

GEOGRAPHIC PREFERENCE: None

INDUSTRY PREFERENCE BY FIRM: Technological Orientation (e.g., Electronics, Communication, Medical Instrumentation, Specialty Materials, Optoelectronics)

INDUSTRY PREFERENCES BY INDIVIDUAL FIRM MEMBERS: N/A

YEAR COMPANY ESTABLISHED: 1982 (previous name was Ven-Tech Two, Inc.)

FUNDS UNDER MANAGEMENT AT COST: N/A

MINIMUM SIZE INVESTMENT: No minimum

PREFERRED SIZE INVESTMENT: $500,000—$1,000,000

WILL FIRM SERVE AS LEAD INVESTOR: Yes

NUMBER OF DEALS COMPLETED IN THE LAST 12 MONTHS: 18

AMOUNT INVESTED IN LAST 12 MONTHS: $9 million

AVERAGE TIME REQUIRED TO COMPLETE A DEAL: 1–2 months
(From Initial Contact to Closing)

FIRM NAME: **Hallador, Inc.**

ADDRESS: 1435 River Park Dr.
                  Suite 505
                  Sacramento, CA 95815

PHONE: (916) 920–0191

SBIC ___ VENTURE CAPITAL FUND _X_ MESBIC ___ OTHER ___

TYPES OF FINANCING PREFERRED (Stages): Seed/first and second stages

MINIMUM DATA REQUIRED TO CONSIDER FINANCING: Business plan

GEOGRAPHIC PREFERENCE: West Coast

INDUSTRY PREFERENCE BY FIRM: Electronic Instruments/Electronic Test
Equipment/Media/Computer Peripherals and Enhancement Devices/Communications

INDUSTRY PREFERENCES BY INDIVIDUAL FIRM MEMBERS: Initial inquiries to Chris L. Branscum, Vice-president—Venture Capital

YEAR COMPANY ESTABLISHED: 1979

FUNDS UNDER MANAGEMENT AT COST: $5 million

MINIMUM SIZE INVESTMENT: $100,000

PREFERRED SIZE INVESTMENT: $250,000–$500,000

WILL FIRM SERVE AS LEAD INVESTOR: Yes

NUMBER OF DEALS COMPLETED IN THE LAST 12 MONTHS: 6

AMOUNT INVESTED IN LAST 12 MONTHS: $2 million

AVERAGE TIME REQUIRED TO COMPLETE A DEAL: 60 days
(From Initial Contact to Closing)

FIRM NAME: **Hambrecht & Quist Venture Partners**

ADDRESS: 235 Montgomery St.
                  San Francisco, CA 94104

PHONE: (415) 576–3333

SBIC ___ VENTURE CAPITAL FUND ___ MESBIC ___ OTHER _X_
(Venture capital fund manager)

TYPES OF FINANCING PREFERRED (Stages): All stages

MINIMUM DATA REQUIRED TO CONSIDER FINANCING: Business plan

GEOGRAPHIC PREFERENCE: USA

INDUSTRY PREFERENCE BY FIRM: All high-technology industries

INDUSTRY PREFERENCES BY INDIVIDUAL FIRM MEMBERS: N/A

YEAR COMPANY ESTABLISHED: 1968

FUNDS UNDER MANAGEMENT AT COST: Over $350 million

MINIMUM SIZE INVESTMENT: None

PREFERRED SIZE INVESTMENT: $500,000 plus

WILL FIRM SERVE AS LEAD INVESTOR: Yes, preferably

NUMBER OF DEALS COMPLETED IN THE LAST 12 MONTHS: 118

AMOUNT INVESTED IN LAST 12 MONTHS: $95 million

AVERAGE TIME REQUIRED TO COMPLETE A DEAL: 2 months
(From Initial Contact to Closing)

FIRM NAME: **Happ Ventures**

ADDRESS: 444 Castro St.
                  Suite 400
                  Mountain View, CA 94041

PHONE: (415) 961–1115

SBIC _____   VENTURE CAPITAL FUND _X_   MESBIC _____   OTHER _____

TYPES OF FINANCING PREFERRED (Stages): R&D partnerships/seed/first round

MINIMUM DATA REQUIRED TO CONSIDER FINANCING: Preliminary business plan

GEOGRAPHIC PREFERENCE: None

INDUSTRY PREFERENCE BY FIRM: Communications/Computer Related/Electronic Components and Instrumentation/Industrial Products and Equipment/Medical–Health Related

INDUSTRY PREFERENCES BY INDIVIDUAL FIRM MEMBERS:
William D. Happ

YEAR COMPANY ESTABLISHED: 1982

FUNDS UNDER MANAGEMENT AT COST: N/A

MINIMUM SIZE INVESTMENT: $100,000

PREFERRED SIZE INVESTMENT: $300,000–$600,000

WILL FIRM SERVE AS LEAD INVESTOR: Yes

NUMBER OF DEALS COMPLETED IN THE LAST 12 MONTHS: 3

AMOUNT INVESTED IN LAST 12 MONTHS: N/A

AVERAGE TIME REQUIRED TO COMPLETE A DEAL: 4–6 months
(From Initial Contact to Closing)

FIRM NAME: Hawaii–Pacific Venture Capital Corp.

ADDRESS: 2121 S. El Camino Real
Suite 1000
San Mateo, CA 94403

PHONE: (415) 573–0806

SBIC ____ VENTURE CAPITAL FUND _X_ MESBIC ____ OTHER ____

TYPES OF FINANCING PREFERRED (Stages): All stages

MINIMUM DATA REQUIRED TO CONSIDER FINANCING: N/A

GEOGRAPHIC PREFERENCE: USA, Europe, and Asia

INDUSTRY PREFERENCE BY FIRM: Any

INDUSTRY PREFERENCES BY INDIVIDUAL FIRM MEMBERS:
Michael Yang, President
Raymond Y. C. Ho, Chairman

YEAR COMPANY ESTABLISHED: 1984

FUNDS UNDER MANAGEMENT AT COST: N/A

MINIMUM SIZE INVESTMENT: $100,000 or less

PREFERRED SIZE INVESTMENT: $100,000–$200,000

WILL FIRM SERVE AS LEAD INVESTOR: N/A

NUMBER OF DEALS COMPLETED IN THE LAST 12 MONTHS: N/A

AMOUNT INVESTED IN LAST 12 MONTHS: N/A

AVERAGE TIME REQUIRED TO COMPLETE A DEAL: N/A
(From Initial Contact to Closing)

FIRM NAME: Health/Medical Investments, Inc.

ADDRESS: 2121 S. El Camino Real
Suite 1000
San Mateo, CA 94403

PHONE: (415) 345–8500

SBIC ____ VENTURE CAPITAL FUND _X_ MESBIC ____ OTHER ____

TYPES OF FINANCING PREFERRED (Stages): All stages

MINIMUM DATA REQUIRED TO CONSIDER FINANCING: N/A

GEOGRAPHIC PREFERENCE: USA, Europe, and Asia

INDUSTRY PREFERENCE BY FIRM: Health/Medical/Biotechnology

INDUSTRY PREFERENCES BY INDIVIDUAL FIRM MEMBERS:
Norman Brown—Health/Medical and Biotechnology
Linda Mak—Health/Medical and Biotechnology

YEAR COMPANY ESTABLISHED: 1983

FUNDS UNDER MANAGEMENT AT COST: N/A

MINIMUM SIZE INVESTMENT: $100,000 or less

PREFERRED SIZE INVESTMENT: $100,000–$200,000

WILL FIRM SERVE AS LEAD INVESTOR: Yes

NUMBER OF DEALS COMPLETED IN THE LAST 12 MONTHS: N/A

AMOUNT INVESTED IN LAST 12 MONTHS: N/A

AVERAGE TIME REQUIRED TO COMPLETE A DEAL: N/A
(From Initial Contact to Closing)

FIRM NAME: **Health/Medical Ventures**

ADDRESS: 2121 S. El Camino Real
Suite 1000
San Mateo, CA 94403

PHONE: (415) 345–8500

SBIC ____   VENTURE CAPITAL FUND _X_   MESBIC ____   OTHER ____

TYPES OF FINANCING PREFERRED (Stages): All stages

MINIMUM DATA REQUIRED TO CONSIDER FINANCING: N/A

GEOGRAPHIC PREFERENCE: California

INDUSTRY PREFERENCE BY FIRM: Health/Medical/Biotechnology

INDUSTRY PREFERENCES BY INDIVIDUAL FIRM MEMBERS:
Norman Brown, President
Anthony J. D'Eustachio, Vice-chairman

YEAR COMPANY ESTABLISHED: 1985

FUNDS UNDER MANAGEMENT AT COST: N/A

MINIMUM SIZE INVESTMENT: $100,000 or less

PREFERRED SIZE INVESTMENT: $100,000–$200,000

WILL FIRM SERVE AS LEAD INVESTOR: Yes

NUMBER OF DEALS COMPLETED IN THE LAST 12 MONTHS: N/A

AMOUNT INVESTED IN LAST 12 MONTHS: N/A

AVERAGE TIME REQUIRED TO COMPLETE A DEAL: N/A
(From Initial Contact to Closing)

FIRM NAME: **Hoebich Venture Management, Inc.**

ADDRESS: 850 Hamilton Ave.
Palo Alto, CA 94301

PHONE: (415) 326–5590

SBIC ____   VENTURE CAPITAL FUND ____   MESBIC ____   OTHER _X_

TYPES OF FINANCING PREFERRED (Stages): Start-up

MINIMUM DATA REQUIRED TO CONSIDER FINANCING: Experienced people

GEOGRAPHIC PREFERENCE: Northern California, 15 minutes from office

INDUSTRY PREFERENCE BY FIRM: Technology

INDUSTRY PREFERENCES BY INDIVIDUAL FIRM MEMBERS:
Christian Hoebich

YEAR COMPANY ESTABLISHED: 1971

FUNDS UNDER MANAGEMENT AT COST: N/A

MINIMUM SIZE INVESTMENT: $5,000–$10,000

PREFERRED SIZE INVESTMENT: $50,000

WILL FIRM SERVE AS LEAD INVESTOR: Yes

NUMBER OF DEALS COMPLETED IN THE LAST 12 MONTHS: 3

AMOUNT INVESTED IN LAST 12 MONTHS: $100,000

AVERAGE TIME REQUIRED TO COMPLETE A DEAL: 4 weeks
(From Initial Contact to Closing)

FIRM NAME: **Inodsuez Technology Group**

ADDRESS: 3000 Sand Hill Rd.
Building 4, Suite 130
Menlo Park, CA 94025

PHONE: (415) 854–0587

SBIC ___ VENTURE CAPITAL FUND _X_ MESBIC ___ OTHER ___

TYPES OF FINANCING PREFERRED (Stages): All

MINIMUM DATA REQUIRED TO CONSIDER FINANCING: Business plan, complete financials (actual or forecast)

GEOGRAPHIC PREFERENCE: West Coast

INDUSTRY PREFERENCE BY FIRM: Electronics/Computer Related Including Applications/Biotechnology/Health Care

INDUSTRY PREFERENCES BY INDIVIDUAL FIRM MEMBERS:
Philippe Sevin—All Areas
David Gold—All Areas

YEAR COMPANY ESTABLISHED: 1985

FUNDS UNDER MANAGEMENT AT COST: Approximately $30 million

MINIMUM SIZE INVESTMENT: Any

PREFERRED SIZE INVESTMENT: Up to $1.0 million

WILL FIRM SERVE AS LEAD INVESTOR: Yes

NUMBER OF DEALS COMPLETED IN THE LAST 12 MONTHS: 8 in the last 6 months

AMOUNT INVESTED IN LAST 12 MONTHS: Approximately $3.5 million in the last 6 months

AVERAGE TIME REQUIRED TO COMPLETE A DEAL: Varies; typically measured in months
(From Initial Contact to Closing)

FIRM NAME: **Institutional Venture Partners**

ADDRESS: 3000 Sand Hill Rd.
Building II, Suite 290
Menlo Park, CA 94025

PHONE: (415) 854–0132

SBIC ——   VENTURE CAPITAL FUND _X_   MESBIC ——   OTHER ——

TYPES OF FINANCING PREFERRED (Stages): Seed financings/start-up/second and third round financings/bridge financings of mature companies/buyouts

MINIMUM DATA REQUIRED TO CONSIDER FINANCING: N/A

GEOGRAPHIC PREFERENCE: Start-ups: West Coast/later round financings: other Western states/Buyouts: national

INDUSTRY PREFERENCE BY FIRM: Biomedical Products/Communications/ Computer Hardware and Software/Electronic Data Processing/Electronics and Electrical Components/High Technology/Environmental Control/Manufacturing/Medical Equipment and Instrumentation/Metallurgy/Optics and Lasers/Pharmaceuticals/Molecular Biology

INDUSTRY PREFERENCES BY INDIVIDUAL FIRM MEMBERS:
Reid W. Dennis   Samuel D. Colella
Mary Jane Elmore   John K. Poitras

YEAR COMPANY ESTABLISHED: N/A

FUNDS UNDER MANAGEMENT AT COST: N/A

MINIMUM SIZE INVESTMENT: $600,000

PREFERRED SIZE INVESTMENT: $600,000–$2,000,000

WILL FIRM SERVE AS LEAD INVESTOR: N/A

NUMBER OF DEALS COMPLETED IN THE LAST 12 MONTHS: N/A

AMOUNT INVESTED IN LAST 12 MONTHS: N/A

AVERAGE TIME REQUIRED TO COMPLETE A DEAL: N/A
(From Initial Contact to Closing)

FIRM NAME: **InterVen Management Co.**

ADDRESS: 515 S. Figuerea St.   1300 SW Fifth Ave.
#1900   #2323
Los Angeles, CA 90071   Portland, OR 97201

PHONE: (213) 622–1922   (503) 223–4334

SBIC ——   VENTURE CAPITAL FUND _X_   MESBIC ——   OTHER ——

TYPES OF FINANCING PREFERRED (Stages): Seed capital/buyout/start-up/first stage

MINIMUM DATA REQUIRED TO CONSIDER FINANCING: Business plan

GEOGRAPHIC PREFERENCE: Southern California and Pacific Northwest

INDUSTRY PREFERENCE BY FIRM: Semiconductors/Data Communications/Medical Devices/Instrumentation

INDUSTRY PREFERENCES BY INDIVIDUAL FIRM MEMBERS: N/A

YEAR COMPANY ESTABLISHED: 1985

FUNDS UNDER MANAGEMENT AT COST: $30 million

MINIMUM SIZE INVESTMENT: $500,000

PREFERRED SIZE INVESTMENT: $1 million

WILL FIRM SERVE AS LEAD INVESTOR: Yes

NUMBER OF DEALS COMPLETED IN THE LAST 12 MONTHS: 15

AMOUNT INVESTED IN LAST 12 MONTHS: $8 million

AVERAGE TIME REQUIRED TO COMPLETE A DEAL: 90 days
(From Initial Contact to Closing)

FIRM NAME: **Irvine Technology Fund**

ADDRESS: 4600 Campus Dr.
                    Newport Beach, CA 92660

PHONE: N/A

SBIC ____   VENTURE CAPITAL FUND _X_   MESBIC ____   OTHER ____

TYPES OF FINANCING PREFERRED (Stages): Early stage/expansion

MINIMUM DATA REQUIRED TO CONSIDER FINANCING: N/A

GEOGRAPHIC PREFERENCE: Southern California

INDUSTRY PREFERENCE BY FIRM: Medical/Health Care/Audio/Video/Computer/High Technology

INDUSTRY PREFERENCES BY INDIVIDUAL FIRM MEMBERS:
   H. D. Thoreau   Walter Cruttenden
   Greg Presson   J. C. MacRae

YEAR COMPANY ESTABLISHED: 1980

FUNDS UNDER MANAGEMENT AT COST: $17 million

MINIMUM SIZE INVESTMENT: $100,000

PREFERRED SIZE INVESTMENT: $250,000–$500,000

WILL FIRM SERVE AS LEAD INVESTOR: Yes, in local area only

NUMBER OF DEALS COMPLETED IN THE LAST 12 MONTHS: 8

AMOUNT INVESTED IN LAST 12 MONTHS: Less than $5 million

AVERAGE TIME REQUIRED TO COMPLETE A DEAL: 3–4 months
(From Initial Contact to Closing)

FIRM NAME: **Ivanhoe Venture Capital, Ltd.**

ADDRESS: 737 Pearl St.
Suite 201
La Jolla, CA 92037

PHONE: (619) 454–8882

SBIC _X_ VENTURE CAPITAL FUND ___ MESBIC ___ OTHER ___

TYPES OF FINANCING PREFERRED (Stages): Mezzanine/bridge/second round/third round

MINIMUM DATA REQUIRED TO CONSIDER FINANCING: Business plan/marketing plan/5-year projections

GEOGRAPHIC PREFERENCE: Western USA

INDUSTRY PREFERENCE BY FIRM: Diversified

INDUSTRY PREFERENCES BY INDIVIDUAL FIRM MEMBERS: None

YEAR COMPANY ESTABLISHED: 1982

FUNDS UNDER MANAGEMENT AT COST: $1 million

MINIMUM SIZE INVESTMENT: $50,000

PREFERRED SIZE INVESTMENT: $100,000

WILL FIRM SERVE AS LEAD INVESTOR: Yes

NUMBER OF DEALS COMPLETED IN THE LAST 12 MONTHS: 4

AMOUNT INVESTED IN LAST 12 MONTHS: $270,000

AVERAGE TIME REQUIRED TO COMPLETE A DEAL: 3 months
(From Initial Contact to Closing)

FIRM NAME: **Julian, Cole and Stein**

ADDRESS: 11777 San Vicente Blvd.
Suite 522
Los Angeles, CA 90049

PHONE: (213) 826–8002

SBIC ___ VENTURE CAPITAL FUND _X_ MESBIC ___ OTHER ___

TYPES OF FINANCING PREFERRED (Stages): Seed/start-up/first stage

MINIMUM DATA REQUIRED TO CONSIDER FINANCING: Business plan, management team resumes, market description

GEOGRAPHIC PREFERENCE: Primary focus on Southern California

INDUSTRY PREFERENCE BY FIRM: Computer Technology/Communications/ Specialized Semiconductors/Health Care/Factory Automation

INDUSTRY PREFERENCES BY INDIVIDUAL FIRM MEMBERS: N/A

YEAR COMPANY ESTABLISHED: 1983

FUNDS UNDER MANAGEMENT AT COST: $35 million

MINIMUM SIZE INVESTMENT: $500,000 (seed)–$300,000

PREFERRED SIZE INVESTMENT: $500,000–$1,000,000

WILL FIRM SERVE AS LEAD INVESTOR: Yes

NUMBER OF DEALS COMPLETED IN THE LAST 12 MONTHS: 5

AMOUNT INVESTED IN LAST 12 MONTHS: $5.1 million

AVERAGE TIME REQUIRED TO COMPLETE A DEAL: 30–60 days
   (From Initial Contact to Closing)

FIRM NAME: **Leong Ventures**

ADDRESS: 146 Atherton Ave.
                Atherton, CA 94025

PHONE: (415) 327–8970

SBIC ___   VENTURE CAPITAL FUND _X_   MESBIC ___   OTHER ___

TYPES OF FINANCING PREFERRED (Stages): First round financing

MINIMUM DATA REQUIRED TO CONSIDER FINANCING: Business plan with
   all patents

GEOGRAPHIC PREFERENCE: Santa Clara, San Mateo, and Alameda counties,
   California

INDUSTRY PREFERENCE BY FIRM: Biomedical/Medical Technology/Health

INDUSTRY PREFERENCES BY INDIVIDUAL FIRM MEMBERS:
   George Leong
   Helen Leong

YEAR COMPANY ESTABLISHED: 1978

FUNDS UNDER MANAGEMENT AT COST: $1.075 million

MINIMUM SIZE INVESTMENT: $100,000

PREFERRED SIZE INVESTMENT: $300,000

WILL FIRM SERVE AS LEAD INVESTOR: Yes

NUMBER OF DEALS COMPLETED IN THE LAST 12 MONTHS: 1

AMOUNT INVESTED IN LAST 12 MONTHS: $1 million

AVERAGE TIME REQUIRED TO COMPLETE A DEAL: 60 days
   (From Initial Contact to Closing)

FIRM NAME: **Donald L. Lucas (No company name)**

ADDRESS: 3000 Sand Hill Rd.
                #3
                Menlo Park, CA 94025

PHONE: (415) 854–4223

SBIC ___   VENTURE CAPITAL FUND _X_   MESBIC ___   OTHER ___

TYPES OF FINANCING PREFERRED (Stages): N/A

MINIMUM DATA REQUIRED TO CONSIDER FINANCING: Business plan, current financials

GEOGRAPHIC PREFERENCE: USA

INDUSTRY PREFERENCE BY FIRM: High-technology Computer-software-related services

INDUSTRY PREFERENCES BY INDIVIDUAL FIRM MEMBERS: N/A

YEAR COMPANY ESTABLISHED: 1967

FUNDS UNDER MANAGEMENT AT COST: N/A

MINIMUM SIZE INVESTMENT: $500,000

PREFERRED SIZE INVESTMENT: N/A

WILL FIRM SERVE AS LEAD INVESTOR: Yes

NUMBER OF DEALS COMPLETED IN THE LAST 12 MONTHS: N/A

AMOUNT INVESTED IN LAST 12 MONTHS: N/A

AVERAGE TIME REQUIRED TO COMPLETE A DEAL: N/A
(From Initial Contact to Closing)

FIRM NAME: **Manning & Co**

ADDRESS: 29438 Quailwood Dr.
                Rancho Palos Verdes, CA 90274

PHONE: (213) 377–4335

SBIC ⎯⎯ VENTURE CAPITAL FUND ⎯X⎯ MESBIC ⎯⎯ OTHER ⎯⎯

TYPES OF FINANCING PREFERRED (Stages): Start-up/first stage/second stage/buyout and acquisition financing

MINIMUM DATA REQUIRED TO CONSIDER FINANCING: Annual sales history and 3-year profit and loss projection

GEOGRAPHIC PREFERENCE: Southwest USA

INDUSTRY PREFERENCE BY FIRM: Computer Related/Distribution/Manufacturing/Medical Services/Real Estate Investments/Real-estate-related Services/Technology/Leisure Products and Services

INDUSTRY PREFERENCES BY INDIVIDUAL FIRM MEMBERS:
Christopher A. Manning, President

YEAR COMPANY ESTABLISHED: 1971

FUNDS UNDER MANAGEMENT AT COST: Low seven figures

MINIMUM SIZE INVESTMENT: No minimum

PREFERRED SIZE INVESTMENT: $100,000

WILL FIRM SERVE AS LEAD INVESTOR: Yes

NUMBER OF DEALS COMPLETED IN THE LAST 12 MONTHS: N/A

AMOUNT INVESTED IN LAST 12 MONTHS: N/A

AVERAGE TIME REQUIRED TO COMPLETE A DEAL: N/A
(From Initial Contact to Closing)

FIRM NAME: James A. Matzdorff & Co./Capital Development Group

ADDRESS: 249 S. Lafayette Park Pl.
                  Suite 132
                  Los Angeles, CA 90057

PHONE: (213) 384–4449

SBIC ____ VENTURE CAPITAL FUND _X_ MESBIC ____ OTHER ____

TYPES OF FINANCING PREFERRED (Stages): All types of financing; prefer second and third stages

MINIMUM DATA REQUIRED TO CONSIDER FINANCING: Completed package containing resumes of individuals involved and history of company and financials available

GEOGRAPHIC PREFERENCE: Western part of USA; prefer California

INDUSTRY PREFERENCE BY FIRM: High Technology, Food Related: Manufacturing, Industrial, and Wholesale Distributors

INDUSTRY PREFERENCES BY INDIVIDUAL FIRM MEMBERS: N/A

YEAR COMPANY ESTABLISHED: 1978

FUNDS UNDER MANAGEMENT AT COST: N/A

MINIMUM SIZE INVESTMENT: $500,000

PREFERRED SIZE INVESTMENT: $500,000 plus

WILL FIRM SERVE AS LEAD INVESTOR: Yes

NUMBER OF DEALS COMPLETED IN THE LAST 12 MONTHS: 7

AMOUNT INVESTED IN LAST 12 MONTHS: N/A

AVERAGE TIME REQUIRED TO COMPLETE A DEAL: 30–90 days
(From Initial Contact to Closing)

FIRM NAME: Leonard Mautner Associates

ADDRESS: 1434 Sixth St.
                  Santa Monica, CA 90401

PHONE: (213) 393–9788

SBIC ____ VENTURE CAPITAL FUND ____ MESBIC ____ OTHER _X_
(Consulting firm evaluating ventures, arranging private placements)

TYPES OF FINANCING PREFERRED (Stages): Seed/first stage/buyout

MINIMUM DATA REQUIRED TO CONSIDER FINANCING: Good business plan

GEOGRAPHIC PREFERENCE: Within 2 hours of office

INDUSTRY PREFERENCE BY FIRM: Computer Related/Automation/Data Communications/Medical Instruments/Optics Technology

INDUSTRY PREFERENCES BY INDIVIDUAL FIRM MEMBERS:
Leonard Mautner

YEAR COMPANY ESTABLISHED: 1969

FUNDS UNDER MANAGEMENT AT COST: N/A

MINIMUM SIZE INVESTMENT: $100,000–$300,000

PREFERRED SIZE INVESTMENT: $100,000–$300,000

WILL FIRM SERVE AS LEAD INVESTOR: Will arrange for

NUMBER OF DEALS COMPLETED IN THE LAST 12 MONTHS: 3

AMOUNT INVESTED IN LAST 12 MONTHS: N/A

AVERAGE TIME REQUIRED TO COMPLETE A DEAL: 2–3 months
(From Initial Contact to Closing)

FIRM NAME: **Mayfield Fund**

ADDRESS: 2200 Sand Hill Rd.
Menlo Park, CA 94025

PHONE: (415) 854–5560

SBIC ____   VENTURE CAPITAL FUND _X_   MESBIC ____   OTHER ____

TYPES OF FINANCING PREFERRED (Stages): Seed/start-up/second and third
round financing

MINIMUM DATA REQUIRED TO CONSIDER FINANCING: Detailed business
plan, market analysis, financial projections

GEOGRAPHIC PREFERENCE: Western USA

INDUSTRY PREFERENCE BY FIRM: High-technology companies on the leading
edge in computers or computer-related areas, electronics, health care and
medical areas, robotics or proprietary technology. Will generally decline service industry areas.

INDUSTRY PREFERENCES BY INDIVIDUAL FIRM MEMBERS: N/A

YEAR COMPANY ESTABLISHED: 1969

FUNDS UNDER MANAGEMENT AT COST: $200 million

MINIMUM SIZE INVESTMENT: $100,000 initial

PREFERRED SIZE INVESTMENT: $2 million

WILL FIRM SERVE AS LEAD INVESTOR: Yes

NUMBER OF DEALS COMPLETED IN THE LAST 12 MONTHS: 37

AMOUNT INVESTED IN LAST 12 MONTHS: $30 million

AVERAGE TIME REQUIRED TO COMPLETE A DEAL: 2 months
(From Initial Contact to Closing)

FIRM NAME: **Melchor Venture Management, Inc.**

ADDRESS: 170 State St.
Suite 220
Los Altos, CA 94022

PHONE: (415) 941–6565

SBIC ____   VENTURE CAPITAL FUND _X_   MESBIC ____   OTHER ____

TYPES OF FINANCING PREFERRED (Stages): Seed financings/start-ups

MINIMUM DATA REQUIRED TO CONSIDER FINANCING: N/A

GEOGRAPHIC PREFERENCE: Northern California

INDUSTRY PREFERENCE BY FIRM: Communications/Computer Hardware/ Electronic Data Processing/High Technology/Electronics and Electrical Components/Medical Equipment and Instrumentation/Optics and Lasers/Proprietary Technology/Software

INDUSTRY PREFERENCES BY INDIVIDUAL FIRM MEMBERS:
Richard H. Frank
Gregory S. Young

YEAR COMPANY ESTABLISHED: N/A

FUNDS UNDER MANAGEMENT AT COST: N/A

MINIMUM SIZE INVESTMENT: $50,000

PREFERRED SIZE INVESTMENT: $500,000

WILL FIRM SERVE AS LEAD INVESTOR: N/A

NUMBER OF DEALS COMPLETED IN THE LAST 12 MONTHS: N/A

AMOUNT INVESTED IN LAST 12 MONTHS: N/A

AVERAGE TIME REQUIRED TO COMPLETE A DEAL: N/A
(From Initial Contact to Closing)

FIRM NAME: **Merrill, Pickard, Anderson, & Eyre**

ADDRESS: 2 Palo Alto Square
                 Suite 425
                 Palo Alto, CA 94306

PHONE: (415) 856–8880

SBIC ___   VENTURE CAPITAL FUND _X_   MESBIC ___   OTHER ___

TYPES OF FINANCING PREFERRED (Stages): Seed/first and second rounds

MINIMUM DATA REQUIRED TO CONSIDER FINANCING: Business plan summary

GEOGRAPHIC PREFERENCE: West Coast/North Coast

INDUSTRY PREFERENCE BY FIRM: High-technology Manufacturing

INDUSTRY PREFERENCES BY INDIVIDUAL FIRM MEMBERS: N/A

YEAR COMPANY ESTABLISHED: 1980

FUNDS UNDER MANAGEMENT AT COST: $93 million

MINIMUM SIZE INVESTMENT: $750,000

PREFERRED SIZE INVESTMENT: $1 million

WILL FIRM SERVE AS LEAD INVESTOR: Yes

NUMBER OF DEALS COMPLETED IN THE LAST 12 MONTHS: 16

AMOUNT INVESTED IN LAST 12 MONTHS: $11 million

AVERAGE TIME REQUIRED TO COMPLETE A DEAL: 2 weeks–1½ months
(From Initial Contact to Closing)

FIRM NAME: **Metropolitan Venture Company, Inc.**
ADDRESS: 5757 Wilshire Blvd.
                  #670
                  Los Angeles, CA 90036
PHONE: (213) 938–3488

SBIC __X__ VENTURE CAPITAL FUND ____ MESBIC ____ OTHER ____

TYPES OF FINANCING PREFERRED (Stages): Later stage

MINIMUM DATA REQUIRED TO CONSIDER FINANCING: N/A

GEOGRAPHIC PREFERENCE: Southern California

INDUSTRY PREFERENCE BY FIRM: Real Estate, Diversified

INDUSTRY PREFERENCES BY INDIVIDUAL FIRM MEMBERS: N/A

YEAR COMPANY ESTABLISHED: 1980

FUNDS UNDER MANAGEMENT AT COST: N/A

MINIMUM SIZE INVESTMENT: $75,000

PREFERRED SIZE INVESTMENT: $100,000

WILL FIRM SERVE AS LEAD INVESTOR: Yes

NUMBER OF DEALS COMPLETED IN THE LAST 12 MONTHS: 5

AMOUNT INVESTED IN LAST 12 MONTHS: $500,000

AVERAGE TIME REQUIRED TO COMPLETE A DEAL: 6 weeks
  (From Initial Contact to Closing)

FIRM NAME: **Microtechnology Investments Ltd.**
ADDRESS: 46 Red Birch Ct.   3400 Comserv Dr.
                  Danville, CA 94526   Eagan, MN 55122
PHONE: (415) 838–9319   (612) 681–7581

SBIC ____ VENTURE CAPITAL FUND __X__ MESBIC ____ OTHER ____

TYPES OF FINANCING PREFERRED (Stages): Early stages

MINIMUM DATA REQUIRED TO CONSIDER FINANCING: Business plan

GEOGRAPHIC PREFERENCE: West and Midwest

INDUSTRY PREFERENCE BY FIRM: Focus on software products on microcom-
  puters

INDUSTRY PREFERENCES BY INDIVIDUAL FIRM MEMBERS:
  M. M. Stuckey makes investment decisions

YEAR COMPANY ESTABLISHED: 1983

FUNDS UNDER MANAGEMENT AT COST: Confidential

MINIMUM SIZE INVESTMENT: No minimums

PREFERRED SIZE INVESTMENT: $250,000

WILL FIRM SERVE AS LEAD INVESTOR: Yes

NUMBER OF DEALS COMPLETED IN THE LAST 12 MONTHS: All early stage

AMOUNT INVESTED IN LAST 12 MONTHS: Confidential

AVERAGE TIME REQUIRED TO COMPLETE A DEAL: 6 months
   (From Initial Contact to Closing)

FIRM NAME: **Miller & LaHaye**

ADDRESS: 606 Wilshire Blvd.
                Suite 602
                Santa Monica, CA 90401

PHONE: (213) 458–1441

SBIC ____ VENTURE CAPITAL FUND _X_ MESBIC ____ OTHER ____

TYPES OF FINANCING PREFERRED (Stages): Early stage and subsequent rounds

MINIMUM DATA REQUIRED TO CONSIDER FINANCING: Business plan and
   supporting documentation

GEOGRAPHIC PREFERENCE: None

INDUSTRY PREFERENCE BY FIRM: Growth situations, generally with emphasis
   on high technology

INDUSTRY PREFERENCES BY INDIVIDUAL FIRM MEMBERS: N/A

YEAR COMPANY ESTABLISHED: 1981

FUNDS UNDER MANAGEMENT AT COST: $43 million

MINIMUM SIZE INVESTMENT: $100,000

PREFERRED SIZE INVESTMENT: $750,000 for initial participation

WILL FIRM SERVE AS LEAD INVESTOR: Yes

NUMBER OF DEALS COMPLETED IN THE LAST 12 MONTHS: 11

AMOUNT INVESTED IN LAST 12 MONTHS: $7.6 million

AVERAGE TIME REQUIRED TO COMPLETE A DEAL: 8 weeks
   (From Initial Contact to Closing)

FIRM NAME: **Montgomery Securities**   **Montgomer Medical Ventures**
                Montgomery Bridge Funds   **Montgomery Ventures**

ADDRESS: 600 Montgomery St.
                San Francisco, CA 94111

PHONE: (415) 627–2000

SBIC ____ VENTURE CAPITAL FUND _X_ MESBIC ____ OTHER ____

TYPES OF FINANCING PREFERRED (Stages): Early stage to bridge

MINIMUM DATA REQUIRED TO CONSIDER FINANCING: Business plan

GEOGRAPHIC PREFERENCE: None

INDUSTRY PREFERENCE BY FIRM: Technology/Medical/Consumer/Specialty
Chemical/Finance

INDUSTRY PREFERENCES BY INDIVIDUAL FIRM MEMBERS: N/A

YEAR COMPANY ESTABLISHED: 1969

FUNDS UNDER MANAGEMENT AT COST: $180 million

MINIMUM SIZE INVESTMENT: $250,000

PREFERRED SIZE INVESTMENT: $1 million

WILL FIRM SERVE AS LEAD INVESTOR: Yes

NUMBER OF DEALS COMPLETED IN THE LAST 12 MONTHS: 45

AMOUNT INVESTED IN LAST 12 MONTHS: $18.8 million

AVERAGE TIME REQUIRED TO COMPLETE A DEAL: 90 days
(From Initial Contact to Closing)

FIRM NAME: **Myriad Capital, Inc.**

ADDRESS: 2225 W. Commonwealth Ave.
                  Suite 111
                  Alhambra, CA 91801

PHONE: (818) 289–5689

SBIC ___   VENTURE CAPITAL FUND ___   MESBIC _X_   OTHER ___

TYPES OF FINANCING PREFERRED (Stages): Second or third

MINIMUM DATA REQUIRED TO CONSIDER FINANCING: Business plan; audited financial statements

GEOGRAPHIC PREFERENCE: California

INDUSTRY PREFERENCE BY FIRM: Instrumentation/Computer/Electronics/
Engineering/Consulting/Real Estate

INDUSTRY PREFERENCES BY INDIVIDUAL FIRM MEMBERS: N/A

YEAR COMPANY ESTABLISHED: 3–5 years

FUNDS UNDER MANAGEMENT AT COST: N/A

MINIMUM SIZE INVESTMENT: $50,000

PREFERRED SIZE INVESTMENT: $200,000–$400,000

WILL FIRM SERVE AS LEAD INVESTOR: Yes

NUMBER OF DEALS COMPLETED IN THE LAST 12 MONTHS: 10

AMOUNT INVESTED IN LAST 12 MONTHS: $1.2 million invested

AVERAGE TIME REQUIRED TO COMPLETE A DEAL: 1–2 months
(From Initial Contact to Closing)

FIRM NAME: National Investment Management, Inc.

ADDRESS: Suite 300
              23133 Hawthorne Blvd.
              Torrance, CA 90505

PHONE: (213) 373–8944

SBIC ____   VENTURE CAPITAL FUND __X__   MESBIC ____   OTHER ____

TYPES OF FINANCING PREFERRED (Stages): Later stage/leveraged buyouts

MINIMUM DATA REQUIRED TO CONSIDER FINANCING: 5-year financial

GEOGRAPHIC PREFERENCE: USA

INDUSTRY PREFERENCE BY FIRM: Any

INDUSTRY PREFERENCES BY INDIVIDUAL FIRM MEMBERS: N/A

YEAR COMPANY ESTABLISHED: 1976

FUNDS UNDER MANAGEMENT AT COST: $20 million

MINIMUM SIZE INVESTMENT: $500,000

PREFERRED SIZE INVESTMENT: N/A

WILL FIRM SERVE AS LEAD INVESTOR: Yes

NUMBER OF DEALS COMPLETED IN THE LAST 12 MONTHS: N/A

AMOUNT INVESTED IN LAST 12 MONTHS: N/A

AVERAGE TIME REQUIRED TO COMPLETE A DEAL: N/A
    (From Initial Contact to Closing)

FIRM NAME: Newtek Ventures

ADDRESS: 500 Washington St.
              Suite 720
              San Francisco, CA 94111

PHONE: (415) 986–5711

SBIC ____   VENTURE CAPITAL FUND __X__   MESBIC ____   OTHER ____

TYPES OF FINANCING PREFERRED (Stages): Early stage/first and second
    rounds

MINIMUM DATA REQUIRED TO CONSIDER FINANCING: N/A

GEOGRAPHIC PREFERENCE: West Coast

INDUSTRY PREFERENCE BY FIRM: Semiconductor Capital Equipment/
    Computers/Energy/Telecommunications/Robotics–Automation/Lasers/Optics/
    Medical Instrumentation/Biotechnology

INDUSTRY PREFERENCES BY INDIVIDUAL FIRM MEMBERS: N/A

YEAR COMPANY ESTABLISHED: 1983

FUNDS UNDER MANAGEMENT AT COST: One fund capitalized at $20 million

MINIMUM SIZE INVESTMENT: $250,000

PREFERRED SIZE INVESTMENT: $500,000

WILL FIRM SERVE AS LEAD INVESTOR: Yes

NUMBER OF DEALS COMPLETED IN THE LAST 12 MONTHS: 9 deals

AMOUNT INVESTED IN LAST 12 MONTHS: Approximately $4 million

AVERAGE TIME REQUIRED TO COMPLETE A DEAL: N/A
   (From Initial Contact to Closing)

FIRM NAME: **New West Ventures**

ADDRESS: 4350 Executive Dr.   4600 Campus Dr.
                 #206   #103
                 San Diego, CA 92121   Newport Beach, CA 92660

PHONE: (619) 457–0722   (714) 756–8940

SBIC __X__ VENTURE CAPITAL FUND ____ MESBIC ____ OTHER ____

TYPES OF FINANCING PREFERRED (Stages): Second round

MINIMUM DATA REQUIRED TO CONSIDER FINANCING: Business plan

GEOGRAPHIC PREFERENCE: Open

INDUSTRY PREFERENCE BY FIRM: Open

INDUSTRY PREFERENCES BY INDIVIDUAL FIRM MEMBERS: N/A

YEAR COMPANY ESTABLISHED: 1981

FUNDS UNDER MANAGEMENT AT COST: $10 million

MINIMUM SIZE INVESTMENT: $250,000

PREFERRED SIZE INVESTMENT: $1.5 million

WILL FIRM SERVE AS LEAD INVESTOR: Yes

NUMBER OF DEALS COMPLETED IN THE LAST 12 MONTHS: 11

AMOUNT INVESTED IN LAST 12 MONTHS: $2.5 million

AVERAGE TIME REQUIRED TO COMPLETE A DEAL: 5 weeks
   (From Initial Contact to Closing)

FIRM NAME: **Oak Grove Ventures**

ADDRESS: 173 Jefferson Dr.
                 Menlo Park, CA 94025

PHONE: (415) 324–2276

SBIC ____ VENTURE CAPITAL FUND __X__ MESBIC ____ OTHER ____

TYPES OF FINANCING PREFERRED (Stages): Seed/start-up financing/first round

MINIMUM DATA REQUIRED TO CONSIDER FINANCING: Depends on circumstances

GEOGRAPHIC PREFERENCE: West Coast

INDUSTRY PREFERENCE BY FIRM: Communications/Computer Related/ Electronic Components and Instrumentation/Genetic Engineering/Industrial Products and Equipment/Medical

INDUSTRY PREFERENCES BY INDIVIDUAL FIRM MEMBERS:

Paul M. Cook, General Partner	No formal division of industry
James J. Horthal, General Partner	preferences among individual
Duane C. Montopoli, General Partner	firm members

YEAR COMPANY ESTABLISHED: 1972

FUNDS UNDER MANAGEMENT AT COST: $15 million

MINIMUM SIZE INVESTMENT: $100,000–$300,000

PREFERRED SIZE INVESTMENT: $300,000–$600,000

WILL FIRM SERVE AS LEAD INVESTOR: Yes

NUMBER OF DEALS COMPLETED IN THE LAST 12 MONTHS: 4

AMOUNT INVESTED IN LAST 12 MONTHS: $1.6 million

AVERAGE TIME REQUIRED TO COMPLETE A DEAL: 6–8 weeks (From Initial Contact to Closing)

FIRM NAME: **Orange County Area Investments**

ADDRESS: 1430 Santanella Terrace
                  Corona del Mar, CA 92625

PHONE: (714) 720–9033

SBIC ____   VENTURE CAPITAL FUND __X__   MESBIC ____   OTHER ____

TYPES OF FINANCING PREFERRED (Stages): All stages

MINIMUM DATA REQUIRED TO CONSIDER FINANCING: N/A

GEOGRAPHIC PREFERENCE: Orange County

INDUSTRY PREFERENCE BY FIRM: No preferences

INDUSTRY PREFERENCES BY INDIVIDUAL FIRM MEMBERS:
Sandford T. Waddell, President
Jean Leitz, Vice-chairman

YEAR COMPANY ESTABLISHED: 1985

FUNDS UNDER MANAGEMENT AT COST: N/A

MINIMUM SIZE INVESTMENT: $100,000 or less

PREFERRED SIZE INVESTMENT: $100,000–$200,000

WILL FIRM SERVE AS LEAD INVESTOR: Yes

NUMBER OF DEALS COMPLETED IN THE LAST 12 MONTHS: N/A

AMOUNT INVESTED IN LAST 12 MONTHS: N/A

AVERAGE TIME REQUIRED TO COMPLETE A DEAL: N/A (From Initial Contact to Closing)

FIRM NAME: Oscco Ventures

ADDRESS: 3000 Sand Hill Rd.
                  #4–140
                  Menlo Park, CA 94025

PHONE: (415) 854–2222

SBIC ___   VENTURE CAPITAL FUND _X_   MESBIC ___   OTHER ___

TYPES OF FINANCING PREFERRED (Stages): Seed/start-up/first and second
   rounds

MINIMUM DATA REQUIRED TO CONSIDER FINANCING: Summary plan

GEOGRAPHIC PREFERENCE: West and Southwest

INDUSTRY PREFERENCE BY FIRM: Unique and proprietary products with significant economic advantage

INDUSTRY PREFERENCES BY INDIVIDUAL FIRM MEMBERS:
   James G. Rudolph—Computers/Medical/Semiconductor/Communications
   F. Ward Paine—Semiconductor Equipment/General
   Stephen E. Halprin—Proprietary Technology/Software

YEAR COMPANY ESTABLISHED: 1962

FUNDS UNDER MANAGEMENT AT COST: $25 million in current fund

MINIMUM SIZE INVESTMENT: $200,000

PREFERRED SIZE INVESTMENT: $750,000 plus

WILL FIRM SERVE AS LEAD INVESTOR: Yes

NUMBER OF DEALS COMPLETED IN THE LAST 12 MONTHS: 4

AMOUNT INVESTED IN LAST 12 MONTHS: $2.5 million

AVERAGE TIME REQUIRED TO COMPLETE A DEAL: 2 months
   (From Initial Contact to Closing)

FIRM NAME: P & C Venture Partners

ADDRESS: 20813 Stevens Creek Blvd.
                  #101
                  Cupertino, CA 95014

PHONE: (408) 446–9693

SBIC ___   VENTURE CAPITAL FUND _X_   MESBIC ___   OTHER ___

TYPES OF FINANCING PREFERRED (Stages): Start-up/first stage

MINIMUM DATA REQUIRED TO CONSIDER FINANCING: Business plan

GEOGRAPHIC PREFERENCE: West Coast

INDUSTRY PREFERENCE BY FIRM: Communications/Computer Related/Elec-
   tronic Components and Instrumentation/Industrial Products and Equipment/
   Medical

INDUSTRY PREFERENCES BY INDIVIDUAL FIRM MEMBERS: N/A

YEAR COMPANY ESTABLISHED: 1984

FUNDS UNDER MANAGEMENT AT COST: N/A

MINIMUM SIZE INVESTMENT: $100,000

PREFERRED SIZE INVESTMENT: $300,000–$600,000

WILL FIRM SERVE AS LEAD INVESTOR: Yes

NUMBER OF DEALS COMPLETED IN THE LAST 12 MONTHS: N/A

AMOUNT INVESTED IN LAST 12 MONTHS: N/A

AVERAGE TIME REQUIRED TO COMPLETE A DEAL: N/A
(From Initial Contact to Closing)

FIRM NAME: **Pacific Capital Fund, Inc.**

ADDRESS: 3420 E. Third Ave.
Foster City, CA 94404

PHONE: (415) 571–5411

SBIC ____ VENTURE CAPITAL FUND ____ MESBIC _X_ OTHER ____

TYPES OF FINANCING PREFERRED (Stages): Second stage/later stage expansion/buyout or acquisition

MINIMUM DATA REQUIRED TO CONSIDER FINANCING: Annual sales: $500,000–$1.5 million/P&L: break-even

GEOGRAPHIC PREFERENCE: West Coast

INDUSTRY PREFERENCE BY FIRM: Computer Related/Distribution/Manufacturing/Medical/Real-estate-related Services/Technology

INDUSTRY PREFERENCES BY INDIVIDUAL FIRM MEMBERS: N/A

YEAR COMPANY ESTABLISHED: 1980

FUNDS UNDER MANAGEMENT AT COST: N/A

MINIMUM SIZE INVESTMENT: $100,000–$300,000

PREFERRED SIZE INVESTMENT: $100,000–$300,000

WILL FIRM SERVE AS LEAD INVESTOR: Will function either as deal originator or investor in deals created by others

NUMBER OF DEALS COMPLETED IN THE LAST 12 MONTHS: N/A

AMOUNT INVESTED IN LAST 12 MONTHS: N/A

AVERAGE TIME REQUIRED TO COMPLETE A DEAL: 1–3 months
(From Initial Contact to Closing)

FIRM NAME: **Paragon Partners**

ADDRESS: 3000 Sand Hill Rd.
Building 2, Suite 190
Menlo Park, CA 94025

PHONE: (415) 854–8000

SBIC _____   VENTURE CAPITAL FUND _X_   MESBIC _____   OTHER _____

TYPES OF FINANCING PREFERRED (Stages): Start-ups/early stage and later stage. Prefer role as deal originator but will also invest in deals created by others.

MINIMUM DATA REQUIRED TO CONSIDER FINANCING: Business plan

GEOGRAPHIC PREFERENCE: None

INDUSTRY PREFERENCE BY FIRM: Communications/Computer Hardware and Software/Electronic Data Processing/Electronics and Electrical Components/Health Services/High Technology/Medical Equipment and Instrumentation/Medium Technology/Metal Fabrication and Processing/Oil and Gas/Optics and Lasers/Pharmaceuticals/Proprietary Technology/Robotics

INDUSTRY PREFERENCES BY INDIVIDUAL FIRM MEMBERS: N/A

YEAR COMPANY ESTABLISHED: 1983

FUNDS UNDER MANAGEMENT AT COST: $40 million

MINIMUM SIZE INVESTMENT: $300,000–$600,000

PREFERRED SIZE INVESTMENT: $1 million

WILL FIRM SERVE AS LEAD INVESTOR: Yes

NUMBER OF DEALS COMPLETED IN THE LAST 12 MONTHS: 5

AMOUNT INVESTED IN LAST 12 MONTHS: $4 million

AVERAGE TIME REQUIRED TO COMPLETE A DEAL: 90–120 days (From Initial Contact to Closing)

FIRM NAME: **Peregrine Associates**

ADDRESS: 606 Wilshire Blvd.
                Suite 602
                Santa Monica, CA 90401

PHONE: (213) 458–1441

SBIC _____   VENTURE CAPITAL FUND _X_   MESBIC _____   OTHER _____

TYPES OF FINANCING PREFERRED (Stages): Early stage and subsequent rounds

MINIMUM DATA REQUIRED TO CONSIDER FINANCING: Business plan

GEOGRAPHIC PREFERENCE: None

INDUSTRY PREFERENCE BY FIRM: Growth situations with emphasis on electronics and medical

INDUSTRY PREFERENCES BY INDIVIDUAL FIRM MEMBERS: N/A

YEAR COMPANY ESTABLISHED: 1981

FUNDS UNDER MANAGEMENT AT COST: $43 million

MINIMUM SIZE INVESTMENT: $100,000

PREFERRED SIZE INVESTMENT: $750,000

WILL FIRM SERVE AS LEAD INVESTOR: Yes

NUMBER OF DEALS COMPLETED IN THE LAST 12 MONTHS: 11

AMOUNT INVESTED IN LAST 12 MONTHS: $7.6 million

AVERAGE TIME REQUIRED TO COMPLETE A DEAL: 8 weeks
(From Initial Contact to Closing)

FIRM NAME: **Robertson Colman & Stephens**

ADDRESS: 1 Embarcadero Center
San Francisco, CA 94111

PHONE: (415) 781-9700

SBIC ____ VENTURE CAPITAL FUND _X_ MESBIC ____ OTHER ____

TYPES OF FINANCING PREFERRED (Stages): Early/middle

MINIMUM DATA REQUIRED TO CONSIDER FINANCING: Business plan; ac-
tual/projected financials

GEOGRAPHIC PREFERENCE: None

INDUSTRY PREFERENCE BY FIRM: Communications/Computer Related/
Components and Instrumentation/Industrial Products/Medical Equipment/
Health Services/Genetic Engineering/Biotechnology

INDUSTRY PREFERENCES BY INDIVIDUAL FIRM MEMBERS: N/A

YEAR COMPANY ESTABLISHED: 1978

FUNDS UNDER MANAGEMENT AT COST: $150 million

MINIMUM SIZE INVESTMENT: $500,000

PREFERRED SIZE INVESTMENT: $1.5–2.0 million

WILL FIRM SERVE AS LEAD INVESTOR: Yes

NUMBER OF DEALS COMPLETED IN THE LAST 12 MONTHS: 12: 6 startups
and 6 follow on

AMOUNT INVESTED IN LAST 12 MONTHS: Approximately $15 million

AVERAGE TIME REQUIRED TO COMPLETE A DEAL: 2–3 months
(From Initial Contact to Closing)

FIRM NAME: **San Joaquin Capital Corp.**

ADDRESS: 1675 Chester Ave.
Suite 330
P.O. Box 2538
Bakersfield, CA 93303

PHONE: (805) 323-7581

SBIC _X_ VENTURE CAPITAL FUND ____ MESBIC ____ OTHER ____

TYPES OF FINANCING PREFERRED (Stages): Second or third round

MINIMUM DATA REQUIRED TO CONSIDER FINANCING: Same information
as required in servicing a bank loan

GEOGRAPHIC PREFERENCE: California

INDUSTRY PREFERENCE BY FIRM: None

INDUSTRY PREFERENCES BY INDIVIDUAL FIRM MEMBERS: None

YEAR COMPANY ESTABLISHED: 1962

FUNDS UNDER MANAGEMENT AT COST: N/A

MINIMUM SIZE INVESTMENT: $50,000

PREFERRED SIZE INVESTMENT: $100,000–$150,000

WILL FIRM SERVE AS LEAD INVESTOR: Yes

NUMBER OF DEALS COMPLETED IN THE LAST 12 MONTHS: 6

AMOUNT INVESTED IN LAST 12 MONTHS: $500,000

AVERAGE TIME REQUIRED TO COMPLETE A DEAL: 60 days
  (From Initial Contact to Closing)

FIRM NAME: **San Jose Capital**

ADDRESS: 100 Park Center Plaza
                Suite 427
                San Jose, CA 95113

PHONE: N/A

SBIC _X_   VENTURE CAPITAL FUND _X_   MESBIC ____   OTHER ____

TYPES OF FINANCING PREFERRED (Stages): Start-up/first stage

MINIMUM DATA REQUIRED TO CONSIDER FINANCING: Business plan

GEOGRAPHIC PREFERENCE: West Coast

INDUSTRY PREFERENCE BY FIRM: N/A

INDUSTRY PREFERENCES BY INDIVIDUAL FIRM MEMBERS: N/A

YEAR COMPANY ESTABLISHED: 1977

FUNDS UNDER MANAGEMENT AT COST: $10 million

MINIMUM SIZE INVESTMENT: $100,000

PREFERRED SIZE INVESTMENT: $300,000

WILL FIRM SERVE AS LEAD INVESTOR: Yes

NUMBER OF DEALS COMPLETED IN THE LAST 12 MONTHS: 6

AMOUNT INVESTED IN LAST 12 MONTHS: $1.5 million

AVERAGE TIME REQUIRED TO COMPLETE A DEAL: 2 months
  (From Initial Contact to Closing)

FIRM NAME: **Schroder Venture Managers Limited**

ADDRESS: 755 Page Mill Rd.
                Building A, Suite 280
                Palo Alto, CA 94304

PHONE: (415) 424–1144

SBIC ____   VENTURE CAPITAL FUND _X_ MESBIC ____   OTHER ____

TYPES OF FINANCING PREFERRED (Stages): Early stage/start-up/seed financings/leveraged buyouts

MINIMUM DATA REQUIRED TO CONSIDER FINANCING: Business plan

GEOGRAPHIC PREFERENCE: East or West Coast USA

INDUSTRY PREFERENCE BY FIRM: N/A

INDUSTRY PREFERENCES BY INDIVIDUAL FIRM MEMBERS:
Jeffrey J. Collinson—Biotechnology and LBO

Michael Hentschel—Telecommunications and Electronics

Judith Schneider—Electronics and Retail

David Walters—Electronics and Retail

YEAR COMPANY ESTABLISHED: 1983

FUNDS UNDER MANAGEMENT AT COST: $37.5 million

MINIMUM SIZE INVESTMENT: Any size

PREFERRED SIZE INVESTMENT: $500,000

WILL FIRM SERVE AS LEAD INVESTOR: Yes

NUMBER OF DEALS COMPLETED IN THE LAST 12 MONTHS: 10

AMOUNT INVESTED IN LAST 12 MONTHS: $7 million

AVERAGE TIME REQUIRED TO COMPLETE A DEAL: 1.5 months
(From Initial Contact to Closing)

FIRM NAME: **Seaport Ventures, Inc.**

ADDRESS: 770 B Street
              Suite 420
              San Diego, CA 92101

PHONE: (619) 232–4069

SBIC _X_ VENTURE CAPITAL FUND ____   MESBIC ____   OTHER ____

TYPES OF FINANCING PREFERRED (Stages): First stage/second stage/leveraged buyouts/occasional third stage

MINIMUM DATA REQUIRED TO CONSIDER FINANCING: Historical financial statements, 3-year financial projections

GEOGRAPHIC PREFERENCE: Continental USA

INDUSTRY PREFERENCE BY FIRM: Will not invest in motion pictures, real estate

INDUSTRY PREFERENCES BY INDIVIDUAL FIRM MEMBERS:
Michael Stolper, President
Carole Rhoades, Vice-president

YEAR COMPANY ESTABLISHED: 1982

FUNDS UNDER MANAGEMENT AT COST: $3 million

MINIMUM SIZE INVESTMENT: $50,000

PREFERRED SIZE INVESTMENT: $250,000

WILL FIRM SERVE AS LEAD INVESTOR: Yes

NUMBER OF DEALS COMPLETED IN THE LAST 12 MONTHS: 9

AMOUNT INVESTED IN LAST 12 MONTHS: $1.375 million

AVERAGE TIME REQUIRED TO COMPLETE A DEAL: 6–10 weeks
   (From Initial Contact to Closing)

FIRM NAME: **Sequoia Capital**

ADDRESS: 3000 Sand Hill Rd.
            Building 4, Suite 280
            Menlo Park, CA 94025

PHONE: (415) 854–3927

SBIC ____   VENTURE CAPITAL FUND __X__   MESBIC ____   OTHER ____

TYPES OF FINANCING PREFERRED (Stages): Seed/first/second

MINIMUM DATA REQUIRED TO CONSIDER FINANCING: Business plan

GEOGRAPHIC PREFERENCE: Western USA and Texas

INDUSTRY PREFERENCE BY FIRM: Computers/Semiconductors/Software/
   Health Care/Peripherals/Communications

INDUSTRY PREFERENCES BY INDIVIDUAL FIRM MEMBERS:
   Donald T. Valentine—Semiconduc-   Walter   Baumgartner—Peripherals/
      tors/Software   Communications
   Pierre R. Lamond—Semiconductor   Jonathan   Hamren—Communica-
      Equipment/Communications   tions/Software
   Gordon Russell—Health Care

YEAR COMPANY ESTABLISHED: 1973

FUNDS UNDER MANAGEMENT AT COST: $180 million

MINIMUM SIZE INVESTMENT: $750,000

PREFERRED SIZE INVESTMENT: $1.5 million

WILL FIRM SERVE AS LEAD INVESTOR: Yes

NUMBER OF DEALS COMPLETED IN THE LAST 12 MONTHS: 29

AMOUNT INVESTED IN LAST 12 MONTHS: $13.73 million

AVERAGE TIME REQUIRED TO COMPLETE A DEAL: 3 months
   (From Initial Contact to Closing)

FIRM NAME: **Sofinnova Inc.**

ADDRESS: 3 Embarcadero
            #2560
            San Francisco, CA 94111

PHONE: (415) 362–4021

SBIC ____   VENTURE CAPITAL FUND __X__   MESBIC ____   OTHER ____

TYPES OF FINANCING PREFERRED (Stages): Early stage/first and second rounds

MINIMUM DATA REQUIRED TO CONSIDER FINANCING: Business plan

GEOGRAPHIC PREFERENCE: West Coast, East Coast

INDUSTRY PREFERENCE BY FIRM: All sectors of electronics technology

INDUSTRY PREFERENCES BY INDIVIDUAL FIRM MEMBERS: N/A

YEAR COMPANY ESTABLISHED: 1976

FUNDS UNDER MANAGEMENT AT COST: $42 million

MINIMUM SIZE INVESTMENT: $300,000

PREFERRED SIZE INVESTMENT: $450,000

WILL FIRM SERVE AS LEAD INVESTOR: Yes

NUMBER OF DEALS COMPLETED IN THE LAST 12 MONTHS: 8

AMOUNT INVESTED IN LAST 12 MONTHS: $3 million

AVERAGE TIME REQUIRED TO COMPLETE A DEAL: 6 weeks
(From Initial Contact to Closing)

FIRM NAME: **Southern California Ventures**

ADDRESS: 9920 La Cienega Bl   2101 Business Center Dr.
               Inglewood CA 90301   Irvine, CA 92715
               (headquarters)   (branch)

PHONE: (213) 216–0544   (714) 752–9341

SBIC ____   VENTURE CAPITAL FUND __X__   MESBIC ____   OTHER ____

TYPES OF FINANCING PREFERRED (Stages): Seed/early stage

MINIMUM DATA REQUIRED TO CONSIDER FINANCING: Tentative business plan

GEOGRAPHIC PREFERENCE: Southern California

INDUSTRY PREFERENCE BY FIRM: Seek high-value-added proprietary products and services

INDUSTRY PREFERENCES BY INDIVIDUAL FIRM MEMBERS: N/A

YEAR COMPANY ESTABLISHED: 1983

FUNDS UNDER MANAGEMENT AT COST: $15 million

MINIMUM SIZE INVESTMENT: $100,000 or less

PREFERRED SIZE INVESTMENT: $300,000–$500,000

WILL FIRM SERVE AS LEAD INVESTOR: Yes

NUMBER OF DEALS COMPLETED IN THE LAST 12 MONTHS: 13

AMOUNT INVESTED IN LAST 12 MONTHS: $3 million

AVERAGE TIME REQUIRED TO COMPLETE A DEAL: 60 days
(From Initial Contact to Closing)

FIRM NAME: **Sutter Hill Ventures**

ADDRESS: 2 Palo Alto Sq.
Suite 700
Palo Alto, CA 94306

PHONE: (415) 493–5600

SBIC ___   VENTURE CAPITAL FUND _X_   MESBIC ___   OTHER ___

TYPES OF FINANCING PREFERRED (Stages): Seed/start-up/first stage

MINIMUM DATA REQUIRED TO CONSIDER FINANCING: N/A

GEOGRAPHIC PREFERENCE: USA

INDUSTRY PREFERENCE BY FIRM: Communications/Computer Related/Electronic Components and Instrumentation/Agricultural/Distribution/Medical/Genetic Engineering/Industrial Products and Equipment

INDUSTRY PREFERENCES BY INDIVIDUAL FIRM MEMBERS: N/A

YEAR COMPANY ESTABLISHED: 1962

FUNDS UNDER MANAGEMENT AT COST: Approximately $500 million

MINIMUM SIZE INVESTMENT: $100,000–$300,000

PREFERRED SIZE INVESTMENT: $750,000–$2,000,000

WILL FIRM SERVE AS LEAD INVESTOR: Yes

NUMBER OF DEALS COMPLETED IN THE LAST 12 MONTHS: 28

AMOUNT INVESTED IN LAST 12 MONTHS: $14.149 million

AVERAGE TIME REQUIRED TO COMPLETE A DEAL: 60 days
(From Initial Contact to Closing)

FIRM NAME: **Technology Funding**

ADDRESS: 2000 Alameda de las Pulgas
Suite 250
San Mateo, CA 94403

PHONE: (415) 345–2200

SBIC ___   VENTURE CAPITAL FUND _X_   MESBIC ___   OTHER ___

TYPES OF FINANCING PREFERRED (Stages): Start-up/company operating 1–2 years: losses/company operating 1–3 years: break-even to profitable

MINIMUM DATA REQUIRED TO CONSIDER FINANCING: Business plan (current)

GEOGRAPHIC PREFERENCE: Far West preferred, but will consider opportunities elsewhere

INDUSTRY PREFERENCE BY FIRM: Most high-technology areas, with exception of consumer products

INDUSTRY PREFERENCES BY INDIVIDUAL FIRM MEMBERS:
Gene J. Fischer, General Partner   David N. Hartford, General Partner
John A. Griner, General Partner   Charles R. Kokesh, General Partner
Frank R. Pope, General Partner   Cowsy J. Wadia, Associate

YEAR COMPANY ESTABLISHED: 1979

FUNDS UNDER MANAGEMENT AT COST: $35 million

MINIMUM SIZE INVESTMENT: $500,000

PREFERRED SIZE INVESTMENT: $750,000–$1,000,000

WILL FIRM SERVE AS LEAD INVESTOR: Yes

NUMBER OF DEALS COMPLETED IN THE LAST 12 MONTHS: 15

AMOUNT INVESTED IN LAST 12 MONTHS: $7.5 million

AVERAGE TIME REQUIRED TO COMPLETE A DEAL: 60 days
    (From Initial Contact to Closing)

FIRM NAME: **Techno World Investments, Inc.**

ADDRESS: 2121 S. El Camino Real
                Suite 1000
                San Mateo, CA 94403

PHONE: (415) 573–0800

SBIC ___   VENTURE CAPITAL FUND _X_ MESBIC ___   OTHER ___

TYPES OF FINANCING PREFERRED (Stages): All Stages

MINIMUM DATA REQUIRED TO CONSIDER FINANCING: N/A

GEOGRAPHIC PREFERENCE: USA, Europe, Asia

INDUSTRY PREFERENCE BY FIRM: Any

INDUSTRY PREFERENCES BY INDIVIDUAL FIRM MEMBERS:
    Allan F. Robb, Vice-chairman
    Flemming Fischer, President

YEAR COMPANY ESTABLISHED: 1984

FUNDS UNDER MANAGEMENT AT COST: N/A

MINIMUM SIZE INVESTMENT: $100,000 or less

PREFERRED SIZE INVESTMENT: $100,000–$200,000

WILL FIRM SERVE AS LEAD INVESTOR: Yes

NUMBER OF DEALS COMPLETED IN THE LAST 12 MONTHS: N/A

AMOUNT INVESTED IN LAST 12 MONTHS: N/A

AVERAGE TIME REQUIRED TO COMPLETE A DEAL: N/A
    (From Initial Contact to Closing)

FIRM NAME: **Union Venture Corporation**

ADDRESS: 445 Figueroa St.
                Los Angeles, CA 90071

PHONE: (213) 236–6292

SBIC _X_ VENTURE CAPITAL FUND ___   MESBIC ___   OTHER ___

TYPES OF FINANCING PREFERRED (Stages): Early stages

MINIMUM DATA REQUIRED TO CONSIDER FINANCING: Complete and detailed business plan

GEOGRAPHIC PREFERENCE: USA only

INDUSTRY PREFERENCE BY FIRM: Computers/Computer Peripherals/Integrated Circuits/Communications/Medical Technologies/Airlines/General Manufacturing

INDUSTRY PREFERENCES BY INDIVIDUAL FIRM MEMBERS: N/A

YEAR COMPANY ESTABLISHED: 1967

FUNDS UNDER MANAGEMENT AT COST: $20 million

MINIMUM SIZE INVESTMENT: $300,000

PREFERRED SIZE INVESTMENT: $500,000–$750,000

WILL FIRM SERVE AS LEAD INVESTOR: Yes

NUMBER OF DEALS COMPLETED IN THE LAST 12 MONTHS: 10

AMOUNT INVESTED IN LAST 12 MONTHS: N/A

AVERAGE TIME REQUIRED TO COMPLETE A DEAL: 2 months
(From Initial Contact to Closing)

FIRM NAME: **United Business Ventures, Inc.**

ADDRESS·   3931 MacArthur Blvd.   130 Monthgomery St.
                Suite 212   6th Floor
                Newport Beach, CA 92660   San Francisco, CA 94104

PHONE: (714) 851–0855   (415) 392–5410

SBIC ____   VENTURE CAPITAL FUND ____   MESBIC _X_   OTHER ____

TYPES OF FINANCING PREFERRED (Stages): Start-ups/second stage/buyouts/acquisitions/owner-occupied facility/equipment

MINIMUM DATA REQUIRED TO CONSIDER FINANCING: 3 years of financial statements and tax returns, business history, management resumes, financial statements of principal, cash flow pro forma

GEOGRAPHIC PREFERENCE: No preference

INDUSTRY PREFERENCE BY FIRM: No preference

INDUSTRY PREFERENCES BY INDIVIDUAL FIRM MEMBERS: N/A

YEAR COMPANY ESTABLISHED: 1975

FUNDS UNDER MANAGEMENT AT COST: $2.5 million

MINIMUM SIZE INVESTMENT: $75,000

PREFERRED SIZE INVESTMENT: $250,000

WILL FIRM SERVE AS LEAD INVESTOR: Yes

NUMBER OF DEALS COMPLETED IN THE LAST 12 MONTHS: 4

AMOUNT INVESTED IN LAST 12 MONTHS: $1 million

AVERAGE TIME REQUIRED TO COMPLETE A DEAL: 45 days
(From Initial Contact to Closing)

FIRM NAME: **Unity Capital Corporation**

ADDRESS: 4343 Morena Blvd.
                  #3-A
                  San Diego, CA 92117

PHONE: (619) 275–6030

SBIC ____ VENTURE CAPITAL FUND ____ MESBIC __X__ OTHER ____

TYPES OF FINANCING PREFERRED (Stages): Ongoing

MINIMUM DATA REQUIRED TO CONSIDER FINANCING: 2–3 years with financial statements

GEOGRAPHIC PREFERENCE: California

INDUSTRY PREFERENCE BY FIRM: Various

INDUSTRY PREFERENCES BY INDIVIDUAL FIRM MEMBERS: N/A

YEAR COMPANY ESTABLISHED: 1979

FUNDS UNDER MANAGEMENT AT COST: $310,000

MINIMUM SIZE INVESTMENT: $15,000

PREFERRED SIZE INVESTMENT: $90,000 (maximum)

WILL FIRM SERVE AS LEAD INVESTOR: Yes

NUMBER OF DEALS COMPLETED IN THE LAST 12 MONTHS: 1

AMOUNT INVESTED IN LAST 12 MONTHS: N/A

AVERAGE TIME REQUIRED TO COMPLETE A DEAL: 3 months
    (From Initial Contact to Closing)

FIRM NAME: **U.S. Venture Partners**

ADDRESS: 2180 Sand Hill Rd.
                  Suite 300
                  Menlo Park, CA 94025

PHONE: (415) 854–9080

SBIC ____ VENTURE CAPITAL FUND __X__ MESBIC ____ OTHER ____

TYPES OF FINANCING PREFERRED (Stages): Seed/start-up/first stage/second
    stage/later stage financings/purchases of secondary positions

MINIMUM DATA REQUIRED TO CONSIDER FINANCING: N/A

GEOGRAPHIC PREFERENCE: West Coast, East Coast, Northwest

INDUSTRY PREFERENCE BY FIRM: Consumer/Distribution/Electronic Components and Instrumentation/Genetic/Engineering/Industrial Products and Equipment/Medical–Health Related/Franchise Businesses

INDUSTRY PREFERENCES BY INDIVIDUAL FIRM MEMBERS:
    William K. Bowes, Jr.—Genetic Engineering/Diagnostic Equipment/Drugs and
        Medicines/Industrial Products and Equipment/Communications/Computers
    Stuart G. Moldaw—Specialty Retailing and Consumer Products

Robert Sackman—Communications/Computers/Electronic Components and Instrumentation/Industrial Products and Equipment

H. Joseph Horowitz—Consumer Products and Services/Food and Beverage Products/Specialty Retailing/Medical and Health Related/Electronic Components and Instrumentation/Industrial Products and Equipment

Jane H. Martin—Communications/Computer Related/Consumer Specialty Retailing/Electronic Components and Instrumentation/Industrial Products and Equipment

YEAR COMPANY ESTABLISHED: 1981

FUNDS UNDER MANAGEMENT AT COST: $160 million

MINIMUM SIZE INVESTMENT: $1 million

PREFERRED SIZE INVESTMENT: $1 million

WILL FIRM SERVE AS LEAD INVESTOR: Yes

NUMBER OF DEALS COMPLETED IN THE LAST 12 MONTHS: 31

AMOUNT INVESTED IN LAST 12 MONTHS: $19.1 million

AVERAGE TIME REQUIRED TO COMPLETE A DEAL: N/A
(From Initial Contact to Closing)

FIRM NAME: **Vista Capital Corporation**

ADDRESS: 701 "B" St.
                Suite 760
                San Diego, CA 92101

PHONE: (619) 236–1800

SBIC _X_ VENTURE CAPITAL FUND ___ MESBIC ___ OTHER ___

TYPES OF FINANCING PREFERRED (Stages): Second or third round

MINIMUM DATA REQUIRED TO CONSIDER FINANCING: Business plan and most recent financial statements

GEOGRAPHIC PREFERENCE: West Coast

INDUSTRY PREFERENCE BY FIRM: High Technology/Biotechnology/Gas and Oil

INDUSTRY PREFERENCES BY INDIVIDUAL FIRM MEMBERS: N/A

YEAR COMPANY ESTABLISHED: 1983

FUNDS UNDER MANAGEMENT AT COST: N/A

MINIMUM SIZE INVESTMENT: $50,000

PREFERRED SIZE INVESTMENT: $100,000

WILL FIRM SERVE AS LEAD INVESTOR: Not usually

NUMBER OF DEALS COMPLETED IN THE LAST 12 MONTHS: 2

AMOUNT INVESTED IN LAST 12 MONTHS: $170,000

AVERAGE TIME REQUIRED TO COMPLETE A DEAL: Varies
(From Initial Contact to Closing)

FIRM NAME: **Walden**

ADDRESS: 303 Sacramento   1001 Logan Bldg.
                San Francisco, CA 94111   Seattle, WA 98101

PHONE: (415) 391–7225   (206) 623–6550

SBIC ____ VENTURE CAPITAL FUND _X_ MESBIC ____ OTHER ____

TYPES OF FINANCING PREFERRED (Stages): All stages

MINIMUM DATA REQUIRED TO CONSIDER FINANCING: N/A

GEOGRAPHIC PREFERENCE: West Coast

INDUSTRY PREFERENCE BY FIRM: None

INDUSTRY PREFERENCES BY INDIVIDUAL FIRM MEMBERS: None

YEAR COMPANY ESTABLISHED: 1975

FUNDS UNDER MANAGEMENT AT COST: $30 million

MINIMUM SIZE INVESTMENT: $500,000

PREFERRED SIZE INVESTMENT: $1 million

WILL FIRM SERVE AS LEAD INVESTOR: Yes

NUMBER OF DEALS COMPLETED IN THE LAST 12 MONTHS: 13

AMOUNT INVESTED IN LAST 12 MONTHS: $4.4 million

AVERAGE TIME REQUIRED TO COMPLETE A DEAL: 30 days
    (From Initial Contact to Closing)

FIRM NAME: **Weiss, Peck & Greer**

ADDRESS: 555 California St.   1 New York Plaza
                San Franciso, CA 94104   New York, NY 10004

PHONE: (415) 622–6864   (212) 908–9500

SBIC ____ VENTURE CAPITAL FUND _X_ MESBIC ____ OTHER ____

TYPES OF FINANCING PREFERRED (Stages): All

MINIMUM DATA REQUIRED TO CONSIDER FINANCING: Complete business
    plan

GEOGRAPHIC PREFERENCE: Nationwide

INDUSTRY PREFERENCE BY FIRM: Diversified

INDUSTRY PREFERENCES BY INDIVIDUAL FIRM MEMBERS:
    San Francisco   New York   Boston
        Philip Greer   E. Theodore Stolberg   Ralph T. Linsalata
        Gunnar Hurtig III   Kim Davis
        Robert J. Loarie   Wes Lang
        John Savage
        Eugene Weber

YEAR COMPANY ESTABLISHED: 1971

FUNDS UNDER MANAGEMENT AT COST: $240 million

MINIMUM SIZE INVESTMENT: $500,000

PREFERRED SIZE INVESTMENT: $1.0–$1.5 million

WILL FIRM SERVE AS LEAD INVESTOR: Yes

NUMBER OF DEALS COMPLETED IN THE LAST 12 MONTHS: 17

AMOUNT INVESTED IN LAST 12 MONTHS: $12 million

AVERAGE TIME REQUIRED TO COMPLETE A DEAL: 6–8 weeks
(From Initial Contact to Closing)

COLORADO

FIRM NAME: **Cambridge Venture Partners**

ADDRESS: 88 Steele St.
                Suite 200
                Denver, CO 80206

PHONE: (303) 393–1111

SBIC ____ VENTURE CAPITAL FUND _X_ MESBIC ____ OTHER ____

TYPES OF FINANCING PREFERRED (Stages): Seed/start-up/R&D/management
buyouts and acquisitions

MINIMUM DATA REQUIRED TO CONSIDER FINANCING: Business plan

GEOGRAPHIC PREFERENCE: Rocky Mountain region and western USA

INDUSTRY PREFERENCE BY FIRM: Medical Technology/Computer Technol-
ogy/Communications Technology

INDUSTRY PREFERENCES BY INDIVIDUAL FIRM MEMBERS:
Bruce B. Paul—Medical and Communications Technology
Duncan M. Davidson—Computer Technology

YEAR COMPANY ESTABLISHED: 1981

FUNDS UNDER MANAGEMENT AT COST: N/A

MINIMUM SIZE INVESTMENT: $50,000

PREFERRED SIZE INVESTMENT: $250,000

WILL FIRM SERVE AS LEAD INVESTOR: Yes

NUMBER OF DEALS COMPLETED IN THE LAST 12 MONTHS: N/A

AMOUNT INVESTED IN LAST 12 MONTHS: N/A

AVERAGE TIME REQUIRED TO COMPLETE A DEAL: 30 days
(From Initial Contact to Closing)

FIRM NAME: **Colorado Growth Capital, Inc.**

ADDRESS: 1600 Broadway
                Suite 2125
                Denver, CO 80202

PHONE: (303) 629–0250

SBIC _X_ VENTURE CAPITAL FUND ____ MESBIC ____ OTHER ____

TYPES OF FINANCING PREFERRED (Stages): Second and third stages

MINIMUM DATA REQUIRED TO CONSIDER FINANCING: Business plan/past and current financials/product literature/resumes of principals/breakdown on use of proceeds/market analysis/competition/etc.

GEOGRAPHIC PREFERENCE: Western and Rocky Mountain region

INDUSTRY PREFERENCE BY FIRM: Operating Manufacturing/Companies who possess patented or proprietary products, with a potential national market

INDUSTRY PREFERENCES BY INDIVIDUAL FIRM MEMBERS: Debra Chavez, Financial Analyst, reviews all potential deals

YEAR COMPANY ESTABLISHED: 1979

FUNDS UNDER MANAGEMENT AT COST: $1.5 million

MINIMUM SIZE INVESTMENT: $50,000

PREFERRED SIZE INVESTMENT: $100,000

WILL FIRM SERVE AS LEAD INVESTOR: Yes

NUMBER OF DEALS COMPLETED IN THE LAST 12 MONTHS: N/A

AMOUNT INVESTED IN LAST 12 MONTHS: N/A

AVERAGE TIME REQUIRED TO COMPLETE A DEAL: 3 months (From Initial Contact to Closing)

FIRM NAME: Colorado Venture Capital Corp.

ADDRESS: 885 Arapahoe Ave.
Boulder, CO 80302

PHONE: (303) 449–9018

SBIC ___ VENTURE CAPITAL FUND _X_ MESBIC ___ OTHER ___

TYPES OF FINANCING PREFERRED (Stages): Expansion capital/bridge financing/leveraged buyouts

MINIMUM DATA REQUIRED TO CONSIDER FINANCING: Business plan

GEOGRAPHIC PREFERENCE: Western USA especially Rocky Mountain region

INDUSTRY PREFERENCE BY FIRM: Medical and Health/Communications/Computer Equipment/Product-oriented Profitable "Lo-Tech"

INDUSTRY PREFERENCES BY INDIVIDUAL FIRM MEMBERS: N/A

YEAR COMPANY ESTABLISHED: 1981

FUNDS UNDER MANAGEMENT AT COST: $5 million

MINIMUM SIZE INVESTMENT: $150,000

PREFERRED SIZE INVESTMENT: $250,000

WILL FIRM SERVE AS LEAD INVESTOR: Yes

NUMBER OF DEALS COMPLETED IN THE LAST 12 MONTHS: 10

AMOUNT INVESTED IN LAST 12 MONTHS: $1,601,256

AVERAGE TIME REQUIRED TO COMPLETE A DEAL: 90 days
   (From Initial Contact to Closing)

FIRM NAME: **Columbine Venture Fund, Ltd.**

ADDRESS: 5613 DTC Parkway
            #510
            Englewood, CO 80111

PHONE: (303) 694–3222

SBIC ____ VENTURE CAPITAL FUND _X_ MESBIC ____ OTHER ____

TYPES OF FINANCING PREFERRED (Stages): Seed and start-up/first round

MINIMUM DATA REQUIRED TO CONSIDER FINANCING: Business plan

GEOGRAPHIC PREFERENCE: Rocky Mountain states

INDUSTRY PREFERENCE BY FIRM: Electronic Systems and Compo-
   nents/Computer and Communication Equipment/Biotechnology/Specialty
   Chemicals and Materials/Medical Electronics

INDUSTRY PREFERENCES BY INDIVIDUAL FIRM MEMBERS: N/A

YEAR COMPANY ESTABLISHED: 1984

FUNDS UNDER MANAGEMENT AT COST: $34 million

MINIMUM SIZE INVESTMENT: $100,000

PREFERRED SIZE INVESTMENT: $500,000

WILL FIRM SERVE AS LEAD INVESTOR: Yes

NUMBER OF DEALS COMPLETED IN THE LAST 12 MONTHS: 13

AMOUNT INVESTED IN LAST 12 MONTHS: $3.7 million

AVERAGE TIME REQUIRED TO COMPLETE A DEAL: 90 days
   (From Initial Contact to Closing)

FIRM NAME: **The Masters Fund**

ADDRESS: 1426 Pearl St.
            Suite 211
            Boulder, CO 80302

PHONE: (303) 443–2460

SBIC ____ VENTURE CAPITAL FUND _X_ MESBIC ____ OTHER ____

TYPES OF FINANCING PREFERRED (Stages): Seed/first round

MINIMUM DATA REQUIRED TO CONSIDER FINANCING: Business summary

GEOGRAPHIC PREFERENCE: None

INDUSTRY PREFERENCE BY FIRM: Computer Hardware, Software, and Services

INDUSTRY PREFERENCES BY INDIVIDUAL FIRM MEMBERS: N/A

YEAR COMPANY ESTABLISHED: 1983

FUNDS UNDER MANAGEMENT AT COST: $12 million

MINIMUM SIZE INVESTMENT: None

PREFERRED SIZE INVESTMENT: $500,000

WILL FIRM SERVE AS LEAD INVESTOR: Yes

NUMBER OF DEALS COMPLETED IN THE LAST 12 MONTHS: 5

AMOUNT INVESTED IN LAST 12 MONTHS: $3 million

AVERAGE TIME REQUIRED TO COMPLETE A DEAL: 3 months
  (From Initial Contact to Closing)

FIRM NAME: **Mile Hi Small Business Investment Co.**

ADDRESS: 3801 E. Florida Ave.
                   Suite 401
                   Denver, CO 80210

PHONE: N/A

SBIC ___   VENTURE CAPITAL FUND ___   MESBIC _X_   OTHER ___

TYPES OF FINANCING PREFERRED (Stages): Prefer expansion financings, will
  consider start-ups, will not consider seed stage deals

MINIMUM DATA REQUIRED TO CONSIDER FINANCING: Written deal summary

GEOGRAPHIC PREFERENCE: Colorado

INDUSTRY PREFERENCE BY FIRM: Communications/Manufacturing/Dis-
  tribution

INDUSTRY PREFERENCES BY INDIVIDUAL FIRM MEMBERS:
  E. Preston Summa, Jr.—Communications/Medical Technology/Electronics

YEAR COMPANY ESTABLISHED: 1984

FUNDS UNDER MANAGEMENT AT COST: $560,000

MINIMUM SIZE INVESTMENT: $75,000

PREFERRED SIZE INVESTMENT: $75,000–$100,000

WILL FIRM SERVE AS LEAD INVESTOR: Yes

NUMBER OF DEALS COMPLETED IN THE LAST 12 MONTHS: 1

AMOUNT INVESTED IN LAST 12 MONTHS: $100,000

AVERAGE TIME REQUIRED TO COMPLETE A DEAL: 90 days
  (From Initial Contact to Closing)

FIRM NAME: **The Rockies Fund, Inc.**

ADDRESS: 8400 E. Prentice
                   #560
                   Englewood, CO 80111

PHONE: (303) 793–3060

SBIC ___   VENTURE CAPITAL FUND _X_   MESBIC ___   OTHER ___

TYPES OF FINANCING PREFERRED (Stages): Third or fourth stages/bridge

MINIMUM DATA REQUIRED TO CONSIDER FINANCING: Full business plan and executive summary

GEOGRAPHIC PREFERENCE: Rocky Mountain region

INDUSTRY PREFERENCE BY FIRM: Broad-based interests

INDUSTRY PREFERENCES BY INDIVIDUAL FIRM MEMBERS: N/A

YEAR COMPANY ESTABLISHED: 1983

FUNDS UNDER MANAGEMENT AT COST: $3 million

MINIMUM SIZE INVESTMENT: $100,000

PREFERRED SIZE INVESTMENT: $200,000

WILL FIRM SERVE AS LEAD INVESTOR: Yes

NUMBER OF DEALS COMPLETED IN THE LAST 12 MONTHS: 6

AMOUNT INVESTED IN LAST 12 MONTHS: $1.5 million

AVERAGE TIME REQUIRED TO COMPLETE A DEAL: 90–120 days
(From Initial Contact to Closing)

FIRM NAME: **Stephenson Merchant Banking**

ADDRESS: 899 Logan St.
                 Denver, CO 80203

PHONE: (303) 837–1700

SBIC ____   VENTURE CAPITAL FUND ____   MESBIC ____   OTHER _X_

TYPES OF FINANCING PREFERRED (Stages): Minimum requirement: break-even. Prefer historical profits. Principally interested in management leveraged buyouts

MINIMUM DATA REQUIRED TO CONSIDER FINANCING: 3 years of financials/business plan and description/management backgrounds/5 year pro formas

GEOGRAPHIC PREFERENCE: Within 2 hours of Denver

INDUSTRY PREFERENCE BY FIRM: Communications/Medical Technology/Financial Services/Mobile Homes/Basic Manufacturing/Transportation/Petroleum Reserves

INDUSTRY PREFERENCES BY INDIVIDUAL FIRM MEMBERS: N/A

YEAR COMPANY ESTABLISHED: 1969

FUNDS UNDER MANAGEMENT AT COST: $100 million

MINIMUM SIZE INVESTMENT: $100,000

PREFERRED SIZE INVESTMENT: $500,000–$1,000,000

WILL FIRM SERVE AS LEAD INVESTOR: Yes

NUMBER OF DEALS COMPLETED IN THE LAST 12 MONTHS: 7

AMOUNT INVESTED IN LAST 12 MONTHS: $3 million

AVERAGE TIME REQUIRED TO COMPLETE A DEAL: 90 days
(From Initial Contact to Closing)

FIRM NAME: **Venture Associates Ltd.**

ADDRESS: 1333 18th St.
               Suite 400
               Denver, CO 80202

PHONE: (303) 297–8670

SBIC ____ VENTURE CAPITAL FUND ____ MESBIC ____
OTHER _X_ (Private venture capital company)

TYPES OF FINANCING PREFERRED (Stages): Concept/start-up/first stage

MINIMUM DATA REQUIRED TO CONSIDER FINANCING: Business plan

GEOGRAPHIC PREFERENCE: USA

INDUSTRY PREFERENCE BY FIRM: All, with the exception of real estate

INDUSTRY PREFERENCES BY INDIVIDUAL FIRM MEMBERS: N/A

YEAR COMPANY ESTABLISHED: 1982

FUNDS UNDER MANAGEMENT AT COST: N/A

MINIMUM SIZE INVESTMENT: $100,000

PREFERRED SIZE INVESTMENT: $500,000

WILL FIRM SERVE AS LEAD INVESTOR: Yes

NUMBER OF DEALS COMPLETED IN THE LAST 12 MONTHS: 3

AMOUNT INVESTED IN LAST 12 MONTHS: $1.2 million

AVERAGE TIME REQUIRED TO COMPLETE A DEAL: 4 months
(From Initial Contact to Closing)

CONNECTICUT

FIRM NAME: **Beacon Partners**

ADDRESS: 71 Strawberry Hill
               Suite 614
               Stanford, CT 06902

PHONE: (203) 348–8858

SBIC ____ VENTURE CAPITAL FUND ____ MESBIC ____ OTHER _X_

TYPES OF FINANCING PREFERRED (Stages): Turnarounds/later stage

MINIMUM DATA REQUIRED TO CONSIDER FINANCING: Business plan

GEOGRAPHIC PREFERENCE: Northeast

INDUSTRY PREFERENCE BY FIRM: Chemicals/Health Care/Food/Textiles/Tele-
communications

INDUSTRY PREFERENCES BY INDIVIDUAL FIRM MEMBERS: N/A

YEAR COMPANY ESTABLISHED: 1975

FUNDS UNDER MANAGEMENT AT COST: N/A

MINIMUM SIZE INVESTMENT: $250,000

PREFERRED SIZE INVESTMENT: $500,000–$1,000,000

WILL FIRM SERVE AS LEAD INVESTOR: Yes

NUMBER OF DEALS COMPLETED IN THE LAST 12 MONTHS: N/A

AMOUNT INVESTED IN LAST 12 MONTHS: N/A

AVERAGE TIME REQUIRED TO COMPLETE A DEAL: 90–120 days
   (From Initial Contact to Closing)

FIRM NAME: **Fairchester Associates**

ADDRESS: 2777 Summer St.
                Suite 414
                Stamford, CT 06905

PHONE: (203) 357–0714

SBIC ___ VENTURE CAPITAL FUND _X_ MESBIC ___ OTHER ___

TYPES OF FINANCING PREFERRED (Stages): Second stage

MINIMUM DATA REQUIRED TO CONSIDER FINANCING: Business plan

GEOGRAPHIC PREFERENCE: East

INDUSTRY PREFERENCE BY FIRM: Health Care/Electronic Components/
   Publishing/Oil Field Service/Energy

INDUSTRY PREFERENCES BY INDIVIDUAL FIRM MEMBERS:
   William R. Knobloch—Health Care/Electronic Components
   Carl W. Knobloch—Oil Field Service/Publishing /Energy

YEAR COMPANY ESTABLISHED: 1962

FUNDS UNDER MANAGEMENT AT COST: $7 million

MINIMUM SIZE INVESTMENT: $250,000

PREFERRED SIZE INVESTMENT: $500,000

WILL FIRM SERVE AS LEAD INVESTOR: Yes

NUMBER OF DEALS COMPLETED IN THE LAST 12 MONTHS: 3

AMOUNT INVESTED IN LAST 12 MONTHS: $2.2 million

AVERAGE TIME REQUIRED TO COMPLETE A DEAL: 3 months
   (From Initial Contact to Closing)

FIRM NAME: **The First Connecticut Small Business Investment Co.**

ADDRESS: 177 State St.
                Bridgeport, CT 06604

PHONE: (203) 366–4726

SBIC _X_ VENTURE CAPITAL FUND ___ MESBIC ___ OTHER ___

TYPES OF FINANCING PREFERRED (Stages): Secondary

MINIMUM DATA REQUIRED TO CONSIDER FINANCING: Current financials and projections

GEOGRAPHIC PREFERENCE: Southern New England, eastern New York, New Jersey, southeast Pennsylvania

INDUSTRY PREFERENCE BY FIRM: General

INDUSTRY PREFERENCES BY INDIVIDUAL FIRM MEMBERS: N/A

YEAR COMPANY ESTABLISHED: 1960

FUNDS UNDER MANAGEMENT AT COST: $33 million

MINIMUM SIZE INVESTMENT: $10,000

PREFERRED SIZE INVESTMENT: $150,000

WILL FIRM SERVE AS LEAD INVESTOR: Yes

NUMBER OF DEALS COMPLETED IN THE LAST 12 MONTHS: 110

AMOUNT INVESTED IN LAST 12 MONTHS: $12 million

AVERAGE TIME REQUIRED TO COMPLETE A DEAL: 10 days to 1 month (From Initial Contact to Closing)

FIRM NAME:	**Grayrock Capital Inc.**
ADDRESS:	36 Grove St.
	New Canaan, CT 06840
PHONE:	(203) 966–8392

SBIC ____ VENTURE CAPITAL FUND ____ MESBIC ____ OTHER __X__

TYPES OF FINANCING PREFERRED (Stages): Start-up financing/first stage financing (up to 1 year old)/second stage financing (1–3 years)/later stage expansion financing/buyout or acquisition financing

MINIMUM DATA REQUIRED TO CONSIDER FINANCING: Annual sales of $500,000/losses and profits projected after two years

GEOGRAPHIC PREFERENCE: Near major metropolitan areas: Midwest/ Northwest/East Coast/West Coast

INDUSTRY PREFERENCE BY FIRM: Communicatons/Computer Services/Office Automation/Consumer Products/Distribution/Electronic Components and Instrumentation/Energy/Natural resources-related products/Genetic Engineering/Health-related Products and Services/Chemicals/Industrial Automation/ Robotics/Retail/Distribution

INDUSTRY PREFERENCES BY INDIVIDUAL FIRM MEMBERS: N/A

YEAR COMPANY ESTABLISHED: 1981

FUNDS UNDER MANAGEMENT AT COST: $6.0 million

MINIMUM SIZE INVESTMENT: $100,000

PREFERRED SIZE INVESTMENT: $250,000–$500,000

WILL FIRM SERVE AS LEAD INVESTOR: Yes

NUMBER OF DEALS COMPLETED IN THE LAST 12 MONTHS: 9

AMOUNT INVESTED IN LAST 12 MONTHS: $2.5 million

AVERAGE TIME REQUIRED TO COMPLETE A DEAL: 3 months
   (From Initial Contact to Closing)

FIRM NAME: **James B. Kobak & Co.**

ADDRESS: 774 Hollow Tree Ridge
                Darien, CT 06820

PHONE: (203) 655–8764

SBIC ___   VENTURE CAPITAL FUND ___   MESBIC ___   OTHER _X_

TYPES OF FINANCING PREFERRED (Stages): Start-up/first stage

MINIMUM DATA REQUIRED TO CONSIDER FINANCING: N/A

GEOGRAPHIC PREFERENCE: None

INDUSTRY PREFERENCE BY FIRM: Mail Order/Publishing

INDUSTRY PREFERENCES BY INDIVIDUAL FIRM MEMBERS:
   James B. Kobak, President
   Hope M. Kobak, Vice-president

YEAR COMPANY ESTABLISHED: 1971

FUNDS UNDER MANAGEMENT AT COST: N/A

MINIMUM SIZE INVESTMENT: $100,000 or less

PREFERRED SIZE INVESTMENT: N/A

WILL FIRM SERVE AS LEAD INVESTOR: N/A

NUMBER OF DEALS COMPLETED IN THE LAST 12 MONTHS: N/A

AMOUNT INVESTED IN LAST 12 MONTHS: N/A

AVERAGE TIME REQUIRED TO COMPLETE A DEAL: N/A
   (From Initial Contact to Closing)

FIRM NAME: **MarketCorp Venture Associates, LP**

ADDRESS: 285 Riverside Ave.
                Westport, CT 06880

PHONE: (203) 222–1000

SBIC ___   VENTURE CAPITAL FUND _X_   MESBIC ___   OTHER ___

TYPES OF FINANCING PREFERRED (Stages): Early stages: start-up and stage I

MINIMUM DATA REQUIRED TO CONSIDER FINANCING: Business plan is
   preferred

GEOGRAPHIC PREFERENCE: Preference is eastern but not limited to

INDUSTRY PREFERENCE BY FIRM: Retailing/Packaged Goods/Health Care/ Communications/Consumer Electronics

INDUSTRY PREFERENCES BY INDIVIDUAL FIRM MEMBERS: N/A

YEAR COMPANY ESTABLISHED: 1984

FUNDS UNDER MANAGEMENT AT COST: $65.651 million

MINIMUM SIZE INVESTMENT: $250,000

PREFERRED SIZE INVESTMENT: $250,000–$1,250,000

WILL FIRM SERVE AS LEAD INVESTOR: Yes

NUMBER OF DEALS COMPLETED IN THE LAST 12 MONTHS: 8

AMOUNT INVESTED IN LAST 12 MONTHS: Approximately $6 million

AVERAGE TIME REQUIRED TO COMPLETE A DEAL: 1–2 months
(From Initial Contact to Closing)

FIRM NAME: **Memhard Investment Bankers**

ADDRESS: 22 Fifth St.
                Stamford, CT 06905

PHONE: (203) 348–6802

SBIC ____   VENTURE CAPITAL FUND ____   MESBIC ____   OTHER _X_

TYPES OF FINANCING PREFERRED (Stages): Prefer role as deal origina-
tor/start-ups/first stage/second stage/later stage expansion/buyout or acquisi-
tion/purchases of secondary positions

MINIMUM DATA REQUIRED TO CONSIDER FINANCING: Annual sales: nominal; P&L: losses (profits projected after 2 years)

GEOGRAPHIC PREFERENCE: East Coast, Midwest, Southeast

INDUSTRY PREFERENCE BY FIRM: Communications/Computer Re-
lated/Consumer/Distribution/Electronic Components and Instrumenta-
tion/Energy–Natural Resources/Industrial Products and Equipment/Medical–
Health Related/Agriculture

INDUSTRY PREFERENCES BY INDIVIDUAL FIRM MEMBERS:
Richard C. Memhard, President
R. Scott Memhard, Vice-president
Laura M. Flemins, Treasurer

YEAR COMPANY ESTABLISHED: 1973

FUNDS UNDER MANAGEMENT AT COST: N/A

MINIMUM SIZE INVESTMENT: $500,000

PREFERRED SIZE INVESTMENT: $500,000–$1,000,000

WILL FIRM SERVE AS LEAD INVESTOR: N/A

NUMBER OF DEALS COMPLETED IN THE LAST 12 MONTHS: 1 (last 6 months)

AMOUNT INVESTED IN LAST 12 MONTHS: $200,000 (last 6 months)

AVERAGE TIME REQUIRED TO COMPLETE A DEAL: N/A
(From Initial Contact to Closing)

FIRM NAME: Oxford Partners

ADDRESS: Soundview Plaza
                 1266 Main St.
                 Stamford, CT 06902

PHONE: (203) 964–0592

SBIC ___ VENTURE CAPITAL FUND _X_ MESBIC ___ OTHER ___

TYPES OF FINANCING PREFERRED (Stages): Early stages/first and second stages

MINIMUM DATA REQUIRED TO CONSIDER FINANCING: Business plan

GEOGRAPHIC PREFERENCE: No preference

INDUSTRY PREFERENCE BY FIRM: Information Industry/Telecommunications Industry/Medical Industry

INDUSTRY PREFERENCES BY INDIVIDUAL FIRM MEMBERS: N/A

YEAR COMPANY ESTABLISHED: 1981

FUNDS UNDER MANAGEMENT AT COST: $80 million

MINIMUM SIZE INVESTMENT: $500,000

PREFERRED SIZE INVESTMENT: $1 million

WILL FIRM SERVE AS LEAD INVESTOR: Yes

NUMBER OF DEALS COMPLETED IN THE LAST 12 MONTHS: 24

AMOUNT INVESTED IN LAST 12 MONTHS: $11.8 million

AVERAGE TIME REQUIRED TO COMPLETE A DEAL: 1 month
(From Initial Contact to Closing)

FIRM NAME: Prime Capital, LP

ADDRESS: One Landmark Sq.
                 Suite 800
                 Stamford, CT 06901

PHONE: (203) 964–0642

SBIC ___ VENTURE CAPITAL FUND _X_ MESBIC ___ OTHER ___

TYPES OF FINANCING PREFERRED (Stages): First or second stage

MINIMUM DATA REQUIRED TO CONSIDER FINANCING: Detailed business plan including 5 year financial projections

GEOGRAPHIC PREFERENCE: USA

INDUSTRY PREFERENCE BY FIRM: Communications/Computer Related/Electronics/Genetic Engineering/Medical/Energy/Industrial

INDUSTRY PREFERENCES BY INDIVIDUAL FIRM MEMBERS: N/A

YEAR COMPANY ESTABLISHED: 1981

FUNDS UNDER MANAGEMENT AT COST: $26.2 million

MINIMUM SIZE INVESTMENT: $300,000–$600,000

PREFERRED SIZE INVESTMENT: $600,000 plus

WILL FIRM SERVE AS LEAD INVESTOR: Yes

NUMBER OF DEALS COMPLETED IN THE LAST 12 MONTHS: 15

AMOUNT INVESTED IN LAST 12 MONTHS: $5.5 million

AVERAGE TIME REQUIRED TO COMPLETE A DEAL: 2–3 months
   (From Initial Contact to Closing)

FIRM NAME: **Regional Financial Enterprises**

ADDRESS: 51 Pine St.   Burlington Executive Center
              New Canaan, CT 06840   315 E. Eisenhower Parkway
                                                   Ann Arbor, MI 48243

PHONE: (203) 966–2800   (313) 769–0941

SBIC ____ VENTURE CAPITAL FUND _X_ MESBIC ____ OTHER ____

TYPES OF FINANCING PREFERRED (Stages): Start-up and early stage/
   expansion/leveraged buyouts

MINIMUM DATA REQUIRED TO CONSIDER FINANCING: Business plan

GEOGRAPHIC PREFERENCE: None

INDUSTRY PREFERENCE BY FIRM: Health-care services and computer related
   account for 60% of activity; balance is diversified

INDUSTRY PREFERENCES BY INDIVIDUAL FIRM MEMBERS:
   Howard C. Landis—Health Care
   George E. Thomassy III—Health Care
   Robert R. Sparacino—Computer Related

YEAR COMPANY ESTABLISHED: 1980

FUNDS UNDER MANAGEMENT AT COST: $65 million

MINIMUM SIZE INVESTMENT: $1 million, except for follow-ons

PREFERRED SIZE INVESTMENT: $2 million

WILL FIRM SERVE AS LEAD INVESTOR: Yes

NUMBER OF DEALS COMPLETED IN THE LAST 12 MONTHS: 23

AMOUNT INVESTED IN LAST 12 MONTHS: $15 million

AVERAGE TIME REQUIRED TO COMPLETE A DEAL: 3 months
   (From Initial Contact to Closing)

FIRM NAME: **Saugatuck Capital Company**

ADDRESS: 999 Summer St.
              Stamford, CT 06905

PHONE: (203) 348–6669

SBIC ____ VENTURE CAPITAL FUND _X_ MESBIC ____ OTHER ____

TYPES OF FINANCING PREFERRED (Stages): First stage/second stage/later stage
   expansion/buyout or acquisition

MINIMUM DATA REQUIRED TO CONSIDER FINANCING: Annual sales: $1.5 million/P&L break-even

GEOGRAPHIC PREFERENCE: N/A

INDUSTRY PREFERENCE BY FIRM: Communications/Consumer/Distribution/ Electronic Components and Instrumentation/Energy–Natural Resources/ Genetic Engineering/Industrial Products and Equipment/Medical–Health Related/Finance and Insurance/Transportation

INDUSTRY PREFERENCES BY INDIVIDUAL FIRM MEMBERS:

Frank J. Hawley, Jr.—Data Communications/Telephone Related/Communications Equipment/Electronics Equipment/Analytical and Scientific Instrumentation/Laser Related/Optics Technology/Oil and Gas Services/Technology-Related Products and Equipment/Finance and Insurance/ Transportation

Alexander H. Dunbar—Consumer Products/Food Products/Industrial Products/Advanced Materials/Chemicals/Equipment and Machinery/Industrial Automation/Plastics/Process Control/Robotics

Norman W. Johnson—Consumer Services/Medical Products/Recombinant DNA (agricultural and industrial) Diagnostic Equipment/Drugs and Medicines/Hospital and Clinical Labs/Medical Services/Theraputic Equipment

YEAR COMPANY ESTABLISHED: 1982

FUNDS UNDER MANAGEMENT AT COST: $25 million

MINIMUM SIZE INVESTMENT: $500,000

PREFERRED SIZE INVESTMENT: $500,000–$1,000,000

WILL FIRM SERVE AS LEAD INVESTOR: Yes

NUMBER OF DEALS COMPLETED IN THE LAST 12 MONTHS: 4

AMOUNT INVESTED IN LAST 12 MONTHS: $6.1 million

AVERAGE TIME REQUIRED TO COMPLETE A DEAL: 60–90 days (From Initial Contact to Closing)

FIRM NAME: **Donald C. Seibert**

ADDRESS: P.O. Box 740
                Old Greenwich, CT 06870

PHONE: (203) 637–1704

SBIC ____   VENTURE CAPITAL FUND __X__   MESBIC ____   OTHER ____

TYPES OF FINANCING PREFERRED (Stages): New start/first stage/leveraged buyout

MINIMUM DATA REQUIRED TO CONSIDER FINANCING: Business plan, resumes of principals

GEOGRAPHIC PREFERENCE: Investment experience mostly in USA but also in Canada and the UK. Any country would be considered but I prefer to invest where I have had experience

INDUSTRY PREFERENCE BY FIRM: Electronic Technology/Resources/Turnaround Management/Others considered

INDUSTRY PREFERENCES BY INDIVIDUAL FIRM MEMBERS: Donald C. Seibert is the only full-time firm member. Preferences as listed above.

YEAR COMPANY ESTABLISHED: 1968

FUNDS UNDER MANAGEMENT AT COST: $2 million

MINIMUM SIZE INVESTMENT: No minimum

PREFERRED SIZE INVESTMENT: $50,000–$1,000,000

WILL FIRM SERVE AS LEAD INVESTOR: Yes

NUMBER OF DEALS COMPLETED IN THE LAST 12 MONTHS: 1

AMOUNT INVESTED IN LAST 12 MONTHS: $150,000

AVERAGE TIME REQUIRED TO COMPLETE A DEAL: 1–2 months
(From Initial Contact to Closing)

FIRM NAME: **Vista Technology Ventures, Inc.**

ADDRESS: 2410 Long Ridge Rd.
                  Stamford, CT 06903

PHONE: (203) 322–0091

SBIC ___ VENTURE CAPITAL FUND ___ MESBIC ___ OTHER _X_
(Consultant investment banker)

TYPES OF FINANCING PREFERRED (Stages): Early stages/leveraged buyouts

MINIMUM DATA REQUIRED TO CONSIDER FINANCING: 1 year of operations

GEOGRAPHIC PREFERENCE: New England, Mid-Atlantic

INDUSTRY PREFERENCE BY FIRM: Electronic/Computers/Instruments/Biotechnology/Specialty Publishing)

INDUSTRY PREFERENCES BY INDIVIDUAL FIRM MEMBERS: N/A

YEAR COMPANY ESTABLISHED: 1969

FUNDS UNDER MANAGEMENT AT COST: As required

MINIMUM SIZE INVESTMENT: $500,000

PREFERRED SIZE INVESTMENT: $1 million

WILL FIRM SERVE AS LEAD INVESTOR: Yes

NUMBER OF DEALS COMPLETED IN THE LAST 12 MONTHS: 3

AMOUNT INVESTED IN LAST 12 MONTHS: $500,000

AVERAGE TIME REQUIRED TO COMPLETE A DEAL: 6 months
(From Initial Contact to Closing)

FIRM NAME: **Vista Ventures**

ADDRESS: 36 Grove St.
                  New Canaan, CT 06840

PHONE: (203) 972–3400

SBIC ___ VENTURE CAPITAL FUND _X_ MESBIC ___ OTHER ___

TYPES OF FINANCING PREFERRED (Stages): Seed/start-up/first stage/second stage/buyout

MINIMUM DATA REQUIRED TO CONSIDER FINANCING: Nominal

GEOGRAPHIC PREFERENCE: None

INDUSTRY PREFERENCE BY FIRM: Information Systems/Communications Systems/Health Care/Life Sciences/Technology

INDUSTRY PREFERENCES BY INDIVIDUAL FIRM MEMBERS: N/A

YEAR COMPANY ESTABLISHED: 1980

FUNDS UNDER MANAGEMENT AT COST: $100 million

MINIMUM SIZE INVESTMENT: $100,000 or less

PREFERRED SIZE INVESTMENT: $600,000 plus

WILL FIRM SERVE AS LEAD INVESTOR: Yes

NUMBER OF DEALS COMPLETED IN THE LAST 12 MONTHS: 20

AMOUNT INVESTED IN LAST 12 MONTHS: $11 million

AVERAGE TIME REQUIRED TO COMPLETE A DEAL: Varies
(From Initial Contact to Closing)

FIRM NAME: **Neal Wehr & Associates**

ADDRESS: 108 I Seaside Ave
Milford, CT 06460

PHONE: (203) 333–0949

SBIC ___ VENTURE CAPITAL FUND ___ MESBIC ___ OTHER _X_

TYPES OF FINANCING PREFERRED (Stages): Leveraged buyouts

MINIMUM DATA REQUIRED TO CONSIDER FINANCING: Full financial disclosure

GEOGRAPHIC PREFERENCE: Connecticut

INDUSTRY PREFERENCE BY FIRM: Manufacturing/Wholesale

INDUSTRY PREFERENCES BY INDIVIDUAL FIRM MEMBERS: N/A

YEAR COMPANY ESTABLISHED: 1975

FUNDS UNDER MANAGEMENT AT COST: N/A

MINIMUM SIZE INVESTMENT: N/A

PREFERRED SIZE INVESTMENT: N/A

WILL FIRM SERVE AS LEAD INVESTOR: N/A

NUMBER OF DEALS COMPLETED IN THE LAST 12 MONTHS: 3

AMOUNT INVESTED IN LAST 12 MONTHS: N/A

AVERAGE TIME REQUIRED TO COMPLETE A DEAL: 3 months
(From Initial Contact to Closing)

FIRM NAME: **Whitehead Associates**

ADDRESS: 15 Valley Dr.
               Greenwich, CT 06830

PHONE: (203) 629–4633

SBIC ____ VENTURE CAPITAL FUND _X_ MESBIC ____ OTHER ____

TYPES OF FINANCING PREFERRED (Stages): Seed/start-up/expansion

MINIMUM DATA REQUIRED TO CONSIDER FINANCING: Comprehensive
   business plan, including product, market, financial, management data

GEOGRAPHIC PREFERENCE: None

INDUSTRY PREFERENCE BY FIRM: Will consider (and have invested in) various industries, but prefer health care, medical devices and instrumentation,
   biotechnology.

INDUSTRY PREFERENCES BY INDIVIDUAL FIRM MEMBERS: N/A

YEAR COMPANY ESTABLISHED: 1980

FUNDS UNDER MANAGEMENT AT COST: Substantial

MINIMUM SIZE INVESTMENT: $100,000

PREFERRED SIZE INVESTMENT: $500,000–$1,000,000

WILL FIRM SERVE AS LEAD INVESTOR: Yes

NUMBER OF DEALS COMPLETED IN THE LAST 12 MONTHS: 9

AMOUNT INVESTED IN LAST 12 MONTHS: $2.8 million

AVERAGE TIME REQUIRED TO COMPLETE A DEAL: 3 months
   (From Initial Contact to Closing)

FIRM NAME: **Xerox Venture Capital**

ADDRESS: 800 Long Ridge Rd.
               Stamford, CT 06904

PHONE: (203) 329–8711

ADDRESS: 2029 Century Park East
               Suite 740
               Los Angeles, CA 90067

PHONE: (213) 278–7940

SBIC ____ VENTURE CAPITAL FUND _X_ MESBIC ____ OTHER ____

TYPES OF FINANCING PREFERRED (Stages): Seed/first round and second round

MINIMUM DATA REQUIRED TO CONSIDER FINANCING: Business plan and
   investment memorandum

GEOGRAPHIC PREFERENCE: None

INDUSTRY PREFERENCE BY FIRM: Communications/Information and Document Processing Systems/Components (hardware and software)/Electronics
   Technology

INDUSTRY PREFERENCES BY INDIVIDUAL FIRM MEMBERS: N/A

YEAR COMPANY ESTABLISHED: 1976

FUNDS UNDER MANAGEMENT AT COST: $50 million

MINIMUM SIZE INVESTMENT: $250,000

PREFERRED SIZE INVESTMENT: $500,000–$1,000,000

WILL FIRM SERVE AS LEAD INVESTOR: Yes

NUMBER OF DEALS COMPLETED IN THE LAST 12 MONTHS: 10

AMOUNT INVESTED IN LAST 12 MONTHS: $7 million

AVERAGE TIME REQUIRED TO COMPLETE A DEAL: 2–6 weeks
(From Initial Contact to Closing)

DISTRICT OF COLUMBIA

FIRM NAME: **Allied Capital Corporation**

ADDRESS: 1625 I St., NW
Suite 603
Washington, DC 20006

PHONE: (202) 331–1112

SBIC ____   VENTURE CAPITAL FUND __X__   MESBIC ____   OTHER ____

TYPES OF FINANCING PREFERRED (Stages): Second and third round financings/growth companies/financing for leveraged buyouts or acquisitions of companies

MINIMUM DATA REQUIRED TO CONSIDER FINANCING: Prior financial statements where applicable, 3 year projections, resumes on key individuals

GEOGRAPHIC PREFERENCE: East of Mississippi with emphasis on Mid-Atlantic and the Southeast

INDUSTRY PREFERENCE BY FIRM: None; we will consider investments in any industry where there is strong growth. We emphasize non-high-technology investment opportunities

INDUSTRY PREFERENCES BY INDIVIDUAL FIRM MEMBERS:
George Williams—Communications
Jon Ledecky—Medical
David Gladstone—Computers and Software

YEAR COMPANY ESTABLISHED: 1958

FUNDS UNDER MANAGEMENT AT COST: $55 million

MINIMUM SIZE INVESTMENT: $100,000

PREFERRED SIZE INVESTMENT: $500,000

WILL FIRM SERVE AS LEAD INVESTOR: Firm has a strong preference for being lead investor

NUMBER OF DEALS COMPLETED IN THE LAST 12 MONTHS: 13

AMOUNT INVESTED IN LAST 12 MONTHS: $13.2 million

AVERAGE TIME REQUIRED TO COMPLETE A DEAL: 2 months
(From Initial Contact to Closing)

FIRM NAME: **Ewing Capital, Inc.**

ADDRESS: 1110 Vermont Ave., NW
Suite 1260
Washington, DC 20005

PHONE: (202) 463-8787

SBIC ____ VENTURE CAPITAL FUND ____ MESBIC ____ OTHER _X_
(Investment banking firm)

TYPES OF FINANCING PREFERRED (Stages): Second stage and above

MINIMUM DATA REQUIRED TO CONSIDER FINANCING: Business plan/5 year
financials or 5 year projections

GEOGRAPHIC PREFERENCE: None

INDUSTRY PREFERENCE BY FIRM: Telecommunicatons/Broadcasting/Manu-
facturing

INDUSTRY PREFERENCES BY INDIVIDUAL FIRM MEMBERS:
Samuel D. Ewing, Jr.

YEAR COMPANY ESTABLISHED: 1981

FUNDS UNDER MANAGEMENT AT COST: N/A

MINIMUM SIZE INVESTMENT: $1 million

PREFERRED SIZE INVESTMENT: N/A

WILL FIRM SERVE AS LEAD INVESTOR: N/A

NUMBER OF DEALS COMPLETED IN THE LAST 12 MONTHS: N/A

AMOUNT INVESTED IN LAST 12 MONTHS: N/A

AVERAGE TIME REQUIRED TO COMPLETE A DEAL: N/A
(From Initial Contact to Closing)

FIRM NAME: **Fulcrum Venture Capital Corporation**

ADDRESS: 2021 K Street, NW
Suite 301
Washington, DC 20006-1085

PHONE: (202) 833-9590

SBIC ____ VENTURE CAPITAL FUND ____ MESBIC _X_ OTHER ____

TYPES OF FINANCING PREFERRED (Stages): Second stage expansions

MINIMUM DATA REQUIRED TO CONSIDER FINANCING: Business plan

GEOGRAPHIC PREFERENCE: USA only

INDUSTRY PREFERENCE BY FIRM: Computer Related/Semiconductors/
Medical Services-Products/Chemical Processing/Communications

INDUSTRY PREFERENCES BY INDIVIDUAL FIRM MEMBERS: N/A

YEAR COMPANY ESTABLISHED: 1978

FUNDS UNDER MANAGEMENT AT COST: $7 million

MINIMUM SIZE INVESTMENT: $100,000

PREFERRED SIZE INVESTMENT: $250,000–$300,000

WILL FIRM SERVE AS LEAD INVESTOR: Yes

NUMBER OF DEALS COMPLETED IN THE LAST 12 MONTHS: 5

AMOUNT INVESTED IN LAST 12 MONTHS: $850,000

AVERAGE TIME REQUIRED TO COMPLETE A DEAL: 90 days
   (From Initial Contact to Closing)

FIRM NAME: **Minority Broadcast Investment Corporation**

ADDRESS: 1220 19th St., NW
                Suite 501
                Washington, DC 20036

PHONE: (202) 293–1166

SBIC ___   VENTURE CAPITAL FUND ___   MESBIC _X_   OTHER ___

TYPES OF FINANCING PREFERRED (Stages): Acquisitions/start-ups

MINIMUM DATA REQUIRED TO CONSIDER FINANCING: 3 year financial history/10 Year financial projections

GEOGRAPHIC PREFERENCE: None

INDUSTRY PREFERENCE BY FIRM: Radio/TV/Cable TV/Cellular Radio/MDS/
   Other telecommunications ventures

INDUSTRY PREFERENCES BY INDIVIDUAL FIRM MEMBERS: N/A

YEAR COMPANY ESTABLISHED: 1979

FUNDS UNDER MANAGEMENT AT COST: $3.2 million

MINIMUM SIZE INVESTMENT: $100,000

PREFERRED SIZE INVESTMENT: $250,000

WILL FIRM SERVE AS LEAD INVESTOR: Yes

NUMBER OF DEALS COMPLETED IN THE LAST 12 MONTHS: 3

AMOUNT INVESTED IN LAST 12 MONTHS: $415,000

AVERAGE TIME REQUIRED TO COMPLETE A DEAL: 60–90 days
   (From Initial Contact to Closing)

FIRM NAME: **Syndicated Communications, Inc.**
                   Syncom Capital Corp.

ADDRESS: 1030 15th St., NW
                Suite 203
                Washington, DC 20005

PHONE: (202) 293–9428

SBIC ___ VENTURE CAPITAL FUND _X_ (SCI) MESBIC _X_ (SCC) OTHER ___

TYPES OF FINANCING PREFERRED (Stages): Start-up

MINIMUM DATA REQUIRED TO CONSIDER FINANCING: Market analysis/corporate structure and management/business plan (5 years)

GEOGRAPHIC PREFERENCE: USA

INDUSTRY PREFERENCE BY FIRM: Communications

INDUSTRY PREFERENCES BY INDIVIDUAL FIRM MEMBERS: N/A

YEAR COMPANY ESTABLISHED: 1977

FUNDS UNDER MANAGEMENT AT COST: $8,614,547

MINIMUM SIZE INVESTMENT: $100,000

PREFERRED SIZE INVESTMENT: $500,000

WILL FIRM SERVE AS LEAD INVESTOR: Yes

NUMBER OF DEALS COMPLETED IN THE LAST 12 MONTHS: N/A

AMOUNT INVESTED IN LAST 12 MONTHS: $1 million

AVERAGE TIME REQUIRED TO COMPLETE A DEAL:
(From Initial Contact to Closing)　　Radio: 3–6 months; Cable: 1–3 years

FIRM NAME:　　**Wachtel & Co., Inc.**

ADDRESS:　　　1101 Fourteenth St., NW
　　　　　　　Washington, DC 20005–5680

PHONE:　　　　(202) 898–1144

SBIC ___ VENTURE CAPITAL FUND ___ MESBIC ___ OTHER _X_

TYPES OF FINANCING PREFERRED (Stages): Will do start-ups but prefer the company to have at least several months of operating history. We are also interested in raising capital for companies in all later stages via both the private and public financing routes

MINIMUM DATA REQUIRED TO CONSIDER FINANCING: P&Ls and balance sheets for 3–5 years if available. If not available, will review same for a shorter period

GEOGRAPHIC PREFERENCE: Eastern half of USA

INDUSTRY PREFERENCE BY FIRM: Primary interest is in service industries and not in industries or companies that are capital intensive

INDUSTRY PREFERENCES BY INDIVIDUAL FIRM MEMBERS:
Sidney B. Wachtel—Consulting/Financial and Data Processing
John D. Sanders—Engineering/Electronics and Telecommunications
Wendie L. Wachtel—Distribution and Services
Bonnie K. Wachtel—Consulting and Computer Services

YEAR COMPANY ESTABLISHED: 1961

FUNDS UNDER MANAGEMENT AT COST: $7–$10 million

MINIMUM SIZE INVESTMENT: $50,000 (private); $500,000 (public)

PREFERRED SIZE INVESTMENT: $100,000–$150,000 (private); $750,000–$1,500,000 (public)

WILL FIRM SERVE AS LEAD INVESTOR: Yes

NUMBER OF DEALS COMPLETED IN THE LAST 12 MONTHS: 8

AMOUNT INVESTED IN LAST 12 MONTHS: $150,000 (start-ups); $899,000 (follow-on)

AVERAGE TIME REQUIRED TO COMPLETE A DEAL: 2–3 months
(From Initial Contact to Closing)

FLORIDA

FIRM NAME: **Business Research Corp.**
(subsidiary of Bay Street Corp.)

ADDRESS: 205 Worth Ave.
Palos Beach, FL 33480

PHONE: (305) 832–2155

SBIC ___   VENTURE CAPITAL FUND _X_   MESBIC ___   OTHER ___

TYPES OF FINANCING PREFERRED (Stages): Second stage/buyouts

MINIMUM DATA REQUIRED TO CONSIDER FINANCING: Preliminary information/summary/5-year plan

GEOGRAPHIC PREFERENCE: East Coast and near Midwest

INDUSTRY PREFERENCE BY FIRM: Communications/Engineered Hard Goods

INDUSTRY PREFERENCES BY INDIVIDUAL FIRM MEMBERS: N/A

YEAR COMPANY ESTABLISHED: 1963

FUNDS UNDER MANAGEMENT AT COST: $50 million

MINIMUM SIZE INVESTMENT: $750,000

PREFERRED SIZE INVESTMENT: $2–$5 million

WILL FIRM SERVE AS LEAD INVESTOR: Yes

NUMBER OF DEALS COMPLETED IN THE LAST 12 MONTHS: 2

AMOUNT INVESTED IN LAST 12 MONTHS: $49 Million

AVERAGE TIME REQUIRED TO COMPLETE A DEAL: 4 months
(From Initial Contact to Closing)

FIRM NAME: **Caribank Capital Corp.**

ADDRESS: 255 East Dania Beach Blvd.
Dania, FL 33004

PHONE: (305) 925–2211

SBIC _X_   VENTURE CAPITAL FUND ___   MESBIC ___   OTHER ___

TYPES OF FINANCING PREFERRED (Stages): Second and third stages

MINIMUM DATA REQUIRED TO CONSIDER FINANCING: Business plan

GEOGRAPHIC PREFERENCE: Southeast USA

INDUSTRY PREFERENCE BY FIRM: High Technology/Oil and Gas/Health Care

INDUSTRY PREFERENCES BY INDIVIDUAL FIRM MEMBERS:
Michael E.Chaney, President—High-technology Industry/Oil and Gas
Harold F. Messner, Vice-president—Health Care/Oil and Gas

YEAR COMPANY ESTABLISHED: 1982

FUNDS UNDER MANAGEMENT AT COST: $2.1 million

MINIMUM SIZE INVESTMENT: $150,000

PREFERRED SIZE INVESTMENT: $200,000

WILL FIRM SERVE AS LEAD INVESTOR: Yes

NUMBER OF DEALS COMPLETED IN THE LAST 12 MONTHS: 5

AMOUNT INVESTED IN LAST 12 MONTHS: $1.2 million

AVERAGE TIME REQUIRED TO COMPLETE A DEAL: 60 days
(From Initial Contact to Closing)

FIRM NAME: **Electro-Science Management Corp.**

ADDRESS: 600 Courtland St.
                Suite 490
                Orlando, FL 32804

PHONE: (305) 645–1188

SBIC ____   VENTURE CAPITAL FUND __X__   MESBIC ____   OTHER ____

TYPES OF FINANCING PREFERRED (Stages): First and second stages

MINIMUM DATA REQUIRED TO CONSIDER FINANCING: Business plan

GEOGRAPHIC PREFERENCE: Southeast

INDUSTRY PREFERENCE BY FIRM: Proprietary products of a technology basis
marketed to commercial customers/Communications/Information Process-
ing/Medical

INDUSTRY PREFERENCES BY INDIVIDUAL FIRM MEMBERS: N/A

YEAR COMPANY ESTABLISHED: 1969

FUNDS UNDER MANAGEMENT AT COST: $7.5–$10 million

MINIMUM SIZE INVESTMENT: $100,000

PREFERRED SIZE INVESTMENT: $100,000–$250,000

WILL FIRM SERVE AS LEAD INVESTOR: Yes

NUMBER OF DEALS COMPLETED IN THE LAST 12 MONTHS: 2

AMOUNT INVESTED IN LAST 12 MONTHS: N/A

AVERAGE TIME REQUIRED TO COMPLETE A DEAL: 90–120 days
(From Initial Contact to Closing)

FIRM NAME: **First American Lending Corporation**

ADDRESS: 401 Northlake Blvd.
                North Palm Beach, FL 33408

PHONE: (305) 863–9826

SBIC ____ VENTURE CAPITAL FUND ____ MESBIC _X_ OTHER ____

TYPES OF FINANCING PREFERRED (Stages): Loans ranging from $25,000 to
  $150,000 secured, or equity investments

MINIMUM DATA REQUIRED TO CONSIDER FINANCING: Tax returns/current
  financial statements/pro formas/histories/comparison, etc.

GEOGRAPHIC PREFERENCE: Florida

INDUSTRY PREFERENCE BY FIRM: N/A

INDUSTRY PREFERENCES BY INDIVIDUAL FIRM MEMBERS: N/A

YEAR COMPANY ESTABLISHED: 1980

FUNDS UNDER MANAGEMENT AT COST: N/A

MINIMUM SIZE INVESTMENT: $25,000

PREFERRED SIZE INVESTMENT: $25,000–$150,000

WILL FIRM SERVE AS LEAD INVESTOR: Yes, $150,000 or less

NUMBER OF DEALS COMPLETED IN THE LAST 12 MONTHS: 3

AMOUNT INVESTED IN LAST 12 MONTHS: Approximately $100,000

AVERAGE TIME REQUIRED TO COMPLETE A DEAL: 30 days
  (From Initial Contact to Closing)

FIRM NAME: **Gold Coast Capital Corp.**

ADDRESS: 3550 Biscayne Blvd.
                # 601
                Miami, FL 33137

PHONE: (305) 576–2012

SBIC _X_ VENTURE CAPITAL FUND ____ MESBIC ____ OTHER ____

TYPES OF FINANCING PREFERRED (Stages): Active at least one year/certain
  select start-ups

MINIMUM DATA REQUIRED TO CONSIDER FINANCING: One year statement
  and personal statement of chief officers

GEOGRAPHIC PREFERENCE: Southeast

INDUSTRY PREFERENCE BY FIRM: Retail Business/Manufacturing/Wholesale
  Business/Land Development

INDUSTRY PREFERENCES BY INDIVIDUAL FIRM MEMBERS: N/A

YEAR COMPANY ESTABLISHED: 1959

FUNDS UNDER MANAGEMENT AT COST: $3 million

MINIMUM SIZE INVESTMENT: $25,000

PREFERRED SIZE INVESTMENT: $100,000

WILL FIRM SERVE AS LEAD INVESTOR: Yes, over $100,000

NUMBER OF DEALS COMPLETED IN THE LAST 12 MONTHS: 13

AMOUNT INVESTED IN LAST 12 MONTHS: $1.2 million

AVERAGE TIME REQUIRED TO COMPLETE A DEAL: 30 days
(From Initial Contact to Closing)

FIRM NAME: **Jets Venture Capital Corporation**

ADDRESS: 615 Park St.
Jacksonville, FL 32204

PHONE: N/A

SBIC __X__ VENTURE CAPITAL FUND ____ MESBIC ____ OTHER ____

TYPES OF FINANCING PREFERRED (Stages): Start-up or first stage

MINIMUM DATA REQUIRED TO CONSIDER FINANCING: Business plan

GEOGRAPHIC PREFERENCE: Southeast

INDUSTRY PREFERENCE BY FIRM: None

INDUSTRY PREFERENCES BY INDIVIDUAL FIRM MEMBERS: None

YEAR COMPANY ESTABLISHED: 1980

FUNDS UNDER MANAGEMENT AT COST: $2.5 million

MINIMUM SIZE INVESTMENT: $50,000

PREFERRED SIZE INVESTMENT: $200,000

WILL FIRM SERVE AS LEAD INVESTOR: Yes

NUMBER OF DEALS COMPLETED IN THE LAST 12 MONTHS: 5

AMOUNT INVESTED IN LAST 12 MONTHS: $1 million

AVERAGE TIME REQUIRED TO COMPLETE A DEAL: 7 days
(From Initial Contact to Closing)

FIRM NAME: **North American Company Limited**

ADDRESS: 111 East Las Olas Blvd.
P.O. Box 14758
Fort Lauderdale, FL 33302

PHONE: (305) 463–0681

SBIC ____ VENTURE CAPITAL FUND __X__ MESBIC ____ OTHER ____

TYPES OF FINANCING PREFERRED (Stages): Start-up/first stage/second
stage/later stage and expansion/buyout or acquisition financing/purchases of
secondary positions

MINIMUM DATA REQUIRED TO CONSIDER FINANCING: N/A

GEOGRAPHIC PREFERENCE: East Coast, Midwest, and Southeası

INDUSTRY PREFERENCE BY FIRM: Computer Related/Distribution/Manufacturing/Medical/Services/Technology

INDUSTRY PREFERENCES BY INDIVIDUAL FIRM MEMBERS: N/A

YEAR COMPANY ESTABLISHED: 1941

FUNDS UNDER MANAGEMENT AT COST: $25 million

MINIMUM SIZE INVESTMENT: $100,000–$300,000

PREFERRED SIZE INVESTMENT: $600,000 plus

WILL FIRM SERVE AS LEAD INVESTOR: Yes

NUMBER OF DEALS COMPLETED IN THE LAST 12 MONTHS: N/A

AMOUNT INVESTED IN LAST 12 MONTHS: N/A

AVERAGE TIME REQUIRED TO COMPLETE A DEAL: 3 months
(From Initial Contact to Closing)

FIRM NAME: **Pro-Med Capital, Inc.**
(subsidiary of Western Financial Capital Corp.)

ADDRESS: 1380 Miami Gardens Dr., NE
Suite 225
North Miami Beach, FL 33179

PHONE: (305) 949–5900

SBIC __X__ VENTURE CAPITAL FUND ____ MESBIC ____ OTHER ____

TYPES OF FINANCING PREFERRED (Stages): Second and third stages/business expansion with marketing in place

MINIMUM DATA REQUIRED TO CONSIDER FINANCING: Complete financials/resumes/business plan

GEOGRAPHIC PREFERENCE: USA

INDUSTRY PREFERENCE BY FIRM: Health care/Medical

INDUSTRY PREFERENCES BY INDIVIDUAL FIRM MEMBERS: N/A

YEAR COMPANY ESTABLISHED: 1979

FUNDS UNDER MANAGEMENT AT COST: $12 million

MINIMUM SIZE INVESTMENT: $50,000

PREFERRED SIZE INVESTMENT: $200,000

WILL FIRM SERVE AS LEAD INVESTOR: Prefer working with others

NUMBER OF DEALS COMPLETED IN THE LAST 12 MONTHS: 45

AMOUNT INVESTED IN LAST 12 MONTHS: $4 million

AVERAGE TIME REQUIRED TO COMPLETE A DEAL: 30 days
(From Initial Contact to Closing)

FIRM NAME: **RLR Securities Group, Inc.**

ADDRESS: 7539 W. Oakland Park Blvd.
                Lauderhill, FL 33379

PHONE: (800) 327-9193

SBIC ____ VENTURE CAPITAL FUND ____ MESBIC ____ OTHER _X_

TYPES OF FINANCING PREFERRED (Stages): First/second/public

MINIMUM DATA REQUIRED TO CONSIDER FINANCING: Full business
    plan/pro formas (audited if available)

GEOGRAPHIC PREFERENCE: N/A

INDUSTRY PREFERENCE BY FIRM: N/A

INDUSTRY PREFERENCES BY INDIVIDUAL FIRM MEMBERS: N/A

YEAR COMPANY ESTABLISHED: 1979

FUNDS UNDER MANAGEMENT AT COST: N/A

MINIMUM SIZE INVESTMENT: $500,000

PREFERRED SIZE INVESTMENT: $1-$2 million

WILL FIRM SERVE AS LEAD INVESTOR: N/A

NUMBER OF DEALS COMPLETED IN THE LAST 12 MONTHS: N/A

AMOUNT INVESTED IN LAST 12 MONTHS: N/A

AVERAGE TIME REQUIRED TO COMPLETE A DEAL: N/A
    (From Initial Contact to Closing)

FIRM NAME: **Universal Financial Services, Inc.**

ADDRESS: 2301 Collins Ave.
                Suite M-109
                Miami Beach, FL 33139

PHONE: (305) 538-5464

SBIC ____ VENTURE CAPITAL FUND ____ MESBIC _X_ OTHER ____

TYPES OF FINANCING PREFERRED (Stages): Buyout/expansion

MINIMUM DATA REQUIRED TO CONSIDER FINANCING: Use of funds' man-
    agement record

GEOGRAPHIC PREFERENCE: Southeast USA and Denver and Utah

INDUSTRY PREFERENCE BY FIRM: Transportation/ Construction

INDUSTRY PREFERENCES BY INDIVIDUAL FIRM MEMBERS: N/A

YEAR COMPANY ESTABLISHED: 1978

FUNDS UNDER MANAGEMENT AT COST: $1.6 million

MINIMUM SIZE INVESTMENT: $25,000

PREFERRED SIZE INVESTMENT: $500,000

WILL FIRM SERVE AS LEAD INVESTOR: Yes

NUMBER OF DEALS COMPLETED IN THE LAST 12 MONTHS: N/A

AMOUNT INVESTED IN LAST 12 MONTHS: $750,000

AVERAGE TIME REQUIRED TO COMPLETE A DEAL: 90 days
   (From Initial Contact to Closing)

FIRM NAME: **Venture Management Associates, Inc.**

ADDRESS: One Southeast Financial Center
                 Miami, FL 33131

PHONE: (305) 375–6470

SBIC __X__ VENTURE CAPITAL FUND ____ MESBIC ____ OTHER ____

TYPES OF FINANCING PREFERRED (Stages): N/A

MINIMUM DATA REQUIRED TO CONSIDER FINANCING: N/A

GEOGRAPHIC PREFERENCE: Southeast

INDUSTRY PREFERENCE BY FIRM: Communications/Computer Re-
   lated/Consumer/Electronic Components and Instrumentation/Energy—Natural Resources/Genetic Engineering/Industrial Products and Equipment/
   Medical–Health Related

INDUSTRY PREFERENCES BY INDIVIDUAL FIRM MEMBERS: N/A

YEAR COMPANY ESTABLISHED: 1968

FUNDS UNDER MANAGEMENT AT COST: $24 million

MINIMUM SIZE INVESTMENT: $300,000

PREFERRED SIZE INVESTMENT: $600,000

WILL FIRM SERVE AS LEAD INVESTOR: Yes

NUMBER OF DEALS COMPLETED IN THE LAST 12 MONTHS: 17

AMOUNT INVESTED IN LAST 12 MONTHS: $4 million

AVERAGE TIME REQUIRED TO COMPLETE A DEAL: N/A
   (From Initial Contact to Closing)

GEORGIA

FIRM NAME: **Advanced Technology Development Fund**

ADDRESS: 430 Tenth St.
                 Suite N 114
                 Atlanta, GA 30318

PHONE: (404) 875–4393

SBIC ____ VENTURE CAPITAL FUND __X__ MESBIC ____ OTHER ____

TYPES OF FINANCING PREFERRED (Stages): Early stage/start-up

MINIMUM DATA REQUIRED TO CONSIDER FINANCING: Business plan with
  financials/management team/proprietary product information/marketing plan

GEOGRAPHIC PREFERENCE: Southeast

INDUSTRY PREFERENCE BY FIRM: Computer Hardware/Software/Electronic/
  Telecommunication/Health Care

INDUSTRY PREFERENCES BY INDIVIDUAL FIRM MEMBERS:
  Ronald W. White
  Daniel D. Ross

YEAR COMPANY ESTABLISHED: 1983

FUNDS UNDER MANAGEMENT AT COST: $11.2 million

MINIMUM SIZE INVESTMENT: $150,000

PREFERRED SIZE INVESTMENT: $350,000–$1,000,000

WILL FIRM SERVE AS LEAD INVESTOR: Yes

NUMBER OF DEALS COMPLETED IN THE LAST 12 MONTHS: 13

AMOUNT INVESTED IN LAST 12 MONTHS: $3,817,953.32

AVERAGE TIME REQUIRED TO COMPLETE A DEAL: 2 months
  (From Initial Contact to Closing)

FIRM NAME: **Investor's Equity, Inc.**

ADDRESS: 2629 First Atlanta Tower
                Atlanta, GA 30383

PHONE: (404) 523–3999

SBIC _X_   VENTURE CAPITAL FUND ___   MESBIC ___   OTHER ___

TYPES OF FINANCING PREFERRED (Stages): Venture (secondary)

MINIMUM DATA REQUIRED TO CONSIDER FINANCING: N/A

GEOGRAPHIC PREFERENCE: Southeast

INDUSTRY PREFERENCE BY FIRM: Light Manufacturing/High Technol-
  ogy/Medical Technology

INDUSTRY PREFERENCES BY INDIVIDUAL FIRM MEMBERS: N/A

YEAR COMPANY ESTABLISHED: 1957

FUNDS UNDER MANAGEMENT AT COST: $500,000

MINIMUM SIZE INVESTMENT: $100,000

PREFERRED SIZE INVESTMENT: $100,000–$1,000,000

WILL FIRM SERVE AS LEAD INVESTOR: Yes

NUMBER OF DEALS COMPLETED IN THE LAST 12 MONTHS: 4

AMOUNT INVESTED IN LAST 12 MONTHS: $300,000

AVERAGE TIME REQUIRED TO COMPLETE A DEAL: 6 weeks
  (From Initial Contact to Closing)

FIRM NAME: **Lendman Capital Associates, LP**

ADDRESS: 5 Piedmont Center
Suite 320
Atlanta, GA 30305

PHONE: (404) 233–9003

SBIC ____   VENTURE CAPITAL FUND __X__   MESBIC ____   OTHER ____

TYPES OF FINANCING PREFERRED (Stages): First and second stages

MINIMUM DATA REQUIRED TO CONSIDER FINANCING: Financials/
references/business plan/management information

GEOGRAPHIC PREFERENCE: Southeast

INDUSTRY PREFERENCE BY FIRM: No preference

INDUSTRY PREFERENCES BY INDIVIDUAL FIRM MEMBERS: No preference

YEAR COMPANY ESTABLISHED: 1983

FUNDS UNDER MANAGEMENT AT COST: $10 million

MINIMUM SIZE INVESTMENT: $250,000

PREFERRED SIZE INVESTMENT: $250,000–$300,000

WILL FIRM SERVE AS LEAD INVESTOR: Yes

NUMBER OF DEALS COMPLETED IN THE LAST 12 MONTHS: 4

AMOUNT INVESTED IN LAST 12 MONTHS: $2 million

AVERAGE TIME REQUIRED TO COMPLETE A DEAL: 3 months
(From Initial Contact to Closing)

ILLINOIS

FIRM NAME: **Allstate Insurance Company**

ADDRESS: Venture Capital Division E-2
Allstate Plaza
Northbrook, IL 60062

PHONE: (312) 291–5681

SBIC ____   VENTURE CAPITAL FUND ____   MESBIC ____
OTHER __X__   (Venture capital division of an insurance company)

TYPES OF FINANCING PREFERRED (Stages): No preference

MINIMUM DATA REQUIRED TO CONSIDER FINANCING: Well-defined business plan addressing a large potential market offering compelling economic
benefits

GEOGRAPHIC PREFERENCE: None

INDUSTRY PREFERENCE BY FIRM: All areas except insurance

INDUSTRY PREFERENCES BY INDIVIDUAL FIRM MEMBERS:
  Leonard A. Batterson—Telecommunications/Computers/Semiconductors/
    Medical Products/Communications
  Donald R. Johnson—Telecommunicatons/Factory Automation/Computer Soft-
    ware
  Robert L. Lestina—Later stage, nontechnical ventures/Leveraged buyouts
  Oliver M. Darden—Urban Investments
  Sharri E. Marcin—Health Care/Office Automation
  Marcy H. Shockey—Medical Products/Marketing/Semiconductors/Computer-
    related Products
  Paul J. Renze—High-growth Companies
  Marc S. Sandroff—Health-care services/Medical Technology/Telecommunica-
    tions/High Technology

YEAR COMPANY ESTABLISHED: Venture Capital Division established 1958

FUNDS UNDER MANAGEMENT AT COST: $200 million (August 1985)

MINIMUM SIZE INVESTMENT: $500,000

PREFERRED SIZE INVESTMENT: $1–$3 million

WILL FIRM SERVE AS LEAD INVESTOR: Yes

NUMBER OF DEALS COMPLETED IN THE LAST 12 MONTHS: 30

AMOUNT INVESTED IN LAST 12 MONTHS: Amounted committed: $32.0 mil-
                                    lion
                                    Dollars out: $29.7 million

AVERAGE TIME REQUIRED TO COMPLETE A DEAL: 10 weeks
(From Initial Contact to Closing)

FIRM NAME: **Amoco Venture Capital Company**

ADDRESS: 200 East Randolph Dr.
              Chicago, IL 60601

PHONE: (312) 856–6523

SBIC ____   VENTURE CAPITAL FUND ____   MESBIC _X_   OTHER ____

TYPES OF FINANCING PREFERRED (Stages): Start-up or second round

MINIMUM DATA REQUIRED TO CONSIDER FINANCING: 4-year financial
  forecast

GEOGRAPHIC PREFERENCE: None

INDUSTRY PREFERENCE BY FIRM: Minority owned and managed businesses
  that are either technically oriented or can provide goods or services to an
  Amoco Co.

INDUSTRY PREFERENCES BY INDIVIDUAL FIRM MEMBERS: N/A

YEAR COMPANY ESTABLISHED: 1970

FUNDS UNDER MANAGEMENT AT COST: $2 million per year

MINIMUM SIZE INVESTMENT: $150,000

PREFERRED SIZE INVESTMENT: $300,000

WILL FIRM SERVE AS LEAD INVESTOR: Yes

NUMBER OF DEALS COMPLETED IN THE LAST 12 MONTHS: 6

AMOUNT INVESTED IN LAST 12 MONTHS: $2.1 million

AVERAGE TIME REQUIRED TO COMPLETE A DEAL: 2 months
(From Initial Contact to Closing)

FIRM NAME: **William Blair Venture Management Company**

ADDRESS: 135 S. LaSalle St.
Chicago, IL 60603

PHONE: (312) 853–8250

SBIC ____   VENTURE CAPITAL FUND _X_   MESBIC ____   OTHER ____

TYPES OF FINANCING PREFERRED (Stages): First stage/second stage/third stage/leveraged buyouts

MINIMUM DATA REQUIRED TO CONSIDER FINANCING: Description of business/historical and financial statements/projections (3–5) years/resumes of key management

GEOGRAPHIC PREFERENCE: USA

INDUSTRY PREFERENCE BY FIRM: None

INDUSTRY PREFERENCES BY INDIVIDUAL FIRM MEMBERS: N/A

YEAR COMPANY ESTABLISHED: 1982

FUNDS UNDER MANAGEMENT AT COST: $50 million

MINIMUM SIZE INVESTMENT: $500,000

PREFERRED SIZE INVESTMENT: $750,000–$1,000,000

WILL FIRM SERVE AS LEAD INVESTOR: Yes

NUMBER OF DEALS COMPLETED IN THE LAST 12 MONTHS: 9

AMOUNT INVESTED IN LAST 12 MONTHS: Approximately $4.7 million

AVERAGE TIME REQUIRED TO COMPLETE A DEAL: 60 days
(From Initial Contact to Closing)

FIRM NAME: **Business Ventures Inc.**

ADDRESS: 20 N. Wacker Dr.
Suite 550
Chicago, IL 60606

PHONE: (312) 346–1581

SBIC _X_ VENTURE CAPITAL FUND ____   MESBIC ____   OTHER ____

TYPES OF FINANCING PREFERRED (Stages): Early

MINIMUM DATA REQUIRED TO CONSIDER FINANCING: Business plan

GEOGRAPHIC PREFERENCE: Chicago metropolitan area

INDUSTRY PREFERENCE BY FIRM: No preferences

INDUSTRY PREFERENCES BY INDIVIDUAL FIRM MEMBERS: N/A

YEAR COMPANY ESTABLISHED: 1982

FUNDS UNDER MANAGEMENT AT COST: N/A

MINIMUM SIZE INVESTMENT: $50,000

PREFERRED SIZE INVESTMENT: Up to $250,000

WILL FIRM SERVE AS LEAD INVESTOR: Yes

NUMBER OF DEALS COMPLETED IN THE LAST 12 MONTHS: 3

AMOUNT INVESTED IN LAST 12 MONTHS: N/A

AVERAGE TIME REQUIRED TO COMPLETE A DEAL: 3 months
   (From Initial Contact to Closing)

FIRM NAME: **Continental Illinois Venture Corporation**

ADDRESS: 231 South LaSalle St.
                  Chicago, IL 60697

PHONE: (312) 828–8021

SBIC __X__ VENTURE CAPITAL FUND ____ MESBIC ____ OTHER ____

TYPES OF FINANCING PREFERRED (Stages): Start-up/expansion/leveraged
   buyouts

MINIMUM DATA REQUIRED TO CONSIDER FINANCING: Business plan

GEOGRAPHIC PREFERENCE: No preference

INDUSTRY PREFERENCE BY FIRM: No preference

INDUSTRY PREFERENCES BY INDIVIDUAL FIRM MEMBERS: N/A

YEAR COMPANY ESTABLISHED: 1970

FUNDS UNDER MANAGEMENT AT COST: N/A

MINIMUM SIZE INVESTMENT: $500,000

PREFERRED SIZE INVESTMENT: $1 million

WILL FIRM SERVE AS LEAD INVESTOR: Yes

NUMBER OF DEALS COMPLETED IN THE LAST 12 MONTHS: 6

AMOUNT INVESTED IN LAST 12 MONTHS: $4.33 million

AVERAGE TIME REQUIRED TO COMPLETE A DEAL: 8 weeks
   (From Initial Contact to Closing)

FIRM NAME: **First Chicago Investment Advisors**

ADDRESS: 3 First National Plaza
                  Suite 0140
                  Chicago, IL 60670

PHONE: (312) 732–4154

SBIC ____ VENTURE CAPITAL FUND __X__ MESBIC ____ OTHER ____

TYPES OF FINANCING PREFERRED (Stages): Start-ups through third stage

MINIMUM DATA REQUIRED TO CONSIDER FINANCING: Business plan or partnership prospectives

GEOGRAPHIC PREFERENCE: None

INDUSTRY PREFERENCE BY FIRM: None

INDUSTRY PREFERENCES BY INDIVIDUAL FIRM MEMBERS:
John H. Mahar—High Technology
Marshall L. Greenwald—Medical/
    Health Care
Dan Mitchell—Electronics/Com-
    munications
T. Bondurant French—Partner-
    ships/General
Patrick A. McGivney—General

YEAR COMPANY ESTABLISHED: 1976

FUNDS UNDER MANAGEMENT AT COST: $150 million

MINIMUM SIZE INVESTMENT: $500,000

PREFERRED SIZE INVESTMENT: $1 million

WILL FIRM SERVE AS LEAD INVESTOR: Yes

NUMBER OF DEALS COMPLETED IN THE LAST 12 MONTHS: 31

AMOUNT INVESTED IN LAST 12 MONTHS: $10.973 million

AVERAGE TIME REQUIRED TO COMPLETE A DEAL: 6–8 weeks
(From Initial Contact to Closing)

FIRM NAME: **First Chicago Venture Capital**

ADDRESS: One First National Plaza
Suite 2628
Chicago, IL 60670

PHONE: (312) 732–5400

SBIC _X_ VENTURE CAPITAL FUND ___ MESBIC ___ OTHER ___

TYPES OF FINANCING PREFERRED (Stages): Start-ups/growth equity/leveraged buyouts/acquisitions

MINIMUM DATA REQUIRED TO CONSIDER FINANCING: Business plan

GEOGRAPHIC PREFERENCE: None

INDUSTRY PREFERENCE BY FIRM: Diversified

INDUSTRY PREFERENCES BY INDIVIDUAL FIRM MEMBERS: N/A

YEAR COMPANY ESTABLISHED: 1961

FUNDS UNDER MANAGEMENT AT COST: $350 million

MINIMUM SIZE INVESTMENT: $750,000

PREFERRED SIZE INVESTMENT: $2–$5 million

WILL FIRM SERVE AS LEAD INVESTOR: Yes

NUMBER OF DEALS COMPLETED IN THE LAST 12 MONTHS: 68

AMOUNT INVESTED IN LAST 12 MONTHS: $124.8 million

AVERAGE TIME REQUIRED TO COMPLETE A DEAL: N/A
(From Initial Contact to Closing)

FIRM NAME: **Funds, Inc.**

ADDRESS: 1930 George St.
Melrose Park, IL 60160

PHONE: (312) 343–6575

SBIC __X__   VENTURE CAPITAL FUND ____   MESBIC ____   OTHER ____

TYPES OF FINANCING PREFERRED (Stages): Second stage financing (generally) of companies 1–3 years old/later stage expansion financing/buyout or acquisition financing/purchases of secondary positions

MINIMUM DATA REQUIRED TO CONSIDER FINANCING: Financial statements and D&B

GEOGRAPHIC PREFERENCE: To be determined

INDUSTRY PREFERENCE BY FIRM: Drugstores/Pharmacies/Clinics

INDUSTRY PREFERENCES BY INDIVIDUAL FIRM MEMBERS: N/A

YEAR COMPANY ESTABLISHED: 1984

FUNDS UNDER MANAGEMENT AT COST: N/A

MINIMUM SIZE INVESTMENT: $100,000

PREFERRED SIZE INVESTMENT: $100,000 or less

WILL FIRM SERVE AS LEAD INVESTOR: Yes

NUMBER OF DEALS COMPLETED IN THE LAST 12 MONTHS: 2

AMOUNT INVESTED IN LAST 12 MONTHS: Approximately $100,000

AVERAGE TIME REQUIRED TO COMPLETE A DEAL: 4–6 weeks
(From Initial Contact to Closing)

FIRM NAME: **Golder, Thoma & Cressey**

ADDRESS: 120 South LaSalle St.
Suite 630
Chicago, IL 60603

PHONE: (312) 853–3322

SBIC ____   VENTURE CAPITAL FUND __X__ MESBIC ____   OTHER ____

TYPES OF FINANCING PREFERRED (Stages): All stages/acquisitions

MINIMUM DATA REQUIRED TO CONSIDER FINANCING: Complete Business
plan

GEOGRAPHIC PREFERENCE: None

INDUSTRY PREFERENCE BY FIRM: Information Services/Health Care and
Medical Products

INDUSTRY PREFERENCES BY INDIVIDUAL FIRM MEMBERS:
Thoma—Information Services
Cressey—Health Care and Medical Products
Rauner—Health Care and Medical Products

YEAR COMPANY ESTABLISHED: 1980

FUNDS UNDER MANAGEMENT AT COST: $160 million

MINIMUM SIZE INVESTMENT: $500,000

PREFERRED SIZE INVESTMENT: $1–$3 million

WILL FIRM SERVE AS LEAD INVESTOR: Yes

NUMBER OF DEALS COMPLETED IN THE LAST 12 MONTHS: N/A

AMOUNT INVESTED IN LAST 12 MONTHS: $21,178,942

AVERAGE TIME REQUIRED TO COMPLETE A DEAL: 3 months
   (From Initial Contact to Closing)

FIRM NAME: **IEG Venture Management, Inc.**

ADDRESS: 401 N. Michigan Ave.
                  #2020
                  Chicago, IL 60611

PHONE: (312) 644–0890

SBIC ____   VENTURE CAPITAL FUND _X_   MESBIC ____   OTHER ____

TYPES OF FINANCING PREFERRED (Stages): Start-up/early stage

MINIMUM DATA REQUIRED TO CONSIDER FINANCING: N/A

GEOGRAPHIC PREFERENCE: Midwest

INDUSTRY PREFERENCE BY FIRM: IEG invests primarily in technology based
   start-up companies in the Midwest

INDUSTRY PREFERENCES BY INDIVIDUAL FIRM MEMBERS: N/A

YEAR COMPANY ESTABLISHED: 1983

FUNDS UNDER MANAGEMENT AT COST: Over $3 million

MINIMUM SIZE INVESTMENT: $250,000–$500,000

PREFERRED SIZE INVESTMENT: N/A

WILL FIRM SERVE AS LEAD INVESTOR: Possibly

NUMBER OF DEALS COMPLETED IN THE LAST 12 MONTHS: 1

AMOUNT INVESTED IN LAST 12 MONTHS: $350,000

AVERAGE TIME REQUIRED TO COMPLETE A DEAL: 3–6 months
   (From Initial Contact to Closing)

FIRM NAME: **Longworth Ventures**

ADDRESS: Suite 616
                  135 S. LaSalle St.
                  Chicago, IL 60603

PHONE: (312) 372–3888

SBIC ____   VENTURE CAPITAL FUND _X_   MESBIC ____   OTHER ____

TYPES OF FINANCING PREFERRED (Stages): Start-up/first stage/second stage/later stage expansion/buyout or acquisition/purchases of secondary positions

MINIMUM DATA REQUIRED TO CONSIDER FINANCING: Financial projections for 5 years/nominal annual sales/profits projected in two years

GEOGRAPHIC PREFERENCE: None

INDUSTRY PREFERENCE BY FIRM: Health Care Related/Computer Related/Communications/Other technology and basic industry leveraged buyouts

INDUSTRY PREFERENCES BY INDIVIDUAL FIRM MEMBERS:
Lawrence Sucsy, General Partner
Thomas Galuhn, General Partner
Andrew Beaurline, General Partner

YEAR COMPANY ESTABLISHED: N/A

FUNDS UNDER MANAGEMENT AT COST: Undisclosed

MINIMUM SIZE INVESTMENT: $100,000

PREFERRED SIZE INVESTMENT: $300,000

WILL FIRM SERVE AS LEAD INVESTOR: Yes

NUMBER OF DEALS COMPLETED IN THE LAST 12 MONTHS: Undisclosed

AMOUNT INVESTED IN LAST 12 MONTHS: Undisclosed

AVERAGE TIME REQUIRED TO COMPLETE A DEAL: 3–8 weeks
(From Initial Contact to Closing)

FIRM NAME: **The Luken Co.**

ADDRESS: 135 S. LaSalle St.
Suite 711
Chicago, IL 60603

PHONE: (312) 263–4015

SBIC ____ VENTURE CAPITAL FUND ____ MESBIC ____
OTHER __X__ (Financial consulting and investment banking firm investing own and associate money)

TYPES OF FINANCING PREFERRED (Stages): All stages except start-ups

MINIMUM DATA REQUIRED TO CONSIDER FINANCING: 1 year operating history

GEOGRAPHIC PREFERENCE: Midwest

INDUSTRY PREFERENCE BY FIRM: No specific industry preference: Service/Distribution/Medium Technology Manufacturing/Applied Technology

INDUSTRY PREFERENCES BY INDIVIDUAL FIRM MEMBERS: N/A

YEAR COMPANY ESTABLISHED: 1981

FUNDS UNDER MANAGEMENT AT COST: N/A

MINIMUM SIZE INVESTMENT: $300,000

PREFERRED SIZE INVESTMENT: $500,000–$2,000,000

WILL FIRM SERVE AS LEAD INVESTOR: Yes

NUMBER OF DEALS COMPLETED IN THE LAST 12 MONTHS: 5

AMOUNT INVESTED IN LAST 12 MONTHS: $1.95 million

AVERAGE TIME REQUIRED TO COMPLETE A DEAL: 60 days
   (From Initial Contact to Closing)

FIRM NAME: **North American Capital Group, Ltd.**

ADDRESS: 7250 N. Cicero
              #201
              Lincolnwood, IL 60646

PHONE: N/A

SBIC ____ VENTURE CAPITAL FUND _X_ MESBIC ____ OTHER ____

TYPES OF FINANCING PREFERRED (Stages): No start-ups/Prefer first, second,
   and third stages/leveraged buyouts

MINIMUM DATA REQUIRED TO CONSIDER FINANCING: Business plan/
   management resumes/product description/marketing/competition/financial/
   operations/etc.

GEOGRAPHIC PREFERENCE: Midwest

INDUSTRY PREFERENCE BY FIRM: Franchising, manufacturing, distribution
   and service companies

INDUSTRY PREFERENCES BY INDIVIDUAL FIRM MEMBERS:
   Gregory I. Kravitt, President
   William Anderson, Executive, vice-president

YEAR COMPANY ESTABLISHED: 1980

FUNDS UNDER MANAGEMENT AT COST: N/A

MINIMUM SIZE INVESTMENT: $100,000

PREFERRED SIZE INVESTMENT: $3.0 million

WILL FIRM SERVE AS LEAD INVESTOR: Yes

NUMBER OF DEALS COMPLETED IN THE LAST 12 MONTHS: 2

AMOUNT INVESTED IN LAST 12 MONTHS: $6.0 million

AVERAGE TIME REQUIRED TO COMPLETE A DEAL: 30–60 day, minimum
   (From Initial Contact to Closing)

FIRM NAME: **Seidman Jackson Fisher & Co.**

ADDRESS: 233 N. Michigan Ave.
              Suite 1812
              Chicago, IL 60601

PHONE: (312) 856–1812

SBIC ___ VENTURE CAPITAL FUND _X_ MESBIC ___ OTHER ___

TYPES OF FINANCING PREFERRED (Stages): Early stage to buyouts

MINIMUM DATA REQUIRED TO CONSIDER FINANCING: Complete business plan

GEOGRAPHIC PREFERENCE: Continental USA

INDUSTRY PREFERENCE BY FIRM: N/A

INDUSTRY PREFERENCES BY INDIVIDUAL FIRM MEMBERS: N/A

YEAR COMPANY ESTABLISHED: 1981

FUNDS UNDER MANAGEMENT AT COST: $45 million

MINIMUM SIZE INVESTMENT: $500,000

PREFERRED SIZE INVESTMENT: $1 million

WILL FIRM SERVE AS LEAD INVESTOR: Yes

NUMBER OF DEALS COMPLETED IN THE LAST 12 MONTHS: 9

AMOUNT INVESTED IN LAST 12 MONTHS: $5 million

AVERAGE TIME REQUIRED TO COMPLETE A DEAL: 90 days
(From Initial Contact to Closing)

FIRM NAME: **Technology Partners**

ADDRESS: 257 E. Main St.   1550 Tiburon Blvd.
               Barrington, IL 60010   Suite A
               Peter J. Gillespie   Belvedere, CA 94920
                                           William Hart

PHONE: (312) 381–2510

SBIC _X_ VENTURE CAPITAL FUND ___ MESBIC ___ OTHER ___

TYPES OF FINANCING PREFERRED (Stages): Early stage: first professional money

MINIMUM DATA REQUIRED TO CONSIDER FINANCING: Letter describing product or service/target market/management competence/investment opportunity

GEOGRAPHIC PREFERENCE: None

INDUSTRY PREFERENCE BY FIRM: Computers/Hardware–Software/Telecommunications/Health Care/Factory Automation/Advance Materials

INDUSTRY PREFERENCES BY INDIVIDUAL FIRM MEMBERS: N/A

YEAR COMPANY ESTABLISHED: 1981

FUNDS UNDER MANAGEMENT AT COST: $3.0 million

MINIMUM SIZE INVESTMENT: $200,000

PREFERRED SIZE INVESTMENT: $500,000

WILL FIRM SERVE AS LEAD INVESTOR: Yes

NUMBER OF DEALS COMPLETED IN THE LAST 12 MONTHS: 5

AMOUNT INVESTED IN LAST 12 MONTHS: $1.0 million

AVERAGE TIME REQUIRED TO COMPLETE A DEAL: 3 months
(From Initial Contact to Closing)

FIRM NAME: **Vanguard Capital Corporation**

ADDRESS: One Northbrook Place
Suite 200
5 Revere Dr.
Northbrook, IL 60062

PHONE: (312) 272–3636

SBIC ___   VENTURE CAPITAL FUND _X_   MESBIC ___   OTHER ___

TYPES OF FINANCING PREFERRED (Stages): Seed/spin-off

MINIMUM DATA REQUIRED TO CONSIDER FINANCING: Resumes

GEOGRAPHIC PREFERENCE: Illinois

INDUSTRY PREFERENCE BY FIRM: Marketing driven companies

INDUSTRY PREFERENCES BY INDIVIDUAL FIRM MEMBERS: N/A

YEAR COMPANY ESTABLISHED: 1961

FUNDS UNDER MANAGEMENT AT COST: N/A

MINIMUM SIZE INVESTMENT: $50,000

PREFERRED SIZE INVESTMENT: $100,000

WILL FIRM SERVE AS LEAD INVESTOR: Yes

NUMBER OF DEALS COMPLETED IN THE LAST 12 MONTHS: 2

AMOUNT INVESTED IN LAST 12 MONTHS: N/A

AVERAGE TIME REQUIRED TO COMPLETE A DEAL: 60 days
(From Initial Contact to Closing)

FIRM NAME: **Walnut Capital Corp.**

ADDRESS: 3 First National Plaza
22nd Floor
Chicago, IL 60602

PHONE: N/A

SBIC _X_   VENTURE CAPITAL FUND ___   MESBIC ___   OTHER ___

TYPES OF FINANCING PREFERRED (Stages): Early

MINIMUM DATA REQUIRED TO CONSIDER FINANCING: Business plan and
current financial information

GEOGRAPHIC PREFERENCE: None

INDUSTRY PREFERENCE BY FIRM: Technology/Research and Development

INDUSTRY PREFERENCES BY INDIVIDUAL FIRM MEMBERS: N/A

YEAR COMPANY ESTABLISHED: 1980

FUNDS UNDER MANAGEMENT AT COST: $2 million

MINIMUM SIZE INVESTMENT: $50,000

PREFERRED SIZE INVESTMENT: $100,000–$250,000

WILL FIRM SERVE AS LEAD INVESTOR: Yes

NUMBER OF DEALS COMPLETED IN THE LAST 12 MONTHS: 7

AMOUNT INVESTED IN LAST 12 MONTHS: $800,000

AVERAGE TIME REQUIRED TO COMPLETE A DEAL: Varies
    (From Initial Contact to Closing)

INDIANA

FIRM NAME: **Biddinger Investment Capital Corp.**

ADDRESS: 9102 North Meridian
                Suite 500
                Indianapolis, IN 46260

PHONE: (317) 844–7390

SBIC ____ VENTURE CAPITAL FUND ____ MESBIC ____ OTHER _X_

TYPES OF FINANCING PREFERRED (Stages): Second stage

MINIMUM DATA REQUIRED TO CONSIDER FINANCING: Business plan/
    audited financials

GEOGRAPHIC PREFERENCE: Southeast

INDUSTRY PREFERENCE BY FIRM: Broadcasting/Food

INDUSTRY PREFERENCES BY INDIVIDUAL FIRM MEMBERS: N/A

YEAR COMPANY ESTABLISHED: 1980

FUNDS UNDER MANAGEMENT AT COST: N/A

MINIMUM SIZE INVESTMENT: $500,000

PREFERRED SIZE INVESTMENT: $500,000–$1,000,000

WILL FIRM SERVE AS LEAD INVESTOR: Yes

NUMBER OF DEALS COMPLETED IN THE LAST 12 MONTHS: 2

AMOUNT INVESTED IN LAST 12 MONTHS: $1.1 million

AVERAGE TIME REQUIRED TO COMPLETE A DEAL: 4–6 months
    (From Initial Contact to Closing)

FIRM NAME: **Corporation for Innovation Development**

ADDRESS: One North Capitol
                Suite 520
                Indianapolis, IN 46204

PHONE: (317) 635–7325

SBIC ___   VENTURE CAPITAL FUND _X_   MESBIC ___   OTHER ___

TYPES OF FINANCING PREFERRED (Stages): All stages plus leveraged buyouts

MINIMUM DATA REQUIRED TO CONSIDER FINANCING: Business plan

GEOGRAPHIC PREFERENCE: Indiana only

INDUSTRY PREFERENCE BY FIRM: All industries except real estate

INDUSTRY PREFERENCES BY INDIVIDUAL FIRM MEMBERS:
    Marion Dietrich—Medical Technology
    Don Taylor—Electronics/Computers
    Archie Leslie—All Other
YEAR COMPANY ESTABLISHED: 1981

FUNDS UNDER MANAGEMENT AT COST: $10 million

MINIMUM SIZE INVESTMENT: $100,000

PREFERRED SIZE INVESTMENT: $300,000–$500,000

WILL FIRM SERVE AS LEAD INVESTOR: Yes

NUMBER OF DEALS COMPLETED IN THE LAST 12 MONTHS: 4

AMOUNT INVESTED IN LAST 12 MONTHS: $1.8 million

AVERAGE TIME REQUIRED TO COMPLETE A DEAL: 3 months
    (From Initial Contact to Closing)

FIRM NAME: **Heritage Venture Group, Inc.**

ADDRESS: 2400 One Indiana Sq.
                Indianapolis, IN 46204

PHONE: (317) 635–5696

SBIC _X_   VENTURE CAPITAL FUND ___   MESBIC ___   OTHER ___

TYPES OF FINANCING PREFERRED (Stages): Emerging growth and ma-
    ture/acquisitions

MINIMUM DATA REQUIRED TO CONSIDER FINANCING: Written business
    plan including management resumes, historical financings

GEOGRAPHIC PREFERENCE: Midwest to continental USA

INDUSTRY PREFERENCE BY FIRM: Communications, including cellular radio
    (telephone), radio and TV broadcasting, cable television/Traditional Manufac-
    turing/Diversified Portfolio

INDUSTRY PREFERENCES BY INDIVIDUAL FIRM MEMBERS: N/A

YEAR COMPANY ESTABLISHED: 1981

FUNDS UNDER MANAGEMENT AT COST: $3 million plus

MINIMUM SIZE INVESTMENT: $100,000

PREFERRED SIZE INVESTMENT: $250,000–$500,000

WILL FIRM SERVE AS LEAD INVESTOR: Yes

NUMBER OF DEALS COMPLETED IN THE LAST 12 MONTHS: N/A

AMOUNT INVESTED IN LAST 12 MONTHS: N/A

AVERAGE TIME REQUIRED TO COMPLETE A DEAL: 6 weeks to 2 months
(From Initial Contact to Closing)

FIRM NAME: **Middlewest Ventures**

ADDRESS: 20 N. Meridian
                Indianapolis, IN 46204

PHONE: (317) 631–8822

SBIC ____   VENTURE CAPITAL FUND _X_   MESBIC ____   OTHER ____

TYPES OF FINANCING PREFERRED (Stages): Seed/early stage

MINIMUM DATA REQUIRED TO CONSIDER FINANCING: Outline of business
plan

GEOGRAPHIC PREFERENCE: Midwest (Indiana, Ohio, Michigan, Illinois, Tennessee, Kentucky, Missouri)

INDUSTRY PREFERENCE BY FIRM: Medical Products and Instrumentation/Information Management/Data Communications/Industrial Automation/Biotechnology

INDUSTRY PREFERENCES BY INDIVIDUAL FIRM MEMBERS: N/A

YEAR COMPANY ESTABLISHED: 1985

FUNDS UNDER MANAGEMENT AT COST: $25 million

MINIMUM SIZE INVESTMENT: $250,000

PREFERRED SIZE INVESTMENT: $1 million

WILL FIRM SERVE AS LEAD INVESTOR: Yes

NUMBER OF DEALS COMPLETED IN THE LAST 12 MONTHS: N/A

AMOUNT INVESTED IN LAST 12 MONTHS: N/A

AVERAGE TIME REQUIRED TO COMPLETE A DEAL: 3 months
(From Initial Contact to Closing)

FIRM NAME: **Mount Vernon Venture Capital Co.**

ADDRESS: P.O. Box 40177
                Indianapolis, IN 46240

PHONE: (317) 846–5106

SBIC _X_ VENTURE CAPITAL FUND ____   MESBIC ____   OTHER ____

TYPES OF FINANCING PREFERRED (Stages): Second stage

MINIMUM DATA REQUIRED TO CONSIDER FINANCING: Business plan

GEOGRAPHIC PREFERENCE: Indiana and Midwest

INDUSTRY PREFERENCE BY FIRM: N/A

INDUSTRY PREFERENCES BY INDIVIDUAL FIRM MEMBERS: N/A

YEAR COMPANY ESTABLISHED: 1983

FUNDS UNDER MANAGEMENT AT COST: $2.1 million

MINIMUM SIZE INVESTMENT: $100,000

PREFERRED SIZE INVESTMENT: $200,000–$300,000

WILL FIRM SERVE AS LEAD INVESTOR: Yes

NUMBER OF DEALS COMPLETED IN THE LAST 12 MONTHS: 4

AMOUNT INVESTED IN LAST 12 MONTHS: $470,000

AVERAGE TIME REQUIRED TO COMPLETE A DEAL: 6 weeks
   (From Initial Contact to Closing)

IOWA

FIRM NAME: **R. W. Allsop & Associates**

ADDRESS: 2750 First Ave., NE   *Also offices at:*   815 E. Mason St.
                Cedar Rapids, IA 52402   Suite 1501
PHONE: (319) 363–8971   P.O. Box 1368

                                                               Milwaukee, WI 53201
                                                               111 W. Port Plaza
                                                               Suite 600
                                                               St. Louis, MO 63146

                                                               35 Corporate Woods
                                                               Suite 244
                                                               9101 W. 110th St.
                                                               Overland Park, KS 66210

PHONE: (319) 363–8971

SBIC ____ VENTURE CAPITAL FUND _X_ MESBIC ____ OTHER ____

TYPES OF FINANCING PREFERRED (Stages): First, second, and third stage financings management/leveraged buyouts

MINIMUM DATA REQUIRED TO CONSIDER FINANCING: Business plan/historical financial statements/3–5 year projections/resumes

GEOGRAPHIC PREFERENCE: Mid-America

INDUSTRY PREFERENCE BY FIRM: Communications/Computer Technology and Applications/Industrial Automation/Medical/Health Care

INDUSTRY PREFERENCES BY INDIVIDUAL FIRM MEMBERS:
    Robert W. Allsop (Iowa) 319/363–8971
    Gregory B. Bultman (Wisconsin) 414/271–6510
    Paul D. Rhines (Iowa) 319/363–8971
    Robert L. Kuk (Missouri) 314/434–1688
    Larry C. Maddox (Kansas) 913/451–3719

YEAR COMPANY ESTABLISHED: 1981

FUNDS UNDER MANAGEMENT AT COST: $45 million

MINIMUM SIZE INVESTMENT: $500,000

PREFERRED SIZE INVESTMENT: $700,000

WILL FIRM SERVE AS LEAD INVESTOR: Yes

NUMBER OF DEALS COMPLETED IN THE LAST 12 MONTHS: 26

AMOUNT INVESTED IN LAST 12 MONTHS: $9.8 million

AVERAGE TIME REQUIRED TO COMPLETE A DEAL: 60 days
   (From Initial Contact to Closing)

KENTUCKY

FIRM NAME: **Bluegrass Capital Corp.**

ADDRESS: 1815 Plantside Dr.
                   P.O. Box 35000
                   Louisville, KY 40232

PHONE: (502) 491–3440

SBIC ___   VENTURE CAPITAL FUND _X_   MESBIC ___   OTHER ___

TYPES OF FINANCING PREFERRED (Stages): Second or subsequent stage/no
   mezzanine financings/no start-ups

MINIMUM DATA REQUIRED TO CONSIDER FINANCING: Full business plan

GEOGRAPHIC PREFERENCE: Midwest, Ohio River Valley

INDUSTRY PREFERENCE BY FIRM: Manufacturing concerns; High-Technology
   content not a prerequisite

INDUSTRY PREFERENCES BY INDIVIDUAL FIRM MEMBERS: Charles S. Ar-
   ensberg, President

YEAR COMPANY ESTABLISHED: 1985

FUNDS UNDER MANAGEMENT AT COST: $1 million

MINIMUM SIZE INVESTMENT: $100,000

PREFERRED SIZE INVESTMENT: $200,00

WILL FIRM SERVE AS LEAD INVESTOR: Only in transactions below $1 million

NUMBER OF DEALS COMPLETED IN THE LAST 12 MONTHS: 3

AMOUNT INVESTED IN LAST 12 MONTHS: $500,000

AVERAGE TIME REQUIRED TO COMPLETE A DEAL: 3–4 months
   (From Initial Contact to Closing)

LOUISIANA

FIRM NAME: **Louisiana Equity Capital Corp.**

ADDRESS: 451 Florida St.
                   P.O. Box 1511
                   Baton Rouge, LA 70821

PHONE: (504) 389–4421

SBIC __X__ VENTURE CAPITAL FUND ___ MESBIC ___ OTHER ___

TYPES OF FINANCING PREFERRED (Stages): All stages of venture financing, excluding R&D

MINIMUM DATA REQUIRED TO CONSIDER FINANCING: Comprehensive business plan with pro forma financial statements

GEOGRAPHIC PREFERENCE: Entire USA when a participating investor. Louisiana only when a lead investor

INDUSTRY PREFERENCE BY FIRM: Wide range of interests

INDUSTRY PREFERENCES BY INDIVIDUAL FIRM MEMBERS:
   Melvin L. Rambin, President
   Jack McDonald, III, Investment Officer (contact person)

YEAR COMPANY ESTABLISHED: 1974

FUNDS UNDER MANAGEMENT AT COST: $8.2 million

MINIMUM SIZE INVESTMENT: $100,000

PREFERRED SIZE INVESTMENT: $250,000–$500,000

WILL FIRM SERVE AS LEAD INVESTOR: Yes, in our local area

NUMBER OF DEALS COMPLETED IN THE LAST 12 MONTHS: 5

AMOUNT INVESTED IN LAST 12 MONTHS: $1.485 million

AVERAGE TIME REQUIRED TO COMPLETE A DEAL: Initial response: 1 week;
   (From Initial Contact to Closing)   closing: 8 weeks

FIRM NAME: **Walnut Street Capital Co.**

ADDRESS: Cotton Exchange Building
              Suite 702
              New Orleans, LA 70130

PHONE: (504) 525–2112

SBIC __X__ VENTURE CAPITAL FUND ___ MESBIC ___ OTHER ___

TYPES OF FINANCING PREFERRED (Stages): All

MINIMUM DATA REQUIRED TO CONSIDER FINANCING: N/A

GEOGRAPHIC PREFERENCE: N/A

INDUSTRY PREFERENCE BY FIRM: N/A

INDUSTRY PREFERENCES BY INDIVIDUAL FIRM MEMBERS: N/A

YEAR COMPANY ESTABLISHED: 1982

FUNDS UNDER MANAGEMENT AT COST: $6 million

MINIMUM SIZE INVESTMENT: $200,000

PREFERRED SIZE INVESTMENT: $300,000

WILL FIRM SERVE AS LEAD INVESTOR: Yes

NUMBER OF DEALS COMPLETED IN THE LAST 12 MONTHS: 6

AMOUNT INVESTED IN LAST 12 MONTHS: $1.25 million

AVERAGE TIME REQUIRED TO COMPLETE A DEAL: 10 weeks
(From Initial Contact to Closing)

MAINE

FIRM NAME: **Maine Capital Corporation**

ADDRESS: 70 Center St.
               Portland, ME 04101

PHONE: (207) 772–1001

SBIC __X__   VENTURE CAPITAL FUND ____   MESBIC ____   OTHER ____

TYPES OF FINANCING PREFERRED (Stages): All stages

MINIMUM DATA REQUIRED TO CONSIDER FINANCING: Business plan

GEOGRAPHIC PREFERENCE: Maine only

INDUSTRY PREFERENCE BY FIRM: N/A

INDUSTRY PREFERENCES BY INDIVIDUAL FIRM MEMBERS: N/A

YEAR COMPANY ESTABLISHED: 1980

FUNDS UNDER MANAGEMENT AT COST: $1 million

MINIMUM SIZE INVESTMENT: $50,000

PREFERRED SIZE INVESTMENT: $100,000

WILL FIRM SERVE AS LEAD INVESTOR: Yes

NUMBER OF DEALS COMPLETED IN THE LAST 12 MONTHS: 3

AMOUNT INVESTED IN LAST 12 MONTHS: $300,000

AVERAGE TIME REQUIRED TO COMPLETE A DEAL: 3 months
(From Initial Contact to Closing)

MARYLAND

FIRM NAME: **ABS Ventures Limited Partnerships**

ADDRESS: 135 East Baltimore St.
               Baltimore, MD 21202

PHONE: (301) 727–1700

SBIC ____   VENTURE CAPITAL FUND __X__   MESBIC ____   OTHER ____

TYPES OF FINANCING PREFERRED (Stages): Start-up/first stage

MINIMUM DATA REQUIRED TO CONSIDER FINANCING: Business plan with
5 year pro forma financials

GEOGRAPHIC PREFERENCE: None

INDUSTRY PREFERENCE BY FIRM: Communications and Information Systems/Computer Services/Engineering and Manufacturing Sytems/Medical Technology and Services/Specialty Retailing

INDUSTRY PREFERENCES BY INDIVIDUAL FIRM MEMBERS:
Edward T. Anderson—Communications and Information Systems
Bruns H. Grayson—Computer Services/Medical Technology/Specialty Retailing
Arthur H. Reidel—Computer Services/Engineering and Manufacturing

YEAR COMPANY ESTABLISHED: 1982

FUNDS UNDER MANAGEMENT AT COST: $108 million

MINIMUM SIZE INVESTMENT: $500,000

PREFERRED SIZE INVESTMENT: $500,000–$1,000,000

WILL FIRM SERVE AS LEAD INVESTOR: Yes

NUMBER OF DEALS COMPLETED IN THE LAST 12 MONTHS: 59

AMOUNT INVESTED IN LAST 12 MONTHS: $22.2 million

AVERAGE TIME REQUIRED TO COMPLETE A DEAL: 2–6 months
(From Initial Contact to Closing)

FIRM NAME: **Broventure Capital Management**

ADDRESS: 16 West Madison St.
                Baltimore, MD 21201

PHONE: (301) 727–4520

SBIC ____ VENTURE CAPITAL FUND _X_ MESBIC ____   OTHER ____

TYPES OF FINANCING PREFERRED (Stages): Start-up/first stage/second stage/purchases or secondary positions

MINIMUM DATA REQUIRED TO CONSIDER FINANCING: Business plan with recent 5 year projections

GEOGRAPHIC PREFERENCE: USA; Mid Atlantic and Southeast favored

INDUSTRY PREFERENCE BY FIRM: Communications/Computer Related/Electronics/Medical

INDUSTRY PREFERENCES BY INDIVIDUAL FIRM MEMBERS:
William M. Gust
Harvey C. Branch
Philip English

YEAR COMPANY ESTABLISHED: 1965

FUNDS UNDER MANAGEMENT AT COST: N/A

MINIMUM SIZE INVESTMENT: $500,000–$750,000

PREFERRED SIZE INVESTMENT: $750,000

WILL FIRM SERVE AS LEAD INVESTOR: Yes

NUMBER OF DEALS COMPLETED IN THE LAST 12 MONTHS: 12

AMOUNT INVESTED IN LAST 12 MONTHS: $6 million

AVERAGE TIME REQUIRED TO COMPLETE A DEAL: N/A
   (From Initial Contact to Closing)

FIRM NAME: **Emerging Growth Partners**

ADDRESS: 400 E. Pratt St.
                Suite 610
                Baltimore, MD 21202

PHONE: (301) 332–1021

SBIC ___ VENTURE CAPITAL FUND _X_ MESBIC ___ OTHER ___

TYPES OF FINANCING PREFERRED (Stages): Second stage/expansions

MINIMUM DATA REQUIRED TO CONSIDER FINANCING: Business Plan

GEOGRAPHIC PREFERENCE: None

INDUSTRY PREFERENCE BY FIRM: None

INDUSTRY PREFERENCES BY INDIVIDUAL FIRM MEMBERS: N/A

YEAR COMPANY ESTABLISHED: 1982

FUNDS UNDER MANAGEMENT AT COST: $100 milion

MINIMUM SIZE INVESTMENT: $500,000

PREFERRED SIZE INVESTMENT: $750,000–$1,500,000

WILL FIRM SERVE AS LEAD INVESTOR: Yes

NUMBER OF DEALS COMPLETED IN THE LAST 12 MONTHS: 6

AMOUNT INVESTED IN LAST 12 MONTHS: $12 million

AVERAGE TIME REQUIRED TO COMPLETE A DEAL: 1 month
   (From Initial Contact to Closing)

FIRM NAME: **Greater Washington Investors, Inc.**

ADDRESS: 5454 Wisconsin Ave.
                Chevy Chase, MD 20815

PHONE: (301) 656–0626

SBIC _X_ VENTURE CAPITAL FUND ___ MESBIC ___ OTHER ___

TYPES OF FINANCING PREFERRED (Stages): Early stage

MINIMUM DATA REQUIRED TO CONSIDER FINANCING: Business plan including management and history

GEOGRAPHIC PREFERENCE: East Coast

INDUSTRY PREFERENCE BY FIRM: Technology-based industries

INDUSTRY PREFERENCES BY INDIVIDUAL FIRM MEMBERS: N/A

YEAR COMPANY ESTABLISHED: 1959

FUNDS UNDER MANAGEMENT AT COST: $22 million

MINIMUM SIZE INVESTMENT: $250,000

PREFERRED SIZE INVESTMENT: $250,000–$500,000

WILL FIRM SERVE AS LEAD INVESTOR: Yes

NUMBER OF DEALS COMPLETED IN THE LAST 12 MONTHS: 16

AMOUNT INVESTED IN LAST 12 MONTHS: $4.7 million

AVERAGE TIME REQUIRED TO COMPLETE A DEAL: 4 months
(From Initial Contact to Closing)

FIRM NAME: **New Enterprise Associates**

ADDRESS: 1119 St. Paul St.   235 Montgomery St.
             Baltimore, MD 21202   Suite 1025
                                        San Francisco, CA 94101

PHONE: (301) 244–0115   (415) 956–1579

SBIC ____ VENTURE CAPITAL FUND _X_ MESBIC ____ OTHER ____

TYPES OF FINANCING PREFERRED (Stages): Seed/start-up/early expansion

MINIMUM DATA REQUIRED TO CONSIDER FINANCING: Complete business
plan with financial projections, management resumes, analysis of market

GEOGRAPHIC PREFERENCE: Invests nationwide

INDUSTRY PREFERENCE BY FIRM: Telecommunications/Computers and Pe-
ripherals/Defense Electronics/Medical and Life Sciences/Health Care/Office
Communications/Semiconductor/Specialty Retailing

INDUSTRY PREFERENCES BY INDIVIDUAL FIRM MEMBERS:
Maryland
        Frank A. Bonsal, Jr.
        Curran W. Harvey, Jr.
        Arthur J. Marks
        Raymond L. Bank
        Charles W. Newhall, III
California
        Cornelius C. Bond
        C. Woodrow Rea, Jr.
        R. John Armor
        C. Richard Kramlich

YEAR COMPANY ESTABLISHED: 1978

FUNDS UNDER MANAGEMENT AT COST: $200 million

MINIMUM SIZE INVESTMENT: $500,000

PREFERRED SIZE INVESTMENT: $1 million for initial investment

WILL FIRM SERVE AS LEAD INVESTOR: Yes

NUMBER OF DEALS COMPLETED IN THE LAST 12 MONTHS: 73

AMOUNT INVESTED IN LAST 12 MONTHS: $41.8 million

AVERAGE TIME REQUIRED TO COMPLETE A DEAL: 2–3 months
(From Initial Contact to Closing)

FIRM NAME: **Suburban Capital Corp.**

ADDRESS: 6610 Rockledge Dr.
Bethesda, MD 20817

PHONE: (301) 493–2083

SBIC _X_ VENTURE CAPITAL FUND ___ MESBIC ___ OTHER ___

TYPES OF FINANCING PREFERRED (Stages): Second and third stages

MINIMUM DATA REQUIRED TO CONSIDER FINANCING: Business plan

GEOGRAPHIC PREFERENCE: East Coast and South

INDUSTRY PREFERENCE BY FIRM: Diversified

INDUSTRY PREFERENCES BY INDIVIDUAL FIRM MEMBERS: N/A

YEAR COMPANY ESTABLISHED:1983

FUNDS UNDER MANAGEMENT AT COST: $8 million

MINIMUM SIZE INVESTMENT: $250,000

PREFERRED SIZE INVESTMENT: $400,000–$500,000

WILL FIRM SERVE AS LEAD INVESTOR: Yes

NUMBER OF DEALS COMPLETED IN THE LAST 12 MONTHS: 8

AMOUNT INVESTED IN LAST 12 MONTHS: $3.5 million

AVERAGE TIME REQUIRED TO COMPLETE A DEAL: 60–90 days
(From Initial Contact to Closing)

MASSACHUSETTS

FIRM NAME: **Acquivest Group, Inc.**

ADDRESS: 10 Speen St.
Framingham, MA 01701

PHONE: (617) 875–3242

SBIC ___ VENTURE CAPITAL FUND ___ MESBIC ___

OTHER _X_ (Managing principal of investment groups)

TYPES OF FINANCING PREFERRED (Stages): 100% acquisition of going busi-
nesses/sponsor of qualified managers to search and acquire busi-
ness/advanced stage venture investing

MINIMUM DATA REQUIRED TO CONSIDER FINANCING: Business plan or equivalent, including financials

GEOGRAPHIC PREFERENCE: Eastern USA

INDUSTRY PREFERENCE BY FIRM: Any field where continuing management has experience

INDUSTRY PREFERENCES BY INDIVIDUAL FIRM MEMBERS: N/A

YEAR COMPANY ESTABLISHED: 1960

FUNDS UNDER MANAGEMENT AT COST: N/A

MINIMUM SIZE INVESTMENT: $1 million

PREFERRED SIZE INVESTMENT: $3 million–$30 million

WILL FIRM SERVE AS LEAD INVESTOR: Yes

NUMBER OF DEALS COMPLETED IN THE LAST 12 MONTHS: N/A

AMOUNT INVESTED IN LAST 12 MONTHS: N/A

AVERAGE TIME REQUIRED TO COMPLETE A DEAL: 3–4 months (From Initial Contact to Closing)

FIRM NAME: **Advanced Technology Ventures**

ADDRESS: Ten Post Office Sq.   1000 El Camino Real
                Suite 1230   Suite 210
                Boston, MA 02109   Menlo Park, CA 94025–4327

PHONE: (617) 423–4050   (415) 321–8601

SBIC ___   VENTURE CAPITAL FUND _X_ MESBIC ___   OTHER ___

TYPES OF FINANCING PREFERRED (Stages): Start-up/first stage/second stage

MINIMUM DATA REQUIRED TO CONSIDER FINANCING: Business plan, including past actual operating results, if any, and pro forma financial forecasts/management profiles

GEOGRAPHIC PREFERENCE: None

INDUSTRY PREFERENCE BY FIRM: Satellite and Microwave Communications/Computer graphics and CAD/CAM/Micro and Minicomputers/Recombinant DNA/Lasers/Optics Technology/Energy Conservation/Semiconductors/Robotics/Microbiology/Office Automation/Monoclonal Antibodies and Hybridomas

INDUSTRY PREFERENCES BY INDIVIDUAL FIRM MEMBERS: N/A

YEAR COMPANY ESTABLISHED: 1980

FUNDS UNDER MANAGEMENT AT COST: $75 million

MINIMUM SIZE INVESTMENT: $300,000–$600,000

PREFERRED SIZE INVESTMENT: $600,000 plus

WILL FIRM SERVE AS LEAD INVESTOR: Yes

NUMBER OF DEALS COMPLETED IN THE LAST 12 MONTHS: 12

AMOUNT INVESTED IN LAST 12 MONTHS: $8,316,715

AVERAGE TIME REQUIRED TO COMPLETE A DEAL: 4 months
(From Initial Contact to Closing)

FIRM NAME: **Aegis Fund Limited Partnership**

ADDRESS: 171 Milk St.
Boston, MA 02109

PHONE: (617) 338–5655

SBIC ____   VENTURE CAPITAL FUND __X__   MESBIC ____   OTHER ____

TYPES OF FINANCING PREFERRED (Stages): Concentrates investment program on seed and early stage investments in emerging technically oriented
enterprises

MINIMUM DATA REQUIRED TO CONSIDER FINANCING: Complete business
plan is preferred

GEOGRAPHIC PREFERENCE: The fund has adopted a policy that it will not normally make investments in enterprises located more than 75 miles from the
center of Boston

INDUSTRY PREFERENCE BY FIRM: Areas of interest include, but are not limited to, analytical instrumentation, medical instrumentation, delivery of medical services, biomedical products, segments of computer electronics software
operating systems, information technology, new computer architecture, communications, office and factory automation, and some aspects of the specialized energy industry.

INDUSTRY PREFERENCES BY INDIVIDUAL FIRM MEMBERS: N/A

YEAR COMPANY ESTABLISHED: 1983

FUNDS UNDER MANAGEMENT AT COST: Aegis I Fund capitalized at
$15,000,000. We are in the process of capitalizing our second fund within the
next couple of months.

MINIMUM SIZE INVESTMENT: $100,000 and $500,000

PREFERRED SIZE INVESTMENT: N/A

WILL FIRM SERVE AS LEAD INVESTOR: Yes

NUMBER OF DEALS COMPLETED IN THE LAST 12 MONTHS: 12

AMOUNT INVESTED IN LAST 12 MONTHS: Aegis I is fully committed at this
time. Aegis II will be closed at
$20 million.

AVERAGE TIME REQUIRED TO COMPLETE A DEAL: 6–12 weeks
(From Initial Contact to Closing)

FIRM NAME: **American Research & Development**

ADDRESS: 45 Milk St.
Boston, MA 02109

PHONE: (617) 423–7500

SBIC ＿＿   VENTURE CAPITAL FUND ＿＿   MESBIC ＿＿   OTHER ＿X＿

TYPES OF FINANCING PREFERRED (Stages): Seed/start-up/first/second/later stage expansion

MINIMUM DATA REQUIRED TO CONSIDER FINANCING: Annual sales: nominal/P&L: losses (profits projected after 2 years)

GEOGRAPHIC PREFERENCE: None

INDUSTRY PREFERENCE BY FIRM: Communications/Computers/Graphics/ Electronic Components/Artificial Intelligence/Genetic Engineering/Robotics/ Medical Diagnostic Equipment

INDUSTRY PREFERENCES BY INDIVIDUAL FIRM MEMBERS: N/A

YEAR COMPANY ESTABLISHED: 1946

FUNDS UNDER MANAGEMENT AT COST: $70 million

MINIMUM SIZE INVESTMENT: $100,000–$300,000

PREFERRED SIZE INVESTMENT: $600,000 plus

WILL FIRM SERVE AS LEAD INVESTOR: Yes

NUMBER OF DEALS COMPLETED IN THE LAST 12 MONTHS: 21

AMOUNT INVESTED IN LAST 12 MONTHS: $13 million

AVERAGE TIME REQUIRED TO COMPLETE A DEAL: Approx. 4 months (From Initial Contact to Closing)

FIRM NAME: **Analog Devices Enterprises**

ADDRESS: 2 Technology Way
                  Norwood, MA 02062

PHONE: (617) 329–4700

SBIC ＿＿   VENTURE CAPITAL FUND ＿X＿   MESBIC ＿＿   OTHER ＿＿

TYPES OF FINANCING PREFERRED (Stages): First round/second round

MINIMUM DATA REQUIRED TO CONSIDER FINANCING: Complete business plan

GEOGRAPHIC PREFERENCE: None

INDUSTRY PREFERENCE BY FIRM: Communications/Technology/Computer Related

INDUSTRY PREFERENCES BY INDIVIDUAL FIRM MEMBERS: N/A

YEAR COMPANY ESTABLISHED: 1980

FUNDS UNDER MANAGEMENT AT COST: $32 million

MINIMUM SIZE INVESTMENT: $500,000

PREFERRED SIZE INVESTMENT: $1,000,000

WILL FIRM SERVE AS LEAD INVESTOR: Yes

NUMBER OF DEALS COMPLETED IN THE LAST 12 MONTHS: 9

AMOUNT INVESTED IN LAST 12 MONTHS: $12 million

AVERAGE TIME REQUIRED TO COMPLETE A DEAL: 3 months
   (From Initial Contact to Closing)

FIRM NAME: Arthur D. Little Enterprises,Inc.

ADDRESS: 20 Acorn Park
               Cambridge, MA 02140

PHONE: (617) 864–5770

SBIC ____ VENTURE CAPITAL FUND ____ MESBIC ____
OTHER _X_ (Venture capital and invention management subsidiary of Arthur
   D. Little, Inc.)

TYPES OF FINANCING PREFERRED (Stages): Seed through second round

MINIMUM DATA REQUIRED TO CONSIDER FINANCING: N/A

GEOGRAPHIC PREFERENCE: Northeast

INDUSTRY PREFERENCE BY FIRM: Technologies and markets that correspond
   to areas of expertise at Arthur D. Little, Inc.
INDUSTRY PREFERENCE BY INDIVIDUAL FIRM MEMBERS:
   Paul J. Ballantine—General high-technology interests
   Walter J. Cairns—General high-technology interests
   David R. Cunningham—Mechanical Apparatus and Energy Systems
   Richard J. Hammond—Biotechnology
   Edward J. Kenney—Chemical Processes and Material
   Samuel W. Tishler—Electronics and Software

YEAR COMPANY ESTABLISHED: 1984

FUNDS UNDER MANAGEMENT AT COST: $15 million

MINIMUM SIZE INVESTMENT: N/A

PREFERRED SIZE INVESTMENT: $400,000–$600,000

WILL FIRM SERVE AS LEAD INVESTOR: Yes

NUMBER OF DEALS COMPLETED IN THE LAST 12 MONTHS: Venture fund
   commenced operations Sept. 1, 1984

AMOUNT INVESTED IN LAST 12 MONTHS: N/A

AVERAGE TIME REQUIRED TO COMPLETE A DEAL: N/A
   (From Initial Contact to Closing)

FIRM NAME: BancBoston Ventures

ADDRESS: 100 Federal St.
               Boston, MA 02110

PHONE: (617) 434–2442

SBIC _X_ VENTURE CAPITAL FUND ____ MESBIC ____ OTHER ____

TYPES OF FINANCING PREFERRED (Stages): Start-ups/first stage/second stage

MINIMUM DATA REQUIRED TO CONSIDER FINANCING: Formal business
plan including company description, market analysis, marketing technology,
manufacturing, management, ownership, organization, funds required, and
financial data

GEOGRAPHIC PREFERENCE: USA (preferably Northeast)

INDUSTRY PREFERENCE BY FIRM: High Technology/Health Care

INDUSTRY PREFERENCES BY INDIVIDUAL FIRM MEMBERS:
Paul F. Hogan   Jeffrey W. Wilson
Diana H. Frazier   Stephen J. O'Leary III

YEAR COMPANY ESTABLISHED: 1957

FUNDS UNDER MANAGEMENT AT COST: $20 million

MINIMUM SIZE INVESTMENT: $500,000

PREFERRED SIZE INVESTMENT: $500,000–$1,000,000

WILL FIRM SERVE AS LEAD INVESTOR: Yes

NUMBER OF DEALS COMPLETED IN THE LAST 12 MONTHS: 21

AMOUNT INVESTED IN LAST 12 MONTHS: N/A

AVERAGE TIME REQUIRED TO COMPLETE A DEAL: 3 months
(From Initial Contact to Closing)

FIRM NAME: **Battery Ventures**

ADDRESS: 60 Batterymarch St.   General Partners:
             Suite 1400   Howard Anderson
             Boston, MA 02110   Robert G. Barrett
PHONE: (617) 542–7710   Richard D. Frisbie

SBIC ____   VENTURE CAPITAL FUND _X_   MESBIC ____   OTHER ____

TYPES OF FINANCING PREFERRED (Stages): Start-up/first and second round
investments

MINIMUM DATA REQUIRED TO CONSIDER FINANCING: N/A

GEOGRAPHIC PREFERENCE: None; seek investments on a national basis

INDUSTRY PREFERENCE BY FIRM: Factory and Office Automation/Infor-
mation Systems/Communications

INDUSTRY PREFERENCES BY INDIVIDUAL FIRM MEMBERS: N/A

YEAR COMPANY ESTABLISHED: 1984

FUNDS UNDER MANAGEMENT AT COST: $34 million

MINIMUM SIZE INVESTMENT: None

PREFERRED SIZE INVESTMENT: $500,000–$750,000, depending on stage

WILL FIRM SERVE AS LEAD INVESTOR: Yes

NUMBER OF DEALS COMPLETED IN THE LAST 12 MONTHS: 7

AMOUNT INVESTED IN LAST 12 MONTHS: $3.5 million

AVERAGE TIME REQUIRED TO COMPLETE A DEAL: N/A
   (From Initial Contact to Closing)

FIRM NAME: **The Boston Venture Fund, Inc.**

ADDRESS: 33 Bedford St.
                Link 7
                Lexington, MA 02143

PHONE: (614) 862–0269

SBIC ____   VENTURE CAPITAL FUND _X_ MESBIC ____   OTHER ____

TYPES OF FINANCING PREFERRED (Stages):Early

MINIMUM DATA REQUIRED TO CONSIDER FINANCING: Complete reference
   list/business plan

GEOGRAPHIC PREFERENCE: New England

INDUSTRY PREFERENCE BY FIRM: Software/Medical

INDUSTRY PREFERENCES BY INDIVIDUAL FIRM MEMBERS: N/A

YEAR COMPANY ESTABLISHED: 1982

FUNDS UNDER MANAGEMENT AT COST: $1 million

MINIMUM SIZE INVESTMENT: $25,000

PREFERRED SIZE INVESTMENT: $100,000

WILL FIRM SERVE AS LEAD INVESTOR: Yes

NUMBER OF DEALS COMPLETED IN THE LAST 12 MONTHS: N/A

AMOUNT INVESTED IN LAST 12 MONTHS: N/A

AVERAGE TIME REQUIRED TO COMPLETE A DEAL: 3 months
   (From Initial Contact to Closing)

FIRM NAME: **Bristol Investment Trust**

ADDRESS: 842A Beacon St.
                Boston, MA 02215

PHONE: (617) 566–5212

SBIC ____   VENTURE CAPITAL FUND ____   MESBIC ____   OTHER _X_

TYPES OF FINANCING PREFERRED (Stages): First, second, and third stages

MINIMUM DATA REQUIRED TO CONSIDER FINANCING: Business plan projection

GEOGRAPHIC PREFERENCE: New England

INDUSTRY PREFERENCE BY FIRM: Distribution: wholesale and re-
   tail/manufacturing: some types/Real Estate: related services, various
   types/Retail: various types

INDUSTRY PREFERENCES BY INDIVIDUAL FIRM MEMBERS: N/A

YEAR COMPANY ESTABLISHED: 1966

FUNDS UNDER MANAGEMENT AT COST: N/A

MINIMUM SIZE INVESTMENT: $25,000

PREFERRED SIZE INVESTMENT: $50,000

WILL FIRM SERVE AS LEAD INVESTOR: Yes

NUMBER OF DEALS COMPLETED IN THE LAST 12 MONTHS: N/A

AMOUNT INVESTED IN LAST 12 MONTHS: N/A

AVERAGE TIME REQUIRED TO COMPLETE A DEAL: N/A
(From Initial Contact to Closing)

FIRM NAME: **Burr, Egan, Delaege & Co.**

ADDRESS: One Post Office Sq.   Three Embarcadero Center
                 Suite 3800   Suite 2560
                 Boston, MA 02109   San Francisco, CA 94111

PHONE: (617) 482–8020   (415) 362–4022

SBIC ____   VENTURE CAPITAL FUND _X_   MESBIC ____   OTHER ____

TYPES OF FINANCING PREFERRED (Stages): Start-up/first stage/second stage/later stage expansion/buyout or acquisition/purchases of secondary positions

MINIMUM DATA REQUIRED TO CONSIDER FINANCING: Business plan with financials and resumes

GEOGRAPHIC PREFERENCE: USA

INDUSTRY PREFERENCE BY FIRM: Communications/Computer Related/Distribution/Electronic Components and Instrumentation/Energy–Natural Resources/Genetic Engineering/Medical

INDUSTRY PREFERENCES BY INDIVIDUAL FIRM MEMBERS:
Boston: San Francisco:

     Craig L. Burr   Brion B. Applegate
     William P. Egan   Shirley Cerrudo
     Jonathan A. Flint   Jean Deleage
     Esther B. Sharp   Jean-Bernard Schmidt
                                Thomas E. Winter

YEAR COMPANY ESTABLISHED: 1979

FUNDS UNDER MANAGEMENT AT COST: $200 million

MINIMUM SIZE INVESTMENT: $750,000 plus

PREFERRED SIZE INVESTMENT: $1 million

WILL FIRM SERVE AS LEAD INVESTOR: Yes

NUMBER OF DEALS COMPLETED IN THE LAST 12 MONTHS: 15

AMOUNT INVESTED IN LAST 12 MONTHS: $25 million

AVERAGE TIME REQUIRED TO COMPLETE A DEAL: 2 months
(From Initial Contact to Closing)

FIRM NAME: **The Charles River Partnerships**

ADDRESS: 133 Federal St.
                   Boston, MA 02110

PHONE: (617) 482–9370

SBIC ____   VENTURE CAPITAL FUND __X__   MESBIC ____   OTHER ____

TYPES OF FINANCING PREFERRED (Stages): Early stage/start-up

MINIMUM DATA REQUIRED TO CONSIDER FINANCING: Business plan

GEOGRAPHIC PREFERENCE: None

INDUSTRY PREFERENCE BY FIRM: No oil, gas, or real estate

INDUSTRY PREFERENCES BY INDIVIDUAL FIRM MEMBERS: N/A

YEAR COMPANY ESTABLISHED: 1970

FUNDS UNDER MANAGEMENT AT COST: $144 million

MINIMUM SIZE INVESTMENT: $300,000

PREFERRED SIZE INVESTMENT: $500,000–$1,500,000

WILL FIRM SERVE AS LEAD INVESTOR: Yes

NUMBER OF DEALS COMPLETED IN THE LAST 12 MONTHS: 10

AMOUNT INVESTED IN LAST 12 MONTHS: $17 million

AVERAGE TIME REQUIRED TO COMPLETE A DEAL: 8 weeks
    (From Initial Contact to Closing)

FIRM NAME: **Eastech Management Company, Inc.**

ADDRESS: One Liberty Sq.
                   Ninth Floor
                   Boston, MA 02109

PHONE: (617) 338–0200

SBIC ____   VENTURE CAPITAL FUND __X__   MESBIC ____   OTHER ____

TYPES OF FINANCING PREFERRED (Stages): Start-up/seed

MINIMUM DATA REQUIRED TO CONSIDER FINANCING: Business plan with
    3-year projections

GEOGRAPHIC PREFERENCE: New England, East Coast

INDUSTRY PREFERENCE BY FIRM: Computer-related Technology

INDUSTRY PREFERENCES BY INDIVIDUAL FIRM MEMBERS:
    G. Bickley Stevens II—Computer Related
    Fontaine K. Richardson—Computer Related
    Michael H. Shanahan—Computer Related

YEAR COMPANY ESTABLISHED: 1981

FUNDS UNDER MANAGEMENT AT COST: $34.4 million

MINIMUM SIZE INVESTMENT: $400,000

PREFERRED SIZE INVESTMENT: $600,000–$750,000

WILL FIRM SERVE AS LEAD INVESTOR: Yes

NUMBER OF DEALS COMPLETED IN THE LAST 12 MONTHS: 17

AMOUNT INVESTED IN LAST 12 MONTHS: $6 million

AVERAGE TIME REQUIRED TO COMPLETE A DEAL: 6 weeks
   (From Initial Contact to Closing)

FIRM NAME: **Fidelity Venture Associates**

ADDRESS: 82 Devonshire St.
              Boston, MA 02109

PHONE: (617) 570–6450

SBIC ____ VENTURE CAPITAL FUND _X_ MESBIC ____ OTHER ____

TYPES OF FINANCING PREFERRED (Stages): Across the board

MINIMUM DATA REQUIRED TO CONSIDER FINANCING: Business plan

GEOGRAPHIC PREFERENCE: None

INDUSTRY PREFERENCE BY FIRM: N/A

INDUSTRY PREFERENCES BY INDIVIDUAL FIRM MEMBERS: N/A

YEAR COMPANY ESTABLISHED: 1969

FUNDS UNDER MANAGEMENT AT COST: N/A

MINIMUM SIZE INVESTMENT: N/A

PREFERRED SIZE INVESTMENT: $500,000–$1,000,000

WILL FIRM SERVE AS LEAD INVESTOR: Yes

NUMBER OF DEALS COMPLETED IN THE LAST 12 MONTHS: 14

AMOUNT INVESTED IN LAST 12 MONTHS: $6 million

AVERAGE TIME REQUIRED TO COMPLETE A DEAL: N/A
   (From Initial Contact to Closing)

FIRM NAME: **Fowler, Anthony & Co.**

ADDRESS: 20 Walnut St.
              Wellesley Hills, MA 02181

PHONE: (617) 237–4201

SBIC ____ VENTURE CAPITAL FUND _X_ MESBIC ____ OTHER ____

TYPES OF FINANCING PREFERRED (Stages): Generally early stage and second
   stage deals

MINIMUM DATA REQUIRED TO CONSIDER FINANCING: Business plan

GEOGRAPHIC PREFERENCE: New England

INDUSTRY PREFERENCE BY FIRM: Will consider any industry; expertise in
   industries such as Semiconductors/Computers—Software/Medical–Health
   Care/Analytical Instruments/Home Health Care/Office Automation

INDUSTRY PREFERENCES BY INDIVIDUAL FIRM MEMBERS:
John A. Quagliaroli (contact person)

YEAR COMPANY ESTABLISHED: 1976

FUNDS UNDER MANAGEMENT AT COST: N/A

MINIMUM SIZE INVESTMENT: $100,000

PREFERRED SIZE INVESTMENT: Up to $500,000

WILL FIRM SERVE AS LEAD INVESTOR: Yes

NUMBER OF DEALS COMPLETED IN THE LAST 12 MONTHS: 3

AMOUNT INVESTED IN LAST 12 MONTHS: N/A

AVERAGE TIME REQUIRED TO COMPLETE A DEAL: 3 months or so
(From Initial Contact to Closing)

FIRM NAME: **Greylock Management Corporation**

ADDRESS: 1 Federal St.
                Boston, MA 02110

PHONE: (617) 423-5525

SBIC ____ VENTURE CAPITAL FUND _X_ MESBIC ____ OTHER ____

TYPES OF FINANCING PREFERRED (Stages): Start-up/first stage/second
stage/buyout or acquisition/purchases or secondary positions

MINIMUM DATA REQUIRED TO CONSIDER FINANCING: Business plan

GEOGRAPHIC PREFERENCE: USA

INDUSTRY PREFERENCE BY FIRM: Communications/Computer Re-
lated/Distribution/Electronic Components and Instrumentation/Energy-
Natural Resources/Genetic Engineering/Medical/Industrial Products and
Equipment

INDUSTRY PREFERENCES BY INDIVIDUAL FIRM MEMBERS:
Daniel S. Gregory   Henry F. McCance
Charles P. Waite   David N. Stohm
Howard E. Cox, Jr.   William W. Helman
Robert P. Henderson

YEAR COMPANY ESTABLISHED: 1965

FUNDS UNDER MANAGEMENT AT COST: Over $150 million

MINIMUM SIZE INVESTMENT: $600,000

PREFERRED SIZE INVESTMENT: $1 million

WILL FIRM SERVE AS LEAD INVESTOR: Prefer role as deal originator

NUMBER OF DEALS COMPLETED IN THE LAST 12 MONTHS: 25

AMOUNT INVESTED IN LAST 12 MONTHS: $11–$15 million

AVERAGE TIME REQUIRED TO COMPLETE A DEAL: 90 days
(From Initial Contact to Closing)

FIRM NAME: John Hancock Venture Capital Management, Inc.

ADDRESS: P.O. Box 111
              Boston, MA 02117

PHONE: (617) 421–6760

SBIC ____   VENTURE CAPITAL FUND _X_   MESBIC ____   OTHER ____

TYPES OF FINANCING PREFERRED (Stages): The fund looks for a balance of early stage, expansion, and later stage financings

MINIMUM DATA REQUIRED TO CONSIDER FINANCING: Business plan summarizing product, market, market opportunity, management resumes, financial projections, financing requirements

GEOGRAPHIC PREFERENCE: USA

INDUSTRY PREFERENCE BY FIRM: Technology based

INDUSTRY PREFERENCES BY INDIVIDUAL FIRM MEMBERS:
    Edward W. Kane   Nancy C. Raulston
    Robert J. Lepkowski   William A. Johnston
    D. Brooks Zug   Laurie J. Thomsen

YEAR COMPANY ESTABLISHED: 1982

FUNDS UNDER MANAGEMENT AT COST: $225 million

MINIMUM SIZE INVESTMENT: $500,000–$1,000,000

PREFERRED SIZE INVESTMENT: Same

WILL FIRM SERVE AS LEAD INVESTOR: Yes

NUMBER OF DEALS COMPLETED IN THE LAST 12 MONTHS: 70

AMOUNT INVESTED IN LAST 12 MONTHS: New investments: $17.2 million; Follow-on: $4.5 million

AVERAGE TIME REQUIRED TO COMPLETE A DEAL: 1–3 months
    (From Initial Contact to Closing)

FIRM NAME: Massachusetts Community Development Finance Corporation

ADDRESS: 131 State St.
              Suite 600
              Boston, MA 02109

PHONE: (617) 742–0366

SBIC ____   VENTURE CAPITAL FUND _X_   MESBIC ____   OTHER ____

TYPES OF FINANCING PREFERRED (Stages): Start-up from developed product stage/first stage (less than 1 year)/second stage (generally 1–3 years)/later stage expansion/buyouts and acquisitions

MINIMUM DATA REQUIRED TO CONSIDER FINANCING: Business plan

GEOGRAPHIC PREFERENCE: Economically distressed areas of Massachusetts

INDUSTRY PREFERENCE BY FIRM: Labor Intensive/Manufacturing or Service

INDUSTRY PREFERENCES BY INDIVIDUAL FIRM MEMBERS:
Charles T. Grigsby, President—Venture Capital
Nancy Nye, Vice-president—Real Estate (community development)
Judith Cranna, Investment Officer—Small Loan Guarantee, Venture Capital

YEAR COMPANY ESTABLISHED: 1975

FUNDS UNDER MANAGEMENT AT COST: $10 million

MINIMUM SIZE INVESTMENT: $75,000

PREFERRED SIZE INVESTMENT: Maximum $300,000

WILL FIRM SERVE AS LEAD INVESTOR: Yes

NUMBER OF DEALS COMPLETED IN THE LAST 12 MONTHS: 16

AMOUNT INVESTED IN LAST 12 MONTHS: $2,868,303

AVERAGE TIME REQUIRED TO COMPLETE A DEAL: 90–120 days
(From Initial Contact to Closing)

FIRM NAME: **Morgan, Holland Ventures Corporation**

ADDRESS: One Liberty Sq.
Boston, MA 02109

PHONE: (617) 423–1765

SBIC ___   VENTURE CAPITAL FUND _X_   MESBIC ___   OTHER ___

TYPES OF FINANCING PREFERRED (Stages): Seed/early stage/later stage/
leveraged buyouts

MINIMUM DATA REQUIRED TO CONSIDER FINANCING: N/A

GEOGRAPHIC PREFERENCE: None

INDUSTRY PREFERENCE BY FIRM: N/A

INDUSTRY PREFERENCES BY INDIVIDUAL FIRM MEMBERS:
James F. Morgan, Chairman—CAD/CAM—Computergraphics/Metals and Ce-
ramics/Super Computers/Chemical Processes
Daniel J. Holland, President—Signal Processing/Telecommunications
Jay A. Delahanty, Vice-president—Semiconductors/Semiconductor Equip-
ment/Communications/Robots/Vision Systems/Energy/CAE/Silicon Com-
pilers/Membrane Technology/Ocean Mining
Robert L. Rosbe, Jr., Vice-president—Software/Artificial Intelligence/Communi-
cations/Leveraged Buyouts/Military Electronics
Edwin M. Kania, Jr., Associate—Genetic Engineering/Medical Services/
Agriculture

YEAR COMPANY ESTABLISHED: 1982

FUNDS UNDER MANAGEMENT AT COST: $58.7 million

MINIMUM SIZE INVESTMENT: None

PREFERRED SIZE INVESTMENT: $500,000–$2,500,000

WILL FIRM SERVE AS LEAD INVESTOR: Yes

NUMBER OF DEALS COMPLETED IN THE LAST 12 MONTHS: 5 start-ups; 5
follow-ons

AMOUNT INVESTED IN LAST 12 MONTHS: $10 million

AVERAGE TIME REQUIRED TO COMPLETE A DEAL: 1–3 months
    (From Initial Contact to Closing)

FIRM NAME: **Nautilus Fund, Inc.**

ADDRESS: 24 Federal St.
                Boston, MA 02110

PHONE: (617) 482–8260

SBIC ___   VENTURE CAPITAL FUND _X_   MESBIC ___   OTHER ___

TYPES OF FINANCING PREFERRED (Stages): First stage investments/later
    stage/follow-on

MINIMUM DATA REQUIRED TO CONSIDER FINANCING: Audited financial
    statements/balance sheet/income statement/funds flow/changes in sharehold-
    ers equity for 2 years/unaudited interim statements/business plan with pro-
    jections pro forma

GEOGRAPHIC PREFERENCE: USA

INDUSTRY PREFERENCE BY FIRM: Technology Related/Computers (Hard-
    ware and Software)/Telecommunications/Electronics/Medical/Natural Re-
    sources/Retail/Chemicals

INDUSTRY PREFERENCES BY INDIVIDUAL FIRM MEMBERS:
    Richard A. Spillane, Jr.—All the above

YEAR COMPANY ESTABLISHED: 1979

FUNDS UNDER MANAGEMENT AT COST: $19 million

MINIMUM SIZE INVESTMENT: $150,000

PREFERRED SIZE INVESTMENT: $500,000

WILL FIRM SERVE AS LEAD INVESTOR: No

NUMBER OF DEALS COMPLETED IN THE LAST 12 MONTHS: 2

AMOUNT INVESTED IN LAST 12 MONTHS: $540,000

AVERAGE TIME REQUIRED TO COMPLETE A DEAL: 1–2 months
    (From Initial Contact to Closing)

FIRM NAME: **Newbury, Rosen & Company**

ADDRESS: One State St.
                Suite 1250
                Boston, MA 02109

PHONE: (617) 227–2707

SBIC ___   VENTURE CAPITAL FUND ___   MESBIC ___   OTHER _X_

TYPES OF FINANCING PREFERRED (Stages): Third stage/bridge/leveraged buy-
    out

MINIMUM DATA REQUIRED TO CONSIDER FINANCING: 3 years historic fi-
    nancials

GEOGRAPHIC PREFERENCE: None

INDUSTRY PREFERENCE BY FIRM: Specialty Chemical/Electronic/Oil and Gas

INDUSTRY PREFERENCES BY INDIVIDUAL FIRM MEMBERS: N/A

YEAR COMPANY ESTABLISHED: 1981

FUNDS UNDER MANAGEMENT AT COST: N/A

MINIMUM SIZE INVESTMENT: $1 million

PREFERRED SIZE INVESTMENT: $5 million

WILL FIRM SERVE AS LEAD INVESTOR: Yes

NUMBER OF DEALS COMPLETED IN THE LAST 12 MONTHS: 6

AMOUNT INVESTED IN LAST 12 MONTHS: N/A

AVERAGE TIME REQUIRED TO COMPLETE A DEAL: N/A
   (From Initial Contact to Closing)

FIRM NAME: **New England MESBIC, Inc.**

ADDRESS: 50 Kearney Rd.
                  Suite 3
                  Needham, MA 02194

PHONE: (617) 449–2066

SBIC ____ VENTURE CAPITAL FUND ____ MESBIC _X_ OTHER ____

TYPES OF FINANCING PREFERRED (Stages): Start-up and existing businesses

MINIMUM DATA REQUIRED TO CONSIDER FINANCING: Complete business
   plan

GEOGRAPHIC PREFERENCE: USA

INDUSTRY PREFERENCE BY FIRM: None

INDUSTRY PREFERENCES BY INDIVIDUAL FIRM MEMBERS: None

YEAR COMPANY ESTABLISHED: 1982

FUNDS UNDER MANAGEMENT AT COST: N/A

MINIMUM SIZE INVESTMENT: $50,000

PREFERRED SIZE INVESTMENT: $50,000 plus

WILL FIRM SERVE AS LEAD INVESTOR: Yes

NUMBER OF DEALS COMPLETED IN THE LAST 12 MONTHS: 4

AMOUNT INVESTED IN LAST 12 MONTHS: $250,000

AVERAGE TIME REQUIRED TO COMPLETE A DEAL: 3–6 months
   (From Initial Contact to Closing)

FIRM NAME: **Palmer Partners**

ADDRESS: 300 Unicorn Park Dr.   831 Carew Tower
                  Woburn, Mass 01801   Cincinnati, OH 45202

PHONE: (617) 933–5445   (513) 621–2331

SBIC ____ VENTURE CAPITAL FUND _X_ MESBIC ____ OTHER ____

TYPES OF FINANCING PREFERRED (Stages): Seed/start-up/commercialization/expansion

MINIMUM DATA REQUIRED TO CONSIDER FINANCING: Losses

GEOGRAPHIC PREFERENCE: N/A

INDUSTRY PREFERENCE BY FIRM: N/A

INDUSTRY PREFERENCES BY INDIVIDUAL FIRM MEMBERS: N/A

YEAR COMPANY ESTABLISHED: 1972

FUNDS UNDER MANAGEMENT AT COST: $31.7 million

MINIMUM SIZE INVESTMENT: $100,000

PREFERRED SIZE INVESTMENT: $500,000

WILL FIRM SERVE AS LEAD INVESTOR: Yes

NUMBER OF DEALS COMPLETED IN THE LAST 12 MONTHS: 12

AMOUNT INVESTED IN LAST 12 MONTHS: $3.5 million

AVERAGE TIME REQUIRED TO COMPLETE A DEAL: 2–6 months
(From Initial Contact to Closing)

FIRM NAME: **Pilgrim Capital Corporation**

ADDRESS: 842A Beacon St.
                Boston, MA 02215

PHONE: (617) 566–5212

SBIC ____ VENTURE CAPITAL FUND ____ MESBIC ____ OTHER _X_

TYPES OF FINANCING PREFERRED (Stages): First stage/second stage/third stage

MINIMUM DATA REQUIRED TO CONSIDER FINANCING: Business plan projections

GEOGRAPHIC PREFERENCE: New England

INDUSTRY PREFERENCE BY FIRM: Distribution/Manufacturing/Real Estate/Retail/Miscellaneous

INDUSTRY PREFERENCES BY INDIVIDUAL FIRM MEMBERS: N/A

YEAR COMPANY ESTABLISHED: 1962

FUNDS UNDER MANAGEMENT AT COST: N/A

MINIMUM SIZE INVESTMENT: $25,000

PREFERRED SIZE INVESTMENT: $50,000

WILL FIRM SERVE AS LEAD INVESTOR: Yes

NUMBER OF DEALS COMPLETED IN THE LAST 12 MONTHS: N/A

AMOUNT INVESTED IN LAST 12 MONTHS: N/A

AVERAGE TIME REQUIRED TO COMPLETE A DEAL: N/A
(From Initial Contact to Closing)

FIRM NAME: **Stan Radler Associates, Inc.**

ADDRESS: 78 Pine Hill Rd.
                Southboro, MA 01772

PHONE: (617) 875–1007

SBIC ____ VENTURE CAPITAL FUND ____ MESBIC ____

OTHER __X__ (Private investor, consultant to corporate investors/ funds, consultant to start-ups)

TYPES OF FINANCING PREFERRED (Stages): Early stages

MINIMUM DATA REQUIRED TO CONSIDER FINANCING: Detailed letter

GEOGRAPHIC PREFERENCE: Massachusetts and New England

INDUSTRY PREFERENCE BY FIRM: All high-technology areas

INDUSTRY PREFERENCES BY INDIVIDUAL FIRM MEMBERS: N/A

YEAR COMPANY ESTABLISHED: 1968

FUNDS UNDER MANAGEMENT AT COST: N/A

MINIMUM SIZE INVESTMENT: $50,000

PREFERRED SIZE INVESTMENT: $250,000–$1,000,000

WILL FIRM SERVE AS LEAD INVESTOR: Yes

NUMBER OF DEALS COMPLETED IN THE LAST 12 MONTHS: 2

AMOUNT INVESTED IN LAST 12 MONTHS: $400,000

AVERAGE TIME REQUIRED TO COMPLETE A DEAL: 4 months
    (From Initial Contact to Closing)

FIRM NAME: **Summit Ventures**

ADDRESS: One Boston Plaza
                Boston, MA 02108

PHONE: (617) 742–5500

SBIC ____ VENTURE CAPITAL FUND __X__ MESBIC ____ OTHER ____

TYPES OF FINANCING PREFERRED (Stages): Emerging Growth Companies/leveraged buyouts

MINIMUM DATA REQUIRED TO CONSIDER FINANCING: Company background/corporate strategy/products/services description/market analysis/competitor analysis/operations/financial summary/capital requirements/ management and personnel resumes

GEOGRAPHIC PREFERENCE: USA and Canada

INDUSTRY PREFERENCE BY FIRM:
    Automated Test Equipment/CAD–CAE–CAM Products/Computer Hardware/Defense Electronics/Data Communications and Telecommunications/Factory Automation Equipment/Health Care/Laser and Fiber Optics/Measurement Instrumentation/Medical Instruments and Electronics/Semiconductor Products

INDUSTRY PREFERENCES BY INDIVIDUAL FIRM MEMBERS: Contact any professional

YEAR COMPANY ESTABLISHED: 1984

FUNDS UNDER MANAGEMENT AT COST: $160 million

MINIMUM SIZE INVESTMENT: $1 million

PREFERRED SIZE INVESTMENT: $2–$2.5 million

WILL FIRM SERVE AS LEAD INVESTOR: Yes

NUMBER OF DEALS COMPLETED IN THE LAST 12 MONTHS: 6

AMOUNT INVESTED IN LAST 12 MONTHS: $11 million

AVERAGE TIME REQUIRED TO COMPLETE A DEAL: 75 days
(From Initial Contact to Closing)

FIRM NAME: **TA Associates**

ADDRESS: 45 Milk St.   525 University Ave.
               Boston, MA 02109   Palo Alto, CA 94301

PHONE: (617) 338–0800   (415) 328–1210

SBIC ____   VENTURE CAPITAL FUND _X_   MESBIC ____   OTHER ____

TYPES OF FINANCING PREFERRED (Stages): All stages. Will buy shares from existing stockholders when company is profitable

MINIMUM DATA REQUIRED TO CONSIDER FINANCING: Business plan preferred, but not required on first contact

GEOGRAPHIC PREFERENCE: USA and Canada

INDUSTRY PREFERENCE BY FIRM: Computer Hardware and Peripherals/Computer Software/Data Communications/Telecommunications/ Instrumentation/Industrial Automation Equipment/Semiconductor Products/Semiconductor Equipment/Health-Care Products and Services/Military Electronics/Specialty Chemicals and Materials/Cable Television and Broadcasting/Cellular Communications

INDUSTRY PREFERENCES BY INDIVIDUAL FIRM MEMBERS:

Peter A. Brooke	Nabil El-Hage
John L. Bunce, Jr.	Stephen F. Gormley
Michael C. Child	Henry Koerner
Jeffrey T. Chambers	Donald J. Kramer
Richard H. Churchill, Jr.	C. Kevin Landry
William P. Collatos	P. Andrews McLane
Brian J. Conway	Jacqueline C. Morby
David D. Croll	James F. Wade
Robert W. Daly	Linda C. Wisnewski

YEAR COMPANY ESTABLISHED: 1968

FUNDS UNDER MANAGEMENT AT COST: $500 million

MINIMUM SIZE INVESTMENT: $1 million

PREFERRED SIZE INVESTMENT: $2–$5 million

WILL FIRM SERVE AS LEAD INVESTOR: Yes

NUMBER OF DEALS COMPLETED IN THE LAST 12 MONTHS: 48

AMOUNT INVESTED IN LAST 12 MONTHS: $87 million

AVERAGE TIME REQUIRED TO COMPLETE A DEAL: 6 weeks
  (From Initial Contact to Closing)

FIRM NAME: **Uum, Morton, Bardcoy & Welling, Inc.**

ADDRESS: 1 Boston Pl.
  Boston, MA 02108

PHONE: (617) 227–0760

SBIC ____ VENTURE CAPITAL FUND ____ MESBIC ____ OTHER __X__

TYPES OF FINANCING PREFERRED (Stages): Second and third stages

MINIMUM DATA REQUIRED TO CONSIDER FINANCING: Financials/
projections/product material

GEOGRAPHIC PREFERENCE: Northeast, especially New England

INDUSTRY PREFERENCE BY FIRM: None

INDUSTRY PREFERENCES BY INDIVIDUAL FIRM MEMBERS:
  Peter A. Uum—Health Care/Retail   Bert Wolling—High Technol-
  Poppy Wortom—Real Estate   ogy/Broadcasting
                                          Mike Hollan—Computer

YEAR COMPANY ESTABLISHED: 1983

FUNDS UNDER MANAGEMENT AT COST: Clients have over $100 million to
invest

MINIMUM SIZE INVESTMENT: $2 million

PREFERRED SIZE INVESTMENT: $5 million plus

WILL FIRM SERVE AS LEAD INVESTOR: Yes

NUMBER OF DEALS COMPLETED IN THE LAST 12 MONTHS: 5

AMOUNT INVESTED IN LAST 12 MONTHS: $25 million

AVERAGE TIME REQUIRED TO COMPLETE A DEAL: 6 months
  (From Initial Contact to Closing)

FIRM NAME: **UNC Ventures**

ADDRESS: 195 State St.
  Suite 700
  Boston, MA 02109

PHONE: (617) 723–8300

SBIC ____ VENTURE CAPITAL FUND __X__ MESBIC ____ OTHER ____

TYPES OF FINANCING PREFERRED (Stages): Early stage/expansion financings/leveraged buyouts

MINIMUM DATA REQUIRED TO CONSIDER FINANCING: Complete business plan

GEOGRAPHIC PREFERENCE: N/A

INDUSTRY PREFERENCE BY FIRM: N/A

INDUSTRY PREFERENCES BY INDIVIDUAL FIRM MEMBERS:
Edward Dugger III   James W. Norton, Jr.
Ursula Z. Loucks   Laurence C. Morse
                       Elaine H. Politis

YEAR COMPANY ESTABLISHED: 1971

FUNDS UNDER MANAGEMENT AT COST: $30 million

MINIMUM SIZE INVESTMENT: $500,000

PREFERRED SIZE INVESTMENT: $500,000–$1,000,000

WILL FIRM SERVE AS LEAD INVESTOR: Yes

NUMBER OF DEALS COMPLETED IN THE LAST 12 MONTHS: 5

AMOUNT INVESTED IN LAST 12 MONTHS: $2.5 Million

AVERAGE TIME REQUIRED TO COMPLETE A DEAL: $1\frac{1}{2}$–3 months
(From Initial Contact to Closing)

FIRM NAME: **The Venture Capital Fund of New England**

ADDRESS: 100 Franklin St.
                Boston, MA 02110

PHONE: (617) 451–2577

SBIC ____ VENTURE CAPITAL FUND __X__ MESBIC ____ OTHER ____

TYPES OF FINANCING PREFERRED (Stages): Early stage

MINIMUM DATA REQUIRED TO CONSIDER FINANCING: Complete business plan

GEOGRAPHIC PREFERENCE: New England

INDUSTRY PREFERENCE BY FIRM: High Technology

INDUSTRY PREFERENCES BY INDIVIDUAL FIRM MEMBERS: N/A

YEAR COMPANY ESTABLISHED: 1981

FUNDS UNDER MANAGEMENT AT COST: $19 Million

MINIMUM SIZE INVESTMENT: $200,000

PREFERRED SIZE INVESTMENT: $400,000

WILL FIRM SERVE AS LEAD INVESTOR: Yes

NUMBER OF DEALS COMPLETED IN THE LAST 12 MONTHS: 8

AMOUNT INVESTED IN LAST 12 MONTHS: $3 million

AVERAGE TIME REQUIRED TO COMPLETE A DEAL: 6 weeks
(From Initial Contact to Closing)

FIRM NAME: **Venture Founders Corp.**

ADDRESS: 100 Fifth Ave.
                  Waltham, MA 02154

PHONE: (617) 890–1000

SBIC ____ VENTURE CAPITAL FUND _X_ MESBIC ____ OTHER ____

TYPES OF FINANCING PREFERRED (Stages): Seed/start-up/first stage

MINIMUM DATA REQUIRED TO CONSIDER FINANCING: Business plan

GEOGRAPHIC PREFERENCE: East Coast, USA, Canada, United Kingdom, Continental Europe

INDUSTRY PREFERENCE BY FIRM: Communications/Computer Related/ Consumer/Distribution/Electronic Components and Instrumentation/Genetic Engineering/Industrial Products and Equipment/Medical–Health Related

INDUSTRY PREFERENCES BY INDIVIDUAL FIRM MEMBERS:

M. Ross Yeiter—Contact person

YEAR COMPANY ESTABLISHED: 1970

FUNDS UNDER MANAGEMENT AT COST: $56 million

MINIMUM SIZE INVESTMENT: $100,000 or less

PREFERRED SIZE INVESTMENT: $100,000–$750,000

WILL FIRM SERVE AS LEAD INVESTOR: Yes

NUMBER OF DEALS COMPLETED IN THE LAST 12 MONTHS: 25

AMOUNT INVESTED IN LAST 12 MONTHS: $8.721 million

AVERAGE TIME REQUIRED TO COMPLETE A DEAL: 2–3 months (From Initial Contact to Closing)

FIRM NAME: **Vimac Corp.**

ADDRESS: 12 Arlington St.
                  Boston, MA 02116

PHONE: (617) 267–2785

SBIC ____ VENTURE CAPITAL FUND ____ MESBIC ____ OTHER _X_

TYPES OF FINANCING PREFERRED (Stages): Seed

MINIMUM DATA REQUIRED TO CONSIDER FINANCING: Business plan/ personal interview

GEOGRAPHIC PREFERENCE: New England

INDUSTRY PREFERENCE BY FIRM: Computer Applications/Health-care Systems

INDUSTRY PREFERENCES BY INDIVIDUAL FIRM MEMBERS: N/A

YEAR COMPANY ESTABLISHED: 1982

FUNDS UNDER MANAGEMENT AT COST: $4 million

MINIMUM SIZE INVESTMENT: $100,000

PREFERRED SIZE INVESTMENT: $300,000

WILL FIRM SERVE AS LEAD INVESTOR: Yes

NUMBER OF DEALS COMPLETED IN THE LAST 12 MONTHS: 5

AMOUNT INVESTED IN LAST 12 MONTHS: $1.5 million

AVERAGE TIME REQUIRED TO COMPLETE A DEAL: 4 months
(From Initial Contact to Closing)

MICHIGAN

FIRM NAME: **Dearborn Capital Corporation**

ADDRESS: P.O. Box 1729
Dearborn, MI 48121

PHONE: (313) 337–8577

SBIC ____ VENTURE CAPITAL FUND ____ MESBIC _X_ OTHER ____

TYPES OF FINANCING PREFERRED (Stages): Second tier growth or acquisition

MINIMUM DATA REQUIRED TO CONSIDER FINANCING: N/A

GEOGRAPHIC PREFERENCE: Continental USA

INDUSTRY PREFERENCE BY FIRM: Suppliers of parts or services to the automotive industry

INDUSTRY PREFERENCES BY INDIVIDUAL FIRM MEMBERS:
Stephen M. Aronson, President
Michael L. LaManes, Vice-president

YEAR COMPANY ESTABLISHED: 1978

FUNDS UNDER MANAGEMENT AT COST: N/A

MINIMUM SIZE INVESTMENT: $50,000

PREFERRED SIZE INVESTMENT: $150,000

WILL FIRM SERVE AS LEAD INVESTOR: Yes

NUMBER OF DEALS COMPLETED IN THE LAST 12 MONTHS: N/A

AMOUNT INVESTED IN LAST 12 MONTHS: N/A

AVERAGE TIME REQUIRED TO COMPLETE A DEAL: N/A
(From Initial Contact to Closing)

FIRM NAME: **Growth Funding, Ltd.**
(subsidiary of Venture Funding, Ltd.)

ADDRESS: 321 Fisher Building
Detroit, MI 48202

PHONE: (313) 871–3606

SBIC ____ VENTURE CAPITAL FUND ____ MESBIC ____ OTHER _X_

TYPES OF FINANCING PREFERRED (Stages): Seed/start-up/first stage

MINIMUM DATA REQUIRED TO CONSIDER FINANCING: Preliminary business plan/patent applications

GEOGRAPHIC PREFERENCE: None

INDUSTRY PREFERENCE BY FIRM: Biotechnology/Biomedical/Health-care Devices and Services/Computer Hardware and Software/Consumer Goods

INDUSTRY PREFERENCES BY INDIVIDUAL FIRM MEMBERS:
Eugene I. Schuster   Monis Schuster
David C. Dawson   Harry Ekblom
Jayson D. Pankin

YEAR COMPANY ESTABLISHED: 1983

FUNDS UNDER MANAGEMENT AT COST: N/A

MINIMUM SIZE INVESTMENT: $100,000

PREFERRED SIZE INVESTMENT: $100,000–$1,000,000

WILL FIRM SERVE AS LEAD INVESTOR: Yes

NUMBER OF DEALS COMPLETED IN THE LAST 12 MONTHS: N/A

AMOUNT INVESTED IN LAST 12 MONTHS: N/A

AVERAGE TIME REQUIRED TO COMPLETE A DEAL: 6 months
(From Initial Contact to Closing)

FIRM NAME: **Houston & Associates, Inc.**

ADDRESS: 1625 Woodward Ave.
Suite 220
Bloomfield Hills, MI 48013–1414

PHONE: (313) 332–1625

SBIC ___   VENTURE CAPITAL FUND ___   MESBIC ___

OTHER _X_ (Financial consultants and investors)

TYPES OF FINANCING PREFERRED (Stages): Start-up/first stage/second stage/buyout or acquisition

MINIMUM DATA REQUIRED TO CONSIDER FINANCING: Annual sales: nominal up to $20 million

GEOGRAPHIC PREFERENCE: Midwest (Michigan in particular)

INDUSTRY PREFERENCE BY FIRM: Communications/Computer Related/Distribution/Consumer/Electronic Components and Instrumentation/Energy–Natural Resources/Industrial Products/Medical

INDUSTRY PREFERENCES BY INDIVIDUAL FIRM MEMBERS: E. James Houston, Jr., President, principal contact on all inquiries

YEAR COMPANY ESTABLISHED: 1971

FUNDS UNDER MANAGEMENT AT COST: $1 million

MINIMUM SIZE INVESTMENT: $100,000

PREFERRED SIZE INVESTMENT: $100,000–$300,000

WILL FIRM SERVE AS LEAD INVESTOR: Prefer role as deal origniator, but will consider deals of others

NUMBER OF DEALS COMPLETED IN THE LAST 12 MONTHS: 1

AMOUNT INVESTED IN LAST 12 MONTHS: $50,000

AVERAGE TIME REQUIRED TO COMPLETE A DEAL: 3 months–1 year
(From Initial Contact to Closing)

FIRM NAME: **L. J. Johnson & Co.**

ADDRESS: 2705 Lowell Rd.
                Ann Arbor, MI 48103

PHONE: (313) 996–8033

SBIC ___ VENTURE CAPITAL FUND _X_ MESBIC ___ OTHER _X_

TYPES OF FINANCING PREFERRED (Stages): Early for technology/late for profit

MINIMUM DATA REQUIRED TO CONSIDER FINANCING: Products/markets

GEOGRAPHIC PREFERENCE: Warm climate, Michigan

INDUSTRY PREFERENCE BY FIRM: Technology/Publishing/Service

INDUSTRY PREFERENCES BY INDIVIDUAL FIRM MEMBERS: N/A

YEAR COMPANY ESTABLISHED: 1979

FUNDS UNDER MANAGEMENT AT COST: N/A

MINIMUM SIZE INVESTMENT: $50,000

PREFERRED SIZE INVESTMENT: N/A

WILL FIRM SERVE AS LEAD INVESTOR: Yes

NUMBER OF DEALS COMPLETED IN THE LAST 12 MONTHS: 4

AMOUNT INVESTED IN LAST 12 MONTHS: $8 million

AVERAGE TIME REQUIRED TO COMPLETE A DEAL: 90 days–9 months
(From Initial Contact to Closing)

FIRM NAME: **Michigan Capital and Service, Inc.**

ADDRESS: 500 First National Building
                201 S. Main St.
                Ann Arbor, MI 48104

PHONE: (313) 663–0702

SBIC _X_ VENTURE CAPITAL FUND ___ MESBIC ___ OTHER ___

TYPES OF FINANCING PREFERRED (Stages): Start-up and first stage financings/second and third stage growth financings/management leveraged buyouts

MINIMUM DATA REQUIRED TO CONSIDER FINANCING: Business plan

GEOGRAPHIC PREFERENCE: Midwest as lead; nationwide as participant

INDUSTRY PREFERENCE BY FIRM: Computer Related/Communications/
Medical Devices and Services/Manufacturing/Energy Related/Automation/
Electronics/Data Devices/Broadcasting

INDUSTRY PREFERENCES BY INDIVIDUAL FIRM MEMBERS: N/A

YEAR COMPANY ESTABLISHED: 1966

FUNDS UNDER MANAGEMENT AT COST: $14.7 million

MINIMUM SIZE INVESTMENT: $250,000

PREFERRED SIZE INVESTMENT: $500,000–$750,000

WILL FIRM SERVE AS LEAD INVESTOR: Yes, in Midwest

NUMBER OF DEALS COMPLETED IN THE LAST 12 MONTHS: 40

AMOUNT INVESTED IN LAST 12 MONTHS: $7 million

AVERAGE TIME REQUIRED TO COMPLETE A DEAL: 60–90 days
(From Initial Contact to Closing)

FIRM NAME: **Michigan Tech Capital Corp.**

ADDRESS: Technology Park
1700 Duncan Ave.
P.O. Box 529
Hubbell, MI 49934

PHONE: (906) 487–2643

SBIC __X__ VENTURE CAPITAL FUND ____ MESBIC ____ OTHER ____

TYPES OF FINANCING PREFERRED (Stages): N/A

MINIMUM DATA REQUIRED TO CONSIDER FINANCING: N/A

GEOGRAPHIC PREFERENCE: N/A

INDUSTRY PREFERENCE BY FIRM:
Computer Related: Application Software/Systems Software
Energy/Natural Resources: Minerals/Wood
Manufacturing: Processing, Basic Industries

INDUSTRY PREFERENCES BY INDIVIDUAL FIRM MEMBERS: N/A

YEAR COMPANY ESTABLISHED: 1982

FUNDS UNDER MANAGEMENT AT COST: $700,000

MINIMUM SIZE INVESTMENT: $25,000

PREFERRED SIZE INVESTMENT: $100,000

WILL FIRM SERVE AS LEAD INVESTOR: Prefer role as deal originator, but will
also invest in deals created by others

NUMBER OF DEALS COMPLETED IN THE LAST 12 MONTHS: 2

AMOUNT INVESTED IN LAST 12 MONTHS: $65,000

AVERAGE TIME REQUIRED TO COMPLETE A DEAL: N/A
(From Initial Contact to Closing)

FIRM NAME: **Motor Enterprises, Inc.**

ADDRESS: 3044 W. Grand Blvd.
               Detroit, MI 48202

PHONE: (313) 556–4273

SBIC ___ VENTURE CAPITAL FUND ___ MESBIC _X_ OTHER ___

TYPES OF FINANCING PREFERRED (Stages): Expansion and some start-up

MINIMUM DATA REQUIRED TO CONSIDER FINANCING: Complete business
   plan

GEOGRAPHIC PREFERENCE: Within a reasonable distance of a major GM plant

INDUSTRY PREFERENCE BY FIRM: Manufacturing/Service/Others

INDUSTRY PREFERENCES BY INDIVIDUAL FIRM MEMBERS: N/A

YEAR COMPANY ESTABLISHED: 1970

FUNDS UNDER MANAGEMENT AT COST: $3.5 million

MINIMUM SIZE INVESTMENT: $10,000

PREFERRED SIZE INVESTMENT: $50,000–$100,000

WILL FIRM SERVE AS LEAD INVESTOR: No

NUMBER OF DEALS COMPLETED IN THE LAST 12 MONTHS: 14

AMOUNT INVESTED IN LAST 12 MONTHS: $1 million

AVERAGE TIME REQUIRED TO COMPLETE A DEAL: 4 weeks
   (From Initial Contact to Closing)

MINNESOTA

FIRM NAME: **Cherry Tree Ventures**

ADDRESS: 640 Northland Executive Center
               3600 West 80th St.
               Minneapolis, MN 55431

PHONE: (612) 893–9012

SBIC ___ VENTURE CAPITAL FUND _X_ MESBIC ___ OTHER ___

TYPES OF FINANCING PREFERRED (Stages): Start-up/first stage/second stage

MINIMUM DATA REQUIRED TO CONSIDER FINANCING: Business plan

GEOGRAPHIC PREFERENCE: Minnesota, upper Midwest

INDUSTRY PREFERENCE BY FIRM: Health Care/Communications/Software/
   Micro Applications

INDUSTRY PREFERENCES BY INDIVIDUAL FIRM MEMBERS:
   Buzz Benson—Health-care Field

Michael Butler—Comunications/Application and Systems Software
Thomas W. Jackson—Consumer-based Products and Services

YEAR COMPANY ESTABLISHED: 1980

FUNDS UNDER MANAGEMENT AT COST: $40 million

MINIMUM SIZE INVESTMENT: None

PREFERRED SIZE INVESTMENT: $500,000

WILL FIRM SERVE AS LEAD INVESTOR: Yes

NUMBER OF DEALS COMPLETED IN THE LAST 12 MONTHS: 31

AMOUNT INVESTED IN LAST 12 MONTHS: $10,235,860

AVERAGE TIME REQUIRED TO COMPLETE A DEAL: 90 days
(From Initial Contact to Closing)

FIRM NAME: Dain Bosworth Inc.

ADDRESS: 100 Dain Tower
               Minneapolis, MN 55402

PHONE: (612) 371–2711

SBIC ____ VENTURE CAPITAL FUND ____ MESBIC ____ OTHER _X_

TYPES OF FINANCING PREFERRED (Stages): Mezzanine rounds/no start-ups

MINIMUM DATA REQUIRED TO CONSIDER FINANCING: Business
plan/historical financials/pro forma projections

GEOGRAPHIC PREFERENCE: Flexible, although particularly strong in Midwest,
Rocky Mountains, and Pacific Northwest

INDUSTRY PREFERENCE BY FIRM: Health Care/Medical Products/Pharmaceuticals/Electronics/Computer/Software/Telecommunications

INDUSTRY PREFERENCES BY INDIVIDUAL FIRM MEMBERS:
Gary Blaver—Software
Edward C. Freeman—Telecommunications/Industrial
Jeffrey P. Greiver—Health Care/Medical Products/Pharmaceuticals
Michael J. Norton—Electronics/Computer
James M. Stearns—Generalist

YEAR COMPANY ESTABLISHED: 1909

FUNDS UNDER MANAGEMENT AT COST: N/A

MINIMUM SIZE INVESTMENT: $1 million

PREFERRED SIZE INVESTMENT: $3–$10 million total size

WILL FIRM SERVE AS LEAD INVESTOR: Yes

NUMBER OF DEALS COMPLETED IN THE LAST 12 MONTHS: 12

AMOUNT INVESTED IN LAST 12 MONTHS: $75 million as agent

AVERAGE TIME REQUIRED TO COMPLETE A DEAL: 2–4 months
(From Initial Contact to Closing)

FIRM NAME: **FBS Venture Capital Company**

ADDRESS: 7515 Wayzata Blvd.
                Suite 110
                Minneapolis, MN 55426

PHONE: (612) 544-2754

SBIC _X_ VENTURE CAPITAL FUND ___ MESBIC ___ OTHER ___

TYPES OF FINANCING PREFERRED (Stages): Seed and early stage

MINIMUM DATA REQUIRED TO CONSIDER FINANCING: Business plan

GEOGRAPHIC PREFERENCE: Minnesota, Arizona, Colorado

INDUSTRY PREFERENCE BY FIRM: N/A

INDUSTRY PREFERENCES BY INDIVIDUAL FIRM MEMBERS: N/A

YEAR COMPANY ESTABLISHED: 1983

FUNDS UNDER MANAGEMENT AT COST: $20 million

MINIMUM SIZE INVESTMENT: None

PREFERRED SIZE INVESTMENT: Less than $500,000

WILL FIRM SERVE AS LEAD INVESTOR: Yes

NUMBER OF DEALS COMPLETED IN THE LAST 12 MONTHS: N/A

AMOUNT INVESTED IN LAST 12 MONTHS: N/A

AVERAGE TIME REQUIRED TO COMPLETE A DEAL: N/A
    (From Initial Contact to Closing)

FIRM NAME: **Minnesota Seed Capital, Inc.**

ADDRESS: Parkdale Plaza
                Suite 146
                1660 South Highway 100
                Minneapolis, MN 55416-1519

PHONE: (612) 545-5684

SBIC ___ VENTURE CAPITAL FUND _X_ MESBIC ___ OTHER ___

TYPES OF FINANCING PREFERRED (Stages): Start-up

MINIMUM DATA REQUIRED TO CONSIDER FINANCING: Complete business
    plan with market analysis

GEOGRAPHIC PREFERENCE: Minnesota only

INDUSTRY PREFERENCE BY FIRM: High Technology

INDUSTRY PREFERENCES BY INDIVIDUAL FIRM MEMBERS: N/A

YEAR COMPANY ESTABLISHED: 1980

FUNDS UNDER MANAGEMENT AT COST: $7 million

MINIMUM SIZE INVESTMENT: $50,000

PREFERRED SIZE INVESTMENT: $50,000-$250,000

WILL FIRM SERVE AS LEAD INVESTOR: Yes

NUMBER OF DEALS COMPLETED IN THE LAST 12 MONTHS: 7

AMOUiVT INVESTED IN LAST 12 MONTHS: N/A

AVERAGE TIME REQUIRED TO COMPLETE A DEAL: 60–90 days
(From Initial Contact to Closing)

FIRM NAME: **Northland Capital Corp.**

ADDRESS: 613 Missabe Building
227 West First St.
Duluth, MN 55802

PHONE: (218) 722–0545 – (218) 722–0546

SBIC _X_ VENTURE CAPITAL FUND ___ MESBIC ___ OTHER ___

TYPES OF FINANCING PREFERRED (Stages): No specialty

MINIMUM DATA REQUIRED TO CONSIDER FINANCING: 3 years audited
statements/business plan if available

GEOGRAPHIC PREFERENCE: None

INDUSTRY PREFERENCE BY FIRM: None

INDUSTRY PREFERENCES BY INDIVIDUAL FIRM MEMBERS: None

YEAR COMPANY ESTABLISHED: 1967

FUNDS UNDER MANAGEMENT AT COST: $3 million

MINIMUM SIZE INVESTMENT: $100,000

PREFERRED SIZE INVESTMENT: $100,000–$200,000

WILL FIRM SERVE AS LEAD INVESTOR: Yes

NUMBER OF DEALS COMPLETED IN THE LAST 12 MONTHS: 5

AMOUNT INVESTED IN LAST 12 MONTHS: $600,000

AVERAGE TIME REQUIRED TO COMPLETE A DEAL: 2 months
(From Initial Contact to Closing)

FIRM NAME: **Norwest Venture Capital Management, Inc.**

ADDRESS: 2800 Piper Jaffray Tower   1300 SW Fifth Ave.
222 S. Ninth St.   Suite 3018
Minneapolis, MN 55402   Portland, OR 97201

PHONE: (612) 372–8770   (503) 223–6622

SBIC _X_ VENTURE CAPITAL FUND ___ MESBIC ___ OTHER ___

TYPES OF FINANCING PREFERRED (Stages): Start-up and early stage/second
round financings/leveraged buyouts

MINIMUM DATA REQUIRED TO CONSIDER FINANCING: Detailed business
plan, including financial projections going out 5 years

GEOGRAPHIC PREFERENCE: Western half of USA

INDUSTRY PREFERENCE BY FIRM: Medical Products and Services/Computer Software/Telecommunications/Computer Related/Biotechnology

INDUSTRY PREFERENCES BY INDIVIDUAL FIRM MEMBERS: N/A

YEAR COMPANY ESTABLISHED: 1961

FUNDS UNDER MANAGEMENT AT COST: $240 million

MINIMUM SIZE INVESTMENT: $750,000–$1,000,000

PREFERRED SIZE INVESTMENT: $1.5–$2.0 million

WILL FIRM SERVE AS LEAD INVESTOR: Yes

NUMBER OF DEALS COMPLETED IN THE LAST 12 MONTHS: 45

AMOUNT INVESTED IN LAST 12 MONTHS: $22.9 million

AVERAGE TIME REQUIRED TO COMPLETE A DEAL: 60–90 days
(From Initial Contact to Closing)

FIRM NAME: **Pathfinder Venture Capital Funds**

ADDRESS: 7300 Metro Blvd.
               Suite 585
               Minneapolis, MN 55435

PHONE: (612) 835–1121

SBIC ____   VENTURE CAPITAL FUND __X__   MESBIC ____   OTHER ____

TYPES OF FINANCING PREFERRED (Stages): Start-up/first/second/third/buyouts

MINIMUM DATA REQUIRED TO CONSIDER FINANCING: Business plan

GEOGRAPHIC PREFERENCE: Close to major metro areas

INDUSTRY PREFERENCE BY FIRM: Medical/Computer/Data Communications/Technology

INDUSTRY PREFERENCES BY INDIVIDUAL FIRM MEMBERS:
Norman Dann—Medical   Robert Astromsky—Medical
Jack Ahrens—Computer   Gary Stoltz—Computer
A.J. Greenshields—General   Marvin Bookin—Computer

YEAR COMPANY ESTABLISHED: 1980

FUNDS UNDER MANAGEMENT AT COST: $73 million

MINIMUM SIZE INVESTMENT: $100,000

PREFERRED SIZE INVESTMENT: $500,000–$1,000,000

WILL FIRM SERVE AS LEAD INVESTOR: Yes

NUMBER OF DEALS COMPLETED IN THE LAST 12 MONTHS: 34

AMOUNT INVESTED IN LAST 12 MONTHS: $9.2 million

AVERAGE TIME REQUIRED TO COMPLETE A DEAL: 90 days
(From Initial Contact to Closing)

FIRM NAME: **Piper Jaffray & Hopwood Inc.**

ADDRESS: Piper Jaffray Tower
             P.O. Box 28
             Minneapolis, MN 55440

PHONE: (612) 342–6000

SBIC ____ VENTURE CAPITAL FUND _X_ MESBIC ____ OTHER ____

TYPES OF FINANCING PREFERRED (Stages): Start-up/second stage/expansion/late stage/buyout

MINIMUM DATA REQUIRED TO CONSIDER FINANCING: Business plan with financial projections and management resumes

GEOGRAPHIC PREFERENCE: None

INDUSTRY PREFERENCE BY FIRM: None

INDUSTRY PREFERENCES BY INDIVIDUAL FIRM MEMBERS:
    R. Hunt Greene, First Vice-president
    Frank B. Bennett, Associate
    Douglas R. Whitaker, Associate

YEAR COMPANY ESTABLISHED: 1895

FUNDS UNDER MANAGEMENT AT COST: $10 million plus

MINIMUM SIZE INVESTMENT: $200,000

PREFERRED SIZE INVESTMENT: $300,000

WILL FIRM SERVE AS LEAD INVESTOR: No

NUMBER OF DEALS COMPLETED IN THE LAST 12 MONTHS: 19 (1984)

AMOUNT INVESTED IN LAST 12 MONTHS: N/A

AVERAGE TIME REQUIRED TO COMPLETE A DEAL: 90 days
    (From Initial Contact to Closing)

FIRM NAME: **Shared Ventures, Inc.**

ADDRESS: 6550 York Ave. S.
             Suite 419
             Minneapolis, MN 55435

PHONE: (612) 925–3411

SBIC _X_ VENTURE CAPITAL FUND ____ MESBIC ____ OTHER ____

TYPES OF FINANCING PREFERRED (Stages): First and later stages

MINIMUM DATA REQUIRED TO CONSIDER FINANCING: Summary business plan

GEOGRAPHIC PREFERENCE: Midwest

INDUSTRY PREFERENCE BY FIRM: Diversified

INDUSTRY PREFERENCES BY INDIVIDUAL FIRM MEMBERS: N/A

YEAR COMPANY ESTABLISHED: 1981

FUNDS UNDER MANAGEMENT AT COST: $1.25 million

MINIMUM SIZE INVESTMENT: No minimum

PREFERRED SIZE INVESTMENT: $100,000

WILL FIRM SERVE AS LEAD INVESTOR: Yes

NUMBER OF DEALS COMPLETED IN THE LAST 12 MONTHS: 5

AMOUNT INVESTED IN LAST 12 MONTHS: $370,000

AVERAGE TIME REQUIRED TO COMPLETE A DEAL: 90 days
(From Initial Contact to Closing)

FIRM NAME: **Threshold Ventures, Inc.**

ADDRESS: 430 Oak Grove St.
Suite 303
Minneapolis, MN 55403

PHONE: (612) 874–7199

SBIC _X_ VENTURE CAPITAL FUND ___ MESBIC ___ OTHER ___

TYPES OF FINANCING PREFERRED (Stages): Seed/early stage

MINIMUM DATA REQUIRED TO CONSIDER FINANCING: Business plan and
interviews

GEOGRAPHIC PREFERENCE: N/A

INDUSTRY PREFERENCE BY FIRM: Electronics/Telecommunications/High
Technology

INDUSTRY PREFERENCES BY INDIVIDUAL FIRM MEMBERS: N/A

YEAR COMPANY ESTABLISHED: N/A

FUNDS UNDER MANAGEMENT AT COST: $1 million

MINIMUM SIZE INVESTMENT: $50,000

PREFERRED SIZE INVESTMENT: $150,000

WILL FIRM SERVE AS LEAD INVESTOR: Yes

NUMBER OF DEALS COMPLETED IN THE LAST 12 MONTHS: 6

AMOUNT INVESTED IN LAST 12 MONTHS: $600,000

AVERAGE TIME REQUIRED TO COMPLETE A DEAL: 45 days
(From Initial Contact to Closing)

MISSOURI

FIRM NAME: **Intercapco West, Inc.**

ADDRESS: 7800 Bonhomme
St. Louis, MO 63105

PHONE: (314) 863–0600

SBIC _X_ VENTURE CAPITAL FUND ___ MESBIC ___ OTHER ___

TYPES OF FINANCING PREFERRED (Stages): Later stages

MINIMUM DATA REQUIRED TO CONSIDER FINANCING: Business plan

GEOGRAPHIC PREFERENCE: Midwest

INDUSTRY PREFERENCE BY FIRM: Diversified

INDUSTRY PREFERENCES BY INDIVIDUAL FIRM MEMBERS: N/A

YEAR COMPANY ESTABLISHED: 1976

FUNDS UNDER MANAGEMENT AT COST: $2.5 million

MINIMUM SIZE INVESTMENT: $100,000

PREFERRED SIZE INVESTMENT: $100,000

WILL FIRM SERVE AS LEAD INVESTOR: Yes

NUMBER OF DEALS COMPLETED IN THE LAST 12 MONTHS: 6

AMOUNT INVESTED IN LAST 12 MONTHS: $600,000

AVERAGE TIME REQUIRED TO COMPLETE A DEAL: 1–6 months
(From Initial Contact to Closing)

MONTANA

FIRM NAME: **Rocky Mountain Ventures, Ltd.**

ADDRESS: 315 Securities Building
                Billings, MT 59101

PHONE: (406) 256–1984

SBIC _X_ VENTURE CAPITAL FUND ___ MESBIC ___ OTHER ___

TYPES OF FINANCING PREFERRED (Stages): Post start-up

MINIMUM DATA REQUIRED TO CONSIDER FINANCING: Complete written
business plan

GEOGRAPHIC PREFERENCE: Montana, Colorado, and contiguous states

INDUSTRY PREFERENCE BY FIRM: None

INDUSTRY PREFERENCES BY INDIVIDUAL FIRM MEMBERS: None

YEAR COMPANY ESTABLISHED: 1983

FUNDS UNDER MANAGEMENT AT COST:$1.1 million

MINIMUM SIZE INVESTMENT: $50,000

PREFERRED SIZE INVESTMENT: $150,000–$200,000

WILL FIRM SERVE AS LEAD INVESTOR: Yes

NUMBER OF DEALS COMPLETED IN THE LAST 12 MONTHS: None

AMOUNT INVESTED IN LAST 12 MONTHS: None

AVERAGE TIME REQUIRED TO COMPLETE A DEAL: 2 months
(From Initial Contact to Closing)

NEW HAMPSHIRE

FIRM NAME: **Granite State Capital, Inc.**
ADDRESS: 10 Fort Eddy Rd.
               Concord, NH 03301
PHONE: N/A
SBIC _X_ VENTURE CAPITAL FUND ___ MESBIC ___ OTHER ___
TYPES OF FINANCING PREFERRED (Stages): Early/second/leveraged buyouts
MINIMUM DATA REQUIRED TO CONSIDER FINANCING: Business plan
GEOGRAPHIC PREFERENCE: New England
INDUSTRY PREFERENCE BY FIRM: Diversified
INDUSTRY PREFERENCES BY INDIVIDUAL FIRM MEMBERS:
    Stuart D. Pompian
YEAR COMPANY ESTABLISHED: 1984
FUNDS UNDER MANAGEMENT AT COST: $1 million
MINIMUM SIZE INVESTMENT: $50,000
PREFERRED SIZE INVESTMENT: $100,000–$150,000
WILL FIRM SERVE AS LEAD INVESTOR: Yes
NUMBER OF DEALS COMPLETED IN THE LAST 12 MONTHS: 2
AMOUNT INVESTED IN LAST 12 MONTHS: $350,000
AVERAGE TIME REQUIRED TO COMPLETE A DEAL: 3–4 months
    (From Initial Contact to Closing)

FIRM NAME: **Hampshire Capital Corp.**
ADDRESS: 500 Spaulding Turnpike
               P.O. Box 3010
               Portsmouth, NH 03801
PHONE: (603) 431-7755
SBIC _X_ VENTURE CAPITAL FUND ___ MESBIC ___ OTHER ___
TYPES OF FINANCING PREFERRED (Stages): Early
MINIMUM DATA REQUIRED TO CONSIDER FINANCING: Complete business
    plan
GEOGRAPHIC PREFERENCE: East Coast; Maine to US Virgin Islands
INDUSTRY PREFERENCE BY FIRM: Franchise Companies
INDUSTRY PREFERENCES BY INDIVIDUAL FIRM MEMBERS: N/A
YEAR COMPANY ESTABLISHED: 1979
FUNDS UNDER MANAGEMENT AT COST: $5 million
MINIMUM SIZE INVESTMENT: None

PREFERRED SIZE INVESTMENT: $100,000

WILL FIRM SERVE AS LEAD INVESTOR: Yes

NUMBER OF DEALS COMPLETED IN THE LAST 12 MONTHS: N/A

AMOUNT INVESTED IN LAST 12 MONTHS: N/A

AVERAGE TIME REQUIRED TO COMPLETE A DEAL: 90–120 days
(From Initial Contact to Closing)

NEW JERSEY

FIRM NAME: **Accel Partners**

ADDRESS: One Palmer Sq.   One Embarcadero Center
                  Princeton, NJ 08542   San Francisco, CA 94111

PHONE: (609) 683–4500   (415) 989–5656

SBIC ___ VENTURE CAPITAL FUND _X_ MESBIC ___ OTHER ___

TYPES OF FINANCING PREFERRED (Stages): Early stage and start-up/leveraged
buyouts

MINIMUM DATA REQUIRED TO CONSIDER FINANCING: Business plan

GEOGRAPHIC PREFERENCE: None

INDUSTRY PREFERENCE BY FIRM: Software/Telecommunications/Health
Care/Factory Automation

INDUSTRY PREFERENCES BY INDIVIDUAL FIRM MEMBERS: N/A

YEAR COMPANY ESTABLISHED: 1983

FUNDS UNDER MANAGEMENT AT COST: $75 million

MINIMUM SIZE INVESTMENT: N/A

PREFERRED SIZE INVESTMENT: N/A

WILL FIRM SERVE AS LEAD INVESTOR: Yes

NUMBER OF DEALS COMPLETED IN THE LAST 12 MONTHS: 21

AMOUNT INVESTED IN LAST 12 MONTHS: $10,135,008

AVERAGE TIME REQUIRED TO COMPLETE A DEAL: N/A
(From Initial Contact to Closing)

FIRM NAME: **DSV Partners**

ADDRESS: 221 Nassau St.
                  Princeton, NJ 08542

PHONE: (609) 924–6420

SBIC ___ VENTURE CAPITAL FUND _X_ MESBIC ___ OTHER ___

TYPES OF FINANCING PREFERRED (Stages): Seed/start-up/first stage/second
stage

MINIMUM DATA REQUIRED TO CONSIDER FINANCING: Annual sales, P&L (projected after 3 years)

GEOGRAPHIC PREFERENCE: None

INDUSTRY PREFERENCE BY FIRM: Communications/Computer Related/ Electronic Components and Instrumentation/Energy/Natural Resources/ Genetic Engineering/Industrial Products and Equipment/Medical

INDUSTRY PREFERENCES BY INDIVIDUAL FIRM MEMBERS: N/A

YEAR COMPANY ESTABLISHED: 1981

FUNDS UNDER MANAGEMENT AT COST: $75 million plus

MINIMUM SIZE INVESTMENT: $250,000

PREFERRED SIZE INVESTMENT: $750,000 plus

WILL FIRM SERVE AS LEAD INVESTOR: Yes

NUMBER OF DEALS COMPLETED IN THE LAST 12 MONTHS: 20

AMOUNT INVESTED IN LAST 12 MONTHS: $7.45 million

AVERAGE TIME REQUIRED TO COMPLETE A DEAL: 3 months (From Initial Contact to Closing)

FIRM NAME: **InnoVen Group**

ADDRESS: Park 80 Plaza West—One
              Saddle Brook, NJ 07662

PHONE: (201) 845–4900

SBIC ____ VENTURE CAPITAL FUND _X_ MESBIC ____ OTHER ____

TYPES OF FINANCING PREFERRED (Stages): Start-up/first stage/second stage

MINIMUM DATA REQUIRED TO CONSIDER FINANCING: Annual sales: nominal/P&L: losses (profits projected after 2 years)

GEOGRAPHIC PREFERENCE: East Coast

INDUSTRY PREFERENCE BY FIRM: Communications/Computer Related/ Electronic Components and Instrumentation/Energy–Natural Resources/Genetic Engineering/Industrial Products and Equipment/Medical/Food and Beverage Manufacturing and Distribution/Entertainment and Services

INDUSTRY PREFERENCES BY INDIVIDUAL FIRM MEMBERS: N/A

YEAR COMPANY ESTABLISHED: 1972

FUNDS UNDER MANAGEMENT AT COST: $48.7 million

MINIMUM SIZE INVESTMENT: $300,000–600,000

PREFERRED SIZE INVESTMENT: $600,000 plus

WILL FIRM SERVE AS LEAD INVESTOR: Yes

NUMBER OF DEALS COMPLETED IN THE LAST 12 MONTHS: 38

AMOUNT INVESTED IN LAST 12 MONTHS: $6.3 Million

AVERAGE TIME REQUIRED TO COMPLETE A DEAL: 3 months
(From Initial Contact to Closing)

FIRM NAME: **Johnson & Johnson Development Corp.**

ADDRESS: One Johnson & Johnson Plaza
New Brunswick, NJ 08933

PHONE: (201) 524–6407

SBIC ___ VENTURE CAPITAL FUND ___ MESBIC ___
OTHER _X_ (Venture capital subsidiary of parent company)

TYPES OF FINANCING PREFERRED (Stages): Start-up/first stage

MINIMUM DATA REQUIRED TO CONSIDER FINANCING: Flexible

GEOGRAPHIC PREFERENCE: None

INDUSTRY PREFERENCE BY FIRM: Medical/Health Care

INDUSTRY PREFERENCES BY INDIVIDUAL FIRM MEMBERS: N/A

YEAR COMPANY ESTABLISHED: 1973

FUNDS UNDER MANAGEMENT AT COST: N/A

MINIMUM SIZE INVESTMENT: No preference

PREFERRED SIZE INVESTMENT: No preference

WILL FIRM SERVE AS LEAD INVESTOR: Yes

NUMBER OF DEALS COMPLETED IN THE LAST 12 MONTHS: N/A

AMOUNT INVESTED IN LAST 12 MONTHS: N/A

AVERAGE TIME REQUIRED TO COMPLETE A DEAL: N/A
(From Initial Contact to Closing)

FIRM NAME: **Johnston Associates Inc.**

ADDRESS: 300 Wall St.
Building O
Princeton, NJ 08540

PHONE: (609) 924–3131

SBIC ___ VENTURE CAPITAL FUND _X_ MESBIC ___ OTHER ___

TYPES OF FINANCING PREFERRED (Stages): Start-up

MINIMUM DATA REQUIRED TO CONSIDER FINANCING: Business plan

GEOGRAPHIC PREFERENCE: Northeast

INDUSTRY PREFERENCE BY FIRM: Medical Instrumentation/Health Care/
Biotechnology

INDUSTRY PREFERENCES BY INDIVIDUAL FIRM MEMBERS: N/A

YEAR COMPANY ESTABLISHED: 1967

FUNDS UNDER MANAGEMENT AT COST: N/A

MINIMUM SIZE INVESTMENT: $300,000

PREFERRED SIZE INVESTMENT: $500,000

WILL FIRM SERVE AS LEAD INVESTOR: Yes

NUMBER OF DEALS COMPLETED IN THE LAST 12 MONTHS: 3

AMOUNT INVESTED IN LAST 12 MONTHS: $1.2 million

AVERAGE TIME REQUIRED TO COMPLETE A DEAL: 5 months
(From Initial Contact to Closing)

FIRM NAME: **Med-Tech Ventures**

ADDRESS: 201 Tabor Rd.
Morris Plains, NJ 07950

PHONE: (201) 540–3457

SBIC ____ VENTURE CAPITAL FUND ____ MESBIC ____ OTHER _X_

TYPES OF FINANCING PREFERRED (Stages): Seed/start-up/first stage

MINIMUM DATA REQUIRED TO CONSIDER FINANCING: Business plan

GEOGRAPHIC PREFERENCE: None

INDUSTRY PREFERENCE BY FIRM: Medical/Diagnostics/Drugs and Medicines/
Therapeutic Equipment/Optics/Consumer Products

INDUSTRY PREFERENCES BY INDIVIDUAL FIRM MEMBERS: N/A

YEAR COMPANY ESTABLISHED: 1983

FUNDS UNDER MANAGEMENT AT COST: $25 million

MINIMUM SIZE INVESTMENT: $250,000

PREFERRED SIZE INVESTMENT: $500,000–$1,000,000

WILL FIRM SERVE AS LEAD INVESTOR: Yes

NUMBER OF DEALS COMPLETED IN THE LAST 12 MONTHS: 4

AMOUNT INVESTED IN LAST 12 MONTHS: $4 million

AVERAGE TIME REQUIRED TO COMPLETE A DEAL: 3 months
(From Initial Contact to Closing)

FIRM NAME: **Unicorn Ventures, Lltd.**

ADDRESS: 14 Commerce Dr.
Cranford, NJ 07016

PHONE: (201) 276–7880

SBIC _X_ VENTURE CAPITAL FUND ____ MESBIC ____ OTHER ____

TYPES OF FINANCING PREFERRED (Stages): Early stage/leveraged buyouts/
start-ups

MINIMUM DATA REQUIRED TO CONSIDER FINANCING: Business plan/3 year
historical financials

GEOGRAPHIC PREFERENCE: None

INDUSTRY PREFERENCE BY FIRM: None

INDUSTRY PREFERENCES BY INDIVIDUAL FIRM MEMBERS: None

YEAR COMPANY ESTABLISHED: 1981

FUNDS UNDER MANAGEMENT AT COST: $35 million

MINIMUM SIZE INVESTMENT: $250,000

PREFERRED SIZE INVESTMENT: $500,000–$1,000,000

WILL FIRM SERVE AS LEAD INVESTOR: Yes

NUMBER OF DEALS COMPLETED IN THE LAST 12 MONTHS: 8

AMOUNT INVESTED IN LAST 12 MONTHS: $4 million

AVERAGE TIME REQUIRED TO COMPLETE A DEAL: 60–120 days
     (From Initial Contact to Closing)

NEW MEXICO

FIRM NAME: **Associated Southwest Investors, Inc.**

ADDRESS: 124 Tenth St., NW
               Albuquerque, NM 87102

PHONE: N/A

SBIC ____   VENTURE CAPITAL FUND ____   MESBIC _X_   OTHER ____

TYPES OF FINANCING PREFERRED (Stages): Start-up/expansion/acquisition

MINIMUM DATA REQUIRED TO CONSIDER FINANCING: Business plan

GEOGRAPHIC PREFERENCE: Southwest

INDUSTRY PREFERENCE BY FIRM: Communications/Diversified

INDUSTRY PREFERENCES BY INDIVIDUAL FIRM MEMBERS: N/A

YEAR COMPANY ESTABLISHED: 1971

FUNDS UNDER MANAGEMENT AT COST: $2.4 million

MINIMUM SIZE INVESTMENT: $75,000

PREFERRED SIZE INVESTMENT: $150,000 plus

WILL FIRM SERVE AS LEAD INVESTOR: Yes

NUMBER OF DEALS COMPLETED IN THE LAST 12 MONTHS: 5

AMOUNT INVESTED IN LAST 12 MONTHS: N/A

AVERAGE TIME REQUIRED TO COMPLETE A DEAL: 90 days
     (From Initial Contact to Closing)

FIRM NAME: **Equity Capital Corporation**

ADDRESS: 231 Washington Ave.
               Suite 2
               Santa Fe, NM 87501

PHONE: (505) 988–4273

SBIC __X__ VENTURE CAPITAL FUND ___ MESBIC ___ OTHER ___

TYPES OF FINANCING PREFERRED (Stages): Later stage

MINIMUM DATA REQUIRED TO CONSIDER FINANCING: N/A

GEOGRAPHIC PREFERENCE: Southwest

INDUSTRY PREFERENCE BY FIRM: None

INDUSTRY PREFERENCES BY INDIVIDUAL FIRM MEMBERS: None

YEAR COMPANY ESTABLISHED: 1984

FUNDS UNDER MANAGEMENT AT COST: $1.3 million

MINIMUM SIZE INVESTMENT: $75,000

PREFERRED SIZE INVESTMENT: $150,000

WILL FIRM SERVE AS LEAD INVESTOR: Yes

NUMBER OF DEALS COMPLETED IN THE LAST 12 MONTHS: 5

AMOUNT INVESTED IN LAST 12 MONTHS: $450,000

AVERAGE TIME REQUIRED TO COMPLETE A DEAL: 45 days
   (From Initial Contact to Closing)

FIRM NAME: **Meadows Resources, Inc.**

ADDRESS: 1650 University, NE
                Suite 500
                Albuquerque, NM 87110

PHONE: (505) 132–7600

SBIC ___ VENTURE CAPITAL FUND __X__ MESBIC ___ OTHER ___

TYPES OF FINANCING PREFERRED (Stages): Start-up/first stage/second stage

MINIMUM DATA REQUIRED TO CONSIDER FINANCING: Full business plan

GEOGRAPHIC PREFERENCE: Southwest, but will consider all locations

INDUSTRY PREFERENCE BY FIRM: Telecommunications/Electronics/Medical
   Technology

INDUSTRY PREFERENCES BY INDIVIDUAL FIRM MEMBERS: N/A

YEAR COMPANY ESTABLISHED: 1981

FUNDS UNDER MANAGEMENT AT COST: $20 million

MINIMUM SIZE INVESTMENT: $250,000

PREFERRED SIZE INVESTMENT: $500,000–$1,000,000

WILL FIRM SERVE AS LEAD INVESTOR: Yes

NUMBER OF DEALS COMPLETED IN THE LAST 12 MONTHS: 8

AMOUNT INVESTED IN LAST 12 MONTHS: $9.8 million

AVERAGE TIME REQUIRED TO COMPLETE A DEAL: 90 days
   (From Initial Contact to Closing)

FIRM NAME: Santa Fe Private Equity Fund

ADDRESS: 524 Camino Del Monte Sol
Santa Fe, NM 87501

PHONE: (505) 983–1769

SBIC ____ VENTURE CAPITAL FUND _X_ MESBIC ____ OTHER ____

TYPES OF FINANCING PREFERRED (Stages): Start-up/first stage/second stage

MINIMUM DATA REQUIRED TO CONSIDER FINANCING: Annual sales: nominal

GEOGRAPHIC PREFERENCE: Within 2 hours of office, Southwest and West Coast

INDUSTRY PREFERENCE BY FIRM: Communications/Computer Related/Distribution/Electronic Components and Instrumentation/Genetic Engineering/Industrial Products and Equipment/Medical

INDUSTRY PREFERENCES BY INDIVIDUAL FIRM MEMBERS:
A. David Silver   Kay Tsunemori
Jesse L. Acker

YEAR COMPANY ESTABLISHED: 1983

FUNDS UNDER MANAGEMENT AT COST: $35 million

MINIMUM SIZE INVESTMENT: $100,000–$300,000

PREFERRED SIZE INVESTMENT: $300,000–$600,000

WILL FIRM SERVE AS LEAD INVESTOR: Yes

NUMBER OF DEALS COMPLETED IN THE LAST 12 MONTHS: 8

AMOUNT INVESTED IN LAST 12 MONTHS: $10 million

AVERAGE TIME REQUIRED TO COMPLETE A DEAL: 120 days
(From Initial Contact to Closing)

FIRM NAME: Southwest Capital Investments, Inc.

ADDRESS: 3500-E Comanche Rd. NE
Albuquerque, NM 87107

PHONE: (505) 884–7161

SBIC _X_ VENTURE CAPITAL FUND ____ MESBIC ____ OTHER ____

TYPES OF FINANCING PREFERRED (Stages): Second or third stage

MINIMUM DATA REQUIRED TO CONSIDER FINANCING: Normal business plan and financials

GEOGRAPHIC PREFERENCE: Western USA

INDUSTRY PREFERENCE BY FIRM: Manufacturing/Communication/Retail/Wholesale

INDUSTRY PREFERENCES BY INDIVIDUAL FIRM MEMBERS: N/A

YEAR COMPANY ESTABLISHED: 1976

FUNDS UNDER MANAGEMENT AT COST: $3,510,655 (audited assets at 12/31/84)

MINIMUM SIZE INVESTMENT: $50,000

PREFERRED SIZE INVESTMENT: $100,000–$150,000

WILL FIRM SERVE AS LEAD INVESTOR: Yes

NUMBER OF DEALS COMPLETED IN THE LAST 12 MONTHS: 9

AMOUNT INVESTED IN LAST 12 MONTHS: $526,150

AVERAGE TIME REQUIRED TO COMPLETE A DEAL: 4–8 weeks
(From Initial Contact to Closing)

NEW YORK

FIRM NAME: **Adler & Co.**

ADDRESS: 375 Park Ave.   1245 Oakmead Parkway
            Suite 3303   Sunnyvale, CA 94086
            New York, NY 10152

PHONE: (212) 759–2800   (408) 720–8700

SBIC ____   VENTURE CAPITAL FUND _X_   MESBIC ____   OTHER ____

TYPES OF FINANCING PREFERRED (Stages): No preference

MINIMUM DATA REQUIRED TO CONSIDER FINANCING: 3-year projections/annual sales: nominal/P&L: losses (profits after 1 year)

GEOGRAPHIC PREFERENCE: None

INDUSTRY PREFERENCE BY FIRM: None

INDUSTRY PREFERENCES BY INDIVIDUAL FIRM MEMBERS:
Frederick R. Adler, New York
James J. Harrison, California
Joy London, New York
Yuval Binur, New York
James E. Long, California
Daniel C. O'Neill, California
John B. Harlow, New York
Les Strauss, New York

YEAR COMPANY ESTABLISHED: 1978

FUNDS UNDER MANAGEMENT AT COST: $220 million

MINIMUM SIZE INVESTMENT: $100,000

PREFERRED SIZE INVESTMENT: $500,000

WILL FIRM SERVE AS LEAD INVESTOR: Yes

NUMBER OF DEALS COMPLETED IN THE LAST 12 MONTHS: 44

AMOUNT INVESTED IN LAST 12 MONTHS: $36.2 million

AVERAGE TIME REQUIRED TO COMPLETE A DEAL: 4 weeks
(From Initial Contact to Closing)

FIRM NAME: **Alimansky Venture Group, Inc.**

ADDRESS: 790 Madison Ave.
Suite 705
New York, NY 10021

PHONE: (212) 472–0502

SBIC ___ VENTURE CAPITAL FUND ___ MESBIC ___ OTHER _X_

TYPES OF FINANCING PREFERRED (Stages): Start-up/first stage/second
stage/third stage/buyout or acquisition financing

MINIMUM DATA REQUIRED TO CONSIDER FINANCING: Background of busi-
ness/description of products and services/resumes of principals/whatever data
are available

GEOGRAPHIC PREFERENCE: USA

INDUSTRY PREFERENCE BY FIRM: Communications/Computer/Consumer
Services/Electronics/Energy–Natural Resources/Genetic Engineering/Medi-
cal—Health Related/Industrial/Agriculture/Finance/Franchise/Publishing/Re-
tail

INDUSTRY PREFERENCES BY INDIVIDUAL FIRM MEMBERS:
Burt Alimansky
Peter Vollers
Adrian Horne

YEAR COMPANY ESTABLISHED: 1980

FUNDS UNDER MANAGEMENT AT COST: Firm has worked with over 50 clients

MINIMUM SIZE INVESTMENT: $300,000

PREFERRED SIZE INVESTMENT: $2–$5 million

WILL FIRM SERVE AS LEAD INVESTOR: Yes

NUMBER OF DEALS COMPLETED IN THE LAST 12 MONTHS: Firm has
worked with over 20 clients in 1984

AMOUNT INVESTED IN LAST 12 MONTHS: N/A

AVERAGE TIME REQUIRED TO COMPLETE A DEAL: Varies
(From Initial Contact to Closing)

FIRM NAME: **AMEV Capital Corporation**

ADDRESS: One World Trade Center
Suite 5001
New York, NY 10048–0024

PHONE: N/A

SBIC _X_ VENTURE CAPITAL FUND ___ MESBIC ___ OTHER ___

TYPES OF FINANCING PREFERRED (Stages): Second stage and beginning/ leveraged buyouts

MINIMUM DATA REQUIRED TO CONSIDER FINANCING: Business plan/financial statements/etc.

GEOGRAPHIC PREFERENCE: USA

INDUSTRY PREFERENCE BY FIRM: Diversified

INDUSTRY PREFERENCES BY INDIVIDUAL FIRM MEMBERS: Diversified

YEAR COMPANY ESTABLISHED: 1979

FUNDS UNDER MANAGEMENT AT COST: $15 million

MINIMUM SIZE INVESTMENT: $500,000

PREFERRED SIZE INVESTMENT: $750,000

WILL FIRM SERVE AS LEAD INVESTOR: Yes

NUMBER OF DEALS COMPLETED IN THE LAST 12 MONTHS: 1 follow-on investment; 9 expansion and LBO

AMOUNT INVESTED IN LAST 12 MONTHS: $3.8 million

AVERAGE TIME REQUIRED TO COMPLETE A DEAL: 6 weeks (From Initial Contact to Closing)

FIRM NAME: **Applied Technology Partners, LP**

ADDRESS: One New York Plaza
                34th Floor
                New York, NY 10004

PHONE: (212) 558–0206

SBIC ___   VENTURE CAPITAL FUND _X_   MESBIC ___   OTHER ___

TYPES OF FINANCING PREFERRED (Stages): Start-ups or second stage

MINIMUM DATA REQUIRED TO CONSIDER FINANCING: Business plan with market, products, people and 5 year financial projections

GEOGRAPHIC PREFERENCE: USA

INDUSTRY PREFERENCE BY FIRM: Computer Hardware–Software/Computer Services/Communications Services/Communications Hardware/Industrial Automation

INDUSTRY PREFERENCES BY INDIVIDUAL FIRM MEMBERS:
Frederick B. Bamber—Computer Software/Robotics
Thomas L. Flaherty—Communications/Software
Michael I. Mayers—Hardware/Robotics

YEAR COMPANY ESTABLISHED: 1981

FUNDS UNDER MANAGEMENT AT COST: N/A

MINIMUM SIZE INVESTMENT: $200,000

PREFERRED SIZE INVESTMENT: $250,000–$500,000

WILL FIRM SERVE AS LEAD INVESTOR: Yes

NUMBER OF DEALS COMPLETED IN THE LAST 12 MONTHS: 6

AMOUNT INVESTED IN LAST 12 MONTHS: $2.7 million

AVERAGE TIME REQUIRED TO COMPLETE A DEAL: 8–12 weeks
(From Initial Contact to Closing)

FIRM NAME: **Bessemer Venture Partners**

ADDRESS: 630 Fifth Ave.   3000 Sand Hill Rd.
                  New York, NY 10111   Building 3, Suite 225
                                             Menlo Park, CA 94025

PHONE: (212) 708–9300   (415) 854–2200

ADDRESS: 83 Walnut St.
                  Wellesley Hills, CA 02181

PHONE: (617) 237–6050

SBIC ____ VENTURE CAPITAL FUND _X_ MESBIC ____ OTHER ____

TYPES OF FINANCING PREFERRED (Stages): Any

MINIMUM DATA REQUIRED TO CONSIDER FINANCING: Varies

GEOGRAPHIC PREFERENCE: Continental USA

INDUSTRY PREFERENCE BY FIRM: N/A

INDUSTRY PREFERENCES BY INDIVIDUAL FIRM MEMBERS: N/A

YEAR COMPANY ESTABLISHED: Over 25 years (including predecessors)

FUNDS UNDER MANAGEMENT AT COST: $100 million

MINIMUM SIZE INVESTMENT: $600,000

PREFERRED SIZE INVESTMENT: $750,000

WILL FIRM SERVE AS LEAD INVESTOR: Yes

NUMBER OF DEALS COMPLETED IN THE LAST 12 MONTHS: 20

AMOUNT INVESTED IN LAST 12 MONTHS: $15 million

AVERAGE TIME REQUIRED TO COMPLETE A DEAL: Varies
(From Initial Contact to Closing)

FIRM NAME: **Biotech Capital**

ADDRESS: 600 Madison Ave.
                  New York, NY 10022

PHONE: (212) 758–7722

SBIC ____ VENTURE CAPITAL FUND _X_ MESBIC ____ OTHER ____

TYPES OF FINANCING PREFERRED (Stages): Start-up/turnaround/later stage
expansion/mezzanine

MINIMUM DATA REQUIRED TO CONSIDER FINANCING: Business plan

GEOGRAPHIC PREFERENCE: USA

INDUSTRY PREFERENCE BY FIRM: Biotechnology/Health Care/Microelectronics/Data Communication/Telecommunications/Industrial Manufacturing

INDUSTRY PREFERENCES BY INDIVIDUAL FIRM MEMBERS: Initial contact to Barbara J. Hann

YEAR COMPANY ESTABLISHED: 1980

FUNDS UNDER MANAGEMENT AT COST: N/A

MINIMUM SIZE INVESTMENT: $250,000

PREFERRED SIZE INVESTMENT: $1 million

WILL FIRM SERVE AS LEAD INVESTOR: Yes

NUMBER OF DEALS COMPLETED IN THE LAST 12 MONTHS: 10

AMOUNT INVESTED IN LAST 12 MONTHS: N/A

AVERAGE TIME REQUIRED TO COMPLETE A DEAL: 2 months
(From Initial Contact to Closing)

FIRM NAME: **Bradford Ventures Ltd.**

ADDRESS: 1212 Avenue of the Americas
New York, NY 10036

PHONE: (212) 221–4620

SBIC _____   VENTURE CAPITAL FUND _X_ MESBIC _____   OTHER _____

TYPES OF FINANCING PREFERRED (Stages): Later stage/leveraged buyouts

MINIMUM DATA REQUIRED TO CONSIDER FINANCING: N/A

GEOGRAPHIC PREFERENCE: USA

INDUSTRY PREFERENCE BY FIRM: N/A

INDUSTRY PREFERENCES BY INDIVIDUAL FIRM MEMBERS: N/A

YEAR COMPANY ESTABLISHED: 1972

FUNDS UNDER MANAGEMENT AT COST: $50 million

MINIMUM SIZE INVESTMENT: $500,000

PREFERRED SIZE INVESTMENT: $2–$4 million

WILL FIRM SERVE AS LEAD INVESTOR: Yes

NUMBER OF DEALS COMPLETED IN THE LAST 12 MONTHS: 6

AMOUNT INVESTED IN LAST 12 MONTHS: $15 million

AVERAGE TIME REQUIRED TO COMPLETE A DEAL: 3 months
(From Initial Contact to Closing)

FIRM NAME: **BT Capital Corporation**

ADDRESS: 280 Park Ave.
New York, NY 10017

PHONE: (212) 850–1916

SBIC _X_ VENTURE CAPITAL FUND ___ MESBIC ___ OTHER ___

TYPES OF FINANCING PREFERRED (Stages): Leveraged buyouts/growth companies (making $250,000 or more after taxes)

MINIMUM DATA REQUIRED TO CONSIDER FINANCING: None

GEOGRAPHIC PREFERENCE: None

INDUSTRY PREFERENCE BY FIRM: No technology and no start-ups

INDUSTRY PREFERENCES BY INDIVIDUAL FIRM MEMBERS: N/A

YEAR COMPANY ESTABLISHED: 1975

FUNDS UNDER MANAGEMENT AT COST: $75 Million

MINIMUM SIZE INVESTMENT: $1 million

PREFERRED SIZE INVESTMENT: $3–5 million

WILL FIRM SERVE AS LEAD INVESTOR: Yes

NUMBER OF DEALS COMPLETED IN THE LAST 12 MONTHS: 10

AMOUNT INVESTED IN LAST 12 MONTHS: $28 million

AVERAGE TIME REQUIRED TO COMPLETE A DEAL: 6 weeks
(From Initial Contact to Closing)

FIRM NAME: **Buffalo Capital Corporation**
                   (affiliate of The Hickman Corp., Arthur Taylor & Co., and Saudi Arabian Investment Co.)

ADDRESS: Mt. Morris Rd.
                   Geneseo, NY 14454

PHONE: (716) 243–4310

SBIC ___ VENTURE CAPITAL FUND ___ MESBIC ___
OTHER _X_ (Merchant banking firm with venture capital activity)

TYPES OF FINANCING PREFERRED (Stages): Start-ups/first through third level

MINIMUM DATA REQUIRED TO CONSIDER FINANCING: Business plan

GEOGRAPHIC PREFERENCE: Northeast, Canada, Florida, Mid-Atlantic

INDUSTRY PREFERENCE BY FIRM: Management Buyouts/Retailing/Wholesaling/Software/Medical Care/Media/Financial Services/Food Concept/Horticulture

INDUSTRY PREFERENCES BY INDIVIDUAL FIRM MEMBERS:
J. H. Hickman—Management Buyouts/Retailing/Wholesaling/Medical Care/Food Concepts/Horticulture
A. R. Taylor—Media/Financial Services/Electronic

YEAR COMPANY ESTABLISHED: 1969

FUNDS UNDER MANAGEMENT AT COST: $5 million plus

MINIMUM SIZE INVESTMENT: $250,000

PREFERRED SIZE INVESTMENT: $500,000 plus

WILL FIRM SERVE AS LEAD INVESTOR: Yes

NUMBER OF DEALS COMPLETED IN THE LAST 12 MONTHS: 5

AMOUNT INVESTED IN LAST 12 MONTHS: $1 million plus

AVERAGE TIME REQUIRED TO COMPLETE A DEAL: 1–2 months
(From Initial Contact to Closing)

FIRM NAME: **Chemical Venture Capital Corporation**

ADDRESS: 277 Park Ave.
New York, NY 10172

PHONE: (212) 310–4949

SBIC _X_   VENTURE CAPITAL FUND ____   MESBIC ____   OTHER ____

TYPES OF FINANCING PREFERRED (Stages): No preference: seed to leveraged
buyouts

MINIMUM DATA REQUIRED TO CONSIDER FINANCING: Business plan with
projections

GEOGRAPHIC PREFERENCE: None

INDUSTRY PREFERENCE BY FIRM: Consumer Goods/Broadcasting/Retail-
ing/Industrial Products/Entertainment/Medical Products/Communications

INDUSTRY PREFERENCES BY INDIVIDUAL FIRM MEMBERS:
Steven J. Gilbert, President   Paige Meili, Associate
Jeffrey C. Walker, Vice-president   David Jaffe, Associate
Barry A. Schwimmer, Associate   Nathaniel Henshaw, Analyst

YEAR COMPANY ESTABLISHED: 1984

FUNDS UNDER MANAGEMENT AT COST: $100 million

MINIMUM SIZE INVESTMENT: $250,000

PREFERRED SIZE INVESTMENT: None

WILL FIRM SERVE AS LEAD INVESTOR: Yes

NUMBER OF DEALS COMPLETED IN THE LAST 12 MONTHS: 12

AMOUNT INVESTED IN LAST 12 MONTHS: $25 million

AVERAGE TIME REQUIRED TO COMPLETE A DEAL: 50–100 days
(From Initial Contact to Closing)

FIRM NAME: **Citicorp Venture Capital Ltd.**

ADDRESS: Citicorp Center
New York, NY 10045

PHONE: (212) 559–1127

SBIC _X_   VENTURE CAPITAL FUND ____   MESBIC ____   OTHER ____

TYPES OF FINANCING PREFERRED (Stages): Early stage/leveraged buyouts

MINIMUM DATA REQUIRED TO CONSIDER FINANCING: Written business
plan

GEOGRAPHIC PREFERENCE: Continental USA

INDUSTRY PREFERENCE BY FIRM: Health Care/Computer Systems/Telecommunications/Broadcast Communications/Office Automation/Factory Automation/Design Automation/Biotechnology

INDUSTRY PREFERENCES BY INDIVIDUAL FIRM MEMBERS: N/A

YEAR COMPANY ESTABLISHED: 1967

FUNDS UNDER MANAGEMENT AT COST: $250 million

MINIMUM SIZE INVESTMENT: $500,000

PREFERRED SIZE INVESTMENT: $1–$2 million

WILL FIRM SERVE AS LEAD INVESTOR: Yes

NUMBER OF DEALS COMPLETED IN THE LAST 12 MONTHS: 73

AMOUNT INVESTED IN LAST 12 MONTHS: $43.781 million

AVERAGE TIME REQUIRED TO COMPLETE A DEAL: 30–60 days
(From Initial Contact to Closing)

FIRM NAME: **CMNY Capital Company, Inc.**

ADDRESS: 77 Water St.
                New York, NY 10005

PHONE: N/A

SBIC _X_ VENTURE CAPITAL FUND ____ MESBIC ____ OTHER ____

TYPES OF FINANCING PREFERRED (Stages): Any

MINIMUM DATA REQUIRED TO CONSIDER FINANCING: Business plan

GEOGRAPHIC PREFERENCE: Various

INDUSTRY PREFERENCE BY FIRM: Various

INDUSTRY PREFERENCES BY INDIVIDUAL FIRM MEMBERS: N/A

YEAR COMPANY ESTABLISHED: 1962

FUNDS UNDER MANAGEMENT AT COST: $2 million

MINIMUM SIZE INVESTMENT: $100,000

PREFERRED SIZE INVESTMENT: $250,000–$500,000

WILL FIRM SERVE AS LEAD INVESTOR: Yes

NUMBER OF DEALS COMPLETED IN THE LAST 12 MONTHS: 15

AMOUNT INVESTED IN LAST 12 MONTHS: $2.5 million

AVERAGE TIME REQUIRED TO COMPLETE A DEAL: 4 weeks
(From Initial Contact to Closing)

FIRM NAME: **Coleman Ventures, Inc.**

ADDRESS: 5909 Northern Blvd.
                East Norwich, NY 11732

PHONE: (516) 626–3642

SBIC ____   VENTURE CAPITAL FUND _X_   MESBIC ____   OTHER ____

TYPES OF FINANCING PREFERRED (Stages): Start-up/buyout/acquisition financing

MINIMUM DATA REQUIRED TO CONSIDER FINANCING: Nominal: break-even; P&L projected after 2 years

GEOGRAPHIC PREFERENCE: East Coast

INDUSTRY PREFERENCE BY FIRM: Communications/Computer Related/Medical/Natural Resources/Technology/Electronic Components/Optics Technology/Semiconductors/Publishing, Education Related/Agriculture/Forestry/Fishing

INDUSTRY PREFERENCES BY INDIVIDUAL FIRM MEMBERS: N/A

YEAR COMPANY ESTABLISHED: 1965

FUNDS UNDER MANAGEMENT AT COST: $5 million

MINIMUM SIZE INVESTMENT: $100,000

PREFERRED SIZE INVESTMENT: $350,000–$500,000

WILL FIRM SERVE AS LEAD INVESTOR: Yes

NUMBER OF DEALS COMPLETED IN THE LAST 12 MONTHS: 6

AMOUNT INVESTED IN LAST 12 MONTHS: $600,000

AVERAGE TIME REQUIRED TO COMPLETE A DEAL: 3 months
(From Initial Contact to Closing)

FIRM NAME: **Consumer Ventures Management, Inc.**

ADDRESS: c/o A. Moro
               21 E. 90th St.
               New York, NY 10028

PHONE: (212) 534–2012

SBIC ____   VENTURE CAPITAL FUND _X_   MESBIC ____   OTHER ____

TYPES OF FINANCING PREFERRED (Stages): Start-up/first and second stages

MINIMUM DATA REQUIRED TO CONSIDER FINANCING: Summary of business plan/resume of key management references

GEOGRAPHIC PREFERENCE: East Coast, Midwest

INDUSTRY PREFERENCE BY FIRM: Consumer-oriented business, products, services, real estate recreational

INDUSTRY PREFERENCES BY INDIVIDUAL FIRM MEMBERS: N/A

YEAR COMPANY ESTABLISHED: 1981

FUNDS UNDER MANAGEMENT AT COST: N/A

MINIMUM SIZE INVESTMENT: $250,000

PREFERRED SIZE INVESTMENT: $500,000

WILL FIRM SERVE AS LEAD INVESTOR: Yes

NUMBER OF DEALS COMPLETED IN THE LAST 12 MONTHS: N/A

AMOUNT INVESTED IN LAST 12 MONTHS: N/A

AVERAGE TIME REQUIRED TO COMPLETE A DEAL: 8 weeks
(From Initial Contact to Closing)

FIRM NAME: **CVC Capital Corporation**

ADDRESS: 506 West 57th St.
                  New York, NY 10019

PHONE: (212) 319-7210

SBIC ____ VENTURE CAPITAL FUND ____ MESBIC _X_ OTHER ____

TYPES OF FINANCING PREFERRED (Stages): Start-up

MINIMUM DATA REQUIRED TO CONSIDER FINANCING: 5 year projections

GEOGRAPHIC PREFERENCE: Continental USA

INDUSTRY PREFERENCE BY FIRM: Radio/TV/Real Estate

INDUSTRY PREFERENCES BY INDIVIDUAL FIRM MEMBERS: N/A

YEAR COMPANY ESTABLISHED: 1977

FUNDS UNDER MANAGEMENT AT COST: $12 million

MINIMUM SIZE INVESTMENT: $500,000

PREFERRED SIZE INVESTMENT: $500,000

WILL FIRM SERVE AS LEAD INVESTOR: Yes

NUMBER OF DEALS COMPLETED IN THE LAST 12 MONTHS: 3

AMOUNT INVESTED IN LAST 12 MONTHS: $1.3 million

AVERAGE TIME REQUIRED TO COMPLETE A DEAL: 1–2 months
(From Initial Contact to Closing)

FIRM NAME: **CW Group, Inc.**

ADDRESS: 1041 Third Ave.
                  New York, NY 10021

PHONE: (212) 308-5266

SBIC ____ VENTURE CAPITAL FUND _X_ MESBIC ____ OTHER ____

TYPES OF FINANCING PREFERRED (Stages): None

MINIMUM DATA REQUIRED TO CONSIDER FINANCING: Project proposal for
seed stage/business plan for all others

GEOGRAPHIC PREFERENCE: None

INDUSTRY PREFERENCE BY FIRM: Biomedical and Health Care, including
early stage R&D projects

INDUSTRY PREFERENCES BY INDIVIDUAL FIRM MEMBERS:
Walter Channing—Biomedical and Health Care
Barry Weinberg—Biomedical and Health Care
Charles Hartman—Biomedical and Health Care

YEAR COMPANY ESTABLISHED: 1982

FUNDS UNDER MANAGEMENT AT COST: $50 million

MINIMUM SIZE INVESTMENT: None

PREFERRED SIZE INVESTMENT: $750,000–$2,000,000

WILL FIRM SERVE AS LEAD INVESTOR: Yes

NUMBER OF DEALS COMPLETED IN THE LAST 12 MONTHS: 11

AMOUNT INVESTED IN LAST 12 MONTHS: $5.4 million

AVERAGE TIME REQUIRED TO COMPLETE A DEAL: 90 days
   (From Initial Contact to Closing)

FIRM NAME: **DeMuth, Folger & Terhune**

ADDRESS: One Exchange Plaza at 55 Broadway
                  New York, NY 10006

PHONE: (212) 509–5580

SBIC ___   VENTURE CAPITAL FUND _X_   MESBIC ___   OTHER ___

TYPES OF FINANCING PREFERRED (Stages): Start-up/early stage/later stage and
   buyouts

MINIMUM DATA REQUIRED TO CONSIDER FINANCING: 3–5 year business
   plan

GEOGRAPHIC PREFERENCE: USA

INDUSTRY PREFERENCE BY FIRM: Telecommunications/Electronics/Data
   Processing/Industrial Automation/Health Care

INDUSTRY PREFERENCES BY INDIVIDUAL FIRM MEMBERS:
   Donald F. DeMuth
   Thomas W. Folger
   J. Michael Terhune

YEAR COMPANY ESTABLISHED: 1983

FUNDS UNDER MANAGEMENT AT COST: $50 million

MINIMUM SIZE INVESTMENT: $500,000

PREFERRED SIZE INVESTMENT: $1 million plus

WILL FIRM SERVE AS LEAD INVESTOR: Yes

NUMBER OF DEALS COMPLETED IN THE LAST 12 MONTHS: 9

AMOUNT INVESTED IN LAST 12 MONTHS: $10 million

AVERAGE TIME REQUIRED TO COMPLETE A DEAL: 60–90 days
   (From Initial Contact to Closing)

FIRM NAME: **Charles B. De Than Group**

ADDRESS: 51 East 67th St.
                  New York, NY 10021

PHONE: (212) 988–5108

SBIC ____ VENTURE CAPITAL FUND ____ MESBIC ____
OTHER _X_ (Venture capital broker, acquisitions and mergers)

TYPES OF FINANCING PREFERRED (Stages): Start-up and stages

MINIMUM DATA REQUIRED TO CONSIDER FINANCING: 3–5 years P&L plus
recent balance sheet and business plan or outline

GEOGRAPHIC PREFERENCE: None

INDUSTRY PREFERENCE BY FIRM: Technology/Electronics–Computer/
Medical–Pharmaceutical. For acquisition: Manufacturing/Service and Distribution. We can look at any worthwhile business plan that makes economic
sense.

INDUSTRY PREFERENCES BY INDIVIDUAL FIRM MEMBERS:
Charles de Than

YEAR COMPANY ESTABLISHED: 1970

FUNDS UNDER MANAGEMENT AT COST: We are brokers; we show deals to
clients with large funds: several million dollars per deal.

MINIMUM SIZE INVESTMENT: $200,000–$300,000

PREFERRED SIZE INVESTMENT: Few million dollars per deal

WILL FIRM SERVE AS LEAD INVESTOR: Not us; our clients may

NUMBER OF DEALS COMPLETED IN THE LAST 12 MONTHS: N/A

AMOUNT INVESTED IN LAST 12 MONTHS: N/A

AVERAGE TIME REQUIRED TO COMPLETE A DEAL: 3–6 months
(From Initial Contact to Closing)

FIRM NAME: **Drexel Burnham Lambert Inc.**
                   The Lambda Funds

ADDRESS: 55 Broad St.
                   15th Floor
                   New York, NY 10004

PHONE: (212) 480–5160

SBIC ____ VENTURE CAPITAL FUND _X_ MESBIC ____ OTHER ____

TYPES OF FINANCING PREFERRED (Stages): All but start-ups

MINIMUM DATA REQUIRED TO CONSIDER FINANCING: Business plan

GEOGRAPHIC PREFERENCE: USA and Canada

INDUSTRY PREFERENCE BY FIRM: None

INDUSTRY PREFERENCES BY INDIVIDUAL FIRM MEMBERS: None

YEAR COMPANY ESTABLISHED: 1979

FUNDS UNDER MANAGEMENT AT COST: $40 million

MINIMUM SIZE INVESTMENT: $400,000

PREFERRED SIZE INVESTMENT: $750,000

WILL FIRM SERVE AS LEAD INVESTOR: Yes

NUMBER OF DEALS COMPLETED IN THE LAST 12 MONTHS: 21

AMOUNT INVESTED IN LAST 12 MONTHS: $9 million

AVERAGE TIME REQUIRED TO COMPLETE A DEAL: 8 weeks
(From Initial Contact to Closing)

FIRM NAME:	**Lewis R. Eisner & Co., Inc.**
ADDRESS:	230 Park Ave.
	New York, NY 10169
PHONE:	(212) 661-2424

SBIC ____ VENTURE CAPITAL FUND ____ MESBIC ____ OTHER _X_

TYPES OF FINANCING PREFERRED (Stages): Specializes in turnaround financing

MINIMUM DATA REQUIRED TO CONSIDER FINANCING: Comparative financial data/projections and fundamental business plan

GEOGRAPHIC PREFERENCE: USA

INDUSTRY PREFERENCE BY FIRM: General

INDUSTRY PREFERENCES BY INDIVIDUAL FIRM MEMBERS: General

YEAR COMPANY ESTABLISHED: 1971

FUNDS UNDER MANAGEMENT AT COST: N/A

MINIMUM SIZE INVESTMENT: $500,000

PREFERRED SIZE INVESTMENT: N/A

WILL FIRM SERVE AS LEAD INVESTOR: N/A

NUMBER OF DEALS COMPLETED IN THE LAST 12 MONTHS: N/A

AMOUNT INVESTED IN LAST 12 MONTHS: N/A

AVERAGE TIME REQUIRED TO COMPLETE A DEAL: 30 days
(From Initial Contact to Closing)

FIRM NAME:	**Elk Associates Funding Corp.**
ADDRESS:	277 Park Ave.
	Suite 4300
	New York, NY 10172
PHONE:	(212) 888-7574

SBIC ____ VENTURE CAPITAL FUND ____ MESBIC _X_ OTHER ____

TYPES OF FINANCING PREFERRED (Stages): Secured financings/second stage

MINIMUM DATA REQUIRED TO CONSIDER FINANCING: Financial statements/appraisals of collateral/credit reports

GEOGRAPHIC PREFERENCE: Northeast

INDUSTRY PREFERENCE BY FIRM: Transportation/Taxicab Finance/Radio Car
  Service Finance/Other Secured Financing

INDUSTRY PREFERENCES BY INDIVIDUAL FIRM MEMBERS: N/A

YEAR COMPANY ESTABLISHED: 1980

FUNDS UNDER MANAGEMENT AT COST: $11 million

MINIMUM SIZE INVESTMENT: $15,000

PREFERRED SIZE INVESTMENT: $75,000–$100,000

WILL FIRM SERVE AS LEAD INVESTOR: Yes

NUMBER OF DEALS COMPLETED IN THE LAST 12 MONTHS: 125

AMOUNT INVESTED IN LAST 12 MONTHS: $6.5 million

AVERAGE TIME REQUIRED TO COMPLETE A DEAL: 30 days
  (From Initial Contact to Closing)

FIRM NAME: **Enventure Capital Group**

ADDRESS: 1000 Guaranty Building
                Buffalo, NY 14202–3985

PHONE: (716) 852–1972

SBIC ____   VENTURE CAPITAL FUND __X__   MESBIC ____   OTHER ____

TYPES OF FINANCING PREFERRED (Stages): Start-up/high technology

MINIMUM DATA REQUIRED TO CONSIDER FINANCING: Business plan

GEOGRAPHIC PREFERENCE: Continental USA

INDUSTRY PREFERENCE BY FIRM: N/A

INDUSTRY PREFERENCES BY INDIVIDUAL FIRM MEMBERS: N/A

YEAR COMPANY ESTABLISHED: 1982

FUNDS UNDER MANAGEMENT AT COST: N/A

MINIMUM SIZE INVESTMENT: N/A

PREFERRED SIZE INVESTMENT: N/A

WILL FIRM SERVE AS LEAD INVESTOR: Yes

NUMBER OF DEALS COMPLETED IN THE LAST 12 MONTHS: 3

AMOUNT INVESTED IN LAST 12 MONTHS: N/A

AVERAGE TIME REQUIRED TO COMPLETE A DEAL: 1 year
  (From Initial Contact to Closing)

FIRM NAME: **Euclid Partners Corp.**

ADDRESS: 50 Rockefeller Plaza
                New York, NY 10020

PHONE: (212) 489–1770

SBIC ____   VENTURE CAPITAL FUND __X__   MESBIC ____   OTHER ____

TYPES OF FINANCING PREFERRED (Stages): Start-up to prepublic offering

MINIMUM DATA REQUIRED TO CONSIDER FINANCING: Business plan

GEOGRAPHIC PREFERENCE: None

INDUSTRY PREFERENCE BY FIRM: High Technology

INDUSTRY PREFERENCES BY INDIVIDUAL FIRM MEMBERS: N/A

YEAR COMPANY ESTABLISHED: 1970

FUNDS UNDER MANAGEMENT AT COST: $25 million

MINIMUM SIZE INVESTMENT: N/A

PREFERRED SIZE INVESTMENT: $500,000

WILL FIRM SERVE AS LEAD INVESTOR: Yes

NUMBER OF DEALS COMPLETED IN THE LAST 12 MONTHS: 6

AMOUNT INVESTED IN LAST 12 MONTHS: N/A

AVERAGE TIME REQUIRED TO COMPLETE A DEAL: 2 months
   (From Initial Contact to Closing)

FIRM NAME: **Ferranti High Technology Inc.**

ADDRESS: 515 Madison Ave.
                  Suite 1225
                  New York, NY 10022

PHONE: N/A

SBIC __X__ VENTURE CAPITAL FUND ____ MESBIC ____ OTHER ____

TYPES OF FINANCING PREFERRED (Stages): Early to middle/no start-ups

MINIMUM DATA REQUIRED TO CONSIDER FINANCING: Product and technical information/executive summary

GEOGRAPHIC PREFERENCE: USA

INDUSTRY PREFERENCE BY FIRM: Semiconductors: Bipolar, ULA, Gate
   Away/Communications: Voice, Data, Satellite, Microwave, Millimeter/Com-
   puters: Advanced Architecture, Fault Tolerance

INDUSTRY PREFERENCES BY INDIVIDUAL FIRM MEMBERS: N/A

YEAR COMPANY ESTABLISHED: 1981

FUNDS UNDER MANAGEMENT AT COST: $3 million

MINIMUM SIZE INVESTMENT: $100,000

PREFERRED SIZE INVESTMENT: $350,000

WILL FIRM SERVE AS LEAD INVESTOR: Yes

NUMBER OF DEALS COMPLETED IN THE LAST 12 MONTHS: 4

AMOUNT INVESTED IN LAST 12 MONTHS: $1.2 million

AVERAGE TIME REQUIRED TO COMPLETE A DEAL: 90–180 days
   (From Initial Contact to Closing)

FIRM NAME: The First Boston Corporation

ADDRESS: 12 East 49th St.
                  New York, NY 10017

PHONE: (212) 909–2000

SBIC ___ VENTURE CAPITAL FUND _X_ MESBIC ___ OTHER ___

TYPES OF FINANCING PREFERRED (Stages): Seed/first stage/second stage/
buyout or acquisition

MINIMUM DATA REQUIRED TO CONSIDER FINANCING: Business plan

GEOGRAPHIC PREFERENCE: None

INDUSTRY PREFERENCE BY FIRM: Communications/Computer Related/
Electronic Components and Instrumentation/Energy–Natural Resources/
Industrial Products and Equipment/Medical–Health Related/Real Estate

INDUSTRY PREFERENCES BY INDIVIDUAL FIRM MEMBERS:
Dennis Newman, Managing Direc-   W. Barry McCarthy, Jr., Vice-presi-
tor   dent
Jeffrey M. Parker, Vice-president   Harold W. Bogle, Associate
John F. Kenny, Jr., Associate   Brian C. Kerester, Analyst

YEAR COMPANY ESTABLISHED: 1978

FUNDS UNDER MANAGEMENT AT COST: $50 million plus

MINIMUM SIZE INVESTMENT: $100,000

PREFERRED SIZE INVESTMENT: $500,000–$1,000,000

WILL FIRM SERVE AS LEAD INVESTOR: Yes

NUMBER OF DEALS COMPLETED IN THE LAST 12 MONTHS: 31

AMOUNT INVESTED IN LAST 12 MONTHS: $14.6 million

AVERAGE TIME REQUIRED TO COMPLETE A DEAL: 4–9 months
(From Initial Contact to Closing)

FIRM NAME: Foster Management Co.

ADDRESS: 437 Madison Ave.
                  New York, NY 10022

PHONE: (212) 753–4810

SBIC ___ VENTURE CAPITAL FUND _X_ MESBIC ___ OTHER ___

TYPES OF FINANCING PREFERRED (Stages): All types

MINIMUM DATA REQUIRED TO CONSIDER FINANCING: 5 year historical financial data (if available) and 5 year business plan

GEOGRAPHIC PREFERENCE: USA only

INDUSTRY PREFERENCE BY FIRM: Health-care Services/Broadcasting/Home
Furnishings/Transportation/Energy/Computer Related

INDUSTRY PREFERENCES BY INDIVIDUAL FIRM MEMBERS:
Timothy E. Foster—Health Care/Energy/Home Furnishings/Computer

John H. Foster—Health Care/Transportation/Home Furnishings
Michael Connelly—Broadcasting/Energy/Health Care

YEAR COMPANY ESTABLISHED: 1972

FUNDS UNDER MANAGEMENT AT COST: $75 million

MINIMUM SIZE INVESTMENT: $500,000

PREFERRED SIZE INVESTMENT: $1.5 million

WILL FIRM SERVE AS LEAD INVESTOR: Yes

NUMBER OF DEALS COMPLETED IN THE LAST 12 MONTHS: 10

AMOUNT INVESTED IN LAST 12 MONTHS: $5.1 million

AVERAGE TIME REQUIRED TO COMPLETE A DEAL: 90 days
(From Initial Contact to Closing)

FIRM NAME: **The Franklin Corp.**

ADDRESS: 1185 Avenue of the Americas
New York, NY 10036

PHONE: (212) 719–4844

SBIC _X_ VENTURE CAPITAL FUND ___ MESBIC ___ OTHER ___

TYPES OF FINANCING PREFERRED (Stages): Intermediate and later stage financings/expansion capital/leveraged buyouts/management buyouts

MINIMUM DATA REQUIRED TO CONSIDER FINANCING: Business plan including prior 3 years financial statements and projection of the next 3 years

GEOGRAPHIC PREFERENCE: Continental USA (with a preference for the Northeast)

INDUSTRY PREFERENCE BY FIRM: Diversified

INDUSTRY PREFERENCES BY INDIVIDUAL FIRM MEMBERS: Diversified

YEAR COMPANY ESTABLISHED: 1959

FUNDS UNDER MANAGEMENT AT COST: $30 million

MINIMUM SIZE INVESTMENT: $200,000

PREFERRED SIZE INVESTMENT: $500,000

WILL FIRM SERVE AS LEAD INVESTOR: Yes

NUMBER OF DEALS COMPLETED IN THE LAST 12 MONTHS: 16

AMOUNT INVESTED IN LAST 12 MONTHS: $4.125 million

AVERAGE TIME REQUIRED TO COMPLETE A DEAL: 60–90 days
(From Initial Contact to Closing)

FIRM NAME: **GeoCapital Ventures**

ADDRESS: 655 Madison Ave.
New York, NY 10021

PHONE: (212) 935–0111

SBIC _____ VENTURE CAPITAL FUND _X_ MESBIC _____ OTHER _____

TYPES OF FINANCING PREFERRED (Stages): Early stage/start-up

MINIMUM DATA REQUIRED TO CONSIDER FINANCING: Description of business or business plan

GEOGRAPHIC PREFERENCE: None

INDUSTRY PREFERENCE BY FIRM: Data Communications/High-value Software/Health Care/Industrial Automation/Computers/Software Services/Semiconductors

INDUSTRY PREFERENCES BY INDIVIDUAL FIRM MEMBERS:
Walter C. Teagle, III
Irwin Lieber
Stephen Clearman

YEAR COMPANY ESTABLISHED: 1984

FUNDS UNDER MANAGEMENT AT COST: $20 million

MINIMUM SIZE INVESTMENT: None

PREFERRED SIZE INVESTMENT: $500,000

WILL FIRM SERVE AS LEAD INVESTOR: Yes

NUMBER OF DEALS COMPLETED IN THE LAST 12 MONTHS: 7

AMOUNT INVESTED IN LAST 12 MONTHS: $2.9 million

AVERAGE TIME REQUIRED TO COMPLETE A DEAL: 60 days
(From Initial Contact to Closing)

FIRM NAME: **Greenhouse Management Corp.**

ADDRESS: 4 Cedar Swamp Rd.
                Glen Cove, NY 11542

PHONE: (516) 759–1188

SBIC _____ VENTURE CAPITAL FUND _X_ MESBIC _____ OTHER _____

TYPES OF FINANCING PREFERRED (Stages): Seed and start-up/later stage follow-on investments

MINIMUM DATA REQUIRED TO CONSIDER FINANCING: Current financial statements and current business plan

GEOGRAPHIC PREFERENCE: Northeast

INDUSTRY PREFERENCE BY FIRM: Information Technology/Biotechnology

INDUSTRY PREFERENCES BY INDIVIDUAL FIRM MEMBERS: N/A

YEAR COMPANY ESTABLISHED: 1981

FUNDS UNDER MANAGEMENT AT COST: $13.444 million

MINIMUM SIZE INVESTMENT: $250,000–$500,000

PREFERRED SIZE INVESTMENT: $500,000–$1,000,000

WILL FIRM SERVE AS LEAD INVESTOR: Yes

NUMBER OF DEALS COMPLETED IN THE LAST 12 MONTHS: 11

AMOUNT INVESTED IN LAST 12 MONTHS: $5,314,027

AVERAGE TIME REQUIRED TO COMPLETE A DEAL: 6 months
(From Initial Contact to Closing)

FIRM NAME: **Hammond, Kennedy & Co., Inc.**

ADDRESS: 230 Park Ave.
Suite 1616
New York, NY 10169

PHONE: (212) 867–1010

SBIC ____   VENTURE CAPITAL FUND ____   MESBIC ____   OTHER _X_

TYPES OF FINANCING PREFERRED (Stages): Financing of management buy-outs of middle-sized ($20 to $100 million) manufacturing companies

MINIMUM DATA REQUIRED TO CONSIDER FINANCING: Meeting with management/three years of history/projections for next two years

GEOGRAPHIC PREFERENCE: East of Rocky Mountains

INDUSTRY PREFERENCE BY FIRM: Light to heavy manufacturing

INDUSTRY PREFERENCES BY INDIVIDUAL FIRM MEMBERS: N/A

YEAR COMPANY ESTABLISHED: 1908

FUNDS UNDER MANAGEMENT AT COST: $5 million

MINIMUM SIZE INVESTMENT: $250,000–$750,000

PREFERRED SIZE INVESTMENT: $500,000–$1,500,000

WILL FIRM SERVE AS LEAD INVESTOR: Yes

NUMBER OF DEALS COMPLETED IN THE LAST 12 MONTHS: 2

AMOUNT INVESTED IN LAST 12 MONTHS: $700,000

AVERAGE TIME REQUIRED TO COMPLETE A DEAL: 120 days
(From Initial Contact to Closing)

FIRM NAME: **Harvest Ventures, Inc.**

ADDRESS: 767 Third Ave.   3000 Sand Hill Rd.
New York, NY 10017   Menlo Park, CA 94025

PHONE: (212) 838–7776   (415) 854–8400

SBIC ____   VENTURE CAPITAL FUND _X_   MESBIC ____   OTHER ____

TYPES OF FINANCING PREFERRED (Stages): Start-up/early stage/follow-on/lead investor

MINIMUM DATA REQUIRED TO CONSIDER FINANCING: Complete business plan/3 year financial projections

GEOGRAPHIC PREFERENCE: USA

INDUSTRY PREFERENCE BY FIRM: Proprietary Technology

INDUSTRY PREFERENCES BY INDIVIDUAL FIRM MEMBERS: N/A

YEAR COMPANY ESTABLISHED: 1981

FUNDS UNDER MANAGEMENT AT COST: $80 million

MINIMUM SIZE INVESTMENT: $750,000

PREFERRED SIZE INVESTMENT: $1 million

WILL FIRM SERVE AS LEAD INVESTOR: Yes

NUMBER OF DEALS COMPLETED IN THE LAST 12 MONTHS: 18

AMOUNT INVESTED IN LAST 12 MONTHS: $12.1 million

AVERAGE TIME REQUIRED TO COMPLETE A DEAL: 6–10 weeks
(From Initial Contact to Closing)

FIRM NAME: **Hutton Venture Investment Partners, Inc.**

ADDRESS: E. F. Hutton & Co., Inc.
One Battery Park Plaza
Suite 1801
New York, NY 10004

PHONE: (212) 742–3722

SBIC ____   VENTURE CAPITAL FUND _X_   MESBIC ____   OTHER ____

TYPES OF FINANCING PREFERRED (Stages): Start-up/company operating 1 to
2 years: losses/company operating 1 to 3 years: break-even to profitable

MINIMUM DATA REQUIRED TO CONSIDER FINANCING: Business plan

GEOGRAPHIC PREFERENCE: None

INDUSTRY PREFERENCE BY FIRM: Technology

INDUSTRY PREFERENCES BY INDIVIDUAL FIRM MEMBERS:
James E. McGrath, President   James F. Wilson, Investment Man-
Timothy E. Noll, Investment Man-   ager
ager

YEAR COMPANY ESTABLISHED: 1981

FUNDS UNDER MANAGEMENT AT COST: $17 million

MINIMUM SIZE INVESTMENT: $250,000

PREFERRED SIZE INVESTMENT: $750,000

WILL FIRM SERVE AS LEAD INVESTOR: Yes

NUMBER OF DEALS COMPLETED IN THE LAST 12 MONTHS: 10

AMOUNT INVESTED IN LAST 12 MONTHS: $5 million

AVERAGE TIME REQUIRED TO COMPLETE A DEAL: 3 months
(From Initial Contact to Closing)

FIRM NAME: **Ibec Agri-Finance Co.**

ADDRESS: 1230 Avenue of the Americas
Suite 760
New York, NY 10020–1576

PHONE: (212) 397–0520

SBIC ____ VENTURE CAPITAL FUND ____ MESBIC ____ OTHER _X_

TYPES OF FINANCING PREFERRED (Stages): Investment banking firm arranging private placements/consulting firm evaluating or preparing venture proposals

MINIMUM DATA REQUIRED TO CONSIDER FINANCING: Management resumes/brief synopsis on idea

GEOGRAPHIC PREFERENCE: None

INDUSTRY PREFERENCE BY FIRM: Agricultural/Agribusiness

INDUSTRY PREFERENCES BY INDIVIDUAL FIRM MEMBERS:
R. B. Halaby, President (212/397–0520)
John R. Crabtree, Midwest Representative (314/821–0204)
Jossely Y. Edwards, West Coast Representative (415/986–5054)

YEAR COMPANY ESTABLISHED: 1983

FUNDS UNDER MANAGEMENT AT COST: N/A

MINIMUM SIZE INVESTMENT: $500,000

PREFERRED SIZE INVESTMENT: N/A

WILL FIRM SERVE AS LEAD INVESTOR: No

NUMBER OF DEALS COMPLETED IN THE LAST 12 MONTHS: 5

AMOUNT INVESTED IN LAST 12 MONTHS: N/A

AVERAGE TIME REQUIRED TO COMPLETE A DEAL: 6 months–1 year
(From Initial Contact to Closing)

FIRM NAME: **Inco Venture Capital Management**

ADDRESS: One New York Plaza
New York, NY 10004

PHONE: (212) 612–5620 or (212) 612–5622

SBIC ____ VENTURE CAPITAL FUND _X_ MESBIC ____ OTHER ____

TYPES OF FINANCING PREFERRED (Stages): Start-up/company operating 1–2 years: losses/company operating 1–3 years: losses, break-even to profitable/ management buyout and acquisition

MINIMUM DATA REQUIRED TO CONSIDER FINANCING: Business plan

GEOGRAPHIC PREFERENCE: None

INDUSTRY PREFERENCE BY FIRM: Biotechnology/Medical Technology/Health Care/Computer and Computer Related Technology/Telecommunications/ Leveraged Buyouts

INDUSTRY PREFERENCES BY INDIVIDUAL FIRM MEMBERS:
Stuart F. Feiner—Buyouts/Biotechnology/Medical Technology
A. Douglas Peabody—Telecommunications/Computer Hardware/Biotechnology
Richard G. Couch—Computer Hardware/Computer Peripherals

YEAR COMPANY ESTABLISHED: 1974

FUNDS UNDER MANAGEMENT AT COST: $70 million

MINIMUM SIZE INVESTMENT: $100,000

PREFERRED SIZE INVESTMENT: $500,000–$1,000,000

WILL FIRM SERVE AS LEAD INVESTOR: Yes

NUMBER OF DEALS COMPLETED IN THE LAST 12 MONTHS: 27

AMOUNT INVESTED IN LAST 12 MONTHS: $7 million

AVERAGE TIME REQUIRED TO COMPLETE A DEAL: 4–8 weeks
(From Initial Contact to Closing)

FIRM NAME: **The Jordan Company**

ADDRESS: 315 Park Avenue South
New York, NY 10010

PHONE: (212) 460–1910

SBIC ___   VENTURE CAPITAL FUND _X_ MESBIC ___   OTHER ___

TYPES OF FINANCING PREFERRED (Stages): Buyouts

MINIMUM DATA REQUIRED TO CONSIDER FINANCING: N/A

GEOGRAPHIC PREFERENCE: None

INDUSTRY PREFERENCE BY FIRM: Any Industry

INDUSTRY PREFERENCES BY INDIVIDUAL FIRM MEMBERS: N/A

YEAR COMPANY ESTABLISHED: 1982

FUNDS UNDER MANAGEMENT AT COST: $100 million

MINIMUM SIZE INVESTMENT: $500,000

PREFERRED SIZE INVESTMENT: $1 million

WILL FIRM SERVE AS LEAD INVESTOR: Yes

NUMBER OF DEALS COMPLETED IN THE LAST 12 MONTHS: 6

AMOUNT INVESTED IN LAST 12 MONTHS: $10 million

AVERAGE TIME REQUIRED TO COMPLETE A DEAL: 2 months
(From Initial Contact to Closing)

FIRM NAME: **Ladenburg, Thalmann & Co., Inc.**

ADDRESS: 540 Madison Ave.
New York, NY 10022

PHONE: (212) 940–0122

SBIC ___   VENTURE CAPITAL FUND ___   MESBIC ___   OTHER _X_

TYPES OF FINANCING PREFERRED (Stages): No preference

MINIMUM DATA REQUIRED TO CONSIDER FINANCING: Business plan/extensive resume of principals with references

GEOGRAPHIC PREFERENCE: None

INDUSTRY PREFERENCE BY FIRM: Medical/Biotechnology/Specialty Retail Stores/Peripheral Computer Equipment/Artificial Intelligence/Electronic

INDUSTRY PREFERENCES BY INDIVIDUAL FIRM MEMBERS: N/A

YEAR COMPANY ESTABLISHED: 1865

FUNDS UNDER MANAGEMENT AT COST: N/A

MINIMUM SIZE INVESTMENT: N/A

PREFERRED SIZE INVESTMENT: N/A

WILL FIRM SERVE AS LEAD INVESTOR: Occasionally

NUMBER OF DEALS COMPLETED IN THE LAST 12 MONTHS: N/A

AMOUNT INVESTED IN LAST 12 MONTHS: N/A

AVERAGE TIME REQUIRED TO COMPLETE A DEAL: 90–120 days
(From Initial Contact to Closing)

FIRM NAME: **Liberty Street Capital**

ADDRESS: 71 Broadway
New York, NY 10006

PHONE: (212) 612–1485

SBIC ____ VENTURE CAPITAL FUND _X_ MESBIC ____
OTHER _X_ (Private investment and banking firm)

TYPES OF FINANCING PREFERRED (Stages): Early stage/buyout financing

MINIMUM DATA REQUIRED TO CONSIDER FINANCING: Strategic plan/principals' backgrounds

GEOGRAPHIC PREFERENCE: Continental USA

INDUSTRY PREFERENCE BY FIRM: Health Care Provider Company/Health Care Cost Containment Companies

INDUSTRY PREFERENCES BY INDIVIDUAL FIRM MEMBERS:
Tom E. Greene III—Above
Clay R. Caroland III—Above

YEAR COMPANY ESTABLISHED: 1980

FUNDS UNDER MANAGEMENT AT COST: N/A

MINIMUM SIZE INVESTMENT: $200,000

PREFERRED SIZE INVESTMENT: $2–$5 million

WILL FIRM SERVE AS LEAD INVESTOR: Yes

NUMBER OF DEALS COMPLETED IN THE LAST 12 MONTHS: 10

AMOUNT INVESTED IN LAST 12 MONTHS: $140 million principal amount of transactions

AVERAGE TIME REQUIRED TO COMPLETE A DEAL: 120 days
(From Initial Contact to Closing)

FIRM NAME: **Manufacturers Hanover Venture Capital Corp.**

ADDRESS: 140 E. 45th St.
                New York, NY 10017

PHONE: (212) 808–0109

SBIC ____ VENTURE CAPITAL FUND ____ MESBIC ____
OTHER __X__ (Venture capital; subsidiary of bank holding company)

TYPES OF FINANCING PREFERRED (Stages): Second stage/latter stage/leveraged
   buyouts

MINIMUM DATA REQUIRED TO CONSIDER FINANCING: Business plan/
   management resumes/audited financial statements

GEOGRAPHIC PREFERENCE: None

INDUSTRY PREFERENCE BY FIRM: Industrial Products/Apparel/Health
   Care/Retailing/Telecommunications/Computers

INDUSTRY PREFERENCES BY INDIVIDUAL FIRM MEMBERS:
   Edward L. Koch III—Health Care/Telecommunications
   Kevin P. Falvey—Retailing
   J. William Drake—Consumer Products
   Bryan J. Carey—Computer and Computer Field

YEAR COMPANY ESTABLISHED: 1981

FUNDS UNDER MANAGEMENT AT COST: $112 million

MINIMUM SIZE INVESTMENT: $500,000

PREFERRED SIZE INVESTMENT: $1.5 million

WILL FIRM SERVE AS LEAD INVESTOR: Yes

NUMBER OF DEALS COMPLETED IN THE LAST 12 MONTHS: 25

AMOUNT INVESTED IN LAST 12 MONTHS: $58.642 million

AVERAGE TIME REQUIRED TO COMPLETE A DEAL: 90 days
   (From Initial Contact to Closing)

FIRM NAME: **Carl Marks & Co., Inc.**

ADDRESS: 77 Water St.
                New York, NY 10005

PHONE: (212) 437–7078

SBIC ____ VENTURE CAPITAL FUND ____ MESBIC ____ OTHER __X__

TYPES OF FINANCING PREFERRED (Stages): Leveraged buyouts

MINIMUM DATA REQUIRED TO CONSIDER FINANCING: Business plan

GEOGRAPHIC PREFERENCE: None

INDUSTRY PREFERENCE BY FIRM: Any

INDUSTRY PREFERENCES BY INDIVIDUAL FIRM MEMBERS: Any

YEAR COMPANY ESTABLISHED: 1925

FUNDS UNDER MANAGEMENT AT COST: $15 million

MINIMUM SIZE INVESTMENT: $500,000

PREFERRED SIZE INVESTMENT: $1 million

WILL FIRM SERVE AS LEAD INVESTOR: Yes

NUMBER OF DEALS COMPLETED IN THE LAST 12 MONTHS: 0

AMOUNT INVESTED IN LAST 12 MONTHS: 0

AVERAGE TIME REQUIRED TO COMPLETE A DEAL: 3 months
(From Initial Contact to Closing)

FIRM NAME: **Matthew Stuart & Co., Inc.**

ADDRESS: 308 Main St.
New Rochelle, NY 10802

PHONE: (914) 235–5730

SBIC ___ VENTURE CAPITAL FUND ___ MESBIC ___
OTHER _X_ (Consulting)

TYPES OF FINANCING PREFERRED (Stages): First and second stages

MINIMUM DATA REQUIRED TO CONSIDER FINANCING: P&L/balance sheet/
5 year pro forma

GEOGRAPHIC PREFERENCE: East

INDUSTRY PREFERENCE BY FIRM: N/A

INDUSTRY PREFERENCES BY INDIVIDUAL FIRM MEMBERS: N/A

YEAR COMPANY ESTABLISHED: 1954

FUNDS UNDER MANAGEMENT AT COST: N/A

MINIMUM SIZE INVESTMENT: $1 million

PREFERRED SIZE INVESTMENT: $1–$5 million

WILL FIRM SERVE AS LEAD INVESTOR: Yes

NUMBER OF DEALS COMPLETED IN THE LAST 12 MONTHS: 12

AMOUNT INVESTED IN LAST 12 MONTHS: $5 million

AVERAGE TIME REQUIRED TO COMPLETE A DEAL: 6 months
(From Initial Contact to Closing)

FIRM NAME: **Medallion Funding Corp.**

ADDRESS: 205 E. 42nd St.
Suite 2020
New York, NY 10017

PHONE: (212) 682–3300

SBIC ___ VENTURE CAPITAL FUND ___ MESBIC _X_ OTHER ___

TYPES OF FINANCING PREFERRED (Stages): Going concern

MINIMUM DATA REQUIRED TO CONSIDER FINANCING: Business plan/fi-
nancial statements

GEOGRAPHIC PREFERENCE: Northeast

INDUSTRY PREFERENCE BY FIRM: Transportation

INDUSTRY PREFERENCES BY INDIVIDUAL FIRM MEMBERS: N/A

YEAR COMPANY ESTABLISHED: 1980

FUNDS UNDER MANAGEMENT AT COST: $21 million

MINIMUM SIZE INVESTMENT: $25,000

PREFERRED SIZE INVESTMENT: $150,000

WILL FIRM SERVE AS LEAD INVESTOR: Yes

NUMBER OF DEALS COMPLETED IN THE LAST 12 MONTHS: 100

AMOUNT INVESTED IN LAST 12 MONTHS: $9 million

AVERAGE TIME REQUIRED TO COMPLETE A DEAL: 3 weeks
(From Initial Contact to Closing)

FIRM NAME: **Merrill Lynch R&D Management Inc.**

ADDRESS: 165 Broadway
New York, NY 10080

PHONE: (212) 637–1307

SBIC ___ VENTURE CAPITAL FUND ___ MESBIC ___
OTHER _X_ (Research and development fund)

TYPES OF FINANCING PREFERRED (Stages): Research and development projects of non-start-up companies

MINIMUM DATA REQUIRED TO CONSIDER FINANCING: Comprehensive, written business plan

GEOGRAPHIC PREFERENCE: None

INDUSTRY PREFERENCE BY FIRM: Health Care and Medical Sciences/Microelectronics/Telecommunications/Biotechnology

INDUSTRY PREFERENCES BY INDIVIDUAL FIRM MEMBERS:
Robert E. Curry—Medical Industry
Robert T. Foley—Electronics Industry
Bruce W. Shewmaker—Telecommunications Industry

YEAR COMPANY ESTABLISHED: 1985

FUNDS UNDER MANAGEMENT AT COST: $60 million plus

MINIMUM SIZE INVESTMENT: $2 million

PREFERRED SIZE INVESTMENT: $4–5 million

WILL FIRM SERVE AS LEAD INVESTOR: Yes

NUMBER OF DEALS COMPLETED IN THE LAST 12 MONTHS: 2

AMOUNT INVESTED IN LAST 12 MONTHS: $10 million

AVERAGE TIME REQUIRED TO COMPLETE A DEAL: 6–8 weeks
(From Initial Contact to Closing)

FIRM NAME: **Merrill Lynch Venture Capital, Inc.**

ADDRESS: 717 Fifth Ave.
                New York, NY 10022

PHONE: (212) 980-0410

SBIC ___   VENTURE CAPITAL FUND _X_   MESBIC ___   OTHER ___

TYPES OF FINANCING PREFERRED (Stages): Early stage financing: start-ups through expansion rounds

MINIMUM DATA REQUIRED TO CONSIDER FINANCING: Complete business plan

GEOGRAPHIC PREFERENCE: USA; will not consider foreign investments. Within USA, no preference

INDUSTRY PREFERENCE BY FIRM: Computer Hardware Systems Peripherals/Artificial Intelligence/Telecommunications/Semiconductors/Electronics/Biotechnology/Health Care

INDUSTRY PREFERENCES BY INDIVIDUAL FIRM MEMBERS: N/A

YEAR COMPANY ESTABLISHED: 1982

FUNDS UNDER MANAGEMENT AT COST: $60 million

MINIMUM SIZE INVESTMENT: $500,000

PREFERRED SIZE INVESTMENT: $750,000–$1,500,000

WILL FIRM SERVE AS LEAD INVESTOR: Yes

NUMBER OF DEALS COMPLETED IN THE LAST 12 MONTHS: 15

AMOUNT INVESTED IN LAST 12 MONTHS: $12.4 million

AVERAGE TIME REQUIRED TO COMPLETE A DEAL: Varies (From Initial Contact to Closing)

FIRM NAME: **New York Securities, Inc.**

ADDRESS: 575 Madison Ave.
                New York, NY 10022

PHONE: N/A

SBIC ___   VENTURE CAPITAL FUND ___   MESBIC ___   OTHER _X_

TYPES OF FINANCING PREFERRED (Stages): First stage/public offering funding

MINIMUM DATA REQUIRED TO CONSIDER FINANCING: N/A

GEOGRAPHIC PREFERENCE: Northeast

INDUSTRY PREFERENCE BY FIRM: Computer Technology and Distribution/Medical Procedures

INDUSTRY PREFERENCES BY INDIVIDUAL FIRM MEMBERS:
    F. Kenneth Melis—Real Estate; Computer Related; Medical Related

YEAR COMPANY ESTABLISHED: 1962

FUNDS UNDER MANAGEMENT AT COST: $250,000

MINIMUM SIZE INVESTMENT: $25,000

PREFERRED SIZE INVESTMENT: $50,000

WILL FIRM SERVE AS LEAD INVESTOR: Yes

NUMBER OF DEALS COMPLETED IN THE LAST 12 MONTHS: 2 Start-ups

AMOUNT INVESTED IN LAST 12 MONTHS: $60,000

AVERAGE TIME REQUIRED TO COMPLETE A DEAL: 120 days
(From Initial Contact to Closing)

FIRM NAME: **Nordic Investors Limited**
c/o Venture Management Advisors
Nordic American Banking Corporation

ADDRESS: 600 Fifth Ave.
New York, NY 10020

PHONE: (212) 315–6532

SBIC ____ VENTURE CAPITAL FUND _X_ MESBIC ____ OTHER ____

TYPES OF FINANCING PREFERRED (Stages): Second and later stages

MINIMUM DATA REQUIRED TO CONSIDER FINANCING: Complete business
plan

GEOGRAPHIC PREFERENCE: None

INDUSTRY PREFERENCE BY FIRM: N/A

INDUSTRY PREFERENCES BY INDIVIDUAL FIRM MEMBERS: N/A

YEAR COMPANY ESTABLISHED: 1983

FUNDS UNDER MANAGEMENT AT COST: $5 million

MINIMUM SIZE INVESTMENT: $250,000

PREFERRED SIZE INVESTMENT: $400,000

WILL FIRM SERVE AS LEAD INVESTOR: If possible

NUMBER OF DEALS COMPLETED IN THE LAST 12 MONTHS: 4

AMOUNT INVESTED IN LAST 12 MONTHS: $1.5 million

AVERAGE TIME REQUIRED TO COMPLETE A DEAL: 90 days
(From Initial Contact to Closing)

FIRM NAME: **Northwood Ventures**

ADDRESS: 420 Madison Ave.
New York, NY 10017

PHONE: (212) 935–2679

SBIC ____ VENTURE CAPITAL FUND _X_ MESBIC ____ OTHER ____

TYPES OF FINANCING PREFERRED (Stages): All

MINIMUM DATA REQUIRED TO CONSIDER FINANCING: Business plan/5 year
   projections

GEOGRAPHIC PREFERENCE: USA, preferably Northeast

INDUSTRY PREFERENCE BY FIRM: None

INDUSTRY PREFERENCES BY INDIVIDUAL FIRM MEMBERS:
   Peter G. Schiff, General Partner

YEAR COMPANY ESTABLISHED: 1983

FUNDS UNDER MANAGEMENT AT COST: $5 million

MINIMUM SIZE INVESTMENT: $100,000

PREFERRED SIZE INVESTMENT: $200,000–$400,000

WILL FIRM SERVE AS LEAD INVESTOR: Yes

NUMBER OF DEALS COMPLETED IN THE LAST 12 MONTHS: 15

AMOUNT INVESTED IN LAST 12 MONTHS: $2.5 million

AVERAGE TIME REQUIRED TO COMPLETE A DEAL: 90 or more days
   (From Initial Contact to Closing)

FIRM NAME: **Alan Patricof Associates, Inc.**

ADDRESS: 545 Madison Ave.   1245 Oakmead Pkwy.
                New York, NY 10022   Suite 105
                                          Sunnyvale, CA

PHONE: (212) 753–6300   (408) 737–8788

ADDRESS: 244 Upper Brook St.   67 Rue de Monceau
                London, W1Y 1PD   Paris, France 75008

PHONE: 493–3633   563–3513

SBIC ____ VENTURE CAPITAL FUND _X_ MESBIC ____ OTHER ____

TYPES OF FINANCING PREFERRED (Stages): Early/first/second/later

MINIMUM DATA REQUIRED TO CONSIDER FINANCING: Business plan/3 year
   projections

GEOGRAPHIC PREFERENCE: None

INDUSTRY PREFERENCE BY FIRM: Computer Hardware and Software/Elec-
   tronics/Communications/Biotechnology/Health Related/Energy/Consumer and
   Industrial Related goods and services

INDUSTRY PREFERENCES BY INDIVIDUAL FIRM MEMBERS:
   Alan J. Patricof, Chairman—General
   Robert G. Faris, President—Energy/Franchises/General
   Lewis Solomon, Executive Vice-president—Communications/Electronics/
      Computers/General High Technology
   W. R. Bottoms, Vice-president—Electronics/General High Technology
   John C. Baker, Vice-president—Computers/General High Technology
   Jonathan Ben-Cnaan, Managing Director—Software/General
   Camilla Jackson, Associate—Medical/Biotechnology/General
   Barbara Lundberg, Associate—Communications/General
   Charles Cheskiewicz, Associate—General High Technology

YEAR COMPANY ESTABLISHED: 1969

FUNDS UNDER MANAGEMENT AT COST: $200 million

MINIMUM SIZE INVESTMENT: $500,000

PREFERRED SIZE INVESTMENT: $1–$3 million

WILL FIRM SERVE AS LEAD INVESTOR: Yes

NUMBER OF DEALS COMPLETED IN THE LAST 12 MONTHS: 35

AMOUNT INVESTED IN LAST 12 MONTHS: $23.5 million

AVERAGE TIME REQUIRED TO COMPLETE A DEAL: N/A
   (From Initial Contact to Closing)

FIRM NAME: **The Pittsford Group, Inc.**

ADDRESS: 8 Lodgepole Rd.
             Pittsford, NY 14534

PHONE: (716) 223–3523

SBIC ____ VENTURE CAPITAL FUND _X_ MESBIC ____ OTHER ____

TYPES OF FINANCING PREFERRED (Stages): All but developmental financials (R&D)

MINIMUM DATA REQUIRED TO CONSIDER FINANCING: Business plan including concept, market feasibility, management team, and 5-year financial projections

GEOGRAPHIC PREFERENCE: North America and Europe; will lead investments in northeastern USA

INDUSTRY PREFERENCE BY FIRM: Health Care/Biotechnology/Other high technology with health-care applications

INDUSTRY PREFERENCES BY INDIVIDUAL FIRM MEMBERS: N/A

YEAR COMPANY ESTABLISHED: 1974

FUNDS UNDER MANAGEMENT AT COST: $30 million

MINIMUM SIZE INVESTMENT: $250,000

PREFERRED SIZE INVESTMENT: $500,000–$1,000,000

WILL FIRM SERVE AS LEAD INVESTOR: Yes

NUMBER OF DEALS COMPLETED IN THE LAST 12 MONTHS: 12

AMOUNT INVESTED IN LAST 12 MONTHS: $7.6 million

AVERAGE TIME REQUIRED TO COMPLETE A DEAL: 60 days
   (From Initial Contact to Closing)

FIRM NAME: **Questec Enterprises, Inc.**

ADDRESS: 328 Main St.
             Huntington, NY 11743

PHONE: (516) 351–1222

SBIC ___ VENTURE CAPITAL FUND _X_ MESBIC ___ OTHER ___

TYPES OF FINANCING PREFERRED (Stages): Early development stage or first round

MINIMUM DATA REQUIRED TO CONSIDER FINANCING: Business plan

GEOGRAPHIC PREFERENCE: None

INDUSTRY PREFERENCE BY FIRM: Equipment, processes, and components related to industrial electronics

INDUSTRY PREFERENCES BY INDIVIDUAL FIRM MEMBERS: N/A

YEAR COMPANY ESTABLISHED: 1983

FUNDS UNDER MANAGEMENT AT COST: $10 million

MINIMUM SIZE INVESTMENT: $500,000

PREFERRED SIZE INVESTMENT: $2 million

WILL FIRM SERVE AS LEAD INVESTOR: Yes

NUMBER OF DEALS COMPLETED IN THE LAST 12 MONTHS: 3

AMOUNT INVESTED IN LAST 12 MONTHS: $7.3 million

AVERAGE TIME REQUIRED TO COMPLETE A DEAL: 5 months
  (From Initial Contact to Closing)

FIRM NAME: **Quiner Partners**

ADDRESS: Box 154
                Glen Head, NY 11545

PHONE: (516) 759–1752

SBIC ___ VENTURE CAPITAL FUND ___ MESBIC ___ OTHER _X_

TYPES OF FINANCING PREFERRED (Stages): Purchase of viable going concerns

MINIMUM DATA REQUIRED TO CONSIDER FINANCING: N/A

GEOGRAPHIC PREFERENCE: USA

INDUSTRY PREFERENCE BY FIRM: N/A

INDUSTRY PREFERENCES BY INDIVIDUAL FIRM MEMBERS: N/A

YEAR COMPANY ESTABLISHED: 1970

FUNDS UNDER MANAGEMENT AT COST: N/A

MINIMUM SIZE INVESTMENT: $5 million

PREFERRED SIZE INVESTMENT: $10–$20 million purchase price

WILL FIRM SERVE AS LEAD INVESTOR: Only as lead investor

NUMBER OF DEALS COMPLETED IN THE LAST 12 MONTHS: 3

AMOUNT INVESTED IN LAST 12 MONTHS: $40 million

AVERAGE TIME REQUIRED TO COMPLETE A DEAL: 2–3 months
  (From Initial Contact to Closing)

FIRM NAME: Rand Capital Corporation; Rand SBIC, Inc.

ADDRESS: 1300 Rand Building
              Buffalo, NY 14203

PHONE: (716) 853-0802

SBIC __X__   VENTURE CAPITAL FUND __X__   MESBIC ____   OTHER ____

TYPES OF FINANCING PREFERRED (Stages): Start-ups/first stage

MINIMUM DATA REQUIRED TO CONSIDER FINANCING: History, nature, and market/resumes/financial statements/pro formas

GEOGRAPHIC PREFERENCE: Northeast, but preferably New York and New Jersey

INDUSTRY PREFERENCE BY FIRM: High Technology/Communications

INDUSTRY PREFERENCES BY INDIVIDUAL FIRM MEMBERS: N/A

YEAR COMPANY ESTABLISHED: 1969

FUNDS UNDER MANAGEMENT AT COST: $8.9 million

MINIMUM SIZE INVESTMENT: $500,000

PREFERRED SIZE INVESTMENT: $75,000-$1,250,000

WILL FIRM SERVE AS LEAD INVESTOR: Yes

NUMBER OF DEALS COMPLETED IN THE LAST 12 MONTHS: 9

AMOUNT INVESTED IN LAST 12 MONTHS: N/A

AVERAGE TIME REQUIRED TO COMPLETE A DEAL: 3 months
    (From Initial Contact to Closing)

FIRM NAME: Regulus International Capital Co., Inc.

ADDRESS: 10 Rockefeller Plaza
              New York, NY 10020

PHONE: N/A

SBIC ____   VENTURE CAPITAL FUND __X__   MESBIC ____   OTHER ____

TYPES OF FINANCING PREFERRED (Stages): R&D/start-up/leveraged buyouts

MINIMUM DATA REQUIRED TO CONSIDER FINANCING: Business plan/resumes/references

GEOGRAPHIC PREFERENCE: East Coast for leveraged buyouts

INDUSTRY PREFERENCE BY FIRM: N/A

INDUSTRY PREFERENCES BY INDIVIDUAL FIRM MEMBERS: N/A

YEAR COMPANY ESTABLISHED: 1975

FUNDS UNDER MANAGEMENT AT COST: N/A

MINIMUM SIZE INVESTMENT: $200,000

PREFERRED SIZE INVESTMENT: $400,000

WILL FIRM SERVE AS LEAD INVESTOR: Yes

NUMBER OF DEALS COMPLETED IN THE LAST 12 MONTHS: N/A

AMOUNT INVESTED IN LAST 12 MONTHS: N/A

AVERAGE TIME REQUIRED TO COMPLETE A DEAL: N/A
(From Initial Contact to Closing)

FIRM NAME: **Revere AE Capital Fund, Inc.**

ADDRESS: 19th Floor
745 Fifth Ave.
New York, NY 10151

PHONE: N/A

SBIC ____ VENTURE CAPITAL FUND __X_ MESBIC ____ OTHER ____

TYPES OF FINANCING PREFERRED (Stages): Second and third round
stage/leveraged buyouts/turnarounds

MINIMUM DATA REQUIRED TO CONSIDER FINANCING: Company must be
in business at least 3 years and have sales greater than $5 million

GEOGRAPHIC PREFERENCE: Northeast, East Coast, California

INDUSTRY PREFERENCE BY FIRM: All areas

INDUSTRY PREFERENCES BY INDIVIDUAL FIRM MEMBERS:
Dora Chio
Clinton Reynolds
Joseph White

YEAR COMPANY ESTABLISHED: 1971

FUNDS UNDER MANAGEMENT AT COST: $37 million

MINIMUM SIZE INVESTMENT: $500,000

PREFERRED SIZE INVESTMENT: $1–$2 million

WILL FIRM SERVE AS LEAD INVESTOR: Yes

NUMBER OF DEALS COMPLETED IN THE LAST 12 MONTHS: 5

AMOUNT INVESTED IN LAST 12 MONTHS: $8 million

AVERAGE TIME REQUIRED TO COMPLETE A DEAL: 4–10 weeks
(From Initial Contact to Closing)

FIRM NAME: **Roundhill Capital & D. H. Blair Co.**

ADDRESS: 44 Wall St.
19th Floor
New York, NY 10005

PHONE: (212) 747–0066

SBIC __X_ VENTURE CAPITAL FUND ____ MESBIC ____ OTHER ____

TYPES OF FINANCING PREFERRED (Stages): Public venture capital/debt or
equity/bridge financing prior to public offering

MINIMUM DATA REQUIRED TO CONSIDER FINANCING: Business plan, including past financials, projections, product review, management background, competition

GEOGRAPHIC PREFERENCE: None

INDUSTRY PREFERENCE BY FIRM: Finance Growth Companies in any industry

INDUSTRY PREFERENCES BY INDIVIDUAL FIRM MEMBERS:
Kevin Kimberlin, Vice-president

YEAR COMPANY ESTABLISHED: 1904

FUNDS UNDER MANAGEMENT AT COST: $65 million

MINIMUM SIZE INVESTMENT: $250,000

PREFERRED SIZE INVESTMENT: $250,000–$5,000,000

WILL FIRM SERVE AS LEAD INVESTOR: Yes

NUMBER OF DEALS COMPLETED IN THE LAST 12 MONTHS: 18

AMOUNT INVESTED IN LAST 12 MONTHS: $45 million

AVERAGE TIME REQUIRED TO COMPLETE A DEAL: 3 months
(From Initial Contact to Closing)

FIRM NAME: **Schroder Venture Managers**

ADDRESS: One State St.   755 Page Mill Road
                New York, NY 10004   Bldg. A, Suite 280
                                           Palo Alto, CA 94303

PHONE: (212) 269–6500   (415) 424–1144

SBIC ____   VENTURE CAPITAL FUND __X__   MESBIC ____   OTHER ____

TYPES OF FINANCING PREFERRED (Stages): Will consider all stages

MINIMUM DATA REQUIRED TO CONSIDER FINANCING: Business
plan/management resumes

GEOGRAPHIC PREFERENCE: USA

INDUSTRY PREFERENCE BY FIRM: Computer Related/Communications/Electronic Components and Instrumentation/Health Care and Biotechnology/Specialty Retailing

INDUSTRY PREFERENCES BY INDIVIDUAL FIRM MEMBERS:
Jeffrey J. Collinson—All   Michael A. Hentschel—All
Judith E. Schneider—All   David Walters—All

YEAR COMPANY ESTABLISHED: 1983

FUNDS UNDER MANAGEMENT AT COST: $37.5 million

MINIMUM SIZE INVESTMENT: Open

PREFERRED SIZE INVESTMENT: $750,000–$1,000,000

WILL FIRM SERVE AS LEAD INVESTOR: Yes

NUMBER OF DEALS COMPLETED IN THE LAST 12 MONTHS: 13

AMOUNT INVESTED IN LAST 12 MONTHS: Approximately $11 million

AVERAGE TIME REQUIRED TO COMPLETE A DEAL: Open
(From Initial Contact to Closing)

FIRM NAME: **Howard M. Singer, Inc.**

ADDRESS: 280 Madison Ave.
                  New York, NY 10016

PHONE: (212) 696–0637

SBIC ___ VENTURE CAPITAL FUND ___ MESBIC ___ OTHER _X_

TYPES OF FINANCING PREFERRED (Stages): First stage

MINIMUM DATA REQUIRED TO CONSIDER FINANCING: N/A

GEOGRAPHIC PREFERENCE: N/A

INDUSTRY PREFERENCE BY FIRM: Oil and Gas/Electronics

INDUSTRY PREFERENCES BY INDIVIDUAL FIRM MEMBERS: N/A

YEAR COMPANY ESTABLISHED: 1976

FUNDS UNDER MANAGEMENT AT COST: N/A

MINIMUM SIZE INVESTMENT: $5 million

PREFERRED SIZE INVESTMENT: $10–$15 million

WILL FIRM SERVE AS LEAD INVESTOR: N/A

NUMBER OF DEALS COMPLETED IN THE LAST 12 MONTHS: 4

AMOUNT INVESTED IN LAST 12 MONTHS: $26 million

AVERAGE TIME REQUIRED TO COMPLETE A DEAL: 4–6 months
    (From Initial Contact to Closing)

FIRM NAME: **Sprout Group**

ADDRESS: 140 Broadway   5700 Stevens Creek Blvd.
                  New York, NY 10005   Suite 320
                                              San Jose, CA 95129

PHONE: (212) 902–2492   (408) 554–1515

ADDRESS: One Center Plaza
                  6th Floor
                  Boston, MA 02108

PHONE: (617) 570–8700

SBIC ___ VENTURE CAPITAL FUND _X_ MESBIC ___ OTHER ___

TYPES OF FINANCING PREFERRED (Stages): Seed/start-up/first and second
    stages/research & development/leveraged buyouts

MINIMUM DATA REQUIRED TO CONSIDER FINANCING: Paramount invest-
    ment consideration is the quality of the management team

GEOGRAPHIC PREFERENCE: None

INDUSTRY PREFERENCE BY FIRM: None; will not consider investments in en-
    tertainment

INDUSTRY PREFERENCES BY INDIVIDUAL FIRM MEMBERS: N/A

YEAR COMPANY ESTABLISHED: 1969

FUNDS UNDER MANAGEMENT AT COST: $150 million

MINIMUM SIZE INVESTMENT: $500,000

PREFERRED SIZE INVESTMENT: $1 million

WILL FIRM SERVE AS LEAD INVESTOR: Yes

NUMBER OF DEALS COMPLETED IN THE LAST 12 MONTHS: 28

AMOUNT INVESTED IN LAST 12 MONTHS: $22 million

AVERAGE TIME REQUIRED TO COMPLETE A DEAL: 60 days
   (From Initial Contact to Closing)

FIRM NAME: **SRK Management Co.**

ADDRESS: 805 Third Ave.
                New York, NY 10022

PHONE: (212) 371–0900

SBIC ___   VENTURE CAPITAL FUND _X_   MESBIC ___   OTHER ___

TYPES OF FINANCING PREFERRED (Stages): Seed/first/second

MINIMUM DATA REQUIRED TO CONSIDER FINANCING: Business plan/financials/references

GEOGRAPHIC PREFERENCE: None

INDUSTRY PREFERENCE BY FIRM: All except retail and real estate

INDUSTRY PREFERENCES BY INDIVIDUAL FIRM MEMBERS:
   Victoria Hamilton—All
   Sidney R. Knafel—All
   Michael S. Willner—Cable Television

YEAR COMPANY ESTABLISHED: 1981

FUNDS UNDER MANAGEMENT AT COST: N/A

MINIMUM SIZE INVESTMENT: $250,000

PREFERRED SIZE INVESTMENT: $500,000–$1,000,000

WILL FIRM SERVE AS LEAD INVESTOR: Yes

NUMBER OF DEALS COMPLETED IN THE LAST 12 MONTHS: 9

AMOUNT INVESTED IN LAST 12 MONTHS: $4 million

AVERAGE TIME REQUIRED TO COMPLETE A DEAL: 3–6 months
   (From Initial Contact to Closing)

FIRM NAME: **Tessler & Cloherty, Inc.**

ADDRESS: 420 Madison Ave.
                New York, NY 10017

PHONE: N/A

SBIC ___   VENTURE CAPITAL FUND _X_   MESBIC ___   OTHER ___

TYPES OF FINANCING PREFERRED (Stages): All stages

MINIMUM DATA REQUIRED TO CONSIDER FINANCING: Executive summary or business plan

GEOGRAPHIC PREFERENCE: Continental USA

INDUSTRY PREFERENCE BY FIRM: All but real estate and finance; concentration in high technology

INDUSTRY PREFERENCES BY INDIVIDUAL FIRM MEMBERS: N/A

YEAR COMPANY ESTABLISHED: 1979

FUNDS UNDER MANAGEMENT AT COST: Approximately $20 million

MINIMUM SIZE INVESTMENT: $250,000 in general; $75,000 in seed stage

PREFERRED SIZE INVESTMENT: $500,000–$1,000,000

WILL FIRM SERVE AS LEAD INVESTOR: Yes

NUMBER OF DEALS COMPLETED IN THE LAST 12 MONTHS: N/A

AMOUNT INVESTED IN LAST 12 MONTHS: Approximately $5 million

AVERAGE TIME REQUIRED TO COMPLETE A DEAL: 120 days
(From Initial Contact to Closing)

FIRM NAME: **Transportation SBIC Inc.**

ADDRESS: 60 East 42nd St.
                 New York, NY 10166

PHONE: (212) 697–4885

SBIC ___   VENTURE CAPITAL FUND ___   MESBIC _X_   OTHER ___

TYPES OF FINANCING PREFERRED (Stages): All

MINIMUM DATA REQUIRED TO CONSIDER FINANCING: Completion of new application

GEOGRAPHIC PREFERENCE: New York City, Boston, and Philadelphia

INDUSTRY PREFERENCE BY FIRM: Taxi Industry/Radio Car Service

INDUSTRY PREFERENCES BY INDIVIDUAL FIRM MEMBERS:
   Robert Silver, Vice-president
   Susan Hirsch, Senior Vice-president

YEAR COMPANY ESTABLISHED: 1979

FUNDS UNDER MANAGEMENT AT COST: $16 million plus

MINIMUM SIZE INVESTMENT: $40,000

PREFERRED SIZE INVESTMENT: $100,000–$200,000

WILL FIRM SERVE AS LEAD INVESTOR: Yes

NUMBER OF DEALS COMPLETED IN THE LAST 12 MONTHS: 100–120

AMOUNT INVESTED IN LAST 12 MONTHS: $12 million

AVERAGE TIME REQUIRED TO COMPLETE A DEAL: 15–20 days
(From Initial Contact to Closing)

FIRM NAME: **Vega Capital Corp.**

ADDRESS: 720 White Plains Rd.
Scarsdale, NY 10583

PHONE: (914) 472–8550

SBIC __X__ VENTURE CAPITAL FUND ____ MESBIC ____ OTHER ____

TYPES OF FINANCING PREFERRED (Stages): Second or later/acquisition financing

MINIMUM DATA REQUIRED TO CONSIDER FINANCING: 3 year history (P&L) plus balance sheet

GEOGRAPHIC PREFERENCE: USA, but prefer Northeast

INDUSTRY PREFERENCE BY FIRM: Manufacturing/Distribution/Certain types of agriculture

INDUSTRY PREFERENCES BY INDIVIDUAL FIRM MEMBERS: N/A

YEAR COMPANY ESTABLISHED: 1968

FUNDS UNDER MANAGEMENT AT COST: $10 million

MINIMUM SIZE INVESTMENT: $100,000

PREFERRED SIZE INVESTMENT: $250,000–$500,00

WILL FIRM SERVE AS LEAD INVESTOR: Yes

NUMBER OF DEALS COMPLETED IN THE LAST 12 MONTHS: 12

AMOUNT INVESTED IN LAST 12 MONTHS: $1 million

AVERAGE TIME REQUIRED TO COMPLETE A DEAL: Varies
(From Initial Contact to Closing)

FIRM NAME: **Vencon Management, Inc.**

ADDRESS: 301 West 53rd St.
New York, NY 10019

PHONE: (212) 581–8787

SBIC ____ VENTURE CAPITAL FUND __X__ MESBIC ____ OTHER ____

TYPES OF FINANCING PREFERRED (Stages): Start-ups to leveraged buyouts

MINIMUM DATA REQUIRED TO CONSIDER FINANCING: Business plan summary/Management resumes

GEOGRAPHIC PREFERENCE: USA

INDUSTRY PREFERENCE BY FIRM: High Technology/Biotechnology/Chemicals/Plastics/Electronics/Agriculture

INDUSTRY PREFERENCES BY INDIVIDUAL FIRM MEMBERS:
Irvin Barash, President—Industry preferences same as above

YEAR COMPANY ESTABLISHED: 1972

FUNDS UNDER MANAGEMENT AT COST: N/A

MINIMUM SIZE INVESTMENT: $250,000

PREFERRED SIZE INVESTMENT: $500,000

WILL FIRM SERVE AS LEAD INVESTOR: Yes

NUMBER OF DEALS COMPLETED IN THE LAST 12 MONTHS: N/A

AMOUNT INVESTED IN LAST 12 MONTHS: N/A

AVERAGE TIME REQUIRED TO COMPLETE A DEAL: 5 months
   (From Initial Contact to Closing)

FIRM NAME: **Venrock Associates**

ADDRESS: 30 Rockefeller Plaza   Two Palo Alto Sq.
            Suite 5508   Suite 210
            New York, NY 10112   Palo Alto, CA 94306

PHONE: (212) 247–3700   (415) 493–5577

SBIC ____ VENTURE CAPITAL FUND _X_ MESBIC ____ OTHER ____

TYPES OF FINANCING PREFERRED (Stages): Does not apply

MINIMUM DATA REQUIRED TO CONSIDER FINANCING: Business plan

GEOGRAPHIC PREFERENCE: USA

INDUSTRY PREFERENCE BY FIRM: Advanced Technology Companies

INDUSTRY PREFERENCES BY INDIVIDUAL FIRM MEMBERS: N/A

YEAR COMPANY ESTABLISHED: 1969

FUNDS UNDER MANAGEMENT AT COST: Confidential

MINIMUM SIZE INVESTMENT: $200,000–$300,000

PREFERRED SIZE INVESTMENT: $300,000–$1,500,000

WILL FIRM SERVE AS LEAD INVESTOR: Yes

NUMBER OF DEALS COMPLETED IN THE LAST 12 MONTHS: 30

AMOUNT INVESTED IN LAST 12 MONTHS: $10 million

AVERAGE TIME REQUIRED TO COMPLETE A DEAL: 2 months
   (From Initial Contact to Closing)

FIRM NAME: **Ventech Partners, C.P.**

ADDRESS: 200 Park Ave.
            Suite 2525
            New York, NY 10017

PHONE: (212) 692–9171

SBIC ____ VENTURE CAPITAL FUND _X_ MESBIC ____ OTHER ____

TYPES OF FINANCING PREFERRED (Stages): Early stages

MINIMUM DATA REQUIRED TO CONSIDER FINANCING: N/A

GEOGRAPHIC PREFERENCE: None

INDUSTRY PREFERENCE BY FIRM: Technology ventures only/Microelec-
   tronics/Computer Systems/Medical Instrumentation

INDUSTRY PREFERENCES BY INDIVIDUAL FIRM MEMBERS: N/A

YEAR COMPANY ESTABLISHED: 1982

FUNDS UNDER MANAGEMENT AT COST: $29 million

MINIMUM SIZE INVESTMENT: $250,000

PREFERRED SIZE INVESTMENT: $750,000–$1,000,000

WILL FIRM SERVE AS LEAD INVESTOR: Yes

NUMBER OF DEALS COMPLETED IN THE LAST 12 MONTHS: 10

AMOUNT INVESTED IN LAST 12 MONTHS: $5 million

AVERAGE TIME REQUIRED TO COMPLETE A DEAL: 1–2 months
(From Initial Contact to Closing)

FIRM NAME: **Welsh, Carson, Anderson & Stowe**

ADDRESS: 45 Wall St.
New York, NY 10005

PHONE: (212) 422–3232

SBIC ____   VENTURE CAPITAL FUND _X_   MESBIC ____   OTHER ____

TYPES OF FINANCING PREFERRED (Stages): Start-up/first stage/leveraged buy-outs

MINIMUM DATA REQUIRED TO CONSIDER FINANCING: Business plan/current financials

GEOGRAPHIC PREFERENCE: USA

INDUSTRY PREFERENCE BY FIRM: Information Processing/Electronics/Health Care

INDUSTRY PREFERENCES BY INDIVIDUAL FIRM MEMBERS: N/A

YEAR COMPANY ESTABLISHED: 1978

FUNDS UNDER MANAGEMENT AT COST: $325 million

MINIMUM SIZE INVESTMENT: $1 million

PREFERRED SIZE INVESTMENT: $2–$5 million

WILL FIRM SERVE AS LEAD INVESTOR: Yes

NUMBER OF DEALS COMPLETED IN THE LAST 12 MONTHS: 27

AMOUNT INVESTED IN LAST 12 MONTHS: $37 million

AVERAGE TIME REQUIRED TO COMPLETE A DEAL: 90 days
(From Initial Contact to Closing)

FIRM NAME: **Winthrop Ventures**

ADDRESS: 74 Trinity Place
New York, NY 10006

PHONE: N/A

SBIC ____   VENTURE CAPITAL FUND ____   MESBIC ____
OTHER _X_   (Private investment banking firm)

TYPES OF FINANCING PREFERRED (Stages): No preference

MINIMUM DATA REQUIRED TO CONSIDER FINANCING: Business plan/past 3 years financials/5 year forecasts

GEOGRAPHIC PREFERENCE: None

INDUSTRY PREFERENCE BY FIRM: Proprietary Manufacturing

INDUSTRY PREFERENCES BY INDIVIDUAL FIRM MEMBERS: N/A

YEAR COMPANY ESTABLISHED: 1972

FUNDS UNDER MANAGEMENT AT COST: N/A

MINIMUM SIZE INVESTMENT: $500,000

PREFERRED SIZE INVESTMENT: N/A

WILL FIRM SERVE AS LEAD INVESTOR: Yes

NUMBER OF DEALS COMPLETED IN THE LAST 12 MONTHS: N/A

AMOUNT INVESTED IN LAST 12 MONTHS: N/A

AVERAGE TIME REQUIRED TO COMPLETE A DEAL: Varies
(From Initial Contact to Closing)

FIRM NAME: **Wood River Capital Corp.**

ADDRESS: 645 Madison Ave.
New York, NY 10022

PHONE: (212) 750–9420

SBIC _X_   VENTURE CAPITAL FUND ____   MESBIC ____   OTHER ____

TYPES OF FINANCING PREFERRED (Stages): Seed and first stage

MINIMUM DATA REQUIRED TO CONSIDER FINANCING: Complete business plan

GEOGRAPHIC PREFERENCE: All areas

INDUSTRY PREFERENCE BY FIRM: All industries except real estate, energy, tax-based deals, entertainment

INDUSTRY PREFERENCES BY INDIVIDUAL FIRM MEMBERS: N/A

YEAR COMPANY ESTABLISHED: 1979

FUNDS UNDER MANAGEMENT AT COST: $25 million equity; $25 million SBIC leverage

MINIMUM SIZE INVESTMENT: $100,000

PREFERRED SIZE INVESTMENT: $300,000–$500,000

WILL FIRM SERVE AS LEAD INVESTOR: Yes

NUMBER OF DEALS COMPLETED IN THE LAST 12 MONTHS: 15

AMOUNT INVESTED IN LAST 12 MONTHS: $4.3 million

AVERAGE TIME REQUIRED TO COMPLETE A DEAL: 2–4 months
(From Initial Contact to Closing)

NORTH CAROLINA

FIRM NAME: **Heritage Capital Corporation**

ADDRESS: 2290 First Union Plaza
                Charlotte, NC 28282

PHONE: (704) 334-2867

SBIC _X_   VENTURE CAPITAL FUND ___   MESBIC ___   OTHER ___

TYPES OF FINANCING PREFERRED (Stages): First and second stages

MINIMUM DATA REQUIRED TO CONSIDER FINANCING: Business plan/
  company background/recent financials

GEOGRAPHIC PREFERENCE: Southeast

INDUSTRY PREFERENCE BY FIRM: No preference

INDUSTRY PREFERENCES BY INDIVIDUAL FIRM MEMBERS: N/A

YEAR COMPANY ESTABLISHED: 1962

FUNDS UNDER MANAGEMENT AT COST: Approximately $6 million

MINIMUM SIZE INVESTMENT: $100,000

PREFERRED SIZE INVESTMENT: $350,000

WILL FIRM SERVE AS LEAD INVESTOR: Yes

NUMBER OF DEALS COMPLETED IN THE LAST 12 MONTHS: 6

AMOUNT INVESTED IN LAST 12 MONTHS: N/A

AVERAGE TIME REQUIRED TO COMPLETE A DEAL: N/A
  (From Initial Contact to Closing)

FIRM NAME: **Kitty Hawk Capital, Ltd.**

ADDRESS: 2030 One Tryon Center
                Charlotte, NC 28284

PHONE: (704) 333-3777

SBIC _X_   VENTURE CAPITAL FUND ___   MESBIC ___   OTHER ___

TYPES OF FINANCING PREFERRED (Stages): Seed/start-up/later stage/follow-
  on/business equity financing/secured term loans/leveraged buyouts

MINIMUM DATA REQUIRED TO CONSIDER FINANCING: Written plan and
  projections

GEOGRAPHIC PREFERENCE: Southeast

INDUSTRY PREFERENCE BY FIRM: High Technology/Energy/Wholesale/
  Manufacturing/Franchise/Publishing/Medical Technology

INDUSTRY PREFERENCES BY INDIVIDUAL FIRM MEMBERS:
  Walter H. Wilkinson, Jr.
  W. Chris Hegele

YEAR COMPANY ESTABLISHED: 1980

FUNDS UNDER MANAGEMENT AT COST: $5.5 million

MINIMUM SIZE INVESTMENT: $250,000

PREFERRED SIZE INVESTMENT: $250,000–$500,000

WILL FIRM SERVE AS LEAD INVESTOR: Yes

NUMBER OF DEALS COMPLETED IN THE LAST 12 MONTHS: 14

AMOUNT INVESTED IN LAST 12 MONTHS: $1.25 million

AVERAGE TIME REQUIRED TO COMPLETE A DEAL: 30–60 days
  (From Initial Contact to Closing)

OHIO

FIRM NAME: **Basic Search**

ADDRESS: Park Place
               10 W. Streetsboro
               Hudson, OH 44236

PHONE: (216) 656–2442

SBIC ____   VENTURE CAPITAL FUND ____   MESBIC ____   OTHER _X_

TYPES OF FINANCING PREFERRED (Stages): Start-ups

MINIMUM DATA REQUIRED TO CONSIDER FINANCING: Must meet entrepreneur only

GEOGRAPHIC PREFERENCE: Ohio, Michigan, Pennsylvania

INDUSTRY PREFERENCE BY FIRM: Manufacturing/Sales/Service

INDUSTRY PREFERENCES BY INDIVIDUAL FIRM MEMBERS:
  Burton D. Morgan—Paper/Printing/Coating
  Jerry Weisz—Rubber/Plastics/Manufacturing

YEAR COMPANY ESTABLISHED: 1970

FUNDS UNDER MANAGEMENT AT COST: $1 million

MINIMUM SIZE INVESTMENT: $50,000

PREFERRED SIZE INVESTMENT: $100,000

WILL FIRM SERVE AS LEAD INVESTOR: Yes

NUMBER OF DEALS COMPLETED IN THE LAST 12 MONTHS: 28

AMOUNT INVESTED IN LAST 12 MONTHS: $1.5 million

AVERAGE TIME REQUIRED TO COMPLETE A DEAL: 7 days
  (From Initial Contact to Closing)

FIRM NAME: **Cardinal Development Capital Fund I**

ADDRESS: 40 South Third St.
               Suite 460
               Columbus, OH 43215

PHONE: (614) 464–5557

SBIC ___ VENTURE CAPITAL FUND _X_ MESBIC ___ OTHER ___

TYPES OF FINANCING PREFERRED (Stages): Start-up/first stage/second stage/buyout or acquisition

MINIMUM DATA REQUIRED TO CONSIDER FINANCING: Annual sales: normal

GEOGRAPHIC PREFERENCE: None

INDUSTRY PREFERENCE BY FIRM: Communications: Telephone Related/Data Communications/Satellite and Microwave Communications/Computer Related: Computer graphics and CAD/CAM and other related fields/Consumer Products/Services/Restaurants

INDUSTRY PREFERENCES BY INDIVIDUAL FIRM MEMBERS: N/A

YEAR COMPANY ESTABLISHED: 1983

FUNDS UNDER MANAGEMENT AT COST: $33 million

MINIMUM SIZE INVESTMENT: $300,000–$600,000

PREFERRED SIZE INVESTMENT: $600,000

WILL FIRM SERVE AS LEAD INVESTOR: Yes

NUMBER OF DEALS COMPLETED IN THE LAST 12 MONTHS: 11

AMOUNT INVESTED IN LAST 12 MONTHS: $4.1 million

AVERAGE TIME REQUIRED TO COMPLETE A DEAL: 90 days (From Initial Contact to Closing)

FIRM NAME: **Center City MESBIC, Inc.**

ADDRESS: 40 South Main St.
Suite 762
Dayton, OH 45402

PHONE: (513) 461–6164

SBIC ___ VENTURE CAPITAL FUND ___ MESBIC _X_ OTHER ___

TYPES OF FINANCING PREFERRED (Stages): Expansions/acquisitions/start-ups

MINIMUM DATA REQUIRED TO CONSIDER FINANCING: Business plan to include past 3 years financial statements and 3 year projection

GEOGRAPHIC PREFERENCE: Southwestern Ohio

INDUSTRY PREFERENCE BY FIRM: Diversified

INDUSTRY PREFERENCES BY INDIVIDUAL FIRM MEMBERS: Diversified

YEAR COMPANY ESTABLISHED: 1981

FUNDS UNDER MANAGEMENT AT COST: $500,000 common; $500,000 preferred stock at 3%

MINIMUM SIZE INVESTMENT: $25,000

PREFERRED SIZE INVESTMENT: $100,000

WILL FIRM SERVE AS LEAD INVESTOR: Yes

NUMBER OF DEALS COMPLETED IN THE LAST 12 MONTHS: 2 acquisitions

AMOUNT INVESTED IN LAST 12 MONTHS: $140,000

AVERAGE TIME REQUIRED TO COMPLETE A DEAL: Approximately 90 days
(From Initial Contact to Closing)

FIRM NAME: **First Ohio Capital Corporation**

ADDRESS: 606 Madison Ave.
Toledo, OH 43604

PHONE: (419) 259–7146

SBIC _X_ VENTURE CAPITAL FUND ___ MESBIC ___ OTHER ___

TYPES OF FINANCING PREFERRED (Stages): Growth firms in the second or
third stage of business development/management buyouts/transfers of own-
ership/acquisitions

MINIMUM DATA REQUIRED TO CONSIDER FINANCING: Business plan

GEOGRAPHIC PREFERENCE: Midwest, with emphasis on Ohio, Michigan, and
Indiana

INDUSTRY PREFERENCE BY FIRM: No strong preference; will consider manufacturing, communications, electronics, and medical

INDUSTRY PREFERENCES BY INDIVIDUAL FIRM MEMBERS: N/A

YEAR COMPANY ESTABLISHED: 1982

FUNDS UNDER MANAGEMENT AT COST: $2.5 million

MINIMUM SIZE INVESTMENT: $100,000

PREFERRED SIZE INVESTMENT: $200,000

WILL FIRM SERVE AS LEAD INVESTOR: Yes

NUMBER OF DEALS COMPLETED IN THE LAST 12 MONTHS: 12

AMOUNT INVESTED IN LAST 12 MONTHS: $1.2 million

AVERAGE TIME REQUIRED TO COMPLETE A DEAL: 90 days
(From Initial Contact to Closing)

FIRM NAME: **Lubrizol Enterprises, Inc.**

ADDRESS: 29400 Lakeland Blvd.
Wickliffe, OH 44092

PHONE: (216) 943–4200

SBIC ___ VENTURE CAPITAL FUND ___ MESBIC ___ OTHER _X_

TYPES OF FINANCING PREFERRED (Stages): N/A

MINIMUM DATA REQUIRED TO CONSIDER FINANCING: N/A

GEOGRAPHIC PREFERENCE: N/A

INDUSTRY PREFERENCE BY FIRM: New and advanced products or processes related to production of specialty chemicals in the following areas: microbiology, mariculture, agriculture, materials science, energy storage and recovery, and custom manufacturing systems

INDUSTRY PREFERENCES BY INDIVIDUAL FIRM MEMBERS:

Donald L. Murfin, President   Bruce H. Grasser, Vice-president
James R. Glynn, Vice-president Fi-   David R. Anderson, Vice-president
  nance

YEAR COMPANY ESTABLISHED: N/A

FUNDS UNDER MANAGEMENT AT COST: $67 million

MINIMUM SIZE INVESTMENT: N/A

PREFERRED SIZE INVESTMENT: $3 million (average)

WILL FIRM SERVE AS LEAD INVESTOR: N/A

NUMBER OF DEALS COMPLETED IN THE LAST 12 MONTHS: N/A

AMOUNT INVESTED IN LAST 12 MONTHS: N/A

AVERAGE TIME REQUIRED TO COMPLETE A DEAL: N/A
(From Initial Contact to Closing)

FIRM NAME: **Miami Valley Capital, Inc.**

ADDRESS: 315 Talbott Tower
                 Dayton, OH 45402

PHONE: (513) 222–7222

SBIC _X_ VENTURE CAPITAL FUND ____ MESBIC ____ OTHER ____

TYPES OF FINANCING PREFERRED (Stages): Stages 1 through 4/no seed

MINIMUM DATA REQUIRED TO CONSIDER FINANCING: Business plan with 3 year forecasted income statements/balance sheets and cash flow statements (by month the first year)

GEOGRAPHIC PREFERENCE: Within 50 miles of Dayton, Ohio

INDUSTRY PREFERENCE BY FIRM: Manufacturing of all types, with proprietary products preferred

INDUSTRY PREFERENCES BY INDIVIDUAL FIRM MEMBERS: N/A

YEAR COMPANY ESTABLISHED: 1980

FUNDS UNDER MANAGEMENT AT COST: $2.7 million

MINIMUM SIZE INVESTMENT: $50,000

PREFERRED SIZE INVESTMENT: $150,000

WILL FIRM SERVE AS LEAD INVESTOR: Yes

NUMBER OF DEALS COMPLETED IN THE LAST 12 MONTHS: 4

AMOUNT INVESTED IN LAST 12 MONTHS: $550,000

AVERAGE TIME REQUIRED TO COMPLETE A DEAL: 3 months
(From Initial Contact to Closing)

FIRM NAME: **Scientific Advances, Inc.**
                   (subsidiary of Battelle Memorial Institute)

ADDRESS: 601 West Fifth Ave.
                  Columbus, OH 43201–3195

PHONE: (614) 294–5541

SBIC ____ VENTURE CAPITAL FUND _X_ MESBIC ____ OTHER ____

TYPES OF FINANCING PREFERRED (Stages): Start-up and expansions/technical companies only/no leveraged buyouts

MINIMUM DATA REQUIRED TO CONSIDER FINANCING: Sensible plan and unique technical capability

GEOGRAPHIC PREFERENCE: Only within USA

INDUSTRY PREFERENCE BY FIRM: Communications/Computer Related/Distribution/Electronic Components and Instrumentation/Energy/Natural Resources/Genetic Engineering/Medical–Health Related/Industrial Products and Equipment

INDUSTRY PREFERENCES BY INDIVIDUAL FIRM MEMBERS: N/A

YEAR COMPANY ESTABLISHED: 1962

FUNDS UNDER MANAGEMENT AT COST: N/A

MINIMUM SIZE INVESTMENT: $500,000

PREFERRED SIZE INVESTMENT: $500,000–$1,000,000

WILL FIRM SERVE AS LEAD INVESTOR: Yes

NUMBER OF DEALS COMPLETED IN THE LAST 12 MONTHS: N/A

AMOUNT INVESTED IN LAST 12 MONTHS: N/A

AVERAGE TIME REQUIRED TO COMPLETE A DEAL: N/A
    (From Initial Contact to Closing)

OKLAHOMA

FIRM NAME: **Bob L. Cartmill & Associates**

ADDRESS: P.O. Box 19316
                  Oklahoma City, OK 73144

PHONE: (405) 685–9945

SBIC ____ VENTURE CAPITAL FUND ____ MESBIC ____ OTHER _X_

TYPES OF FINANCING PREFERRED (Stages): Advanced/no start-ups

MINIMUM DATA REQUIRED TO CONSIDER FINANCING: Usual

GEOGRAPHIC PREFERENCE: Midwest

INDUSTRY PREFERENCE BY FIRM: Manufacturing/Oil Service Related/Food Related

INDUSTRY PREFERENCES BY INDIVIDUAL FIRM MEMBERS: N/A

YEAR COMPANY ESTABLISHED: 1965

FUNDS UNDER MANAGEMENT AT COST: N/A

MINIMUM SIZE INVESTMENT: $2 million

PREFERRED SIZE INVESTMENT: $5–$50 million

WILL FIRM SERVE AS LEAD INVESTOR: No

NUMBER OF DEALS COMPLETED IN THE LAST 12 MONTHS: 5

AMOUNT INVESTED IN LAST 12 MONTHS: None by this firm

AVERAGE TIME REQUIRED TO COMPLETE A DEAL: 6 months
   (From Initial Contact to Closing)

FIRM NAME: **First Oklahoma Investment Capital Corp.**

ADDRESS: 120 N. Robinson
                Suite 880C
                Oklahoma City, OK 73102

PHONE: (405) 272–4693

SBIC _X_ VENTURE CAPITAL FUND ___ MESBIC ___ OTHER ___

TYPES OF FINANCING PREFERRED (Stages): Leveraged buyouts

MINIMUM DATA REQUIRED TO CONSIDER FINANCING: 3 years of financial
   information/Most recent financial statement/proposed financing/pro forma
   results

GEOGRAPHIC PREFERENCE: Southwest

INDUSTRY PREFERENCE BY FIRM: Manufacturers/Wholesalers/Distributors/
   Retailers

INDUSTRY PREFERENCES BY INDIVIDUAL FIRM MEMBERS:
   David H. Pewdley, President

YEAR COMPANY ESTABLISHED: 1978

FUNDS UNDER MANAGEMENT AT COST: $20 million

MINIMUM SIZE INVESTMENT: $50,000

PREFERRED SIZE INVESTMENT: $250,000–$600,000

WILL FIRM SERVE AS LEAD INVESTOR: Yes

NUMBER OF DEALS COMPLETED IN THE LAST 12 MONTHS: 8

AMOUNT INVESTED IN LAST 12 MONTHS: $2 million

AVERAGE TIME REQUIRED TO COMPLETE A DEAL: 60–120 days
   (From Initial Contact to Closing)

FIRM NAME: **First Venture Corporation**

ADDRESS: Venture Bldg.
                The Quarters
                Bartlesville, OK 74006

PHONE: (918) 333–8820

SBIC __X__   VENTURE CAPITAL FUND ___   MESBIC ___   OTHER ___

TYPES OF FINANCING PREFERRED (Stages): First stage and on

MINIMUM DATA REQUIRED TO CONSIDER FINANCING: Business plan

GEOGRAPHIC PREFERENCE: None

INDUSTRY PREFERENCE BY FIRM: Distribution/Manufacturing/Medical/Natural Resources/Computer Technology

INDUSTRY PREFERENCES BY INDIVIDUAL FIRM MEMBERS: N/A

YEAR COMPANY ESTABLISHED: Not provided

FUNDS UNDER MANAGEMENT AT COST: N/A

MINIMUM SIZE INVESTMENT: $100,000

PREFERRED SIZE INVESTMENT: $250,000 in participation

WILL FIRM SERVE AS LEAD INVESTOR: Yes

NUMBER OF DEALS COMPLETED IN THE LAST 12 MONTHS: N/A

AMOUNT INVESTED IN LAST 12 MONTHS: N/A

AVERAGE TIME REQUIRED TO COMPLETE A DEAL: N/A
   (From Initial Contact to Closing)

FIRM NAME: **Western Venture Capital Corp.**

ADDRESS: 4880 S. Lewis
               P.O. Box 702680
               Tulsa, OK 74170

PHONE: N/A

SBIC __X__   VENTURE CAPITAL FUND ___   MESBIC ___   OTHER ___

TYPES OF FINANCING PREFERRED (Stages): Second and third stages/mature companies/leveraged buyouts

MINIMUM DATA REQUIRED TO CONSIDER FINANCING: Business plan

GEOGRAPHIC PREFERENCE: Oklahoma, Texas, Arkansas, Kansas, Missouri, New Mexico, Colorado, Louisiana

INDUSTRY PREFERENCE BY FIRM: Biotechnology/Medical Technology/Leisure–Entertainment/Health Care/Agribusiness/Communications/Computer Technology

INDUSTRY PREFERENCES BY INDIVIDUAL FIRM MEMBERS: Joe D. Tippens

YEAR COMPANY ESTABLISHED: 1980

FUNDS UNDER MANAGEMENT AT COST: $4 million

MINIMUM SIZE INVESTMENT: $250,000

PREFERRED SIZE INVESTMENT: $400,000

WILL FIRM SERVE AS LEAD INVESTOR: No

NUMBER OF DEALS COMPLETED IN THE LAST 12 MONTHS: 7

AMOUNT INVESTED IN LAST 12 MONTHS: $1.4 million

AVERAGE TIME REQUIRED TO COMPLETE A DEAL: 90–120 days
(From Initial Contact to Closing)

OREGON

FIRM NAME: Rosenfeld & Co.

ADDRESS: 625 SW Washington St.
Portland, OR 97205

PHONE: (503) 228–7686

SBIC ___ VENTURE CAPITAL FUND ___ MESBIC ___
OTHER _X_ (Private investment banking firm)

TYPES OF FINANCING PREFERRED (Stages): Third stage/divestitures/buy-outs/workouts/expansion

MINIMUM DATA REQUIRED TO CONSIDER FINANCING: Business plan and/or 3 years financial statements

GEOGRAPHIC PREFERENCE: Pacific Northwest

INDUSTRY PREFERENCE BY FIRM: Medical Technology/All types of manufacturing/All types of services except fast food

INDUSTRY PREFERENCES BY INDIVIDUAL FIRM MEMBERS: N/A

YEAR COMPANY ESTABLISHED: 1977

FUNDS UNDER MANAGEMENT AT COST: N/A

MINIMUM SIZE INVESTMENT: $1 million

PREFERRED SIZE INVESTMENT: $1 million plus

WILL FIRM SERVE AS LEAD INVESTOR: Either lead investor or as agent

NUMBER OF DEALS COMPLETED IN THE LAST 12 MONTHS: 3

AMOUNT INVESTED IN LAST 12 MONTHS: Approximately $4.2 million

AVERAGE TIME REQUIRED TO COMPLETE A DEAL: 4 months
(From Initial Contact to Closing)

FIRM NAME: Shaw Venture Partners

ADDRESS: 851 SW 6th Ave.
Suite 800
Portland, OR 97204

PHONE: N/A

SBIC ___ VENTURE CAPITAL FUND _X_ MESBIC ___ OTHER ___

TYPES OF FINANCING PREFERRED (Stages): Seed/first stage/second stage/buyout/acquisition

MINIMUM DATA REQUIRED TO CONSIDER FINANCING: Business plan

GEOGRAPHIC PREFERENCE: Pacific Northwest, but will consider other areas

INDUSTRY PREFERENCE BY FIRM: Telecommunications/Computer Re-
lated/Electronics/Energy/Genetic Engineering/Industrial Products/Medical
Equipment and Services

INDUSTRY PREFERENCES BY INDIVIDUAL FIRM MEMBERS: N/A

YEAR COMPANY ESTABLISHED: 1983

FUNDS UNDER MANAGEMENT AT COST: $35 million

MINIMUM SIZE INVESTMENT: $300,000–$500,000

PREFERRED SIZE INVESTMENT: $600,000 plus

WILL FIRM SERVE AS LEAD INVESTOR: Yes

NUMBER OF DEALS COMPLETED IN THE LAST 12 MONTHS: 2 follow-on; 2
new

AMOUNT INVESTED IN LAST 12 MONTHS: $1.167 million

AVERAGE TIME REQUIRED TO COMPLETE A DEAL: 3 months
(From Initial Contact to Closing)

PENNSYLVANIA

FIRM NAME: **Capital Corporation of America**

ADDRESS: 225 S. 15th St.
                Suite 920
                Philadelphia, PA 19102

PHONE: (215) 732–1666

SBIC _X_ VENTURE CAPITAL FUND ___ MESBIC ___ OTHER ___

TYPES OF FINANCING PREFERRED (Stages): Acquisition of companies/second
and third stage financings

MINIMUM DATA REQUIRED TO CONSIDER FINANCING: Financial state-
ments/cash flow projections for 5 years

GEOGRAPHIC PREFERENCE: Continental USA

INDUSTRY PREFERENCE BY FIRM: None

INDUSTRY PREFERENCES BY INDIVIDUAL FIRM MEMBERS: None

YEAR COMPANY ESTABLISHED: 1962

FUNDS UNDER MANAGEMENT AT COST: $3 million

MINIMUM SIZE INVESTMENT: $50,000

PREFERRED SIZE INVESTMENT: $250,000

WILL FIRM SERVE AS LEAD INVESTOR: Yes

NUMBER OF DEALS COMPLETED IN THE LAST 12 MONTHS: 3

AMOUNT INVESTED IN LAST 12 MONTHS: $250,000

AVERAGE TIME REQUIRED TO COMPLETE A DEAL: 3–4 weeks
(From Initial Contact to Closing)

FIRM NAME: **First Valley Capital Corporation**

ADDRESS: Hamilton Financial Center
                One Center Sq.
                Suite 201
                Allentown, PA 18101

PHONE: N/A

SBIC _X_ VENTURE CAPITAL FUND ____ MESBIC ____ OTHER ____

TYPES OF FINANCING PREFERRED (Stages): Start-up or later stage

MINIMUM DATA REQUIRED TO CONSIDER FINANCING: Business plan

GEOGRAPHIC PREFERENCE: Eastern Pennsylvania, New Jersey

INDUSTRY PREFERENCE BY FIRM: Diversified

INDUSTRY PREFERENCES BY INDIVIDUAL FIRM MEMBERS: Matthew W.
    Thomas, President

YEAR COMPANY ESTABLISHED: 1983

FUNDS UNDER MANAGEMENT AT COST: $200 thousand

MINIMUM SIZE INVESTMENT: $25 thousand

PREFERRED SIZE INVESTMENT: $25–$50 thousand

WILL FIRM SERVE AS LEAD INVESTOR: Yes

NUMBER OF DEALS COMPLETED IN THE LAST 12 MONTHS: 3

AMOUNT INVESTED IN LAST 12 MONTHS: $200 thousand

AVERAGE TIME REQUIRED TO COMPLETE A DEAL: 4–8 weeks
    (From Initial Contact to Closing)

FIRM NAME: **Fostin Capital Corp.**

ADDRESS: 681 Anderson Dr.   P.O. Box 67
                Pittsburgh, PA 15220   Pittsburgh, PA 15230

PHONE: (412) 928–8900

SBIC ____ VENTURE CAPITAL FUND _X_ MESBIC ____ OTHER ____

TYPES OF FINANCING PREFERRED (Stages): Seed capital/first stage/second
    stage/third stage

MINIMUM DATA REQUIRED TO CONSIDER FINANCING: Business plan

GEOGRAPHIC PREFERENCE: USA

INDUSTRY PREFERENCE BY FIRM: Communications/Computer Re-
    lated/Consumer/Electronic Components and Instrumentation/Energy/Natural
    Resources/Genetic Engineering/Industrial Products and Equipment/Medical

INDUSTRY PREFERENCES BY INDIVIDUAL FIRM MEMBERS:
    William F. Woods—General
    Thomas M. Levine—General
    David M. Martin—Support

YEAR COMPANY ESTABLISHED: 1982

FUNDS UNDER MANAGEMENT AT COST: $60 million (includes nonventure capital assets

MINIMUM SIZE INVESTMENT: $100,000

PREFERRED SIZE INVESTMENT: $250,000–$500,000

WILL FIRM SERVE AS LEAD INVESTOR: Yes

NUMBER OF DEALS COMPLETED IN THE LAST 12 MONTHS: 7

AMOUNT INVESTED IN LAST 12 MONTHS: $1.4 million

AVERAGE TIME REQUIRED TO COMPLETE A DEAL: 3 months
(From Initial Contact to Closing)

FIRM NAME: **Greater Philadelphia Venture Capital Corp.**

ADDRESS: 225 S. 15th St.
                Suite 920
                Philadelphia, PA 19102

PHONE: (215) 732–3415

SBIC ____ VENTURE CAPITAL FUND ____ MESBIC _X_ OTHER ____

TYPES OF FINANCING PREFERRED (Stages): Acquisitions of companies/second and third stages

MINIMUM DATA REQUIRED TO CONSIDER FINANCING: Financial statements and cash flow projections for 5 years

GEOGRAPHIC PREFERENCE: Eastern United States

INDUSTRY PREFERENCE BY FIRM: None

INDUSTRY PREFERENCES BY INDIVIDUAL FIRM MEMBERS: None

YEAR COMPANY ESTABLISHED: 1970

FUNDS UNDER MANAGEMENT AT COST: $3 million

MINIMUM SIZE INVESTMENT: $50,000

PREFERRED SIZE INVESTMENT: $100,000

WILL FIRM SERVE AS LEAD INVESTOR: Yes

NUMBER OF DEALS COMPLETED IN THE LAST 12 MONTHS: 3

AMOUNT INVESTED IN LAST 12 MONTHS: $120,000

AVERAGE TIME REQUIRED TO COMPLETE A DEAL: 3–4 weeks
(From Initial Contact to Closing)

FIRM NAME: **Hillman Ventures, Inc.**

ADDRESS: 2000 Grant Building
                Pittsburgh, PA 15219

PHONE: (412) 281–2620

SBIC ____ VENTURE CAPITAL FUND ____ MESBIC ____ OTHER _X_

TYPES OF FINANCING PREFERRED (Stages): All stages

MINIMUM DATA REQUIRED TO CONSIDER FINANCING: Business plan and reference

GEOGRAPHIC PREFERENCE: None

INDUSTRY PREFERENCE BY FIRM: Computer Software/Electronics/Medical/ Business Services/Telecommunications

INDUSTRY PREFERENCES BY INDIVIDUAL FIRM MEMBERS: N/A

YEAR COMPANY ESTABLISHED: N/A

FUNDS UNDER MANAGEMENT AT COST: In excess of $100 million

MINIMUM SIZE INVESTMENT: $500,000

PREFERRED SIZE INVESTMENT: N/A

WILL FIRM SERVE AS LEAD INVESTOR: Yes

NUMBER OF DEALS COMPLETED IN THE LAST 12 MONTHS: 32

AMOUNT INVESTED IN LAST 12 MONTHS: $15,792,000, follow-on; $43,624,000, new

AVERAGE TIME REQUIRED TO COMPLETE A DEAL: 6 weeks
(From Initial Contact to Closing)

FIRM NAME: **Innovest Group, Inc.**

ADDRESS: 1700 Market St.
               12th Floor
               Philadelphia, PA 19103

PHONE: (215) 564–3960

SBIC ____   VENTURE CAPITAL FUND _X_   MESBIC ____   OTHER ____

TYPES OF FINANCING PREFERRED (Stages): Start-ups/first stage

MINIMUM DATA REQUIRED TO CONSIDER FINANCING: Business plan, including 3 to 5 year financial projections

GEOGRAPHIC PREFERENCE: East and Southeast

INDUSTRY PREFERENCE BY FIRM: Communications/Electronics

INDUSTRY PREFERENCES BY INDIVIDUAL FIRM MEMBERS:
   Richard E. Woosnam—All
   Nila K. Sendzik—All

YEAR COMPANY ESTABLISHED: 1971

FUNDS UNDER MANAGEMENT AT COST: $7 million

MINIMUM SIZE INVESTMENT: $500,000

PREFERRED SIZE INVESTMENT: $500,000–$1,000,000

WILL FIRM SERVE AS LEAD INVESTOR: Yes

NUMBER OF DEALS COMPLETED IN THE LAST 12 MONTHS: 2

AMOUNT INVESTED IN LAST 12 MONTHS: $1.5 million

AVERAGE TIME REQUIRED TO COMPLETE A DEAL: 3 months
(From Initial Contact to Closing)

FIRM NAME: **Meridian Capital Corp.**

ADDRESS: Blue Bell West
                Suite 122
                Blue Bell, PA 19422

PHONE: (215) 278–8907

SBIC _X_ VENTURE CAPITAL FUND ___ MESBIC ___ OTHER ___

TYPES OF FINANCING PREFERRED (Stages): Later stage/leveraged buyouts

MINIMUM DATA REQUIRED TO CONSIDER FINANCING: Complete business
  plan

GEOGRAPHIC PREFERENCE: Mid-Atlantic states

INDUSTRY PREFERENCE BY FIRM: None

INDUSTRY PREFERENCES BY INDIVIDUAL FIRM MEMBERS: None

YEAR COMPANY ESTABLISHED: 1977

FUNDS UNDER MANAGEMENT AT COST: $3 million

MINIMUM SIZE INVESTMENT: $100,000

PREFERRED SIZE INVESTMENT: $200,000

WILL FIRM SERVE AS LEAD INVESTOR: Yes

NUMBER OF DEALS COMPLETED IN THE LAST 12 MONTHS: 4

AMOUNT INVESTED IN LAST 12 MONTHS: $1.048 million

AVERAGE TIME REQUIRED TO COMPLETE A DEAL: 60–90 days
  (From Initial Contact to Closing)

FIRM NAME: **Pennsylvania Growth Investment Corporation**

ADDRESS: 1000 RIDC Plaza
                Suite 311
                Pittsburgh, PA 15238

PHONE: (412) 963–9339

SBIC ___ VENTURE CAPITAL FUND _X_ MESBIC ___ OTHER ___

TYPES OF FINANCING PREFERRED (Stages): Early stages/repeaters/leveraged
  buyouts

MINIMUM DATA REQUIRED TO CONSIDER FINANCING: Resume of princi-
  pals/description of business/brief of business plan/financial statements

GEOGRAPHIC PREFERENCE: Mid-Atlantic

INDUSTRY PREFERENCE BY FIRM: None

INDUSTRY PREFERENCES BY INDIVIDUAL FIRM MEMBERS:
  William L. Mosenson
  Mary G. Dell

YEAR COMPANY ESTABLISHED: 1961

FUNDS UNDER MANAGEMENT AT COST: N/A

MINIMUM SIZE INVESTMENT: $150,000

PREFERRED SIZE INVESTMENT: $250,000–$500,000

WILL FIRM SERVE AS LEAD INVESTOR: Lead or participant

NUMBER OF DEALS COMPLETED IN THE LAST 12 MONTHS: N/A

AMOUNT INVESTED IN LAST 12 MONTHS: N/A

AVERAGE TIME REQUIRED TO COMPLETE A DEAL: Indication of interest in
(From Initial Contact to Closing)   10 days

FIRM NAME: **Seed Ventures, Inc.**

ADDRESS: 5 Great Valley Parkway
                Suite 227
                Malvern, PA 19355

PHONE: N/A

SBIC ___ VENTURE CAPITAL FUND ___ MESBIC ___ OTHER _X_

TYPES OF FINANCING PREFERRED (Stages): Seed/first stage

MINIMUM DATA REQUIRED TO CONSIDER FINANCING: Business plan

GEOGRAPHIC PREFERENCE: Mid-Atlantic

INDUSTRY PREFERENCE BY FIRM: None; however, no real estate or oil and
gas

INDUSTRY PREFERENCES BY INDIVIDUAL FIRM MEMBERS: N/A

YEAR COMPANY ESTABLISHED: 1985

FUNDS UNDER MANAGEMENT AT COST: N/A

MINIMUM SIZE INVESTMENT: $50,000

PREFERRED SIZE INVESTMENT: $50,000–$250,000

WILL FIRM SERVE AS LEAD INVESTOR: Yes

NUMBER OF DEALS COMPLETED IN THE LAST 12 MONTHS: N/A

AMOUNT INVESTED IN LAST 12 MONTHS: N/A

AVERAGE TIME REQUIRED TO COMPLETE A DEAL: N/A
(From Initial Contact to Closing)

FIRM NAME: **TDH II Limited**

ADDRESS: c/o K. S. Sweet Associates
                P.O. Box 249
                King of Prussia, PA 19406

PHONE: (215) 265–5722

SBIC ___ VENTURE CAPITAL FUND _X_ MESBIC ___ OTHER ___

TYPES OF FINANCING PREFERRED (Stages): First choice: later stage/second:
leveraged buyouts/third: start-up

MINIMUM DATA REQUIRED TO CONSIDER FINANCING: Complete business plan and historical financials if available

GEOGRAPHIC PREFERENCE: None

INDUSTRY PREFERENCE BY FIRM: None

INDUSTRY PREFERENCES BY INDIVIDUAL FIRM MEMBERS: None

YEAR COMPANY ESTABLISHED: TDH II Limited, 1983
                          K. S. Sweet Associates, 1971

FUNDS UNDER MANAGEMENT AT COST: TDH II Limited, $18 million

MINIMUM SIZE INVESTMENT: $500,000

PREFERRED SIZE INVESTMENT: $1 million

WILL FIRM SERVE AS LEAD INVESTOR: Yes

NUMBER OF DEALS COMPLETED IN THE LAST 12 MONTHS: 3

AMOUNT INVESTED IN LAST 12 MONTHS: $4.2 million

AVERAGE TIME REQUIRED TO COMPLETE A DEAL: 6 weeks average (From Initial Contact to Closing)

FIRM NAME: **Trivest Venture Fund**

ADDRESS: P.O. Box 36
               Ligonie, PA 15658

PHONE: (412) 471–0151

SBIC ___   VENTURE CAPITAL FUND _X_   MESBIC ___   OTHER ___

TYPES OF FINANCING PREFERRED (Stages): No start-ups, but early stages

MINIMUM DATA REQUIRED TO CONSIDER FINANCING: Business plan

GEOGRAPHIC PREFERENCE: Pennsylvania, Ohio, North Carolina, South Carolina

INDUSTRY PREFERENCE BY FIRM: Medical/High Technology

INDUSTRY PREFERENCES BY INDIVIDUAL FIRM MEMBERS:
    Thomas W. Courtey   James H. Knowles, Jr.
    Kennedy C. O'Herrin   Floyd H. Mone, Jr.

YEAR COMPANY ESTABLISHED: 1984

FUNDS UNDER MANAGEMENT AT COST: $31.1 million

MINIMUM SIZE INVESTMENT: $250,000

PREFERRED SIZE INVESTMENT: $250,000–$1,000,000

WILL FIRM SERVE AS LEAD INVESTOR: Yes

NUMBER OF DEALS COMPLETED IN THE LAST 12 MONTHS: 6

AMOUNT INVESTED IN LAST 12 MONTHS: $3.5 million

AVERAGE TIME REQUIRED TO COMPLETE A DEAL: Can be done in under
(From Initial Contact to Closing)   1 month

FIRM NAME: **Venture Associates**

ADDRESS: 2 Penn Center
                 Suite 410
                 Philadelphia, PA 19102

PHONE: (215) 735–2815

SBIC ___ VENTURE CAPITAL FUND ___ MESBIC ___ OTHER _X_

TYPES OF FINANCING PREFERRED (Stages): Seed/start-up/first round

MINIMUM DATA REQUIRED TO CONSIDER FINANCING: Resumes/summary
of business plan

GEOGRAPHIC PREFERENCE: Mid-Atlantic

INDUSTRY PREFERENCE BY FIRM: High Technology Manufacturing/Tele-
communications/Medical Instruments or Services/Retail/Restaurant/Fran-
chising

INDUSTRY PREFERENCES BY INDIVIDUAL FIRM MEMBERS: N/A

YEAR COMPANY ESTABLISHED: 1982

FUNDS UNDER MANAGEMENT AT COST: N/A

MINIMUM SIZE INVESTMENT: $50,000

PREFERRED SIZE INVESTMENT: $200,000–$500,000

WILL FIRM SERVE AS LEAD INVESTOR: Yes, will join management team in
developing business plan

NUMBER OF DEALS COMPLETED IN THE LAST 12 MONTHS: 8

AMOUNT INVESTED IN LAST 12 MONTHS: Affiliate companies received $10.4
million in capital

AVERAGE TIME REQUIRED TO COMPLETE A DEAL: N/A
(From Initial Contact to Closing)

RHODE ISLAND

FIRM NAME: **Fleet Venture Resources**

ADDRESS: 111 Westminster St.   Fleet Growth Resources
                 Providence, RI 02903   60 State St.
                                            Boston, MA 02109

PHONE: N/A

SBIC _X_ VENTURE CAPITAL FUND _X_ MESBIC ___ OTHER ___

TYPES OF FINANCING PREFERRED (Stages): First, second, third, growth, leveraged buyouts

MINIMUM DATA REQUIRED TO CONSIDER FINANCING: Business plan

GEOGRAPHIC PREFERENCE: East of the Rockies

INDUSTRY PREFERENCE BY FIRM: Electronics/Health Care/Broadcasting/Cable TV/Management Buyouts

INDUSTRY PREFERENCES BY INDIVIDUAL FIRM MEMBERS: N/A

YEAR COMPANY ESTABLISHED: 1967

FUNDS UNDER MANAGEMENT AT COST: $10 million

MINIMUM SIZE INVESTMENT: $250,000

PREFERRED SIZE INVESTMENT: $500,000

WILL FIRM SERVE AS LEAD INVESTOR: Yes

NUMBER OF DEALS COMPLETED IN THE LAST 12 MONTHS: 17

AMOUNT INVESTED IN LAST 12 MONTHS: $4.4 million

AVERAGE TIME REQUIRED TO COMPLETE A DEAL: 90 days
(From Initial Contact to Closing)

FIRM NAME: **Narragansett Capital Corp.**

ADDRESS: 40 Westminster St.
                Providence, RI 02903

PHONE: (401) 751–1000

SBIC ____ VENTURE CAPITAL FUND __X__ MESBIC ____   OTHER ____

TYPES OF FINANCING PREFERRED (Stages): Leveraged buyouts

MINIMUM DATA REQUIRED TO CONSIDER FINANCING: Purchase price from
$10 million to $100 million

GEOGRAPHIC PREFERENCE: None

INDUSTRY PREFERENCE BY FIRM: None

INDUSTRY PREFERENCES BY INDIVIDUAL FIRM MEMBERS: None

YEAR COMPANY ESTABLISHED: 1959

FUNDS UNDER MANAGEMENT AT COST: $185 million

MINIMUM SIZE INVESTMENT: $2 million

PREFERRED SIZE INVESTMENT: $4 million

WILL FIRM SERVE AS LEAD INVESTOR: Yes

NUMBER OF DEALS COMPLETED IN THE LAST 12 MONTHS: 10

AMOUNT INVESTED IN LAST 12 MONTHS: $25 million

AVERAGE TIME REQUIRED TO COMPLETE A DEAL: 90 days
(From Initial Contact to Closing)

SOUTH CAROLINA

FIRM NAME: **Reedy River Ventures**

ADDRESS: P.O. Box 17526
                Greenville, SC 29606

PHONE: (803) 297–9198

ADDRESS: 400 Haywood Rd.
                Greenville, SC 29606

SBIC _X_ VENTURE CAPITAL FUND ____ MESBIC ____ OTHER ____

TYPES OF FINANCING PREFERRED (Stages): Expansion/buyouts/early stage

MINIMUM DATA REQUIRED TO CONSIDER FINANCING: N/A

GEOGRAPHIC PREFERENCE: Southeast

INDUSTRY PREFERENCE BY FIRM: N/A

INDUSTRY PREFERENCES BY INDIVIDUAL FIRM MEMBERS: N/A

YEAR COMPANY ESTABLISHED: 1981

FUNDS UNDER MANAGEMENT AT COST: $3.5 million

MINIMUM SIZE INVESTMENT: $100,000

PREFERRED SIZE INVESTMENT: $250,000–$300,000

WILL FIRM SERVE AS LEAD INVESTOR: Yes

NUMBER OF DEALS COMPLETED IN THE LAST 12 MONTHS: 5

AMOUNT INVESTED IN LAST 12 MONTHS: $780,000

AVERAGE TIME REQUIRED TO COMPLETE A DEAL: 90 days
    (From Initial Contact to Closing)

TENNESSEE

FIRM NAME: **DeSoto Capital Corp.**

ADDRESS: 60 North Third St.
                Memphis, TN 38103

PHONE: (901) 523–6894

SBIC _X_ VENTURE CAPITAL FUND ____ MESBIC ____ OTHER ____

TYPES OF FINANCING PREFERRED (Stages): Expansions/second or third stage

MINIMUM DATA REQUIRED TO CONSIDER FINANCING: Business plan

GEOGRAPHIC PREFERENCE: Sun Belt (preferably in Mid-South)

INDUSTRY PREFERENCE BY FIRM: Low Technology/Manufacturing/Service

INDUSTRY PREFERENCES BY INDIVIDUAL FIRM MEMBERS· N/A

YEAR COMPANY ESTABLISHED: 1976

FUNDS UNDER MANAGEMENT AT COST: $900,000

MINIMUM SIZE INVESTMENT: $50,000

PREFERRED SIZE INVESTMENT: $74,000

WILL FIRM SERVE AS LEAD INVESTOR: Yes

NUMBER OF DEALS COMPLETED IN THE LAST 12 MONTHS: 4

AMOUNT INVESTED IN LAST 12 MONTHS: $260,000

AVERAGE TIME REQUIRED TO COMPLETE A DEAL: 3–4 months
(From Initial Contact to Closing)

FIRM NAME: **Massey Burch Investment Group**

ADDRESS: One Park Plaza
                Suite One
                Nashville, TN 37203

PHONE: (615) 329–9449

SBIC ___   VENTURE CAPITAL FUND _X_   MESBIC ___   OTHER ___

TYPES OF FINANCING PREFERRED (Stages): Seed/early/second stage

MINIMUM DATA REQUIRED TO CONSIDER FINANCING: Business plan

GEOGRAPHIC PREFERENCE: Southeast

INDUSTRY PREFERENCE BY FIRM: Medical, Technology, Service Communication

INDUSTRY PREFERENCES BY INDIVIDUAL FIRM MEMBERS: N/A

YEAR COMPANY ESTABLISHED: 1968

FUNDS UNDER MANAGEMENT AT COST: $100 million plus

MINIMUM SIZE INVESTMENT: $500,000

PREFERRED SIZE INVESTMENT: $2 million

WILL FIRM SERVE AS LEAD INVESTOR: Only

NUMBER OF DEALS COMPLETED IN THE LAST 12 MONTHS: 12

AMOUNT INVESTED IN LAST 12 MONTHS: $15 million

AVERAGE TIME REQUIRED TO COMPLETE A DEAL: 3 months
(From Initial Contact to Closing)

FIRM NAME: **Tennessee Equity Capital Corp.**
               Tennessee Equity Capital Fund

ADDRESS: 1102 Stonewall Jackson
                Nashville, TN 37220

PHONE: (615) 373–4502

SBIC ___   VENTURE CAPITAL FUND _X_   MESBIC _X_   OTHER ___

TYPES OF FINANCING PREFERRED (Stages): Second stage/expansion/merger
and acquisition/business financials

MINIMUM DATA REQUIRED TO CONSIDER FINANCING: Business plan

GEOGRAPHIC PREFERENCE: USA and territories

INDUSTRY PREFERENCE BY FIRM: No preference; diversified

INDUSTRY PREFERENCES BY INDIVIDUAL FIRM MEMBERS:
W. Samuel Cohen

YEAR COMPANY ESTABLISHED: 1979

FUNDS UNDER MANAGEMENT AT COST: N/A

MINIMUM SIZE INVESTMENT: $150,000

PREFERRED SIZE INVESTMENT: $150,000–$2,000,000

WILL FIRM SERVE AS LEAD INVESTOR: Yes

NUMBER OF DEALS COMPLETED IN THE LAST 12 MONTHS: N/A

AMOUNT INVESTED IN LAST 12 MONTHS: N/A

AVERAGE TIME REQUIRED TO COMPLETE A DEAL: 6 weeks
(From Initial Contact to Closing)

FIRM NAME: **Valley Capital Corporation**

ADDRESS: 100 W. Martin Luther King Blvd.
Suite 806, Krystal Building
Chattanooga, TN 37402

PHONE: (615) 265–1557

SBIC ____   VENTURE CAPITAL FUND ____   MESBIC _X_   OTHER ____

TYPES OF FINANCING PREFERRED (Stages): Second and third stages

MINIMUM DATA REQUIRED TO CONSIDER FINANCING: Detailed business
plan

GEOGRAPHIC PREFERENCE: Tennessee Valley service area

INDUSTRY PREFERENCE BY FIRM: Diversified

INDUSTRY PREFERENCES BY INDIVIDUAL FIRM MEMBERS:
Lamar J. Partridge

YEAR COMPANY ESTABLISHED: 1982

FUNDS UNDER MANAGEMENT AT COST: $1 million

MINIMUM SIZE INVESTMENT: $50,000

PREFERRED SIZE INVESTMENT: $150,000

WILL FIRM SERVE AS LEAD INVESTOR: Yes

NUMBER OF DEALS COMPLETED IN THE LAST 12 MONTHS: 2

AMOUNT INVESTED IN LAST 12 MONTHS: $152,500

AVERAGE TIME REQUIRED TO COMPLETE A DEAL: 2 months
(From Initial Contact to Closing)

Texas

FIRM NAME: **Allied Bankshares Capital Corp.**

ADDRESS: 1000 Louisiana
Houston, TX 77002
(P.O. Box 3326, zip 77253)

PHONE: (713) 226–1625

SBIC _X_ VENTURE CAPITAL FUND ____ MESBIC ____ OTHER ____

TYPES OF FINANCING PREFERRED (Stages): Expansion financings and leveraged buyouts/start-ups and turnarounds must meet stiffer criteria

MINIMUM DATA REQUIRED TO CONSIDER FINANCING: Minimum national
annual sales potential of $75,000,000

GEOGRAPHIC PREFERENCE: Southwestern USA; Continental USA

INDUSTRY PREFERENCE BY FIRM: Communications/Computer Related/Trans-
portation/Manufacturing and Processing/Medical and Other Health Products–Services/Natural Resources/Research and Technology

INDUSTRY PREFERENCES BY INDIVIDUAL FIRM MEMBERS: N/A

YEAR COMPANY ESTABLISHED: 1979

FUNDS UNDER MANAGEMENT AT COST: $20 million

MINIMUM SIZE INVESTMENT: $100,000–$300,000

PREFERRED SIZE INVESTMENT: Approximately $500,000

WILL FIRM SERVE AS LEAD INVESTOR: Yes

NUMBER OF DEALS COMPLETED IN THE LAST 12 MONTHS: 12

AMOUNT INVESTED IN LAST 12 MONTHS: $7,126,323

AVERAGE TIME REQUIRED TO COMPLETE A DEAL: 6 weeks
(From Initial Contact to Closing)

FIRM NAME: **Beta Capital Group, Inc.**
(subsidiary of Southwest Securities, Inc.)

ADDRESS: 500 Texas National Bank Bldg.
8235 Douglas Ave.
Dallas, TX 75225

PHONE: (214) 987–7139

SBIC ____ VENTURE CAPITAL FUND ____ MESBIC ____ OTHER _X_

TYPES OF FINANCING PREFERRED (Stages): Leveraged buyouts/bridge financings with right of first release for underwriting subsequent public offerings
and/or mergers, acquisitions

MINIMUM DATA REQUIRED TO CONSIDER FINANCING: Business
plan/historical financial statements

GEOGRAPHIC PREFERENCE: Southwest

INDUSTRY PREFERENCE BY FIRM: N/A

INDUSTRY PREFERENCES BY INDIVIDUAL FIRM MEMBERS: N/A

YEAR COMPANY ESTABLISHED: 1978

FUNDS UNDER MANAGEMENT AT COST: N/A

MINIMUM SIZE INVESTMENT: $1.0 million

PREFERRED SIZE INVESTMENT: $1.0–$2.0 million

WILL FIRM SERVE AS LEAD INVESTOR: Yes

NUMBER OF DEALS COMPLETED IN THE LAST 12 MONTHS: 4

AMOUNT INVESTED IN LAST 12 MONTHS: N/A

AVERAGE TIME REQUIRED TO COMPLETE A DEAL: 2 months
  (From Initial Contact to Closing)

FIRM NAME: **Business Development Partner I & II**

ADDRESS: 10805 Pecan Park Rd.
                Austin, TX 78750

PHONE: (512) 258–1977

SBIC ____   VENTURE CAPITAL FUND _X_   MESBIC ____   OTHER ____

TYPES OF FINANCING PREFERRED (Stages): Seed/start-up/first round

MINIMUM DATA REQUIRED TO CONSIDER FINANCING: Detailed business
  plan

GEOGRAPHIC PREFERENCE: Southwest

INDUSTRY PREFERENCE BY FIRM: Technology-based business

INDUSTRY PREFERENCES BY INDIVIDUAL FIRM MEMBERS:
  Robert L. Brueck, General Partner
  Michael E. Faherty, General Partner

YEAR COMPANY ESTABLISHED: 1981

FUNDS UNDER MANAGEMENT AT COST: N/A

MINIMUM SIZE INVESTMENT: $100,000

PREFERRED SIZE INVESTMENT: $300,000–$1,000,000

WILL FIRM SERVE AS LEAD INVESTOR: Yes

NUMBER OF DEALS COMPLETED IN THE LAST 12 MONTHS: 6

AMOUNT INVESTED IN LAST 12 MONTHS: $2,957,422.30

AVERAGE TIME REQUIRED TO COMPLETE A DEAL: 6 weeks–6 months
  (From Initial Contact to Closing)

FIRM NAME: **Central Texas Small Business Investment Corporation**

ADDRESS: 514 Austin Ave.
                Waco, TX 76703

PHONE: (817) 753–6461

SBIC _X_ VENTURE CAPITAL FUND ___ MESBIC ___ OTHER ___

TYPES OF FINANCING PREFERRED (Stages): Debt and equity

MINIMUM DATA REQUIRED TO CONSIDER FINANCING: Existing business: prior 3 years financial and operating statement with appraisals, accounts receivable, aging and inventory listing when appropriate

GEOGRAPHIC PREFERENCE: Central Texas region

INDUSTRY PREFERENCE BY FIRM: None

INDUSTRY PREFERENCES BY INDIVIDUAL FIRM MEMBERS: None

YEAR COMPANY ESTABLISHED: Over 25 years

FUNDS UNDER MANAGEMENT AT COST: N/A

MINIMUM SIZE INVESTMENT: $25,000

PREFERRED SIZE INVESTMENT: $25,000–$120,000

WILL FIRM SERVE AS LEAD INVESTOR: Yes

NUMBER OF DEALS COMPLETED IN THE LAST 12 MONTHS: N/A

AMOUNT INVESTED IN LAST 12 MONTHS: N/A

AVERAGE TIME REQUIRED TO COMPLETE A DEAL: 2 weeks
(From Initial Contact to Closing)

FIRM NAME: **Charter Venture Group, Inc.**

ADDRESS: Suite 600
                2600 Citadel Plaza Dr.
                Houston, TX 77008

PHONE: (713) 868–0704

SBIC _X_ VENTURE CAPITAL FUND ___ MESBIC ___ OTHER ___

TYPES OF FINANCING PREFERRED (Stages): Latter first stage/second stage/ leveraged buyouts

MINIMUM DATA REQUIRED TO CONSIDER FINANCING: N/A

GEOGRAPHIC PREFERENCE: Southwest

INDUSTRY PREFERENCE BY FIRM: Diversified

INDUSTRY PREFERENCES BY INDIVIDUAL FIRM MEMBERS: N/A

YEAR COMPANY ESTABLISHED: 1980

FUNDS UNDER MANAGEMENT AT COST: $2 million

MINIMUM SIZE INVESTMENT: $100,000

PREFERRED SIZE INVESTMENT: $150,000

WILL FIRM SERVE AS LEAD INVESTOR: Yes

NUMBER OF DEALS COMPLETED IN THE LAST 12 MONTHS: 6

AMOUNT INVESTED IN LAST 12 MONTHS: $520,000

AVERAGE TIME REQUIRED TO COMPLETE A DEAL: 75–90 days
(From Initial Contact to Closing)

FIRM NAME: J. H. Crutchfield & Co.

ADDRESS: 1000 Westlake High Dr.
                  Suite 4B
                  Austin, TX 78746

PHONE: (512) 327–6810

SBIC ____ VENTURE CAPITAL FUND _X_ MESBIC ____ OTHER ____

TYPES OF FINANCING PREFERRED (Stages): Early stage

MINIMUM DATA REQUIRED TO CONSIDER FINANCING: Business plan

GEOGRAPHIC PREFERENCE: Texas

INDUSTRY PREFERENCE BY FIRM: Electronics/Software/Niche Markets

INDUSTRY PREFERENCES BY INDIVIDUAL FIRM MEMBERS:
   J. H. Crutchfield
   G. T. Andron

YEAR COMPANY ESTABLISHED: 1979

FUNDS UNDER MANAGEMENT AT COST: $5 million

MINIMUM SIZE INVESTMENT: $100,000

PREFERRED SIZE INVESTMENT: $250,000–$500,000

WILL FIRM SERVE AS LEAD INVESTOR: Yes

NUMBER OF DEALS COMPLETED IN THE LAST 12 MONTHS: 4

AMOUNT INVESTED IN LAST 12 MONTHS: $1 million

AVERAGE TIME REQUIRED TO COMPLETE A DEAL: 60 days
   (From Initial Contact to Closing)

FIRM NAME: Curtin & Co., Inc.

ADDRESS: 2050 Houston Natural Gas Building
                  Houston, TX 77002

PHONE: (713) 658–9806

SBIC ____ VENTURE CAPITAL FUND ____ MESBIC ____

   OTHER _X_ (Private investment banking)

TYPES OF FINANCING PREFERRED (Stages): Leveraged or management buy-
   outs/research and development/start-up/first round/second round

MINIMUM DATA REQUIRED TO CONSIDER FINANCING: N/A

GEOGRAPHIC PREFERENCE: Texas, Oklahoma, Louisiana

INDUSTRY PREFERENCE BY FIRM: No specific industry preferences; however,
   no interest in real estate, movies, or records

INDUSTRY PREFERENCES BY INDIVIDUAL FIRM MEMBERS: N/A

YEAR COMPANY ESTABLISHED: 1974

FUNDS UNDER MANAGEMENT AT COST: N/A

MINIMUM SIZE INVESTMENT: $500,000

PREFERRED SIZE INVESTMENT: $1–$5 million

WILL FIRM SERVE AS LEAD INVESTOR: Preferred role is to assist companies in accomplishment of venture capital placement

NUMBER OF DEALS COMPLETED IN THE LAST 12 MONTHS: N/A

AMOUNT INVESTED IN LAST 12 MONTHS: N/A

AVERAGE TIME REQUIRED TO COMPLETE A DEAL: 3–6 months
(From Initial Contact to Closing)

FIRM NAME: **D. S. Ventures, Inc.**

ADDRESS: 351 Phalps Coast
                  Irving, TX 75015–2300

PHONE: (214) 659–7205

SBIC ____ VENTURE CAPITAL FUND ____ MESBIC ____
OTHER _X_   (Corporate venture capital subsidiary)

TYPES OF FINANCING PREFERRED (Stages): No strong preference but need to see qualified technology with well-established market potential

MINIMUM DATA REQUIRED TO CONSIDER FINANCING: Business plan/financial forecast/resume of management

GEOGRAPHIC PREFERENCE: None

INDUSTRY PREFERENCE BY FIRM: Chemical Specialties/Electronics/Chemicals/High-technology Materials/Genetics

INDUSTRY PREFERENCES BY INDIVIDUAL FIRM MEMBERS: N/A

YEAR COMPANY ESTABLISHED: 1981

FUNDS UNDER MANAGEMENT AT COST: $5.5 million

MINIMUM SIZE INVESTMENT: N/A

PREFERRED SIZE INVESTMENT: $500,000–$1,000,000

WILL FIRM SERVE AS LEAD INVESTOR: No

NUMBER OF DEALS COMPLETED IN THE LAST 12 MONTHS: 3

AMOUNT INVESTED IN LAST 12 MONTHS: $2 million committed

AVERAGE TIME REQUIRED TO COMPLETE A DEAL: N/A
(From Initial Contact to Closing)

FIRM NAME: **Enterprise Capital Corporation**

ADDRESS: 3115 Allen Parkway
                  First Floor
                  Houston, TX 77019

PHONE: (713) 526–8070

SBIC _X_ VENTURE CAPITAL FUND ____ MESBIC ____ OTHER ____

TYPES OF FINANCING PREFERRED (Stages): All

MINIMUM DATA REQUIRED TO CONSIDER FINANCING: Business plan/past financial history

GEOGRAPHIC PREFERENCE: Nationwide; prefer Houston and close proximity

INDUSTRY PREFERENCE BY FIRM: Medical/Aerospace/Manufacturing

INDUSTRY PREFERENCES BY INDIVIDUAL FIRM MEMBERS: N/A

YEAR COMPANY ESTABLISHED: 1970

FUNDS UNDER MANAGEMENT AT COST: $10 million

MINIMUM SIZE INVESTMENT: $150,000

PREFERRED SIZE INVESTMENT: $250,000

WILL FIRM SERVE AS LEAD INVESTOR: Yes

NUMBER OF DEALS COMPLETED IN THE LAST 12 MONTHS: 12

AMOUNT INVESTED IN LAST 12 MONTHS: $3.8 million

AVERAGE TIME REQUIRED TO COMPLETE A DEAL: 2 months
(From Initial Contact to Closing)

FIRM NAME: **Financial Services—Austin, Inc.**

ADDRESS: P.O. Box 1987
                 Austin, TX 78767

PHONE: (512) 472–7171

SBIC ____   VENTURE CAPITAL FUND ____   MESBIC ____
OTHER __X__   (Investment banker with venture funds available)

TYPES OF FINANCING PREFERRED (Stages): All stages except mezzanine financings

MINIMUM DATA REQUIRED TO CONSIDER FINANCING: Business plan/management and customer references/5 year financial projection

GEOGRAPHIC PREFERENCE: Texas

INDUSTRY PREFERENCE BY FIRM: None

INDUSTRY PREFERENCES BY INDIVIDUAL FIRM MEMBERS: N/A

YEAR COMPANY ESTABLISHED: 1979

FUNDS UNDER MANAGEMENT AT COST: Affiliated fund manages over $15 million

MINIMUM SIZE INVESTMENT: $1.0 million private placement; affiliated fund will take less

PREFERRED SIZE INVESTMENT: $2.0 million private placement

WILL FIRM SERVE AS LEAD INVESTOR: Yes

NUMBER OF DEALS COMPLETED IN THE LAST 12 MONTHS: 4

AMOUNT INVESTED IN LAST 12 MONTHS: N/A

AVERAGE TIME REQUIRED TO COMPLETE A DEAL: 3–4 months
(From Initial Contact to Closing)

FIRM NAME: **InterFirst Venture Corporation**

ADDRESS: P.O. Box 83644
                Dallas, TX 75283

PHONE: N/A

SBIC _X_ VENTURE CAPITAL FUND ____ MESBIC ____ OTHER ____

TYPES OF FINANCING PREFERRED (Stages): Early stage/leverage buyouts

MINIMUM DATA REQUIRED TO CONSIDER FINANCING: Business plan

GEOGRAPHIC PREFERENCE: Southwest

INDUSTRY PREFERENCE BY FIRM: N/A

INDUSTRY PREFERENCES BY INDIVIDUAL FIRM MEMBERS: N/A

YEAR COMPANY ESTABLISHED: 1962

FUNDS UNDER MANAGEMENT AT COST: $40 million

MINIMUM SIZE INVESTMENT: $500,000

PREFERRED SIZE INVESTMENT: $1 million

WILL FIRM SERVE AS LEAD INVESTOR: Yes

NUMBER OF DEALS COMPLETED IN THE LAST 12 MONTHS: 12

AMOUNT INVESTED IN LAST 12 MONTHS: $10 million

AVERAGE TIME REQUIRED TO COMPLETE A DEAL: 3–6 months
    (From Initial Contact to Closing)

FIRM NAME: **Richard Jaffe & Co., Inc.**

ADDRESS: 7318 Royal Circle
                Dallas, TX 75230

PHONE: (214) 739–1845

SBIC ____ VENTURE CAPITAL FUND _X_ MESBIC ____ OTHER ____

TYPES OF FINANCING PREFERRED (Stages): Early

MINIMUM DATA REQUIRED TO CONSIDER FINANCING: Complete business
    plan

GEOGRAPHIC PREFERENCE: Southwest

INDUSTRY PREFERENCE BY FIRM: Computer Related to industrial solutions,
    not consumer/Information Services/Real-estate Development

INDUSTRY PREFERENCES BY INDIVIDUAL FIRM MEMBERS: N/A

YEAR COMPANY ESTABLISHED: 1965

FUNDS UNDER MANAGEMENT AT COST: $3 million

MINIMUM SIZE INVESTMENT: $100,000–$300,000

PREFERRED SIZE INVESTMENT: $100,000–$300,000

WILL FIRM SERVE AS LEAD INVESTOR: Sometimes

NUMBER OF DEALS COMPLETED IN THE LAST 12 MONTHS: 2

AMOUNT INVESTED IN LAST 12 MONTHS: $350,000

AVERAGE TIME REQUIRED TO COMPLETE A DEAL: 120 days
(From Initial Contact to Closing)

FIRM NAME: **MESBIC Financial Corporation of Dallas**

ADDRESS: 7701 North Stemmons Freeway
Suite 836
Dallas, TX 75247

PHONE: (214) 637–0445

SBIC ____ VENTURE CAPITAL FUND ____ MESBIC _X_ OTHER ____

TYPES OF FINANCING PREFERRED (Stages): All stages

MINIMUM DATA REQUIRED TO CONSIDER FINANCING: Complete business
plan

GEOGRAPHIC PREFERENCE: Southwest

INDUSTRY PREFERENCE BY FIRM: None

INDUSTRY PREFERENCES BY INDIVIDUAL FIRM MEMBERS: N/A

YEAR COMPANY ESTABLISHED: 1970

FUNDS UNDER MANAGEMENT AT COST: $4 million

MINIMUM SIZE INVESTMENT: $50,000

PREFERRED SIZE INVESTMENT: $150,000

WILL FIRM SERVE AS LEAD INVESTOR: Yes

NUMBER OF DEALS COMPLETED IN THE LAST 12 MONTHS: 12

AMOUNT INVESTED IN LAST 12 MONTHS: $900,000

AVERAGE TIME REQUIRED TO COMPLETE A DEAL: 120 days
(From Initial Contact to Closing)

FIRM NAME: **MSI Capital Corp.**

ADDRESS: 6510 Abrams Rd.
Suite 650
Dallas, TX 75231

PHONE: (214) 341–1553

SBIC ____ VENTURE CAPITAL FUND _X_ MESBIC ____ OTHER ____

TYPES OF FINANCING PREFERRED (Stages): Expansion capital

MINIMUM DATA REQUIRED TO CONSIDER FINANCING: Business plan

GEOGRAPHIC PREFERENCE: Texas

INDUSTRY PREFERENCE BY FIRM: None

INDUSTRY PREFERENCES BY INDIVIDUAL FIRM MEMBERS: N/A

YEAR COMPANY ESTABLISHED: 1976

FUNDS UNDER MANAGEMENT AT COST: $15 million (2 funds) [MSI Capital co-managers Traid Ventures Limited, a $14,000,000 Texas general industries fund. Traid started operations November 30, 1984.]

MINIMUM SIZE INVESTMENT: $100,000 (small fund); $250,000 (Triad Ventures Ltd.)

PREFERRED SIZE INVESTMENT: $100,000 (small fund); $500,000 (Triad Ventures Ltd.)

WILL FIRM SERVE AS LEAD INVESTOR: Yes

NUMBER OF DEALS COMPLETED IN THE LAST 12 MONTHS: 3

AMOUNT INVESTED IN LAST 12 MONTHS: $1.3 million

AVERAGE TIME REQUIRED TO COMPLETE A DEAL: 6 months
(From Initial Contact to Closing)

FIRM NAME: **MVenture Corp.**

ADDRESS: P.O. Box 662090
               Dallas, TX 75266–2090

PHONE: (241) 741–1469

SBIC __X__   VENTURE CAPITAL FUND ____   MESBIC ____   OTHER ____

TYPES OF FINANCING PREFERRED (Stages): Third stage and later

MINIMUM DATA REQUIRED TO CONSIDER FINANCING: Complete business plan (upon our expression of initial interest)

GEOGRAPHIC PREFERENCE: Primarily Texas; secondarily Southwest

INDUSTRY PREFERENCE BY FIRM: Diversified; will consider most industries, but low priority is given to (1) designers and developers of software, (2) most retail operations, (3) real-estate developing and leasing

INDUSTRY PREFERENCES BY INDIVIDUAL FIRM MEMBERS:
Joseph G. Longino, Jr., Executive Vice-president
J. Wayne Gaylor, Executive Vice-president
Edwin A. Walker, Investment Officer
Michael D. Brown, Investment Officer
Thomas F. Bartlett, Investment Associate

YEAR COMPANY ESTABLISHED: 1976

FUNDS UNDER MANAGEMENT AT COST: $60 million

MINIMUM SIZE INVESTMENT: $250,000

PREFERRED SIZE INVESTMENT: $500,000–$1,000,000

WILL FIRM SERVE AS LEAD INVESTOR: Yes

NUMBER OF DEALS COMPLETED IN THE LAST 12 MONTHS: 33

AMOUNT INVESTED IN LAST 12 MONTHS: $21.8 million

AVERAGE TIME REQUIRED TO COMPLETE A DEAL: 60 days
(From Initial Contact to Closing)

FIRM NAME: **Republic Venture Group, Inc.**

ADDRESS: P.O. Box 225961
                  Dallas, TX 75265

PHONE: (214) 922–5078

SBIC _X_ VENTURE CAPITAL FUND ____ MESBIC ____ OTHER ____

TYPES OF FINANCING PREFERRED (Stages): Second round or later, but will occasionally consider earlier stages

MINIMUM DATA REQUIRED TO CONSIDER FINANCING: Complete business plan

GEOGRAPHIC PREFERENCE: Southwest, but have often invested in other areas of the USA

INDUSTRY PREFERENCE BY FIRM: Technology/Communications/Medical Products/Oil and Gas Related/Leveraged Buyouts

INDUSTRY PREFERENCES BY INDIVIDUAL FIRM MEMBERS: N/A

YEAR COMPANY ESTABLISHED: 1961

FUNDS UNDER MANAGEMENT AT COST: $24 million

MINIMUM SIZE INVESTMENT: $250,000

PREFERRED SIZE INVESTMENT: $500,000

WILL FIRM SERVE AS LEAD INVESTOR: Yes

NUMBER OF DEALS COMPLETED IN THE LAST 12 MONTHS: 11

AMOUNT INVESTED IN LAST 12 MONTHS: $3.5 million

AVERAGE TIME REQUIRED TO COMPLETE A DEAL: 2–4 months
   (From Initial Contact to Closing)

FIRM NAME: **Retzloff Capital Corporation**

ADDRESS: P.O. Box 41250
                  Houston, TX 77240–1250

PHONE: (713) 466–4690

SBIC _X_ VENTURE CAPITAL FUND ____ MESBIC ____ OTHER ____

TYPES OF FINANCING PREFERRED (Stages): Early stage/start-up/first round/second round/expansion

MINIMUM DATA REQUIRED TO CONSIDER FINANCING: Full business plan with 5 year projections/current balance sheet

GEOGRAPHIC PREFERENCE: USA

INDUSTRY PREFERENCE BY FIRM: Fully diversified

INDUSTRY PREFERENCES BY INDIVIDUAL FIRM MEMBERS:
   James K. Hines, President
   Steven F. Retzloff, Secretary/Investments Manager
   Diana Langdon, Investment Analyst

YEAR COMPANY ESTABLISHED: 1983

FUNDS UNDER MANAGEMENT AT COST: $2.5 million

MINIMUM SIZE INVESTMENT: $100,000

PREFERRED SIZE INVESTMENT: $300,000

WILL FIRM SERVE AS LEAD INVESTOR: Yes

NUMBER OF DEALS COMPLETED IN THE LAST 12 MONTHS: 4

AMOUNT INVESTED IN LAST 12 MONTHS: $1.5 million

AVERAGE TIME REQUIRED TO COMPLETE A DEAL: 2–6 months
(From Initial Contact to Closing)

FIRM NAME: **R. Patrick Rowles & Co., Inc.**

ADDRESS: 3336 Richmond Ave.
               Suite 202
               Houston, TX 77098

PHONE: (713) 521–0388

SBIC ___ VENTURE CAPITAL FUND ___ MESBIC ___ OTHER _X_

TYPES OF FINANCING PREFERRED (Stages): Start-up/first stage/second stage

MINIMUM DATA REQUIRED TO CONSIDER FINANCING: Comprehensive
business plan

GEOGRAPHIC PREFERENCE: Texas, Louisiana

INDUSTRY PREFERENCE BY FIRM: Microcomputer Software/Energy–Natural
Resources/Genetic Engineering/Medical–Health Related/Finance/Publishing

INDUSTRY PREFERENCES BY INDIVIDUAL FIRM MEMBERS:
R. Patrick Rowles
Nancy Arbuckle

YEAR COMPANY ESTABLISHED: 1981

FUNDS UNDER MANAGEMENT AT COST: N/A

MINIMUM SIZE INVESTMENT: $150,000

PREFERRED SIZE INVESTMENT: $400,000–$600,000

WILL FIRM SERVE AS LEAD INVESTOR: Yes

NUMBER OF DEALS COMPLETED IN THE LAST 12 MONTHS: 2

AMOUNT INVESTED IN LAST 12 MONTHS: $1.055 million

AVERAGE TIME REQUIRED TO COMPLETE A DEAL: 3 months
(From Initial Contact to Closing)

FIRM NAME: **San Antonio Venture Group, Inc.**

ADDRESS: 2300 W. Commerce
               San Antonio, TX 78209

PHONE: N/A

SBIC _X_ VENTURE CAPITAL FUND ___ MESBIC ___ OTHER ___

TYPES OF FINANCING PREFERRED (Stages): Second tier

MINIMUM DATA REQUIRED TO CONSIDER FINANCING: Business plan

GEOGRAPHIC PREFERENCE: San Antonio, Texas

INDUSTRY PREFERENCE BY FIRM: N/A

INDUSTRY PREFERENCES BY INDIVIDUAL FIRM MEMBERS: N/A

YEAR COMPANY ESTABLISHED: 1976

FUNDS UNDER MANAGEMENT AT COST: $1 million

MINIMUM SIZE INVESTMENT: $50,000

PREFERRED SIZE INVESTMENT: $100,000–$150,000

WILL FIRM SERVE AS LEAD INVESTOR: Yes

NUMBER OF DEALS COMPLETED IN THE LAST 12 MONTHS: 2

AMOUNT INVESTED IN LAST 12 MONTHS: $190,000

AVERAGE TIME REQUIRED TO COMPLETE A DEAL: 3–4 months
   (From Initial Contact to Closing)

FIRM NAME: **SBI Capital Corp.**

ADDRESS: P.O. Box 771668
               Houston, TX 77215–1668

PHONE: (713) 975–1188

SBIC __X__ VENTURE CAPITAL FUND ____ MESBIC ____ OTHER ____

TYPES OF FINANCING PREFERRED (Stages): First stage/second stage/buyout
   or acquisition

MINIMUM DATA REQUIRED TO CONSIDER FINANCING: P&L: break-
   even/annual sales of $500,000–$1.5 million

GEOGRAPHIC PREFERENCE: Texas, Southwestern USA

INDUSTRY PREFERENCE BY FIRM: Communications/Computer Related/Con-
   sumer Products/Electronic Components and Instruments/Energy–Natural
   Resources/Genetic Engineering/Medical

INDUSTRY PREFERENCES BY INDIVIDUAL FIRM MEMBERS: N/A

YEAR COMPANY ESTABLISHED: 1980

FUNDS UNDER MANAGEMENT AT COST: $3 million

MINIMUM SIZE INVESTMENT: $150,000–$300,000

PREFERRED SIZE INVESTMENT: $200,000–$300,000

WILL FIRM SERVE AS LEAD INVESTOR: Yes

NUMBER OF DEALS COMPLETED IN THE LAST 12 MONTHS: 7

AMOUNT INVESTED IN LAST 12 MONTHS: $1,037,799

AVERAGE TIME REQUIRED TO COMPLETE A DEAL: 3–6 months
   (From Initial Contact to Closing)

FIRM NAME: **Texas Capital Corporation**

ADDRESS: 333 Clay St.
Suite 2100
Houston, TX 77002

PHONE: N/A

SBIC __X__ VENTURE CAPITAL FUND __X__ MESBIC ____ OTHER ____

TYPES OF FINANCING PREFERRED (Stages): Second stage/expansion financing

MINIMUM DATA REQUIRED TO CONSIDER FINANCING: Complete business plan

GEOGRAPHIC PREFERENCE: Southwest

INDUSTRY PREFERENCE BY FIRM: N/A

INDUSTRY PREFERENCES BY INDIVIDUAL FIRM MEMBERS:
David Manklin, Vice president

YEAR COMPANY ESTABLISHED: 1959

FUNDS UNDER MANAGEMENT AT COST: $25 million

MINIMUM SIZE INVESTMENT: $300,000

PREFERRED SIZE INVESTMENT: $500,000

WILL FIRM SERVE AS LEAD INVESTOR: Not typically

NUMBER OF DEALS COMPLETED IN THE LAST 12 MONTHS: 3

AMOUNT INVESTED IN LAST 12 MONTHS: $2 million

AVERAGE TIME REQUIRED TO COMPLETE A DEAL: 90–120 days
(From Initial Contact to Closing)

FIRM NAME: **Texas Commerce Investment Company**
TexCom Venture Capital, Inc.

ADDRESS: P.O. Box 2558
Houston, TX 77252–8082

PHONE: (713) 236–4719

SBIC __X__ VENTURE CAPITAL FUND ____ MESBIC ____ OTHER __X__
(Venture capital subsidiary of commercial bank)

TYPES OF FINANCING PREFERRED (Stages): First stage/second stage/later stage expansion/buyout or acquisition

MINIMUM DATA REQUIRED TO CONSIDER FINANCING: 5 year plan

GEOGRAPHIC PREFERENCE: None

INDUSTRY PREFERENCE BY FIRM: None

INDUSTRY PREFERENCES BY INDIVIDUAL FIRM MEMBERS: None

YEAR COMPANY ESTABLISHED: 1982

FUNDS UNDER MANAGEMENT AT COST: $9.3 million

MINIMUM SIZE INVESTMENT: $100,000

PREFERRED SIZE INVESTMENT: $500,000

WILL FIRM SERVE AS LEAD INVESTOR: Yes

NUMBER OF DEALS COMPLETED IN THE LAST 12 MONTHS: 13

AMOUNT INVESTED IN LAST 12 MONTHS: $4.9 million

AVERAGE TIME REQUIRED TO COMPLETE A DEAL: 6 weeks
(From Initial Contact to Closing)

FIRM NAME: **Triad Ventures Limited**

ADDRESS: P.O. Box 1987
                Austin, TX 78767

PHONE: (512) 472-7171

SBIC ____ VENTURE CAPITAL FUND _X_ MESBIC ____ OTHER ____

TYPES OF FINANCING PREFERRED (Stages): All stages except pure start-up

MINIMUM DATA REQUIRED TO CONSIDER FINANCING: Business
plan/management and customer references/minimum 5 year financial projections

GEOGRAPHIC PREFERENCE: Southwest USA, primarily Texas

INDUSTRY PREFERENCE BY FIRM: N/A

INDUSTRY PREFERENCES BY INDIVIDUAL FIRM MEMBERS: N/A

YEAR COMPANY ESTABLISHED: 1984

FUNDS UNDER MANAGEMENT AT COST: $13.5 million

MINIMUM SIZE INVESTMENT: $300,000

PREFERRED SIZE INVESTMENT: $500,000–$750,000

WILL FIRM SERVE AS LEAD INVESTOR: Yes

NUMBER OF DEALS COMPLETED IN THE LAST 12 MONTHS: 4

AMOUNT INVESTED IN LAST 12 MONTHS: $1.5 million

AVERAGE TIME REQUIRED TO COMPLETE A DEAL: 3–4 months
(From Initial Contact to Closing)

FIRM NAME: **T.V.P. Associates**

ADDRESS: 2777 Stemmons Freeway
                #1741
                Dallas, TX 75205

PHONE: (214) 631–0600

SBIC ____ VENTURE CAPITAL FUND _X_ MESBIC ____ OTHER ____

TYPES OF FINANCING PREFERRED (Stages): Seed/start-up/first stage

MINIMUM DATA REQUIRED TO CONSIDER FINANCING: Annual sales: nominal

GEOGRAPHIC PREFERENCE: Prefer Southwest, but will consider projects in other areas

INDUSTRY PREFERENCE BY FIRM: Communications/Computer Related/Consumer/Distribution/Electronic Components and Instrumentation/Energy–Natural Resources/Industrial Products and Equipment/Medical–Health Related

INDUSTRY PREFERENCES BY INDIVIDUAL FIRM MEMBERS: N/A

YEAR COMPANY ESTABLISHED: 1983

FUNDS UNDER MANAGEMENT AT COST: N/A

MINIMUM SIZE INVESTMENT: $250,000

PREFERRED SIZE INVESTMENT: $500,000–$1 million

WILL FIRM SERVE AS LEAD INVESTOR: N/A

NUMBER OF DEALS COMPLETED IN THE LAST 12 MONTHS: 4 (6 months)

AMOUNT INVESTED IN LAST 12 MONTHS: $2.8 million (6 months)

AVERAGE TIME REQUIRED TO COMPLETE A DEAL: N/A
(From Initial Contact to Closing)

FIRM NAME: **United Mercantile Capital Corp.**

ADDRESS: 444 Executive Center Blvd.
Suite 222
El Paso, TX 79902

PHONE: (915) 533–6375

SBIC __X__ VENTURE CAPITAL FUND ____ MESBIC ____ OTHER ____

TYPES OF FINANCING PREFERRED (Stages): Start-up or second stage

MINIMUM DATA REQUIRED TO CONSIDER FINANCING: Business plan or prospectus

GEOGRAPHIC PREFERENCE: Texas, New Mexico, and Arizona

INDUSTRY PREFERENCE BY FIRM: N/A

INDUSTRY PREFERENCES BY INDIVIDUAL FIRM MEMBERS: N/A

YEAR COMPANY ESTABLISHED: 1977

FUNDS UNDER MANAGEMENT AT COST: $2 million

MINIMUM SIZE INVESTMENT: $50,000

PREFERRED SIZE INVESTMENT: $75,000

WILL FIRM SERVE AS LEAD INVESTOR: Yes

NUMBER OF DEALS COMPLETED IN THE LAST 12 MONTHS: 10

AMOUNT INVESTED IN LAST 12 MONTHS: $500,000

AVERAGE TIME REQUIRED TO COMPLETE A DEAL: 60 days
(From Initial Contact to Closing)

FIRM NAME: **West Central Capital Corp.**

ADDRESS: 440 Northlake Center
               Suite 206
               Dallas, TX 75238

PHONE: (214) 348–3969

SBIC ___ VENTURE CAPITAL FUND ___ MESBIC ___ OTHER _X_

TYPES OF FINANCING PREFERRED (Stages): Second and third stages

MINIMUM DATA REQUIRED TO CONSIDER FINANCING: Prefer 2 to 3 years
     previous financial statements or tax returns

GEOGRAPHIC PREFERENCE: Dallas–Fort Worth Metroplex; Southwest

INDUSTRY PREFERENCE BY FIRM: N/A

INDUSTRY PREFERENCES BY INDIVIDUAL FIRM MEMBERS: N/A

YEAR COMPANY ESTABLISHED: 1964

FUNDS UNDER MANAGEMENT AT COST: N/A

MINIMUM SIZE INVESTMENT: N/A

PREFERRED SIZE INVESTMENT: N/A

WILL FIRM SERVE AS LEAD INVESTOR: N/A

NUMBER OF DEALS COMPLETED IN THE LAST 12 MONTHS: N/A

AMOUNT INVESTED IN LAST 12 MONTHS: N/A

AVERAGE TIME REQUIRED TO COMPLETE A DEAL: N/A
     (From Initial Contact to Closing)

VIRGINIA

FIRM NAME: **Atlantic Venture Partners**

ADDRESS: P.O. Box 1493
               Richmond, VA 23212

PHONE: (804) 644–5496

SBIC ___ VENTURE CAPITAL FUND _X_ MESBIC ___ OTHER ___

TYPES OF FINANCING PREFERRED (Stages): Start-up/second and third
     stages/leveraged buyouts/bridge mezzanine

MINIMUM DATA REQUIRED TO CONSIDER FINANCING: Business plan

GEOGRAPHIC PREFERENCE: Southeastern USA

INDUSTRY PREFERENCE BY FIRM: None

INDUSTRY PREFERENCES BY INDIVIDUAL FIRM MEMBERS: N/A

YEAR COMPANY ESTABLISHED: 1982

FUNDS UNDER MANAGEMENT AT COST: $18 million

MINIMUM SIZE INVESTMENT: $250,000

PREFERRED SIZE INVESTMENT: $500,000–$1,000,000

WILL FIRM SERVE AS LEAD INVESTOR: Yes

NUMBER OF DEALS COMPLETED IN THE LAST 12 MONTHS: 10

AMOUNT INVESTED IN LAST 12 MONTHS: $6 million

AVERAGE TIME REQUIRED TO COMPLETE A DEAL: 4 weeks
(From Initial Contact to Closing)

FIRM NAME: **Basic Investment Corporation**

ADDRESS: 6723 Whittier Ave.
Office 201
McLean, VA 22101

PHONE: (703) 356–4300

SBIC ___   VENTURE CAPITAL FUND ___   MESBIC _X_   OTHER ___

TYPES OF FINANCING PREFERRED (Stages): Initial seed/expansion

MINIMUM DATA REQUIRED TO CONSIDER FINANCING: Application
forms/tax return/projected P&L

GEOGRAPHIC PREFERENCE: Metropolitan area

INDUSTRY PREFERENCE BY FIRM: Motel/Diversified

INDUSTRY PREFERENCES BY INDIVIDUAL FIRM MEMBERS: N/A

YEAR COMPANY ESTABLISHED: 1983

FUNDS UNDER MANAGEMENT AT COST: N/A

MINIMUM SIZE INVESTMENT: $10,000

PREFERRED SIZE INVESTMENT: $15,000–$50,000

WILL FIRM SERVE AS LEAD INVESTOR: Will consider

NUMBER OF DEALS COMPLETED IN THE LAST 12 MONTHS: 0

AMOUNT INVESTED IN LAST 12 MONTHS: 0

AVERAGE TIME REQUIRED TO COMPLETE A DEAL: 30 days
(From Initial Contact to Closing)

FIRM NAME: **Hillcrest Group**

ADDRESS: 9 S. 12th St.
Richmond, VA 23219

PHONE: (804) 643–7358

SBIC _X_ VENTURE CAPITAL FUND ___   MESBIC ___   OTHER ___

TYPES OF FINANCING PREFERRED (Stages): Second or later stage/leveraged
buyouts

MINIMUM DATA REQUIRED TO CONSIDER FINANCING: Business plan

GEOGRAPHIC PREFERENCE: Area between Washington, D.C., and Atlanta, Georgia

INDUSTRY PREFERENCE BY FIRM: Diversified

INDUSTRY PREFERENCES BY INDIVIDUAL FIRM MEMBERS: N/A

YEAR COMPANY ESTABLISHED: 1981

FUNDS UNDER MANAGEMENT AT COST: $6.5 million

MINIMUM SIZE INVESTMENT: $250,000

PREFERRED SIZE INVESTMENT: $500,000

WILL FIRM SERVE AS LEAD INVESTOR: Yes

NUMBER OF DEALS COMPLETED IN THE LAST 12 MONTHS: 6

AMOUNT INVESTED IN LAST 12 MONTHS: $1.65 million

AVERAGE TIME REQUIRED TO COMPLETE A DEAL: 60–90 days
(From Initial Contact to Closing)

WASHINGTON

FIRM NAME: **Capital Resource Corporation/Walden**

ADDRESS: 1001 Logan Building
                  Seattle, WA 98101

PHONE: (202) 623–6550

SBIC _X_ VENTURE CAPITAL FUND _X_ MESBIC ___ OTHER ___

TYPES OF FINANCING PREFERRED (Stages): All

MINIMUM DATA REQUIRED TO CONSIDER FINANCING: Business plan

GEOGRAPHIC PREFERENCE: National, but prefer West Coast

INDUSTRY PREFERENCE BY FIRM: Computer/Communications/Medical/ Manufacturing/Specialty Retailing/Software

INDUSTRY PREFERENCES BY INDIVIDUAL FIRM MEMBERS: N/A

YEAR COMPANY ESTABLISHED: 1980

FUNDS UNDER MANAGEMENT AT COST: $30 million, total

MINIMUM SIZE INVESTMENT: $500,000

PREFERRED SIZE INVESTMENT: $750,000

WILL FIRM SERVE AS LEAD INVESTOR: Yes

NUMBER OF DEALS COMPLETED IN THE LAST 12 MONTHS: 5

AMOUNT INVESTED IN LAST 12 MONTHS: $2 million

AVERAGE TIME REQUIRED TO COMPLETE A DEAL: 1 month
(From Initial Contact to Closing)

FIRM NAME: **Palms & Company, Inc.**

ADDRESS: 6702 139th Ave., NE
               Suite 760
               Redmond, WA 98052

PHONE: (206) 883–3580

SBIC ____ VENTURE CAPITAL FUND __X__ MESBIC ____ OTHER ____

TYPES OF FINANCING PREFERRED (Stages): Start-up/second stage company operating 1–2 years: losses/company operating 3 years: break-even profitable/management buyouts/initial public offerings

MINIMUM DATA REQUIRED TO CONSIDER FINANCING: Balance sheet/profit and loss statement/personal financial statements of principals/business plan

GEOGRAPHIC PREFERENCE: Idaho, Oregon, Washington, Alaska, Western Texas, New Mexico, Arizona, southern Colorado, southwestern Kansas, southeastern Utah, Hawaii

INDUSTRY PREFERENCE BY FIRM: Manufacturing/Distribution/Service/Athletic Clubs/Theme Parks/Casinos/Wineries/Motion Pictures/Franchisors/Alternative Energy/Fishing/Real Estate over $10 million/Time Share

INDUSTRY PREFERENCES BY INDIVIDUAL FIRM MEMBERS:
Peter J. Palms IV—Manufacturing/Distribution/Motion Pictures/Wineries
Carol Sarko—Theme Parks/Casinos/Real Estate
Judy Evans—Franchisors/Alternative Energy/Fisheries
Israel Rothman—High Technology
Dave Shank—Debt Financing
Deana Noel—Medical Technology

YEAR COMPANY ESTABLISHED: 1968

FUNDS UNDER MANAGEMENT AT COST: $25 million

MINIMUM SIZE INVESTMENT: $300,000

PREFERRED SIZE INVESTMENT: Equity venture capital: $500,000; Real estate $10 million

WILL FIRM SERVE AS LEAD INVESTOR: Yes

NUMBER OF DEALS COMPLETED IN THE LAST 12 MONTHS: 10

AMOUNT INVESTED IN LAST 12 MONTHS: $20.6 million

AVERAGE TIME REQUIRED TO COMPLETE A DEAL: 6 months
(From Initial Contact to Closing)

FIRM NAME: **Rainier Venture Partners**

ADDRESS: 9725 SE 36th St.
               Suite 300
               Mercer Island, WA 98040

PHONE: (206) 232–6720

SBIC ____ VENTURE CAPITAL FUND __X__ MESBIC ____ OTHER ____

TYPES OF FINANCING PREFERRED (Stages): Early stages, but not seed round

MINIMUM DATA REQUIRED TO CONSIDER FINANCING: Complete business plan

GEOGRAPHIC PREFERENCE: Western USA

INDUSTRY PREFERENCE BY FIRM: Computer Hardware/Computer Software/Computer System Applications/Microelectronics/Test and Measurement/Robotics/Medical Instruments/Telecommunications

INDUSTRY PREFERENCES BY INDIVIDUAL FIRM MEMBERS: N/A

YEAR COMPANY ESTABLISHED: 1983

FUNDS UNDER MANAGEMENT AT COST: $25 million

MINIMUM SIZE INVESTMENT: $250,000

PREFERRED SIZE INVESTMENT: $500,000–$1,000,000

WILL FIRM SERVE AS LEAD INVESTOR: Yes

NUMBER OF DEALS COMPLETED IN THE LAST 12 MONTHS: 8

AMOUNT INVESTED IN LAST 12 MONTHS: $5.3 million

AVERAGE TIME REQUIRED TO COMPLETE A DEAL: 90 days
(From Initial Contact to Closing)

FIRM NAME: **Venture Sum**

ADDRESS: N. 2610 Van Marter
#1
Spokane, WA 99206

PHONE: (509) 926–3720

SBIC ____   VENTURE CAPITAL FUND __X__   MESBIC ____   OTHER ____

TYPES OF FINANCING PREFERRED (Stages): Start-up and secondary

MINIMUM DATA REQUIRED TO CONSIDER FINANCING: Complete business plan

GEOGRAPHIC PREFERENCE: Northwestern USA

INDUSTRY PREFERENCE BY FIRM: High Technology/Communications

INDUSTRY PREFERENCES BY INDIVIDUAL FIRM MEMBERS: N/A

YEAR COMPANY ESTABLISHED: 1981

FUNDS UNDER MANAGEMENT AT COST: N/A

MINIMUM SIZE INVESTMENT: $10,000

PREFERRED SIZE INVESTMENT: $100,000

WILL FIRM SERVE AS LEAD INVESTOR: Yes

NUMBER OF DEALS COMPLETED IN THE LAST 12 MONTHS: 5

AMOUNT INVESTED IN LAST 12 MONTHS: $1 million

AVERAGE TIME REQUIRED TO COMPLETE A DEAL: 1 month
(From Initial Contact to Closing)

WISCONSIN

FIRM NAME:	**Robert W. Beard & Co., Inc.**
ADDRESS:	777 E. Wisconsin Ave. Milwaukee, WI 53202 Attn: J. S. Anderson
PHONE:	(414) 765-3889

SBIC ___ VENTURE CAPITAL FUND ___ MESBIC ___ OTHER _X_

TYPES OF FINANCING PREFERRED (Stages): Second and third stages

MINIMUM DATA REQUIRED TO CONSIDER FINANCING: Business plan

GEOGRAPHIC PREFERENCE: Midwest

INDUSTRY PREFERENCE BY FIRM: N/A

INDUSTRY PREFERENCES BY INDIVIDUAL FIRM MEMBERS: N/A

YEAR COMPANY ESTABLISHED: N/A

FUNDS UNDER MANAGEMENT AT COST: N/A

MINIMUM SIZE INVESTMENT: $500,000

PREFERRED SIZE INVESTMENT: N/A

WILL FIRM SERVE AS LEAD INVESTOR: N/A

NUMBER OF DEALS COMPLETED IN THE LAST 12 MONTHS: N/A

AMOUNT INVESTED IN LAST 12 MONTHS: N/A

AVERAGE TIME REQUIRED TO COMPLETE A DEAL: N/A
    (From Initial Contact to Closing)

FIRM NAME:	**Capital Investments, Inc.**
ADDRESS:	744 N. Fourth St. Milwaukee, WI 53203
PHONE:	(414) 273-6560

SBIC _X_ VENTURE CAPITAL FUND ___ MESBIC ___ OTHER ___

TYPES OF FINANCING PREFERRED (Stages): Second stage (generally companies 1–3 years old)/later stage expansion/buyout or acquisition

MINIMUM DATA REQUIRED TO CONSIDER FINANCING: P&L: break-even

GEOGRAPHIC PREFERENCE: None

INDUSTRY PREFERENCE BY FIRM: Manufacturing/Technology/Medical/Value-added Distributors/Service: Technical Orientation

INDUSTRY PREFERENCES BY INDIVIDUAL FIRM MEMBERS: N/A

YEAR COMPANY ESTABLISHED: 1959

FUNDS UNDER MANAGEMENT AT COST: $13 million

MINIMUM SIZE INVESTMENT: $150,000

PREFERRED SIZE INVESTMENT: $200,000–$600,000

WILL FIRM SERVE AS LEAD INVESTOR: Yes

NUMBER OF DEALS COMPLETED IN THE LAST 12 MONTHS: 5

AMOUNT INVESTED IN LAST 12 MONTHS: $1.3 million

AVERAGE TIME REQUIRED TO COMPLETE A DEAL: N/A
(From Initial Contact to Closing)

FIRM NAME: **Impact Seven, Inc.**

ADDRESS: Industrial Road
                Turtle Lake, WI 54889

PHONE: (715) 986–4171

SBIC ___ VENTURE CAPITAL FUND ___ MESBIC ___ OTHER _X_
(Community development corporation)

TYPES OF FINANCING PREFERRED (Stages): All stages

MINIMUM DATA REQUIRED TO CONSIDER FINANCING: Business plan

GEOGRAPHIC PREFERENCE: Wisconsin

INDUSTRY PREFERENCE BY FIRM: No preference

INDUSTRY PREFERENCES BY INDIVIDUAL FIRM MEMBERS: No preference

YEAR COMPANY ESTABLISHED: 1970

FUNDS UNDER MANAGEMENT AT COST: N/A

MINIMUM SIZE INVESTMENT: $50,000

PREFERRED SIZE INVESTMENT: $300,000–$500,000

WILL FIRM SERVE AS LEAD INVESTOR: Yes

NUMBER OF DEALS COMPLETED IN THE LAST 12 MONTHS: N/A

AMOUNT INVESTED IN LAST 12 MONTHS: N/A

AVERAGE TIME REQUIRED TO COMPLETE A DEAL: Varies
(From Initial Contact to Closing)

FIRM NAME: **Madison Capital Corporation**

ADDRESS: 102 State St.
                Madison, WI 53703

PHONE: (608) 256–8185

SBIC _X_ VENTURE CAPITAL FUND ___ MESBIC ___ OTHER ___

TYPES OF FINANCING PREFERRED (Stages): Early stage/seed financings/start-
up/expansion: unprofitable but shipping; profitable, needs expansion capital
bridge to public offering/turnaround investment/leveraged buyout

MINIMUM DATA REQUIRED TO CONSIDER FINANCING: Complete business
plan covering company, product, market, competition, marketing, organization, financial history, pro formas, capitalization, critical risks

GEOGRAPHIC PREFERENCE: Two hour radius of Madison

INDUSTRY PREFERENCE BY FIRM: N/A

INDUSTRY PREFERENCES BY INDIVIDUAL FIRM MEMBERS: N/A

YEAR COMPANY ESTABLISHED: 1982

FUNDS UNDER MANAGEMENT AT COST: $1.51 million

MINIMUM SIZE INVESTMENT: $50,000

PREFERRED SIZE INVESTMENT: $100,000

WILL FIRM SERVE AS LEAD INVESTOR: Yes

NUMBER OF DEALS COMPLETED IN THE LAST 12 MONTHS: 2

AMOUNT INVESTED IN LAST 12 MONTHS: $260,000

AVERAGE TIME REQUIRED TO COMPLETE A DEAL: 90–180 days
   (From Initial Contact to Closing)

FIRM NAME: **Marine Venture Capital, Inc.**

ADDRESS: 111 E. Wisconsin Ave.
                Milwaukee, WI 53202

PHONE: (414) 765–2274

SBIC _X_ VENTURE CAPITAL FUND ___ MESBIC ___ OTHER ___

TYPES OF FINANCING PREFERRED (Stages): First, second, and third stages

MINIMUM DATA REQUIRED TO CONSIDER FINANCING: N/A

GEOGRAPHIC PREFERENCE: None

INDUSTRY PREFERENCE BY FIRM: Manufacturing/Distribution/Medical Technology/Biotechnology/Chemicals/Avionics

INDUSTRY PREFERENCES BY INDIVIDUAL FIRM MEMBERS:
   H. Wayne Foreman—Low-Technology Manufacturing/Distribution/Factory Automation/Process Control
   Reed R. Prior—Medical Technology/Biotechnology/Avionics/Chemicals/Instrumentation

YEAR COMPANY ESTABLISHED: 1984

FUNDS UNDER MANAGEMENT AT COST: $3 million

MINIMUM SIZE INVESTMENT: $200,000

PREFERRED SIZE INVESTMENT: $400,000

WILL FIRM SERVE AS LEAD INVESTOR: Yes

NUMBER OF DEALS COMPLETED IN THE LAST 12 MONTHS: 4

AMOUNT INVESTED IN LAST 12 MONTHS: $1.3 million

AVERAGE TIME REQUIRED TO COMPLETE A DEAL: 90 days
   (From Initial Contact to Closing)

FIRM NAME: **Wind Point Partners, L.P.**

ADDRESS: 1525 Howe St.
                Racine, WI 53403

PHONE: (414) 631–4030

SBIC _____ VENTURE CAPITAL FUND _X_ MESBIC _____ OTHER _____

TYPES OF FINANCING PREFERRED (Stages): Start-ups/growth equity/leveraged management buyouts

MINIMUM DATA REQUIRED TO CONSIDER FINANCING: Initial proposal/management resumes/prior to funding: business plan

GEOGRAPHIC PREFERENCE: None

INDUSTRY PREFERENCE BY FIRM: None

INDUSTRY PREFERENCES BY INDIVIDUAL FIRM MEMBERS:
    Arthur DelVesco—Telecommunications/Broadcasting
    James E. Daverman—Electronics/Health-care Services
    S. Curtis Johnson—Medical Products/Consumer Products
    Richard R. Kracum—Health-care Services/Medical Products

YEAR COMPANY ESTABLISHED: 1983

FUNDS UNDER MANAGEMENT AT COST: $36 million

MINIMUM SIZE INVESTMENT: $500,000

PREFERRED SIZE INVESTMENT: $1 million

WILL FIRM SERVE AS LEAD INVESTOR: Yes

NUMBER OF DEALS COMPLETED IN THE LAST 12 MONTHS: 11

AMOUNT INVESTED IN LAST 12 MONTHS: $10 million

AVERAGE TIME REQUIRED TO COMPLETE A DEAL: 1–3 months (From Initial Contact to Closing)

WYOMING

FIRM NAME: Capital Corporation of Wyoming, Inc.

ADDRESS: P.O. Box 612
                Casper, WY 82602

PHONE: N/A

SBIC _X_ VENTURE CAPITAL FUND _____ MESBIC _____ OTHER _____

TYPES OF FINANCING PREFERRED (Stages): Start-up to third stage

MINIMUM DATA REQUIRED TO CONSIDER FINANCING: Business plan; emphasis on marketing

GEOGRAPHIC PREFERENCE: Wyoming only

INDUSTRY PREFERENCE BY FIRM: Diversified

INDUSTRY PREFERENCES BY INDIVIDUAL FIRM MEMBERS: N/A

YEAR COMPANY ESTABLISHED: 1979

FUNDS UNDER MANAGEMENT AT COST: $12 million

MINIMUM SIZE INVESTMENT: No minimum

PREFERRED SIZE INVESTMENT: $100,000

WILL FIRM SERVE AS LEAD INVESTOR: Yes

NUMBER OF DEALS COMPLETED IN THE LAST 12 MONTHS: 18

AMOUNT INVESTED IN LAST 12 MONTHS: $1 million

AVERAGE TIME REQUIRED TO COMPLETE A DEAL: 3 months
  (From Initial Contact to Closing)

CANADA

FIRM NAME: **Alta-Can Telecom, Inc.**

ADDRESS: 411 - 1 Street SE
              Floor 26H
              Calgary, Alberta T2G 4Y5
              Canada

PHONE: (403) 231–8535

SBIC ____   VENTURE CAPITAL FUND __X__   MESBIC ____   OTHER ____

TYPES OF FINANCING PREFERRED (Stages): Research and development/start-up/turnaround/expansion/leveraged buyout/technology transfer

MINIMUM DATA REQUIRED TO CONSIDER FINANCING: N/A

GEOGRAPHIC PREFERENCE: Alberta, Canada

INDUSTRY PREFERENCE BY FIRM: Electronics manufacturing and distribution with emphasis on telecommunications, microelectronics product development, and software (invest only in technology situations)

INDUSTRY PREFERENCES BY INDIVIDUAL FIRM MEMBERS:
  Archie A. MacKinnon   David F. Campbell
  Harry W. Truderung

YEAR COMPANY ESTABLISHED: 1982

FUNDS UNDER MANAGEMENT AT COST: $10 million

MINIMUM SIZE INVESTMENT: $150,000

PREFERRED SIZE INVESTMENT: $400,000–$1,000,000

WILL FIRM SERVE AS LEAD INVESTOR: Yes

NUMBER OF DEALS COMPLETED IN THE LAST 12 MONTHS: 1

AMOUNT INVESTED IN LAST 12 MONTHS: $1 million

AVERAGE TIME REQUIRED TO COMPLETE A DEAL: 3 months
  (From Initial Contact to Closing)

FIRM NAME: **Androcan Inc.**

ADDRESS: 50 Bartor Rd.
              Weston, Ontario M9M 2G5
              Canada

PHONE: (416) 745–3333

SBIC ___ VENTURE CAPITAL FUND ___ MESBIC ___ OTHER _X_

TYPES OF FINANCING PREFERRED (Stages): Cash/cash and bank-guaranteed debt

MINIMUM DATA REQUIRED TO CONSIDER FINANCING: N/A

GEOGRAPHIC PREFERENCE: USA (especially West Coast), Toronto, Ontario, Western Canada, London (U.K.)

INDUSTRY PREFERENCE BY FIRM: Do-It-Yourself Products/Housewares and Hardware Products/Proprietary Items/Specialty Distribution/Industrial Specialty Products

INDUSTRY PREFERENCES BY INDIVIDUAL FIRM MEMBERS: N/A

YEAR COMPANY ESTABLISHED: 1970

FUNDS UNDER MANAGEMENT AT COST: N/A

MINIMUM SIZE INVESTMENT: $1 million

PREFERRED SIZE INVESTMENT: Manufacturers: Sales exceeding $10 million
                           Distributors: Sales exceeding $20 million

WILL FIRM SERVE AS LEAD INVESTOR: Yes

NUMBER OF DEALS COMPLETED IN THE LAST 12 MONTHS: 3

AMOUNT INVESTED IN LAST 12 MONTHS: $4 million

AVERAGE TIME REQUIRED TO COMPLETE A DEAL: 12–14 weeks (From Initial Contact to Closing)

FIRM NAME: **Canadian Enterprise Development Corp., Ltd.**

ADDRESS: 199 Bay St.   1100 Melville St.
                Suite 1100   Suite 880
                Toronto, Ontario M5J 1L4 Vancouver, B.C. V6E 4A6
                Canada   Canada

PHONE: (416) 366–7607   (604) 684–3271

SBIC ___ VENTURE CAPITAL FUND _X_ MESBIC ___ OTHER ___

TYPES OF FINANCING PREFERRED (Stages): Seed round through mezzannine

MINIMUM DATA REQUIRED TO CONSIDER FINANCING: Business plan/technology checks/meetings with key personnel

GEOGRAPHIC PREFERENCE: West Coast, East Coast

INDUSTRY PREFERENCE BY FIRM: Electronics/Health

INDUSTRY PREFERENCES BY INDIVIDUAL FIRM MEMBERS: N/A

YEAR COMPANY ESTABLISHED: 1962

FUNDS UNDER MANAGEMENT AT COST: $15 million

MINIMUM SIZE INVESTMENT: $150,000

PREFERRED SIZE INVESTMENT: $350,000–$500,000

WILL FIRM SERVE AS LEAD INVESTOR: Yes

NUMBER OF DEALS COMPLETED IN THE LAST 12 MONTHS: 2

AMOUNT INVESTED IN LAST 12 MONTHS: $4 million

AVERAGE TIME REQUIRED TO COMPLETE A DEAL: 7 weeks
(From Initial Contact to Closing)

FIRM NAME: **Capwest Capital Services Ltd.**

ADDRESS: 1102 Empire Building
                  10080 Jasper Ave.
                  Edmonton, Alberta T5J 1V9
                  Canada

PHONE: (403) 426-7117

SBIC ____ VENTURE CAPITAL FUND ____ MESBIC ____ OTHER _X_

TYPES OF FINANCING PREFERRED (Stages): Preference for merchant banking
operations rather than for pure venture capital investments

MINIMUM DATA REQUIRED TO CONSIDER FINANCING: N/A

GEOGRAPHIC PREFERENCE: N/A

INDUSTRY PREFERENCE BY FIRM: No limitations

INDUSTRY PREFERENCES BY INDIVIDUAL FIRM MEMBERS: N/A

YEAR COMPANY ESTABLISHED: 1973

FUNDS UNDER MANAGEMENT AT COST: N/A

MINIMUM SIZE INVESTMENT: $250,000

PREFERRED SIZE INVESTMENT: $3 million maximum

WILL FIRM SERVE AS LEAD INVESTOR: Yes

NUMBER OF DEALS COMPLETED IN THE LAST 12 MONTHS: N/A

AMOUNT INVESTED IN LAST 12 MONTHS: N/A

AVERAGE TIME REQUIRED TO COMPLETE A DEAL: 2 months
(From Initial Contact to Closing)

FIRM NAME: **Charterhouse Canada Limited**

ADDRESS: 800 - 150 York St.
                  Toronto, Ontario M5H 3S5
                  Canada

PHONE: (416) 362-7791

SBIC ____ VENTURE CAPITAL FUND _X_ MESBIC ____ OTHER ____

TYPES OF FINANCING PREFERRED (Stages): Later stage/mature situations

MINIMUM DATA REQUIRED TO CONSIDER FINANCING: Business plan

GEOGRAPHIC PREFERENCE: North America

INDUSTRY PREFERENCE BY FIRM: Open

INDUSTRY PREFERENCES BY INDIVIDUAL FIRM MEMBERS: Open

YEAR COMPANY ESTABLISHED: 1952

FUNDS UNDER MANAGEMENT AT COST: $18 million

MINIMUM SIZE INVESTMENT: $300,000

PREFERRED SIZE INVESTMENT: $1 million

WILL FIRM SERVE AS LEAD INVESTOR: Yes

NUMBER OF DEALS COMPLETED IN THE LAST 12 MONTHS: 3 buyouts

AMOUNT INVESTED IN LAST 12 MONTHS: $3 million

AVERAGE TIME REQUIRED TO COMPLETE A DEAL: 4 weeks
   (From Initial Contact to Closing)

FIRM NAME: **Citicorp Capital Investors Ltd.**

ADDRESS: University Place
                  123 Front St. W
                  Suite 1900
                  Toronto, Ontario M5J 2M3
                  Canada

PHONE: (416) 947–5805

SBIC ____   VENTURE CAPITAL FUND __X__   MESBIC ____   OTHER ____

TYPES OF FINANCING PREFERRED (Stages): Development/leveraged buyouts

MINIMUM DATA REQUIRED TO CONSIDER FINANCING: Detailed business
   plan

GEOGRAPHIC PREFERENCE: Canada only

INDUSTRY PREFERENCE BY FIRM: N/A

INDUSTRY PREFERENCES BY INDIVIDUAL FIRM MEMBERS: N/A

YEAR COMPANY ESTABLISHED: 1981

FUNDS UNDER MANAGEMENT AT COST: $25 million

MINIMUM SIZE INVESTMENT: $250,000

PREFERRED SIZE INVESTMENT: $700,000

WILL FIRM SERVE AS LEAD INVESTOR: Yes

NUMBER OF DEALS COMPLETED IN THE LAST 12 MONTHS: 6

AMOUNT INVESTED IN LAST 12 MONTHS: $4 million

AVERAGE TIME REQUIRED TO COMPLETE A DEAL: 3 months
   (From Initial Contact to Closing)

FIRM NAME: **Commerce City Investments**

ADDRESS: 1645 Russell Rd.
                  Ottawa, Ontario K1G 4G5
                  Canada

PHONE: (613) 733–1781

SBIC ___   VENTURE   CAPITAL   FUND ___   MESBIC ___   OTHER _X_
   (Private venture capital company)

TYPES OF FINANCING PREFERRED (Stages): Start-up/joint ventures

MINIMUM DATA REQUIRED TO CONSIDER FINANCING: Business and financial plan

GEOGRAPHIC PREFERENCE: Canada and USA

INDUSTRY PREFERENCE BY FIRM: Real Estate/Micro Computerware/Manufacturing

INDUSTRY PREFERENCES BY INDIVIDUAL FIRM MEMBERS: N/A

YEAR COMPANY ESTABLISHED: 1965

FUNDS UNDER MANAGEMENT AT COST: N/A

MINIMUM SIZE INVESTMENT: $10,000–$1,000,000

PREFERRED SIZE INVESTMENT: $100,000–$500,000

WILL FIRM SERVE AS LEAD INVESTOR: Yes

NUMBER OF DEALS COMPLETED IN THE LAST 12 MONTHS: 2

AMOUNT INVESTED IN LAST 12 MONTHS: $1.5 million plus

AVERAGE TIME REQUIRED TO COMPLETE A DEAL: 4 months
   (From Initial Contact to Closing)

FIRM NAME: **Corporate Growth Assistance Ltd.**

ADDRESS: 19 York Ridge Rd.
            Willowdale, Ontario M2P 1R8
            Canada

PHONE: (416) 927–1700 or (416) 222–7772 (after 6:00 pm)

SBIC ___   VENTURE CAPITAL FUND _X_   MESBIC ___   OTHER ___

TYPES OF FINANCING PREFERRED (Stages): Second stage/mezzanine

MINIMUM DATA REQUIRED TO CONSIDER FINANCING: Detailed business plan plus 3 years audited financials

GEOGRAPHIC PREFERENCE: Southern Ontario, Canada and USA

INDUSTRY PREFERENCE BY FIRM: N/A

INDUSTRY PREFERENCES BY INDIVIDUAL FIRM MEMBERS: N/A

YEAR COMPANY ESTABLISHED: 1966

FUNDS UNDER MANAGEMENT AT COST: $4.0 million

MINIMUM SIZE INVESTMENT: $150,000

PREFERRED SIZE INVESTMENT: $750,000

WILL FIRM SERVE AS LEAD INVESTOR: Yes

NUMBER OF DEALS COMPLETED IN THE LAST 12 MONTHS: 6

AMOUNT INVESTED IN LAST 12 MONTHS: $750,000

AVERAGE TIME REQUIRED TO COMPLETE A DEAL: 3 months
   (From Initial Contact to Closing)

FIRM NAME: **Investissements Novacap Inc.**

ADDRESS: 1981 McGill College
                   Suite 380
                   Montreal, Quebec H3A 3A9
                   Canada

PHONE: (514) 282–1383

SBIC ____   VENTURE CAPITAL FUND _X_   MESBIC ____   OTHER ____

TYPES OF FINANCING PREFERRED (Stages): Development/expansion/buyout

MINIMUM DATA REQUIRED TO CONSIDER FINANCING: Budget and business plan

GEOGRAPHIC PREFERENCE: Quebec, Canada, and USA

INDUSTRY PREFERENCE BY FIRM: Manufacturing with growth strategy; avoid real estate, resources, and high-capital intensive

INDUSTRY PREFERENCES BY INDIVIDUAL FIRM MEMBERS: N/A

YEAR COMPANY ESTABLISHED: 1981

FUNDS UNDER MANAGEMENT AT COST: $20 million

MINIMUM SIZE INVESTMENT: $50,000

PREFERRED SIZE INVESTMENT: $1 million

WILL FIRM SERVE AS LEAD INVESTOR: Yes

NUMBER OF DEALS COMPLETED IN THE LAST 12 MONTHS: 10

AMOUNT INVESTED IN LAST 12 MONTHS: $3 million

AVERAGE TIME REQUIRED TO COMPLETE A DEAL: 2 months
   (From Initial Contact to Closing)

FIRM NAME: **IPS Industrial Promotion Services, Ltd.**

ADDRESS: 797 Don Mills Rd.
                   Suite 904
                   Don Mills, Ontario M3C 1V2
                   Canada

PHONE: (416) 422–5026

SBIC ____   VENTURE CAPITAL FUND _X_   MESBIC ____   OTHER ____

TYPES OF FINANCING PREFERRED (Stages): Minority equity positions are preferred. Investments are made in a combination of debt and equity. Representation on the board of directors and active participation in policy are essential.

MINIMUM DATA REQUIRED TO CONSIDER FINANCING: N/A

GEOGRAPHIC PREFERENCE: Canada and USA

INDUSTRY PREFERENCE BY FIRM: Food/Agriculture/Manufacturing/Wholesaling/Distribution/Services

INDUSTRY PREFERENCES BY INDIVIDUAL FIRM MEMBERS: N/A

YEAR COMPANY ESTABLISHED: N/A

FUNDS UNDER MANAGEMENT AT COST: N/A

MINIMUM SIZE INVESTMENT: $100,000

PREFERRED SIZE INVESTMENT: Maximum: $1 million; Average: $300,000

WILL FIRM SERVE AS LEAD INVESTOR: N/A

NUMBER OF DEALS COMPLETED IN THE LAST 12 MONTHS: N/A

AMOUNT INVESTED IN LAST 12 MONTHS: N/A

AVERAGE TIME REQUIRED TO COMPLETE A DEAL: N/A
   (From Initial Contact to Closing)

FIRM NAME: **Kanata Genesis Fund Ltd.**

ADDRESS: 201–4019 Carling Ave.
                 Kanata, Ontario K2K 2A3
                 Canada

PHONE: (613) 592–6453

SBIC ___   VENTURE CAPITAL FUND _X_   MESBIC ___   OTHER ___

TYPES OF FINANCING PREFERRED (Stages): Early stage

MINIMUM DATA REQUIRED TO CONSIDER FINANCING: Business plan

GEOGRAPHIC PREFERENCE: Ontario only, especially Ottawa area

INDUSTRY PREFERENCE BY FIRM: Knowledge based (high technology)

INDUSTRY PREFERENCES BY INDIVIDUAL FIRM MEMBERS: N/A

YEAR COMPANY ESTABLISHED: 1982

FUNDS UNDER MANAGEMENT AT COST: $1.3 million

MINIMUM SIZE INVESTMENT: None

PREFERRED SIZE INVESTMENT: $50,000–$250,000

WILL FIRM SERVE AS LEAD INVESTOR: Yes

NUMBER OF DEALS COMPLETED IN THE LAST 12 MONTHS: 2

AMOUNT INVESTED IN LAST 12 MONTHS: $100,000

AVERAGE TIME REQUIRED TO COMPLETE A DEAL: 3 months
   (From Initial Contact to Closing)

FIRM NAME: **Small Business Equity Limited**

ADDRESS: P.O. Box 3638
                 Halifax, Nova Scotia B3V 3K6
                 Canada

PHONE: (902) 422–9260

SBIC ___   VENTURE CAPITAL FUND _X_   MESBIC ___   OTHER ___

TYPES OF FINANCING PREFERRED (Stages): Any

MINIMUM DATA REQUIRED TO CONSIDER FINANCING: N/A

GEOGRAPHIC PREFERENCE: Nova Scotia

INDUSTRY PREFERENCE BY FIRM: All except real estate, retail, wholesale

INDUSTRY PREFERENCES BY INDIVIDUAL FIRM MEMBERS: N/A

YEAR COMPANY ESTABLISHED: 1980

FUNDS UNDER MANAGEMENT AT COST: $1.5 million

MINIMUM SIZE INVESTMENT: $100,000

PREFERRED SIZE INVESTMENT: $150,000

WILL FIRM SERVE AS LEAD INVESTOR: Yes

NUMBER OF DEALS COMPLETED IN THE LAST 12 MONTHS: 5

AMOUNT INVESTED IN LAST 12 MONTHS: $700,000

AVERAGE TIME REQUIRED TO COMPLETE A DEAL: 4 weeks
    (From Initial Contact to Closing)

Appendix D

Incubator Directory

CONNECTICUT

INCUBATOR FIRM NAME: New Enterprise Center

ADDRESS: Science Park Development Corporation
                            Five Science Park
                            New Haven, CT 06511

PHONE: (203) 786–5005

CONTACT: Courtney Richardson

SERVICES/FINANCING/ASSISTANCE PROVIDED:
Typing   Financial advice
Computer rentals   Business plan assistance
Word processing   Marketing assistance
Mail distribution   Low rent with all utilities included
Telephone answering   24-hour security parking
Business management support   Yale University resource support

ILLINOIS

INCUBATOR FIRM NAME: **Business Center for New Technology**

ADDRESS: c/o Reed Chatwood
                            1220 Rock St.
                            Rockford, IL 61101–1437

PHONE: (815) 968–4087

CONTACT: Art Cornwell, Director Small Business Service Center

SERVICES/FINANCING/ASSISTANCE PROVIDED:
Business counseling   Government procurement assistance
Typing   Subsidized rents (for a limited time)
Telephone answering   Computer access
Loans at low interest   Small business library
    (for a limited time)   Photocopy machine
Technical assistance   Facsimile equipment
Cafeteria

MASSACHUSETTS

INCUBATOR FIRM NAME: **J. B. Blood**

ADDRESS: 20 Wheller St.
                            Lynne, MA 01901

PHONE: (617) 592–2361

CONTACT: William Kyriakakis, Executive Director
            Lynne Office of Economic Development
            One Market Sq.
            Lynne, MA 01901

SERVICES/FINANCING/ASSISTANCE PROVIDED:
   Financings: Start-up through Lynne Municipal Development
      S.B.A. 7A & 503
      I.R.B.
   Assistance: Management assistance available

MINNESOTA

INCUBATOR FIRM NAME: **Saint Paul Small Business Incubator**

ADDRESS: 2325 Endicott St.
                           Saint Paul, MN 55114

PHONE: (612) 292–1577

CONTACT: Robert W. Kessler
               St. Paul Department of Planning & Economic Development
               1000 City Hall Annex
               St. Paul, MN 55102

SERVICES/FINANCING/ASSISTANCE PROVIDED: Business planning, Loan packaging, Accounting referral and other services as necessary or appropriate

INCUBATOR FIRM NAME: **Shari Ost**

ADDRESS: Minneapolis Technology Center
                           1313 5th St. SE
                           Minneapolis, MN 55414

PHONE: N/A

CONTACT: N/A

SERVICES/FINANCING/ASSISTANCE PROVIDED:
   Offices   Telephone answering
   Workshops   Secretarial services
   Development and start-up areas   Accounting
   Conference rooms   Word processing
   Kitchen facilities   Typing
   Beverage area   Computer access
   Off-street parking   Copying machine
   Rental van   Insurance program
   Shipping and receiving area   Office supplies
   Receptionist

MISSISSIPPI

INCUBATOR FIRM NAME: **Jackson Technology Center**

ADDRESS: P.O. Box 12321
                           Jackson, MS 39211

PHONE: N/A

CONTACT: Pete Everett

SERVICES/FINANCING/ASSISTANCE PROVIDED: Under development

NEW YORK

INCUBATOR FIRM NAME: **Broome County Industrial Development Agency**
                            Broome County Industrial Incubator

ADDRESS: 19 Chenago St.
                            Suite 702
                            P.O. Box 1026
                            Binghamton, New York 13902

PHONE: (607) 772–8212

CONTACT: Robert Max, Deputy Director of Development

SERVICES/FINANCING/ASSISTANCE PROVIDED:
    Fixed asset revolving loan program
    Technical, management, financial, and clerical assistance

INCUBATOR FIRM NAME: **Incubator Center Associates**

ADDRESS: 100 E. Onondaga St.
                            Syracuse, New York 13202

PHONE: (315) 470–1343

CONTACT: Samuel W. Williams, Jr.

SERVICES/FINANCING/ASSISTANCE PROVIDED:
    Management counseling
    Secretarial service
    Common meeting room
    Technical services

OHIO

INCUBATOR FIRM NAME: **Akron Summit Industrial Incubator**

ADDRESS: 100 Lincoln St.
                            Akron, OH 44308

PHONE: (216) 253–1918

CONTACT: Greg Balbierz, Economic Development Specialist
            (216) 375–2133
            Michael Lehere, Incubator Manager
            (216) 253–1918

SERVICES/FINANCING/ASSISTANCE PROVIDED:
    Tenant firms are provided with management assistance from the Service Corps
    of Retired Executives (SCORE), the Small Business Enterprise Center (SBEC)—

a cadre of technical advisors available to business expansions and start-ups—
and programs from the University of Akron's Business School Small Business
Institute (SBI).

Provided by on-site and Office of Economic Development personnel, assistance is available in:
    Government grants and loans
    Government procurement procedures
    Government contract preparation
    Equity and debt financing
General services assistance includes:
    Clerical service
    Shipping and receiving
    Word processing
    Bookkeeping
    Conference room
    Security
    Parking
    etc.

INCUBATOR FIRM NAME: **The Innovators Fund**

ADDRESS: Dayton Technology Enterprise Center
                            111 East Fourth St.
                            Dayton, OH 45402

PHONE: (513) 461–4332

CONTACT: Robert Sammons

SERVICES/FINANCING/ASSISTANCE PROVIDED:
    Center under construction
    Venture fund in place

INCUBATOR FIRM NAME: **Ohio University Innovation Center**

ADDRESS: One President St.
                            Athens, Ohio 45701

PHONE: (614) 594–6682

CONTACT: Dinah Adkins
            Assistant to the Director

SERVICES/FINANCING/ASSISTANCE PROVIDED:
    Receptionist
    Secretarial
    Word-processing
    Basic accounting/spread sheets, etc.
    Low-overhead flexible space
    Assistance in obtaining state and federal grants and venture capital
        and other investments
    Access to sophisticated university laboratories and equipment
    Access to business consulting
    Access to technical consulting/research expertise

Access to university machine and electronics shops
Access to university computer facilities
Access to library facilities
    Innovation Center library of more than 850 volumes
    University library, 1 million plus volumes
Access to below-market accounting and legal services (local firms)
Patent help
Idea evaluation
Prototype construction
Basic furniture
Basic janitorial
Security
Access to business workshops
Assistance in preparing business plans

PENNSYLVANIA

INCUBATOR FIRM NAME: **Girard Area Industrial Corporation**

ADDRESS: 227 Hathaway St. East
                                        Girard, Pa 16417

PHONE: (814) 774–9339

CONTACT: Damon Homich

SERVICES/FINANCING/ASSISTANCE PROVIDED:
    Basic Services
        Management Services
            Management assistance/counseling
            Assistance in the preparation of business plans
            Assistance in the preparation of relocation plans
        Financial Services
            Insurance/risk management
            Technical assistance in applying for government grants and loans
            Technical assistance in applying for equity and debt financing
    Services Available
        General Services
            Mail
            Copier
            Clerical/receptionist
            Access to computer
            Computing and information processing assistance
            24-hour answering service
            Group purchasing
            24-hour security, janitorial/maintenance
            Furniture
            Conference room
            Snow removal
            Fork lift
            10 shipping/receiving docks

INCUBATOR FIRM NAME: **Greater Easton Technical Center**

ADDRESS: 201 Ferry St.
                           2nd Floor
                           Easton, PA 18042

PHONE: (215) 263–0600

CONTACT: Charles R. Diacont

SERVICES/FINANCING/ASSISTANCE PROVIDED:

Offices	Telephone answering
Workshops	Secretarial services
Development and start-up areas	Accounting
Conference rooms	Word processing
Kitchen facilities	Typing
Beverage area	Computer access
Off-street parking	Copyng machine
Rental van	Insurance program
Shipping and receiving area	Office supplies
Receptionist	

INCUBATOR FIRM NAME: **Greenville Business Incubator**
                           Sponsor: Greenville Area Economic Development
                           Corporation (GAEDC)

ADDRESS: 12 N. Diamond St. (or)
                           P.O. Box 131
                           Greenville, PA 16125

PHONE: (412) 588–1161

CONTACT: William D. McNeilly, President, GAEDC
             Gladys C. Corpuz-Ross, Incubator Administrative Assistant

SERVICES/FINANCING/ASSISTANCE PROVIDED: N/A

INCUBATOR FIRM NAME: **Hunting Park West Business Center**

ADDRESS: 2783–2781 Roberts Ave. (or)
                           3201–3200 Stokely St.
                           Philadelphia, PA 19144

PHONE: 1(215)843–2000

CONTACT: George A. Wisnoski

SERVICES/FINANCING/ASSISTANCE PROVIDED:
    Shared office systems
    Employee placement assistance
    Management assistance
    Legal/accounting services
    Capital resources available

INCUBATOR FIRM NAME: The Meadville Industrial Condominium
                              An industrial project by the Meadville
                              Redevelopment Authority

ADDRESS: 628 Arch St.
                              Building A
                              Meadville, PA 16335

PHONE: (814) 724–2975

CONTACT: Victor C. Leap, Executive Director
              Steven L. Kohler, Industrial Development Coordinator

SERVICES/FINANCING/ASSISTANCE PROVIDED:
    General Services
        Mail
        Copier
        Business development assistance (defense contract procurement)
    Physical services
        Security
        Janitorial/maintenance—common area
        Furniture
        Conference room
        Loading facilities—common area
        Tow motor—separate fee on time-sharing basis
        Office construction
        Electrical services—tenant shop areas
The General Services listed have been provided on an as needed basis. The
copier use does include an additional copy fee. This fee charge only applies
to the cost of paper for the copier. All other General Services are provided at
no cost to the tenants. Business development assistance has included defense
contract procurement assistance and seminars for business management and
improvement. These services carry no charges.

The Physical Services listed are provided on an as needed basis. There are no
added costs for these services with the exception of an hourly charge for tow
motor usage. This charge is necessary in order to maintain this piece of equipment.
    Management Services
        Management assistance/counseling
        Assistance in the preparation of business plans
        Assistance in the preparation of relocation plans
    Financial Services
        Insurance/risk management
        Technical assistance in applying for government grants and loans
        Technical assistance in applying for equity and debt financing
All the above services shall be implemented and in place by the end of the
Ben Franklin Program year. The Redevelopment Authority staff designated
for this project has the necessary background experience to effectively assist
the incubator tenants by providing the above basic services.

INCUBATOR FIRM NAME: Eric Siegel

ADDRESS: Paoli Technology Center
                              19 East Central Ave.
                              Paoli, PA 19301

PHONE: (215) 251–0505

CONTACT: N/A

SERVICES/FINANCING/ASSISTANCE PROVIDED:

Offices	Telephone answering
Workshops	Secretarial services
Development and start-up areas	Accounting
Conference rooms	Word processing
Kitchen facilities	Typing
Beverage area	Computer access
Off-street parking	Copying machine
Rental van	Insurance program
Shipping and receiving area	Office supplies
Receptionist	Auditorium

INCUBATOR FIRM NAME: **Technology Centers International**

ADDRESS: 1060 Route 309
                         Montgomeryville, PA 18936

PHONE: (215) 646–7800

CONTACT: Loren A. Schultz or Eric Pavlak

SERVICES/FINANCING/ASSISTANCE PROVIDED: Establishes and helps run
business incubator centers. First center established in 1976.

INCUBATOR FIRM NAME: **The Technology Fund**

ADDRESS: 1060 Route 309
                         Montgomeryville, PA 18936

PHONE: 215) 646–7800

CONTACT: Robert Hutton

SERVICES/FINANCING/ASSISTANCE PROVIDED: Venture Capital Fund

INCUBATOR FIRM NAME: **University City Science Center**

ADDRESS: 3624 Market St.
                         Philadelphia, PA 19104

PHONE: (215) 387–2255

CONTACT: Gordon Carlisle, Vice-president, Real Estate

SERVICES/FINANCING/ASSISTANCE PROVIDED:

Program development and market-ing	Athletic facilities
Contract administration	Conference facilities
Health insurance	Audiovisual equipment
Computing	Fine arts
Word processing	Financing and venture capital
Secretarial support	Marketing assistance
Printing and binding	Legal advice
Libraries	

INCUBATOR FIRM NAME: **Jean Vandegrift**

ADDRESS: Lansdale Business Center
                           650 North Cannon Ave.
                           Lansdale, PA 19446

PHONE: (215) 855–6700

CONTACT: N/A

SERVICES/FINANCING/ASSISTANCE PROVIDED:

Offices	Telephone answering
Workshops	Secretarial services
Development and start-up areas	Accounting
Conference rooms	Word processing
Kitchen facilities	Typing
Beverage area	Computer Access
Off-street parking	Copying machne
Rental van	Insurance program
Shipping and receiving area	Office supplies
Receptionist	Railroad siding

VERMONT

INCUBATOR FIRM NAME: **Bennington County Industrial Corporation**

ADDRESS: P.O. Box 357, Water St.
                           North Bennington, VT 05257

PHONE: (802) 442–4392
                           (802) 447–0750

CONTACT: Jay Zwynenburg, Executive Director
            Melany Johnson, Office Manager

SERVICES/FINANCING/ASSISTANCE PROVIDED:
    Leasehold improvement loans
    Copy machine
    Data processing; IBM PC XT
    Maintenance, communication areas, and building
    Security, 24 hours, 7 days
    Typing
    Packaging SBA, VIDA, and bank loans

Appendix E

Deal-Doing Lawyer Directory

ARIZONA

FIRM NAME: **Streich, Lang, Weeks & Cardon, P.A.**

ADDRESS: 2100 First Interstate Bank Plaza
100 West Washington
Phoenix, AZ 85003
(for mailing purposes:
P. O. Box 471
Phoenix, AZ 85001)

PHONE: (602) 257–0999

CONTACT: Jock Patton

CALIFORNIA

FIRM NAME: **Aylward, Kintz, Stiska, Wassenaar & Shannahan**

ADDRESS: 225 Broadway   7855 Ivanhoe Ave.
Suite 2100   Suite 420
San Diego, CA 92101   La Jolla, CA 92037

PHONE: (619) 234–1966   (619) 454–3237

CONTACT: John C. Stiska, Esq.
Craig S. Andrews, Esq.

FIRM NAME: **Brobeck, Phleger & Harrison**

ADDRESS: One Market Plaza   Two Embarcadero Place
San Francisco, CA 94105   2200 Geng Rd.
Palo Alto, CA 94303

PHONE: (415) 442–0900   (415) 424–0160

CONTACT: John W. Larson, Esq.   Edward M. Leonard, Esq.
Ronald B. Moskovitz, Esq.   Richard C. Spalding, Esq.

FIRM NAME: **Cooley, Godward, Castro, Huddleson & Tatum**

ADDRESS: One Maritime Plaza   Five Palo Alto Square
20th Floor   4th Floor
San Francisco, CA 94111   Palo Alto, CA 94306

PHONE: (415) 981–5252   (415) 494–7622

CONTACT: Craig E. Dauchy (S.F.)   Lee F. Benton (P.A.)
Robert V. Gunderson

FIRM NAME: **Dinkelspiel, Donovan & Reder**

ADDRESS: One Embarcadero Center
#2701
San Francisco, CA 94111

PHONE: (415) 788–1100

CONTACT: Barry Reder

FIRM NAME: **Fabian, Graham & Englese**

ADDRESS: 120 Montgomery St.
Suite 670
San Francisco, CA 94104

PHONE: (415) 433–8300

CONTACT: Robert E. Graham, Esq.
Patrick H. Fabian, Esq.

FIRM NAME :   **Paul, Hastings, Janofsky & Walker**

ADDRESS:	PHONE:	CONTACT:
1299 Ocean Ave. 5th Floor Santa Monica, CA 90401	(213) 451–1200	Alan J. Barton Richard K. Roeder
555 S. Flower St. 22nd Floor Los Angeles, CA 90071	(213) 489–4000	Michael J. Connell Steven K. Hazen
695 Town Center Dr. 17th Floor Costa Mesa, CA 92626	(714) 641–1100	James W. Hamilton Michael K. Lindsey

FIRM NAME: **Rodi, Pollock, Pettker, Galbraith & Phillips**

ADDRESS: 611 West Sixth St.
Suite 1600
Los Angeles, CA 90017

PHONE: (213) 680–0823

CONTACT: Michael P. Ridley

FIRM NAME: **Rutan & Tucker**

ADDRESS: 611 Anton Blvd.
                 Suite 1400
                 Costa Mesa, CA 92626

PHONE: (714) 641–5100

CONTACT: Ronald P. Arrington, Esq.

FIRM NAME: **Sheppard, Mullin, Richter & Hampton**

ADDRESS: 333 South Hope St.   4000 MacArthur Blvd.
                 48th Floor   Suite 500
                 Los Angeles, CA 90071   Newport Beach, CA 92660

PHONE: (213) 620–1780   (714) 752–6400

CONTACT: John D. Hussey   Robert R. Burge
                 John J. Malloy III
                 T. William Opdyke
                 Arthur William Brown, Jr.

FIRM NAME: **Stradling, Yocca, Carlson & Rauth**

ADDRESS: 660 Newport Center Dr.
                 Suite 1600
                 Newport Beach, CA 92660–6401

PHONE: (714) 640–7035

CONTACT: C. Craig Carlson

FIRM NAME: **Wilson, Sonsini, Goodrich & Rosati**

ADDRESS: Two Palo Alto Square
                 Palo Alto, CA 94306

PHONE: (415) 493–9300

CONTACT: Larry W. Sonsini, Esq.

COLORADO

FIRM NAME: **Ducker, Gurko & Roble, P.C.**

ADDRESS: 1560 Broadway
                 Suite 1500
                 Denver, CO 80202

PHONE: (303) 861–2828

CONTACT: Bruce Ducker

FIRM NAME: **Holland & Hart**

ADDRESS: 555 Seventeenth St.
Suite 2900
Denver, CO 80202

PHONE: (303) 295–8176

CONTACT: H. Gregory Austin

FIRM NAME: **Olsen & Matsukage**

ADDRESS: 600 Grant St.
Suite 500
Denver, CO 80203

PHONE: (303) 832–6500

CONTACT: Robert E. Olsen
Fay M. Matsukage

CONNECTICUT

FIRM NAME: **Cummings & Lockwood**

ADDRESS: P.O. Box 120
Ten Stamford Forum
Stamford, CT 06904

PHONE: (203) 327–1700

CONTACT: Edward W. Wellman, Jr. Esq.

FIRM NAME: **Goldman, Rosen & Willinger**

ADDRESS: 177 State St.
Bridgeport, CT 06604

PHONE: (203) 366–3939

CONTACT: Jerome Goldman, Esq.

FIRM NAME: **Schatz & Schatz, Ribicoff & Kotkin**

ADDRESS: 2 Landmark Square
Stamford, CT 06901

PHONE: (203) 964–0027

CONTACT: Michael L. Widland

FIRM NAME: **Shipman & Goodwin**

ADDRESS: 799 Main St.
Hartford, CT 06103

PHONE: (203) 549–4770

CONTACT: Frank J. Marco, Esq.

DISTRICT OF COLUMBIA

FIRM NAME: **Michaels & Wishner, P.C.**

ADDRESS: 1726 M. St., NW
               Suite 500
               Washington, D.C. 20036

PHONE: (202) 223–9212

CONTACT: Mark J. Wishner, Esq.

FLORIDA

FIRM NAME: **Peirsol, Boroughs, Grimm, Bennett & Griffin,
               Professional Association**

ADDRESS: 201 E. Pine St.
               Suite 520
               Orlando, FL 32801

PHONE: (305) 841–3353

CONTACT: William A. Grimm

FIRM NAME: **Zemel and Kaufman, P.A.**

ADDRESS: National Bank of Florida Building
               3550 Biscayne Blvd.
               Suite 603
               Miami, FL 33137

PHONE: (305) 573–1811

CONTACT: Herbert C. Zemel

GEORGIA

FIRM NAME: **Robert W. Fisher, P.C.**

ADDRESS: 2630 First Atlanta Tower
               Atlanta, GA 30383

PHONE: (404) 658–1002

CONTACT: Robert W. Fisher

FIRM NAME: **Investor's Equity, Inc.**

ADDRESS: 2629 First Atlanta Tower
               Atlanta, GA 30383

PHONE: (404) 523–3999

CONTACT: Robert W. Fisher

FIRM NAME: **Troutman, Sanders, Lockerman and Ashmore**

ADDRESS: Candler Building
127 Peachtree St., NE
Suite 1400
Atlanta, GA 30043

PHONE: (404) 658–8000

CONTACT: Robert W. Grout, Esq.
William B. Marianes, Esq.

ILLINOIS

FIRM NAME: **Kanter & Eisenberg**

ADDRESS: Three First National Plaza
22nd Floor
Chicago, IL 60602

PHONE: (312) 726–0800

CONTACT: Burton W. Kanter
Robert D. Zimelis
Charles H. Winkler

FIRM NAME: **Kirkland & Ellis**

ADDRESS: 200 East Randolph Dr.
Chicago, IL 60601

PHONE: (312) 861–2004

CONTACT: Jack S. Levin, Partner

Kirkland & Ellis is a law firm with an active practice in representing venture capitalists, start-up and growing businesses, businesses engaged in public offerings, and acquiring target companies in mergers, acquisitions, etc.

FIRM NAME: **Lord, Bissell & Brook**

ADDRESS: 115 South La Salle St.
Chicago, IL 60603

PHONE: (312) 443–0700

CONTACT: John K. O'Connor
(312) 443–0265
David B. Weinberg
(312) 443–0615

FIRM NAME: **McBride, Baker & Coles**

ADDRESS: Three First National Plaza
38th Floor
Chicago, IL 60602

PHONE: (312) 346–6191

CONTACT: Lawrence A. Coles, Jr.

INDIANA

FIRM NAME: **Mount Vernon Venture Capital Company**

ADDRESS: 9102 N. Meridian St.
P.O. Box 40177
Indianapolis, IN 46240

PHONE: (317) 632–3030
CONTACT: Bernard Landman, Jr.
Landman & Beatty
400 Union Federal Building
Indianapolis, IN 46204

MASSACHUSETTS

FIRM NAME: **Choate, Hall & Stewart**

ADDRESS: Exchange Place
53 State St.
Boston, MA 02109

PHONE: (617) 227–5020

CONTACT: Andrew L. Nichols, Esq.

FIRM NAME: **Hale and Dorr**

ADDRESS: 60 State St.
Boston, MA 02109

PHONE: (617) 742–9100

CONTACT: Gabor Garai, Esq.

FIRM NAME: **Testa, Hurwitz & Thibeault**

ADDRESS: 60 State St.
Boston, MA 02110

PHONE: (617) 367–7500

CONTACT: Richard J. Testa

MINNESOTA

FIRM NAME: **Dorsey & Whitney**

ADDRESS: 2200 First Bank Place East
Minneapolis, MN 55402

PHONE: (612) 340–2600

CONTACT: George P. Flannery, (612) 340–2720
Michael Trucano, (612) 340–2673
Richard G. Swanson, (612) 340–2715

FIRM NAME:	**Fredrikson & Byron, P.A.**
ADDRESS:	1100 International Centre 900 Second Ave. South Minneapolis, MN 55402
PHONE:	(612) 347–7000
CONTACT:	Keith A. Libbey

NEW MEXICO

FIRM NAME:	**Mitchell, Alley & Rubin**
ADDRESS:	First Northern Plaza P.O. Box 2005 Santa Fe, NM 87504–2005
PHONE:	(505) 982–3512
CONTACT:	James B. Alley, Jr.

FIRM NAME:	**Modrall, Sperling, Roehl, Harris & Sisk, P.A.**
ADDRESS:	P.O. Box 2168 Suite 1000—Sunwest Building 500 Fourth St., NW Albuquerque, NM 87103–2168
PHONE:	(505) 848–1800
CONTACT:	Paul M. Fish, Esq.

FIRM NAME:	**Ross B. Perkal**
ADDRESS:	124 Tenth St., NW Albuquerque, NM 87102
PHONE:	(505) 247–9400
CONTACT:	Ross B. Perkal

NEW YORK

FIRM NAME:	**Aronsson, Kerker & Ferst Attorneys at Law**
ADDRESS:	1114 Avenue of the Americas New York, NY 10036
PHONE:	(212) 921–2888
CONTACT:	Jeffry M. Aronsson

FIRM NAME: **Robert W. Cross**

ADDRESS: 521 Fifth Ave.
New York, NY 10175

PHONE: (212) 575–6454

CONTACT: Robert W. Cross (turnarounds and workouts)

FIRM NAME: **Granoff & Walker**

ADDRESS: 277 Park Ave.
Suite 4300
New York, NY 10172

PHONE: (212) 888–7574

CONTACT: Gary C. Granoff

FIRM NAME: **Morgan, Lewis & Bockius**

CONTACT: Samuel B. Fortenbaugh III
Morgan, Lewis & Bockius
101 Park Ave.
New York, NY 10178
(212) 309–6070

David R. King
Morgan, Lewis & Bockius
2000 One Logan Square
Philadelphia, PA 19103
(215) 963–05371

Richard M. McGonigal
Morgan, Lewis & Bockius
3200 Miami Center
100 Chopin Plaza
Miami, FL 33131
(305) 579–0330

Michael L. Klowden
Morgan, Lewis & Bockius
611 West Sixth St.
Los Angeles, CA 90017
(213) 612–2520

Lloyd H. Feller
Morgan, Lewis & Bockius
1800 M St., NW
Washington, DC 20036
(202) 872–3932

FIRM NAME: **O'Sullivan, Graev, Karabell & Gross**

ADDRESS: 30 Rockefeller Plaza
New York, NY 10112

PHONE: (212) 408–2400

CONTACT: Lawrence G. Graev, Esq.

FIRM NAME: **Reavis & McGrath**

ADDRESS: 345 Park Ave.
New York, NY 10154

PHONE: (212) 486–9500

CONTACT: Paul Jacobs, Esq.

NORTH CAROLINA

FIRM NAME: **Helms, Mulliss & Johnston**

ADDRESS: 227 North Tryon St.
Charlotte, NC 28202

PHONE: (704) 372–9510

CONTACT: B. Bernard Burns, Jr.

OHIO

FIRM NAME: **Smith & Schnacke**

ADDRESS: 2000 Courthouse Plaza NE
P.O. Box 1817
Dayton, OH 45401

PHONE: (513) 226–6500

CONTACT: J. Michael Herr, Esq.
Richard A. Broock, Esq.

OREGON

FIRM NAME: **Perkins Coie**

ADDRESS: 111 SW Fifth Ave.
Suite 2500
Portland, OR 97204

PHONE: (503) 295–4400

CONTACT: William J. Glasgow

PENNSYLVANIA

FIRM NAME: **McCausland, Keen & Buckman**

ADDRESS: 671 Moore Rd.
Suite 220
King of Prussia, PA 19406

PHONE: (215) 337–4555

CONTACT: Peter McCausland, Esq.

FIRM NAME: **Meyer, Unkovic & Scott**

ADDRESS: 1300 Oliver Building
           Pittsburgh, PA 15222

PHONE: (412) 456–2800

CONTACT: Lawrence B. Niemann

FIRM NAME: **Wissahickon Partners**

ADDRESS: 671 Moore Rd.
           Suite 220
           King of Prussia, PA 19406

PHONE: (215) 337–4555

CONTACT: Peter McCausland
           Gordon L. Keen, Jr.
           Craig L. Battle

RHODE ISLAND

FIRM NAME: **Edwards & Angell**

ADDRESS: 2700 Hospital Trust Tower
           Providence, RI 02903

PHONE: (401) 274–9200

CONTACT: David K. Duffell

TEXAS

FIRM NAME: **Baker & Kirk, P.C.**

ADDRESS: 1020 Holcombe
           Suite 444
           Houston, TX 77030

PHONE: (713) 790–9316

CONTACT: Michael A. Baker, Esq.

FIRM NAME: **Emmott & Arbuckle, P.C.**

ADDRESS: 2640 Fountainview
           Suite 100
           Houston, TX 77057

PHONE: (713) 977–1481

CONTACT: Kurt Arbuckle

FIRM NAME: **Hughes & Luce**

ADDRESS: 1000 Dallas Building
Dallas, TX 75201

PHONE: (214) 760–5500

CONTACT: Alan J. Bogdanow

FIRM NAME: **Jenkens & Gilchrist**

ADDRESS: 2200 InterFirst One
Dallas, TX 75202

PHONE: (214) 653–4500

CONTACT: John R. Holzgraefe

FIRM NAME: **Winstead, McGuire, Sechrest & Minick**

ADDRESS: 1700 MBank Dallas Building
Dallas, TX 75201

PHONE: (214) 742–1700

CONTACT: Darrel A. Rice
Thomas W. Hughes

VIRGINIA

FIRM NAME: **Hunton & Williams**

ADDRESS: 707 East Main St.   4011 Chain Bridge Rd.
P.O. Box 1535   Fairfax, VA 22030
Richmond, VA 23212

BB&T Building
333 Fayetteville St.
P.O. Box 109
Raleigh, NC 27602

PHONE: (804) 788–8200

CONTACT: C. Porter Vaughan III   (804) 788–8285
Thurston R. Moore   (804) 788–8295

WASHINGTON

FIRM NAME: **Efrem Z. Agranoff, Attorney at Law**

ADDRESS: 3114-A Oakes Ave.
Everett, WA 98201

PHONE: (206) 259–8158; 745–9531

CONTACT: Efrem Z. Agranoff

SUBJECT INDEX

INDEX OF VENTURE CAPITAL FIRMS BY STATE

INDEX OF VENTURE CAPITAL FIRMS

INDEX OF
INCUBATOR FIRMS

INDEX OF
DEAL-DOING LAWYERS